# Financial Sector Reforms in the World

# Financial Sector Reforms in the World

*Edited by :*

**V.B. Jugale, Ph.D.**

*Professor and Head*
*Department of Economics*
*Shivaji University*
*Kolhapur-416004 (India)*

**SERIALS PUBLICATIONS**
**NEW DELHI**

First Published : 2006

**ISBN: 81-8387-005-8**



*Published by*

***Office*** : **SERIALS PUBLICATIONS**
4830/24, Ansari Road, Darya Ganj
New Delhi-110002 (India)
Phone : 91-11-23245225
Fax : 91-11-23272135
E-mail: serials@satyam.net.in,
serialspublications@vsnl.net
Website : www.seriealspub.com

# Preface

Financial sector in fact is the brain of the body economy. The traditional economists have never considered the significance of the finance. The finance in reality was given a status of second class citizen in the economic literature. Obviously, the need has emerged to rewrite the monetary economics in the framework of this background. There is an urgent need to explore the general theory of finance in a given economic system with inbuilt linkages with other development agents.

Since the new classical economics, the financial super structure became one of the development activities. Finance since then plays a significant role in solving the development problems of the developing economies. The Financial Liberalization School and the Neo-Liberalization approach has further led the foundation of the Basel-I and II. The *Narsimham Committee* I & II paved the play to have macro-level policy initiatives required for positive business performance of the financial institutions. But the customer centric approach cannot be denied. In fact there should be a trade off between business centric and customer centric approaches. However proper plinth has been constructed by the *Narsimham Committees*. The final financial superstructure is yet be erected in the frame work of financial liberalization approach.

An attempt has been made through this volume to acknowledge the world experiences in financial sector reforms. There are six articles on Indian financial sector reforms. Two belongs to the general category; while four articles are devoted to specific area of analysis. *J.P. Bhosale, H.D. Thorat,* and *A.C. Bhavsar* have concentrated their exploration towards PACS in the framework of FSRs. *Mohod. Izhar Ahmad* has looked into the cooperative sector reforms. *P.S. Subbarao* has analyzed the role of corporate governce in Indian Banking. *Ganesh S. Mani* and *Srivyal Vuyyuri* has empirically identified the determinants of saving in India. While *B.S. Bodla* and *M.S. Turan* has empirically conducted a study related to investment preferences of retail equity investers. Profitability aspect has been exposed by *V. Nagarajan Naidu* and *Manju S. Nair.* The papers by *K. Rani & M. Manickam* and *Thakor Devendrasingh Vijaysingh* and *Ravi M. Tirlapur* and *G. Nagesha* belongs to general category of the overall impact studies. The internal aspects have been highlighted by *Geetanjali Sharma* and *Sandeepa Malhotra.* A global approach towards impact of globalization of financial market has been analytically discussed by *S. VijayKumar* and *N. Namasivayam. Kapil Sharma* has systematically explained the role of IMF in financial management of the deve loping economies. Similarly, *Masudul Alam Choudhury* and *Mohammad Ziaul Hoque* has analytically developed an epistenological approach for anchoring the real and money sector linkages in gold standards. *Thilak Ranaweera* has extended his views on gaps in external financing. *M.M. Metwally* has attempted to measure the impact of growth on market capitalization. *S.K. Sharma and Shudha Chandra* have introduced the changing face of Banking Sector Real Time Gross Settlement.

Country studies have been focused by a few paper writers. *B.S. Bodla* and *M.S. Turan* tried to acknowledge the facts in concern to risk and rewards in Asia Stock Markets. *Mazhar M. Islam* has accounted the growth and performance of local commercial banks in Oman. *Ste Ven Li, Simon S. Gao* and *Jane Zhang* have assessed the financial risk management involved in derivatives in China. *J.V. Menash* and *I.K. Acheampong* has assessed the impact of FSR's in Ghana in general.

The area specific study related to venture capital was conducted by *T. Satyanrayana Chary,* marketing of banking services by *Baby M.D,* micro-credit by *Amrit Patel* and the pros and cons of FSR's during the post reform period and the unfinished agenda or uncertain future of public sector banks is discussed by *Manoj S. Kamat* and *Branda Rodrigues.*

This volume is an attempt to introduce the degree and dignity of FSR's in the world. Of late, the Basel-II has been accorded. This, of course, would be the future agenda of the financial sector in the world. The financial sector, obviously is playing a vital role in developing the economies in general. Its impact studies will a continuous phenomenon. We believe that more number of papers will be contributed by the potential researchers to our next publications.

The reader's responses to this volume is highly appreciating and recognizing. I personally convey my warm regards to the paper contributors. My thanks are due to *Shri. S.K. Jha* and the team of Serial Publications for their pains taking job of publishing and marketing this volume.

**Dr. V.B. Jugale**

Date : 11 May, 2005

# Contents

# 1

# The Impact of Financial Sector Reforms in India

*Ravi M. Tirlapur and Nagesha G.**

## Introduction

Finance refers to the transfer of funds from surplus units to deficit units, that is, from savers to investors. The finançial sector encompassing the financial intermediaries, financial markets, and financial institutions plays a crucial role in the process of economic development. The financial development facilitates economic development in various ways; augments savings, provides funds for investment, allocates investible resources among the competing users, and thereby plays an important role in fostering the growth of income, output and employment. The financial sector has played an important role in India's economic development too. With the view of utilizing the scarce financial resources for speedy economic development, the financial sector in India was subjected to numerous controls and regulations. This 'Control Raj' became more pronounced in the late 1960's in the aftermath of the famous bank nationalization. This and several other measures definitely helped in accelerating the financial and economic development. However the financial sector at a

* Department of Economics, Bangalore University, Bangalore-560056.

later stage started suffering from the so called 'financial repression' as argued by McKinnon and Shaw (1973), where the real interest rates turned out to be negative or zero, thus discouraging savings, investment and adversely effecting the pace of economic development. The highly regulated and controlled regime also adversely affected the financial heath of the banks and other financial institutions.

In this background, the financial sector reforms were launched in 1990's and have been an integral part of the massive economic reform liberalisation measures initiated during that period. The present paper makes a modest attempt at giving an account of the financial sector reforms carried on in India since early 1990's and assess the impact of the reform measures on the rest of the economy in general and on the working of the financial sector in specific.

## Financial Sector on the Eve of 1991

The Indian financial sector was crying for correction on the eve of 1991. It was typically experiencing the 'financial repression' as characterized by "high reserve requirements, interest rate controls, and directed credit to favoured sectors"; thus causing harm to resource mobilisation and resource allocation. The scarce financial resources with the financial sector were pre-empted by way of CRR and SLR requirements which had reached a high of 15 percent and 38.5 percent respectively (as opposed to 15 percent and 25 percent in 1960s and 1970s). These high requirements impounded more than 50 percent of the resources of the financial system. In addition to this the 40 percent of the remaining resources were to be earmarked for the priority sector lending under the directed credit program. These high requirements by way of CRR, SLR, PSL, by taking away about three fourth of their funds robbed the very commercial nature of the banks and other financial institutions. To make the matters worse the banks and financial institutions were subjected to administered/

regulated interested interest rate regime, where all sorts of interest rates were determined by the government/ monetary authorities.

These factors along with lax prudential regulation and supervision, predominance of public sector and lack of competition, political interference and organisational inefficiencies crippled the financial sector (Rangarajan and Jadhav 1992, Joshi and Little1996). Therefore "by 1991 the country had created an unprofitable, inefficient and financially unsound banking" and financial sector" (Joshi and Little1996). The average rate of return on the assets were less than 1 percent (0.15 percent to be precise), capital reserves averaged around 1.5 percent of thc total assets, very low both by Asian and international standards. The application of new accounting criteria revealed that on an average 24 percent of the advances of the public sector banks (PSBs) were non-performing. Thus the sector was abound with various structural anomalies with low profit, low efficiency low portfolio quality and high non-performing assets (NPAs), transaction costs, distorted allocation of resources. The high quantitative achievements since bank nationalisation of 1969-like-rapid expansion of bank branches, deposit mobilisation, lending etc., were marred by the low achievements on the quality side, thus threatening the very existence of the sector and the resultant adverse consequences for the real economy.

## The Financial Sector Reforms Since 1991

The high powered committee for the restructuring the monetary system, popularly known as the Chakravarthy Committee had come forward with a set of recommendations "to improve the monetary regulation to promote price stability"(Gupta S B, 1995). Several steps were taken up following the report. However the real boost to the launch of the financial sector reforms came due to the Narasimhan Committee reports I and II, once in early and the other later in late 1990s. The Government of India promptly initiated the reforms with the objective of removing the shades of financial repression prevalent in the system; improve the financial health and allocative efficiency of the sector. This was sought to be achieved by erecting market oriented, competitive and transparent financial system. Some of the major reforms are listed as below:

**Measures to Improve the Policy Environment**

- Relaxing the statutory requirements by reducing SLR, CRR.
- Phased reduction of Bank Rate.
- Deregulation of interest rates-both deposit and lending rates.
- Doing away with the automatic monetisation of budget deficit of the central government by replacing the adhocs with Ways and Means Advances.
- Setting up special debt recovery tribunals, Bureau of Financial Supervision, OTCEI, and NSE etc.

**Measures to Improve the Financial Health of the System**

- Adoption of prudential and capital adequacy norms as per the Basle Convention framework.
- Recapitalisation and restructuring of the Public sector banks.
- Improving the quality of the loan portfolio.
- Increase the competition by allowing for the private sector participation (both domestic and foreign) in banking, mutual fund and insurance sectors.

**Reforms in the Primary and Secondary Capital Markets**

- Globalization and economic liberalization of the markets with foreign private participation.

- Disinvestment in the public sector.
- Modernisation of stock exchanges.
- Introduction of electronic trading system.
- Relaxation of interest rate regulations.

**Reforms in the Government Securities Market**

- Introduction of 364 and 182 days treasury bills.
- Discount and Finance House of India limited for the reform in the securities market.
- The institutions of primary dealers in the government securities market.
- Reserve repo facility with RBI in government dated securities.
- State governments and provident funds allowed to participate in 91 day treasury bills.

**Reforms in the External Financial Markets**

- Flexible exchange rates system introduced.
- Indian companies permitted to access international capital markets through various instruments including euro issues.
- Rupee made fully convertible on current account and partially convertible in capital account of Balance of Payments.
- RBI made a single window agency for receipt and disposal of proposals for overseas investments by Indian companies.
- The replacement of FERA 1973 by FEMA to facilitate easy capital flows.

**The Impact of Reforms**

The reform is a continuing process and that makes the task of analysing the impact of the reform difficult. However the following paragraphs attempt to assess the impact of financial sector reforms under different heads.

## The Indicators of Financial Development

The many of indicators of the indicators of financial development have shown improvements in the 1990s in the aftermath of the financial sector reforms.

**Table 1 : Indicators of Financial Development**

| *Year* | *Finance Ratio* | *Financial Interrelatios Ratio* | *New Issue Ratio* | *Inter-mediation Ratio* |
|---|---|---|---|---|
| 1984-85 | 0.22 | 2.94 | 1.70 | 0.73 |
| 1985-86 | 0.20 | 2.27 | 1.31 | 0.73 |
| 1986-87 | 0.24 | 2.94 | 1.78 | 0.65 |
| 1987-88 | 0.19 | 2.09 | 1.16 | 0.79 |
| 1988-89 | 0.25 | 2.32 | 1.33 | 0.74 |
| 1989-90 | - | - | - | - |
| 1990-91 | 0.23 | 1.74 | 1.00 | 0.74 |
| 1991-92 | 0.28 | 2.92 | 1.61 | 0.80 |
| 1992-93 | 0.21 | 2.18 | 1.18 | 0.84 |
| 1993-94 | 0.25 | 2.82 | 1.48 | 0.89 |
| 1994-95 | 0.25 | 2.43 | 1.16 | 1.09 |
| 1995-96 | 0.29 | 2.26 | 1.32 | 0.70 |

*Source:* RBI Report on Currency and Finance, Various Issues.

- The *Finance Ratio* showing the ratio of primary issues (i.e. the issues by all the sectors other than banks and other financial institutions) to national income has moved up from 0.23 in 1990-91to 0.29 in 1995-96. This shows that the industrial and stock market slump and periodic scams have not dampened the spirits of the investor class. Thus the primary market has shown the signs of readiness to cater to the needs of the corporate sector.
- The *Financial Interrelations Ratio* is the ratio of total issues to the domestic capital formation and shows the relationship between the financial development and the growth of physical investment.

This ratio has climbed to 2.26 (1995-96) from 1.75 (1990-91).

- Similarly the *Issue Ratio* reflecting the ratio of primary issue to the net domestic capital formation has increased from 1.005 to 1.33.
- The other important indicator, *Intermediation Ratio* is defined as the ratio of secondary issue (issue by banks and other financial institutions) to primary issues. In other words, this ratio indicates the proportion of claims issued by the financial institutions to the non-financial sector and it has gone up from 0.74 in 1990-910 to 1.1 in 1994-95 before dipping to 0.70 in 1995-96.

## Indicators of Financial Health

The ill health of the banks and financial institutions has been one of the important reasons for the initiation of the financial sector reforms. Hence it is of great interest to note if there is some improvement on this front as indicated by the extent of profits and the NPAs. The public sector banks have been the major contributors, in the past, to the losses and mounting NPAs incurred by the financial system. These indicators, however, have shown some improvement in the recent years, though there is much to be achieved. Both the operating and net profits have recorded significant improvements. For instance the net profit as percent of total assets of all the PSBs has moved up from 0.27 in 1991 to about 0.6 in the late 1990s.Thanks to the strict adherence to the capital adequacy and prudential norms and increased competition from the private sector.

The extent of NPAs is the other important indicator of the financial health. Though the gross and the net NPAs of the scheduled commercial banks have gone up in the recent years (except foreign banks), the same in relative terms i.e. as a percent of advances and total assets have shown a declining trend. The gross NPAs as percent of total assets have declined from 4 percent in 1994-95 to about 3 percent in the late 1990s. Level of NPAs still continues to be high by international standards despite the RBI/Government of India having taken several steps both preventive and remedial, to facilitate arrest of the NPA levels and the management of NPAs is proving to be a challenging task in terms of sheer magnitude and spread.

The other important achievement has been the adoptions of capital adequacy norms. Most of the banks have also adhered to the capital adequacy and prudential norms as stipulated from time to time. Now majority of the PSBs have CRAR at 9 to 10 percent (except for one bank, for which it was negative). Apart from the capitalisation from the government, some of the PSBs are also raising capital from the market through IPOs (Initial Public Offers) to strengthen their capital base.

**Composition of Savings**

Gross domestic saving after peaking at about 25 percent of GDP during mid 1990's has slid down to early 1990's levels at 23 percent. The main spoiler has been the public sector saving which has turned negative in late 1990's mainly due to "an increase in the dissaving of government administrative departments" (Economic Survey, GOI, 2003-04). The much talked about fiscal reforms – tax and yet to be tackled expenditure reforms- have not yielded any results in this direction.

Due to this reason, contribution of private savings- which made smart gains in moving from 20 percent (1990-91) to about 26 percent (2000-01), more so, the household savings which moved from 17 percent to about 21 percent during the period- has been camouflaged. Indeed, the private sector has responded vigorously to the financial reforms viz. the increase in the real interest rate, availability of wide portfolio of assets (not just the bank and post office deposits), vibrancy in the stock market (primary as well as secondary). Within the household sector savings, there has been shift in favour of financial savings (since mid 1990s) which augurs well for the real sector.

**Table 2 : Composition of Savings**

| | *1990-91* | *1991-92* | *1992-93* | *1993-94* | *1994-95* | *1995-96* | *1996-97* | *1997-98* | *1998-99* | *1999-00* | *2000-01* | *2001-02 (P)* | *2002-03 (Q)* |
|---|---|---|---|---|---|---|---|---|---|---|---|---|---|
| **Gross Domestic Savings** | 23.10 | 22.00 | 21.80 | 22.50 | 24.80 | 25.10 | 23.20 | 23.10 | 21.70 | 24.2 | 23.7 | 23.5 | 24.2 |
| **Public** | 1.10 | 2.00 | 1.60 | 0.06 | 1.70 | 2.00 | 1.70 | 1.30 | -1.00 | -1.0 | -2.3 | -2.7 | -1.9 |
| **Private** | 22.00 | 20.10 | 20.20 | 21.90 | 23.20 | 23.10 | 21.50 | 21.80 | 22.70 | 25.2 | 26.1 | 26.2 | 26.1 |
| Household | 19.30 | 17.00 | 17.50 | 18.40 | 19.70 | 18.20 | 17.00 | 17.60 | 18.90 | 20.9 | 21.9 | 22.7 | 22.6 |
| Financial | - | - | - | - | 11.90 | 8.90 | 10.40 | 9.60 | 10.50 | 10.6 | 10.7 | 11.1 | 10.3 |
| Physical | - | - | - | - | 7.80 | 9.30 | 6.70 | 8.00 | 8.40 | 10.3 | 11.3 | 11.6 | 12.3 |
| Private Corporate | 2.70 | 3.10 | 2.70 | 3.50 | 3.50 | 4.90 | 4.50 | 4.20 | 3.70 | 4.4 | 4.1 | 3.5 | 3.4 |

*Source*: Economic Survey, GOI, Various Issues.

## Interest Rate Deregulation

One of the important achievements of financial libralisation has been the dismantling of administered interest rate regime and the progressive movement towards market determined interest rate regime. The progress has been gradual, but definite. Ever since the process began, there has been continuous southward movement in the nominal rates. Importantly, the real interest have turned positive (and are increasing) thus getting freedom from the clutches of the financial repression. Though this means high cost of funds for the corporate sector, there is no cause for worry as the corporate sector now has the option of raising funds from the capital market (both domestic and international). Moreover the positive real interest rates has augured well for the savings, as seen in the increase in private sector savings from about 20 percent in 1991-92 to about 26 percent in 2000-01. It is another story that public savings have declined, but it is well known that these savings are not sensitive to changes in interest rates.

## External Financial Indicators

The biggest success of the New Economic Policy since 1991 is the emergence of a vibrant external sector. Wide varieties of measures have been initiated aimed at liberlising the external finance. These mainly include- movement towards market determined exchange rate (Rupee, now is fully convertible on current account and partially on capital account.), libralisation of foreign investment, permission to Indian companies to raise money from the foreign market etc. Results are these to see for every one. The perennial foreign exchange constraints are now things of the past and India now has moved a long way from the nightmare of balance of payments crisis of 1991.

The foreign exchange reserves consisting of foreign currency assets, SDRs and gold holdings of RBI have shown increasing trend throughout and currently stand at over

**Table 3 : External Financial Indicators**

| Year | Forex Reserves | NEER 5 Country Index | NEER 10 Country Index | NEER 36 country Index | REER 5 Country Index | REER 10 Country Index | REER 36 Country Index | Ex. Rate Rupee-Dollar |
|---|---|---|---|---|---|---|---|---|
| 1990-91 | 5834 | - | - | - | - | - | - | 17.94 |
| 1991-92 | 9220 | 143.92 | 142.4 | - | 105.88 | 105.57 | - | 24.47 |
| 1992-93 | 9832 | 118.75 | 117.37 | - | 96.06 | 95.52 | - | 30.65 |
| 1993-94 | 19254 | 110.21 | 116.36 | 61.59 | 95.51 | 96.8 | 44.69 | 31.37 |
| 1994-95 | 25186 | 106.31 | 106.8 | 66.04 | 101.17 | 101.72 | 43.37 | 31.4 |
| 1995-96 | 21687 | 97.57 | 97.35 | 63.62 | 97.99 | 97.75 | 39.73 | 33.45 |
| 1996-97 | 26423 | 95.68 | 95.37 | 63.81 | 101.12 | 100.78 | 38.97 | 35.5 |
| 1997-98 | 29367 | 95.05 | 96.52 | 67.02 | 105.19 | 106.4 | 40.01 | 37.17 |
| 1998-99 | 32490 | 84.09 | 85.33 | 63.44 | 101.06 | 101.89 | 36.34 | 42.07 |
| 1999-00 | 38036 | 81.4 | 83.95 | 63.30 | 99.68 | 102.08 | 35046 | 43.33 |
| 2000-01 | 425231 | 80.37 | 84.45 | 66.53 | 99.08 | 103.04 | 35.42 | 45.68 |
| 2001-02 | 48112 | 79.49 | 83.49 | 68.43 | 102.35 | 105.84 | 35.75 | 47.69 |

*Note* : For 5 country and 10 country index Base: 1995=100, 36 country index Base: 1985=100.

*Source*: Economic Survey, GOI, Various Issues.

100 billion US dollars, sufficient for more than 12 months of import requirements. Foreign Investment- both FII and FDI- has also shown steady increase.

The exchange rate movement has shown considerable stability, with occasional pressure on rupee (both upward and downward), though the nominal Rupee-USD exchange rate has moved from about Rs.18 a Dollar to about Rs.48 now. The five country, ten country, 36 country NEER has in fact appreciated. Where as the REER shown greater stability with occasional bursts of appreciation and depreciation. Thanks to timely and adequate of intervention by RBI these bouts of pressures the have been smoothened.

## The Macroeconomic Indicators

It is difficult to ascertain precisely the contribution of financial sector to the growth of real GDP. But the financial sector must have contributed immensely in this direction, by—

- Affecting the cost and availability of credit,
- Impacting on the real interest rate and the subsequent effect on the rate of savings, investment and GDP growth.
- Making available variety of financial instruments both to the corporate, households and the government sector.
- Maintaining the vibrant external sector by way of removing foreign exchange shortage, maintaining healthy BOP position.
- Giving autonomy to the central bank and thereby regulating the money supply and inflation rate at appropriate and safe level.
- Providing more say to the market forces and removing government interference in the financial sector.

**Table 4 : Macro Economic Indicators**

| *YEAR* | *GDP-* *GR* | *INDL.* *GR* | *SAV.* *RATE* | *INV.* *RATE* | *INFLATION* *RATE* |
|---|---|---|---|---|---|
| 1990-91 | 5.6 | 7.4 | 23.1 | 24.1 | - |
| 1991-92 | 1.3 | -1 | 22.0 | 21.9 | - |
| 1992-93 | 5.1 | 4.3 | 21.8 | 23.8 | - |
| 1993-94 | 5.9 | 5.6 | 22.5 | 21.3 | - |
| 1994-95 | 7.3 | 10.3 | 24.8 | 23.4 | 12.6 |
| 1995-96 | 7.3 | 12.3 | 25.1 | 26.9 | 8 |
| 1996-97 | 7.8 | 7.7 | 23.2 | 24.5 | 4.6 |
| 1997-98 | 4.8 | 3.8 | 23.1 | 24.6 | 4.4 |
| 1998-99 | 6.5 | 3.8 | 21.5 | 22.6 | 5.9 |
| 1999-00 | 6.1 | 5.2 | 24.2 | 25.8 | 3.3 |
| 2000-01 | 4.4 | 6.5 | 23.7 | 24.4 | 7.2 |
| 2001-02 | 5.8 | 3.4 | 23.5 | 23.1 | 3.6 |

*Source*: Economic Survey, GOI, Various Issues.

## Conclusion

India has travelled a long way from being the financially repressed economy to one where there is great amount of financial libralisation. The market forces now have greater say and government interference has decreased to a great extent. While the financial health of the sector has improved, that is not the end in itself. The financial liberalisation and lack of adequate regulation in the initial stages contributed to the proliferation of scams starting with stock scams, UTI scandal, MS shoes issue, to latest Cooperative bank scandal. While the competition, efficiency, transparency, profit etc, are important, the needs of the social, agricultural and other sectors of the society at large, where the market forces fail cannot be brushed aside.

## REFERENCES

Bhalla V.K. (1998), "Indian Financial System." Anmol Publications, New Delhi.

Bhole L.M. (2002), "Financial Institutions and Markets." Tata McGraw Hill.

Economic Survey, Government of India, Various issues.

Jalan Biman (Edited) (1992), "The Indian Economy: Problems and Prospects." Penguin Publications.

Joshi Vijay and Little IMD (1998), "India's Economic Reform 1991-2001."Oxferd University Press, New Delhi.

Rangarajan. (1999), "Indian Economy: Essays on Money and Finance." UBSPD Publications.

Rangarajan C.and Jadhav Narendra,"Issues in Financial Sector Reform." In Jalan Biman Edited (1992), "The Indian Economy: Problems and Prospects." Penguin Publications.

RBI Report on Currency and Finance, Various issues.

# 2

# Role of Corporate Governance in Indian Banking

*P. Srinivas Subbarao**

## Introduction

The concept of corporate governance, which emerged as a response to corporate failures and widespread dissatisfaction with the many corporate functions, has become one of the wide and deep discussions around the globe recently. The concept of corporate governance primarily hinges on complete transparency, integrity and accountability of the management. There is also an increasingly greater focus on investor protection and public interest.

Governance is the process whereby people in power make decisions that create, destroy or maintain social system, structures and processes. Corporate governance is therefore the process whereby people in power direct, monitor and lead corporations, and thereby either create, modify or destroy the structures and systems under which they operate. Corporate governors are both potential agents for change and also guardians of existing ways of working. As such, they are therefore a significant part of the fabric of our society.

* Asst. Professor Department of Management Studies, P.G. Courses· M.R. College (Affiliated to Andhra University).

Corporate governance has become an issue of worldwide importance. The corporation has a vital role to play in promoting economic development and social progress. It is the engine of growth internationally, and increasingly responsible for providing employment, public and private services, goods and infrastructure. The efficiency and accountability of the corporation is now a matter of both private and public interest, and governance has thereby come to the head of the International agenda.

Corporate governance is concerned with the values, vision and visibility. It is about the value orientation of the organization, ethical norms for its performance, the direction of development and social accomplishment of the organization and the visibility of its performance and practices. The concept of good governance connotes that ethics is as important as economics, fair play as crucial as financial success, morals as vital as market share. Good governance is critical to the success of an organization has been emphasized umpteen times. Volumes have been written on the subject, and a plethora of reports have been published besides OECD and World Bank.

**Indian Banking Industry**

Indian banking has around 200 years of history has undergone many transformations since independence (1947). But, LPG (liberalisation, Privatisation and Globalisation) and IT (Information Technology) are currently transforming the Indian banking radically. The metamorphosis in the Indian banking is taking place significantly in the areas of ownership, structure system, process, marketplace, delivery channel, products, technology, etc.

Indian banking consisting of commercial banks, cooperative banks and regional rural banks. Around 60,000 branches of 27 public sector banks (PSBs) and 196 regional rural banks and another 4,700 branches of 55 smaller private sector banks and 200 branches of various foreign banks are working by providing employment to eight lakhs employees. Besides there are 94000 cooperative societies or branches of cooperative banks, augmented by another 24,000 Non Banking Finance Companies are exist in the country. A total of 140,000 institutional outlets servicing the rural sector and the poor implies the availability of one outlet for every 5,600 persons—in theory, a very favorable ratio for catering to the financial needs of the poor.

Earlier banking was virtually a monopoly of the public sector banks with full protection from the State. But the process of reforms in the Indian banking system has thrown them out to more liberal and free market forces. Now the banks, more particularly the public sector, feel the real heat of the competition. The interest rate cuts, dwindling margins and more number of players to serve a reduced number of bankable clients; have all added to the worries of the banks. The customer has finally come to hold the center-stage and all banking products are tailor-made to suit his tastes and preferences. This sudden change in the banking environment in the country has bereaved the banks of all their comforts and many of them are finding it extremely difficult to cope with the change.

## Need of Corporate Governance in Banks

Since banks are important players in the financial system in India, special focus on the Corporate Governance in the banking sector becomes critical. Secondly, the Reserve Bank of India, as regulator, has the responsibility on the nature of Corporate Governance in the banking sector. Thirdly, to the extent that banks have systemic implications, Corporate Governance in the banks is of critical importance. Fourth, given the dominance of public ownership in the banking system in India, corporate practices in the banking sector would also set the standards for Corporate Governance in private sector. Finally, with a view to reducing the possible fiscal burden of recapitulating the PSBs, attention toward Corporate Governance in the banking sector assumes added importance. Since PSBs must be in a position to assure the market that there system of

Corporate Governance is such that they can be trusted with shareholders' money.

The broad connotation of the term Good Corporate Governance covers at least three types of issues viz.,

## Ethical Issues

Ethical issues are concerned about corporate frauds. We have been hearing about several unhealthy manipulations and malpractice's including from some of the best-managed companies in India and abroad. They involve cheating of investors and depositors, payment defaults, insider trading an cornering of stock, violation of laws and norms, evasion of excise duties, indifference to the rights of minorities and institutional share holders and nexus with corrupt officials and politicians. This has badly shaken the confidence of public—both internal and external—and is responsible for the society to become overtly conscious about the need for Good Corporate Governance. The World Bank Annual Report (2002) has observed that the loss of US $1 trillion in banking crises in the 1980s and 1990s in equal to the total flow of official development assistance to developing countries from 1950s to the present date.

## Efficiency Issues

Banking companies in a Capitalist society depends upon public participation in equity. In these, individuals through mutual funds, retirement funds and tax funds make a large proportion of Investment. In addition to these, direct investment by small shareholders continues to remain important, especially in India where the mutual funds industry is still at a nascent stage. However, most of the investors, whose returns depend upon the efficiency of management, do not have any worthwhile say in the management of these companies.

## Accountability Issues

The accountability issues involve the need for transparency of management in the conduct of affairs of the company. This is felt in the interests of stakeholders, workers and customers. Whose fortunes are closely linked with these companies. Further questions also arise with regard to social responsibility of these companies in the broader sense of the term.

## Prerequisites for Good Governance

A review of the literature on corporate governance, including the Reports of various committees, suggests that there are some pre-requisites for good corporate governance. They are:

- A proper system consisting of clearly defined and adequate structure of roles, authority and responsibility.
- Vision, principles and norms which indicate development path, normative considerations and guidelines and norms for performance.
- A proper system for guiding, monitoring, reporting and control.

## Recommendation of the Birla Committee

The Report of the Committee on corporate Governance, set up by the SEBI, (Securities and Exchange board of India, Government of India Organisation) under the chairmanship of Kumar Mangalam Birla, is the first formal and comprehensive attempt to evolve a Code of Corporate Governance, in the context of prevailing condition of governance in Indian companies, as well as the state of capital markets.

The committee has identified the three key constituents of corporate governance as the Shareholders, the Board of Directors and the Management and has attempted to identify in respect of each of these constituents, their roles and responsibilities as also their rights in the context of good corporate governance. Fundamental to this examination and permeating throughout this exercise is the recognition of the three key aspects of corporate governance, namely;

accountability, transparency and equality of treatment for all stakeholders.

### Shareholders Role

The shareholders role in corporate governance is to appoint the directors and the auditors and to hold the board accountable for the proper governance of the company by requiring the board to provide them periodically with the requisite information, in transparent fashion, of the activities and progress of the company.

### Board of Directors Role

The board of directors performs the pivotal role in any system of corporate governance. It is accountable to the stakeholders and directs and controls the Management. It stewards the company, sets its strategic aim and financial goals and oversees their implementation, puts in place adequate internal controls and periodically reports the activities and progress of the company in a transparent manner to the stakeholders.

### Management Role

The responsibility of the management is to undertake the management of the company in terms of the direction provided by the board, to put in place adequate control systems and to ensure their operation and to provide information to the board on a timely basis and in a transparent manner to enable the board to monitor the accountability of Management to it.

### Basel Committee Recommendation

The Basel Committee published a paper for banking organisations in September 1999. The committee suggested that it is the responsibility of the banking supervisors to ensure that there is effective corporate governance in the banking industry. The Committee highlighted the need for having appropriate accountability and checks and balances within each bank to ensure sound corporate governance, which in turn would lead to effective and more meaningful supervision.

The Basel committee underscores the need for banks to set strategies for their operations and insists banks to establish accountability for executing these strategies. Unless there is transparency of information related to decisions and actions, it would be difficult for shareholders to make management accountable.

The Committee issued various papers highlighting the importance of corporate governance on matters namely interest rate risk, framework for internal control system in banking organisations and principles for the management of credit risk. For the purpose of establishing strategic objectives and set of corporate values, the Basel Committee says that it is difficult to conduct the activities of an organisation unless there are strategic objectives or guiding corporate values. Thus, the Board should establish the strategies that will direct the ongoing activities of the bank. From the point of view of banking industry, the corporate governance should also include in its sphere the manner in which the Board of Directors govern the business affairs of individual institutions and their functional relationship with senior management. The committee has given more stress on the following points.

## Need of Effective Board of Directors

The Board of Directors should ensure that the senior management implements the policies that prohibit activities and relationship that diminish the quality of corporate governance, such as,

- Conflicts of interests,
- Lending to officers and employees and other forms of self-dealing (i.e., internal lending should be limited to lending consistent with market terms and to certain types of loans, and reports of insider lending should be provided to board and to be subject to review by internal and external auditors), and

- Providing preferential treatment to related parties to Board and other favored entities (e.g., lending on highly favorable terms covering trading losses, waiving commissions).

Proper system should be established that allows the Board to monitor compliance with these policies and ensure that deviations are reported to an appropriate level of management.

For the purpose of establishing practices and enforcing clear lines of responsibility and accountability, the Basel Committee says that effective Board of Directors should clearly define the authorities and key responsibilities for themselves, as well as senior management. The Committee stipulates that the Board of Directors is ultimately responsible for the operations and financial soundness of the bank. It must receive on timely basis sufficient information to judge the performance of management. The Board members should be capable of exercising judgement independent of the views of management, large shareholders or the Government. Inclusion of qualified directors that are not members of the bank's management on the board can enhance independence and objectivity.

**Role of Senior Management**

In order to keep proper oversight on the activities of the bank, the Basel Committee says that senior management is a key component of corporate governance. Just like the Board of Directors provides checks and balances to senior managers, senior managers should assume the oversight role with respect to line managers in specified business areas and activities. Even in very small banks, key management decisions should be made by more than one person.

In view of the Basel Committee, it is desirable to avoid assigning oversight functions to senior managers who are—

- Overly involved in business line decision-making;

- Assigned in area to manage without necessary prerequisite skills or knowledge;
- Unwilling to discipline successful or key employees, when they go wrong, for fear of losing them.

**Role of Internal and External Auditors**

The Basel Committee has put special responsibility on the Board to recognize and acknowledge that the internal and external auditors are their critically important agents. In particular, the Board should utilise the work of the auditors as an independent check on the information received from management on the operations and performance of the bank.

**Importance of Transparency**

The Committee has given lot of importance to transparency. It says that it is difficult to hold the Board of Directors and senior management accountable for their actions and performance when there is a lack of transparency. Transparency can alone reinforce sound corporate governance, and hence public disclosure is desirable in the following areas:

- board structure with regard to size, membership, qualifications and committees;
- senior management structure regarding responsibilities, reporting lines, qualifications, and experience;
- basic organisational structure in respect of like of business structure, legal entity structure;
- information about incentive structure of the bank in relation to remuneration policies, executive compensation, bonuses, stock option; and
- Nature and extent of transactions with affiliates and related parties.

## Basel II Revolution

The New Basel Capital Accord (the New Accord) which is popularly known as 'Basel II' raised lot of dust among banking circles around the globe. The accord is scheduled to be implemented by the end of 2006. All the banking supervisors may have to join the Accord reluctantly, as Basel II is the ultimate goal of all countries including India, in bringing in the stability in the financial world.

Even the domestic banks in addition to internationally active banks may have to conform to the Accord principles in the coming decades. Instead of rejecting the Accord altogether, it is better to adopt its principles, which are sound and scientific. The following three main pillars of the Accord are relevant and influence the Indian banking.

## Capital Adequacy

The existing prudential capital adequacy norms (CRAR) will be completely overhauled by the proposed Basel II norms in future. The new norms for calculation of risk weighted assets are aimed at improving the present system of assessment of risk and to make them more meaningful. The major departure of the New Accord is in recognising the need for assessment of 'Operational Risks' which is absent in the present norms.

Another innovation of the Accord is IRB (Internal Rating Based) approach to the credit risks which is based on modern risk management principles and tools that involve quantitative assessment of risk. Banks in India, will soon realise the hard truth/that they are moving towards the new capital adequacy norms as proposed in Basel II.

## Banking Supervision

Banking supervision in India will reach new heights by 2010. It had already switched over to 'Risk Based Supervision' from, the old "CAMELS" based approach, under the influence of Basel II. The following are some of the Basel Committee on Banking Supervision prescribed key principles for effective banking supervision as:

- Sound capital assessment and comprehensive assessment of risks.
- On-site, Off-site review/evaluation/surveillance and 'Stress-Test' for banks.
- Excessive holdings of capital over and above the required norms.
- Early intervention and prompt corrective action.

The above core principles are the true pillars of the foundation for 'Effective Banking Supervision'.

**Disclosure Norms/Market Discipline**

It is our experience that the deficiencies in transparency and disclosures by various international financial institutions, organisations and even governments were the main contributors for the financial/political turmoil around the globe, during eighties/nineties.

Banks balance sheets in India will be subject to stringent disclosure norms and further rationalisation/ standardisation of accounting norms. True and transparent disclosures lead to a stable, safe and sound banking in India. The guiding principles suggested by Basel II for disclosure requirements will certainly have influence on Indian Banking.

**Factors Influencing Corporate Governance in Indian Banking Industry**

***The Ownership Structure***

The structure of ownership of a company determines, to a considerable extent, how a corporation is managed and controlled. The ownership structure can be either dispersed among individual and institutional shareholders as in the US and UK or can be concentrated in the hands of a few large shareholders as in Germany and Japan.

But the pattern of shareholding is not as simple as the above statement seeks to convey. The pattern varies across the globe.

Indian banking sector is characterised by the co-existence of state owned (PSBs), private and multinational enterprises. The shares of these enterprises (except those belonging to the public sector) are held by institutional as well as small investors. Specially, shares are held by (i) the term lending institutions (ii) institutional investors, comprising government owned mutual funds, Unit Trust of Indian and the Government owned the insurance corporations (iii) Corporate bodies (iv) directors and their relatives and (v) foreign investors. Apart from these block-holdings there is a sizeable equity holding by small investors.

Which pattern of shareholding, dispersed or concentrated, is ideal for good corporate performance? Large shareholders tend to be active in corporate governance wither through their representatives on company boards or through their active participation in annual general body meetings. Reliance Industries Ltd. have demonstrated this, which has the highest number of equity shareholders spread across the country. Block holding too has not proved to be a failure either. Dominant shareholders are better informed than the dispersed shareholders.

## The Financial Structure

The financial structure of the company i.e., proportions between debt and equity, has implications for the quality of governance. Contrary to the Modigliani-Miller hypothesis that the financial structure of the firm has no relationship to the value of a firm, recent research has shown that the financial structure does matter. It is no secret that the lenders exercise significant influence on the way a company is managed and controlled.

## The Structure and Functioning of the Company Boards

The structure of the company boards has considerable influence on the way the companies are managed and controlled. The board of direction is responsible for establishing corporate objectives, developing broad policies and selecting top-level executives to carry out those objectives and policies. Company boards are permitted to vary in size, composition and structure so as to best serve the interests of the corporation and the shareholders. Board membership may be including both inside directors and outside directors. Again, boards can be single-tired or two-tired.

With regard to the size of board, opinions and practices vary. Some argue that the adequate size is to range from nine to fifteen. Some others put the figure at ten and yet others recommend a minimum of five and a maximum of ten. It should be noted that it is the quality of the directors, the interests they take, and the roles that they assume which are more important than mere numbers or composition.

The Board of Directors adds strength to the good corporate governance of a bank if they—

- Understand their oversight role and their "duty of loyalty" to the bank and its shareholders,
- Serve as a "checks and balance" function vis-à-vis the day-to-day management of the bank,
- Feel empowered to question the management and can comfortably insist upon, straightforward explanations from management,
- Recommend sound practices gleaned from other situations,
- Provide dispassionate advice,
- Are not over extended

- Avoid conflicts of interest in their activities with, an commitments to other organisations, meet regularly with senior management and internal audit to establish and approve policies, establish line of communication and monitor progress of corporate objectives.
- Absent themselves from discussions when they are incapable of providing objective advice.
- Do not participate in day-to-day management of the bank.

## The Institutional Environment

The legal, regulatory, and political environment within which a bank operates determines in large measure the quality of corporate governance. Infact corporate governance mechanisms are economic and legal institutions and often the outcome of political decisions. For example, the extent to which shareholders can control the management depends on their voting rights as defined in company law, the extent to which creditors will be able to exercise financial claims on a bankrupt unit will depend on bankruptcy laws and procedures; and the extent to which the market for corporate control efficiency operates to discipline under performing management will depend on take-over regulations.

## Conclusion

Strong corporate governance is thus indispensable to resilient and vibrant capital markets and is an important instrument of investor protection. It is the blood that fills the veins of transparent corporate disclosure and high-quality accounting practices. It is the muscle that moves a viable and accessible financial reporting structure. Without financial reporting premised on sound, honest number, capital markets will collapse upon themselves.

Corporate governance has assumed vital importance and significance due to globalisation and liberalisation. With the opening of economy and to be in line with WTO requirements, if the Indian corporate have to survive and succeed amidst increasing competition globally, it can only be through transparency in operations. The excellence in terms of customer satisfaction, in terms of return, in terms of product and service, in terms of return to promoters and in terms of social responsibilities towards society and people cannot be achieved without practicing good corporate governance.

## REFERENCES

Annapurniah G, 'Issues and Solutions in Implementing Corporate Governance in Banks', IBA Bulletin, April, 2003.

'Enhancing Corporate Governance for Banking Organisations' by Basel Committee on Banking Supervision, Bank for international Settlements (B.I.S), Basle, Switzerland, September, 1999.

Kirit S. Parikh, 'India Development Report 1999-2000, p. 203.

Swapan Bakshi, 'Corporate Governance in Transformation Times' IBA Bulletin Special Issue, March, 2003.

S.S. Kohli, 'Corporate Governance in Banks: Towards Best Practices' IBA Bulletin Special Issue, March, 2003.

Vepa Kamesam, "Corporate Governance," "RBI Bulletin, January, 2002.

Y.V. Reddy, 'Corporate Governance in the Financial Sector 'RBI Bulletin, August, 1999.

# 3
# External Financing Gap: "Ghost" or Real?

*Thilak Ranaweera**

## Introduction

The publication by the World Bank entitled "Assessing Aid: What Works, What Doesn't, and Why," (see, The World Bank, 1998), has generated a great deal of debate among, academics, professional economists, and policy makers.[1] The World Bank report asserted that aid does help to increase growth in countries with sound economic management. The main message of the report both to aid recipients as well as donors was that aid should be allocated to recipient countries in accordance with their policy environments. These ideas about aid effectiveness, future of development aid, and policy conditionality associated with the new approach to aid have come under considerable criticism (see for example, Dalgaard and Hansen (2001), Doornbos (2001), Guillaumont and Chauvet (2001), Hermes and Lensink

* Thanks are due to Michael Lewin and Nina Budina (World Bank) and Sarath Rajapatirana (American Enterprise Institute) for helpful comments. However, all remaining errors are the responsibility of the author. The opinions expressed are purely personal and have no relationship to those of the World Bank.

1 See also, the background studies to that report by Burnside and Dollar (1997 and 2000) and Collier and Dollar (1999).

(2001), Hoeven (2001), Hansen and Tarp (2000), Lensink and White (2000).

One aspect of this has not received a great deal of discussion until recently relates to the question of analytical models for determining the extent of aid requirements of a country. In his study on "The Ghost of the Financing Gap: How the Harrod-Domar Model still Haunts Development Economics" Easterly (1999, see also 1997) pointed out that the Harrod-Domar model is still being used by leading international financial institutions (IMF, WB, etc) and regional agencies to measure foreign resource requirements, to allocate aid, and to provide advice to developing countries on economic policy. He observed tat the Harrod-Domar model was not intended as a growth model, and was in fact repudiated by one of its authors four decades ago. Easterly encouraged the academic/professional development community to closely evaluate the analytical models used by international financial institutions for determining foreign aid.

In response to Easterly's challenge, in an article in the Journal of Post-Keynesian Economics (Fall 2001) titled "Exorcising the ghost: An alternative model for measuring the financing gap in developing countries", Nureldin Hussain (2001) presented an "alternative" approach to address "interrelated questions of how to predict growth, how to measure the financing gap, and how to allocate aid and measure its development effectiveness." Hussain stated that so far there has not been a credible alternative to the Harrod-Domar model and that this creates a dilemma for policy makers. In this view, the "dominant think tank of World Bank is now shifting from the aid-financial investment toward a new paradigm—good policies plus money," but "this new paradigm has no uniform philosophy to address the interrelated questions" of aid and development. To address such questions, Hussain advocates the use of the so-called "Balance of Payments Constrained Growth Model" of Thirlwall and Hussain (1982)—referred to as the T-H model. According to Hussain, this latter model "introduces a convenient methodology backed by a growth model to estimate resource requirements, as well as providing "new" insights with regard to the formulation of development policies and assessing the effectiveness of development assistance."

Hussain presented a very interesting form of the T-H model with actual applications for a number of African countries. While simplicity and clarity are virtues that any user would appreciate, the T-H model, unfortunately, does not present a "credible alternative." In part, the problem seems to emanate from the particular presentation of the T-model: it is not a complete model. Thus, the T-H model ends up with an incomplete estimate of the financing gap. It appears that Hussain has somewhat misunderstood the so-called World Bank model and Easterly's observations on the "ghost of financing gap". To clarify these issues, we first begin with a very brief description of a stylized version of the "standard" model used by the World Bank for country operations work, which Easterly took to task. Second, a comparison of this "standard" version with the T-H model reveals that the latter is almost an exact copy of one of he key relationships of the former. The T-H model leaves out other key relationship such as the investment-savings gap, the fiscal gap and the monetary implications of the balance of payments. Thus, the T-H model fails to address the fundamental question raised by Easterly, and cannot be considered an "alternative". Furthermore, it is also clear that both Easterly and Hussain have failed to appreciate how the World Bank and IMF models are used in practice: that is, how Bank/IMF economists, policy makers, and donors have used these models in a very flexible way to overcome some of their well-known shortcomings. Thus, it appears that both Easterly and Hussain are ghost-busters chasing after elusive, if not almost non-existent "ghosts."

## The "Standard" Framework of the "Three-Gap" Model of International Financial Institutions[2]

In the following paragraphs, as an example, a description of a popular World Bank model is given with the variables expressed in level terms. While this model can be given in a more compact form to show its properties, we opt to give a description of the actual working model used by the country economists in the World Bank. The "standard" model used by many World Bank country management units (known as the Revised Minimum Standards Model Extended-RMSM-X) belongs to a class of "three-gap" models widely used by developing countries (see Bacha (1990), Iqbal (1997), Khan (), Sepehri, Moshiri and Doudongee (2000), Taylor (1990) that is an extended version of the "two gap" model introduced by Chenery and Strout (1966). It consists of two modules: the flow of funds module that sets the accounting identities and a few behavioral equations (FOF), and a external debt module that brings in information of external debt related transactions (DM). The basic version contains four economic agents or "sectors"" Central Government, the Monetary System (Central Bank and Deposit Money Banks), the "Private" Sector[3] ("Rest of the Economy" including households and private firms, non-central government agencies, parastatal enterprises, and non-monetary financial institutions) and the Foreign Sector.

## Equations of the "Standard" Model[4]

The savings-investment gap:

$$Y - (Cg + Cp) - (Ig + Ip) = X - IM \tag{1}$$

---

[2] The "standard" three-gap model has come under a great deal of criticism from World Bank economists, and there had been a number of attempts to find alternatives that are capable of handling old issues and new demands, including poverty-related work (see, Devarajan et al (1994), Agenor, et al (2000).

[3] The so-called 'Private Sector' should be interpreted as a residual sector covering those sectors not explicitly recognized in the model.

[4] For the symbols used, see appendix 1.

The foreign exchange gap:

$$X - IM + NFY + NCT + KT_{fg} + DFI + POR + NLT + NST + dRES = GAPF \quad (2)$$

The fiscal gap:

$$NTXpg + Td + (Ti - Sub) + NCTfg + NFfg + NFgp + Krev - Ig - NKTRgp =$$

$$= Lmg + Lps + KTfg + NLTfg + NSTfg \quad (3)$$

The monetary sector flows are summarized by equation (4) below:

$$L_{mp} + L_{mg} + dRES = dM + dNOL \quad (4)$$

Ignoring many sectoral details, this stylized version of the model can be summarized to consist of 4 equations and 33 variables.[5] To obtain a numerical solution (33-4) variables should be assigned values. In this process, a number of important variables are "endogenized" by specifying several appropriate behavioral equations. Some of these are discussed below in the section on typical behavioral structure of the model. For the remainder, several different methods of exogenously specifying the expected values for the variables are adopted. These, in fact, could also be considered as sub-models depending on the degree of details accommodated.

## Typical Behavioral Equations of the Model

The money demand function:

$$M = P\, y / v \quad (5)$$

The investment/output relation:

$$I(t) = ICOR\,(t + 1) * [y(t - 1) - y\,(t)] \quad (6)$$

Private consumption function:

$$Cp = c * (Y - T + NCTR + NFY) \quad (7)$$

---

[5] The 5th equation of the system, i.e. that for the private sector is redundant according to Walras' law.

Import functions:

$$IMi = f(y_e, RERi) \quad (8)$$

Manufacturing exports function:

$$Xm = f(yf, RERm) \quad (9)$$

Other exports:

$$Xi = (1 + gxi) * Xi(t - 1) \quad (10)$$

The model can be solved using one of several approaches. First, all resource flows could be specified exogenously and the model could than be solved for the implied growth and inflation rates.[6] Second, resource requirements (including the additional foreign exchange needs) could be estimated for given growth and inflation assumptions. Most users of the model adopt the latter approach for computational convenience. Either approach could be considered as a first step in an iterative process that converges to a feasible solution to the model.[7]

To evaluate the external sustainability of the country, a module that incorporates external debt information supplements the flow-of-funds framework. This enables the calculation of the debt servicing capacity of the country taking into account the existing stock of external debt and changes in that stock as a result of the projected balance of payments outcomes as given by the flow-of-funds part of the model. In other words, the interaction of the information on external debt flows and the flow-of-funds facilitates the mapping of the implications of alternative profiles of aid-financing to the balance of payments.

## Investment-Savings Behavior and the Calculation of "Financing Gap"

For the last two decades, the Harrod-Domar specification embodied in equation (6) above had been under challenge

---

6 In World Bank terminology this is called the "availabilities" approach to model solution.

7 Since no explicit objective function is used, the solution is best described as a feasible one. The importance of iteration in this process cannot be overemphasized.

by numerous academics, World Bank/IMF economists and other users of this type of "standard" model.[8] However, Easterly added a new dimension to that challenge by alluding to the "ghost of financing gap" by emphasizing the implications to an important outcome of the model, namely foreign aid allocation. And this important variable has also an equally significant bearing on the lending programs and policies of the World Bank/IMF, other multi-lateral and bilateral donors. After a critical evaluation of the "financing gap" model in light of growth theory, Easterly (1999) concluded that "...in the short run, there is no theoretical reason in standard neoclassical and endogenous growth models to expect the ICOR to be a measure of investment quality, to be the derivative of growth with respect to investment, or to be constant during transitions." Considering a number of specific country experiences, Easterly (1999) then went on to assert that the "financing gap" model has little empirical validity. From a fairly rigorous viewpoint, these indeed were very valid criticisms of the type of models in question. Unfortunately, however, Easterly did not propose any alternative models that the international financial institutions could possibly use in the given context.

### Comparison of "Three-Gap" and T-H Models

The "standard" model can easily be presented in such a way as to conform to the T-H model by appropriately aggregating variables so as to retain only those that are used by T-H and expressing the results in growth rate form. However, by retaining the details that actually are considered within the framework of the "standard" model, we also want to emphasize the fact that a great deal of information and empirical work goes into the use of the framework than appears at first sight. For example, a function may be

---

8 Some have in fact opted to drop the relationship between investment and growth and have instead adopted an output adjustment mechanism in the Keynesian tradition (see, Bacha, 1990 and Taylor, 1994.

developed for direct foreign investment into the particular country under study or the value assumed may be based on already approved projects (such as oil pipelines, hydro-electric dams, etc) from available reports etc.

The important point to note is that by considering a subset of variables in equation (2), one can easily arrive at the result shown by the T-H model's equation (5) in growth rate form (see, Hussain (2001)). It is clear that the sub-set of the variables considered by Hussain in his equations (2), (3), and (4) —and therefore, in the resulting equation (5)—is the sum of the current and capital account transactions of the balance of payments. Hence, of course the origin of the term "balance of payments constrained growth." Ignoring the richer details in the World Bank presentation, it appears that the T-H model is based on the same aggregative import/ export elasticties that underpin the World Bank's balance of payments equations. However, while focusing on the balance of payments gap is unavoidable, it is not the same thing as asserting that the external gap is the only constraint and that it is the "dominant constraint on output growth". In some developing countries, this may not be the case. It is precisely because of this reason that Chenery and Strout (1966) laid emphasis on the "two gap" approach and the inter-related nature of the savings-investment and foreign exchange gaps.

In contrast of the World Bank's model that incorporates three-related gaps, the T-H model is focused exclusively on one gap: the balance of payments constraint. The T-H model has no explicit savings-investment gap, which is given in equation (1) above. Neither does the T-H model contain a fiscal gap. In the T-M model, therefore, one has to assume that the savings-investment gap and the fiscal gap are actually implicit. To claim that the T-M model is indeed an "alternative" in the context under consideration, it is necessary to explicitly show how the balance of payments constrained growth is related to the investment-savings gap and the fiscal gap. As can be seen from the World Bank's model, this can be done only in a consistent accounting framework that is based on behavioral relations explaining aggregate growth, savings and investment that are consistent with the balance of payments (or vice-versa) and the fiscal variables. The essence of Easterly's criticism was that the Harrod-Domar based simple investment/growth behavioral relation assumed in the World Bank model was neither theoretically satisfying nor empirically valid, especially in the short-run. Easterly was well disposed to make that statement as he had substantially contributed to the evolution of the current form of the World Bank's model. Sweeping this problem under the carpet in the T-H model is not a satisfactory solution as the savings-investment gap and the fiscal gap cannot disappear into this air.

The T-H estimate of foreign exchange requirements to achieve a given target rate of growth (see, his equations 8 and 9) is only a partial representation of the total foreign exchange needs of a country. Considering the more comprehensive balance of payments account given in equation (2) above, it is clear that the T-H model does not explicitly show the foreign exchange requirements relating to the maintenance of a desired (or target) level of foreign reserves (dRES), which is a very important variable in a policy dialogue. It is possible to argue that the change in reserves is somehow embedded in the two parameters of the T-H model relating to the proportions of the total import bill financed by export earnings and capital flows. If this is the case, it is a somewhat confusing way to take account of this factor and is bound to cause problems in practical implementation of the T-H model. The desired or target level of net foreign assets is a key element of the IMF financial programming framework, which is underpinned by the monetary model of the balance of payments. Maintaining an adequate level of foreign assets to meet import payments is a crucial foreign exchange requirement facing many developing countries. Thus, the foreign financing gap estimate of the T-H model is only a partial estimate requirements as it fails to account for the total foreign exchange requirements of a country, including the need to build up external reserves.

Considering the T-H model in the context of explaining growth rate differences by demand constrains associated with the balance of payments, Elliot and Rhodd (1999) came to the conclusion that the T-H model "to be less than complete because it omitted the effect of debt servicing." Elliot and Rhodd demonstrated that the simple Harrod multiplier will over-predict growth if the rate of change in debt servicing is greater than the rate of capital inflows, and the model will under-predict if the rate of capital inflows is greater than the rate of change in debt servicing.

Furthermore, and important shortcoming of the T-H model is that it fails to trace the monetary implications of the balance of payments outcomes, which is at the heart of the IMF's financial programming framework. The Fund's framework integrates monetary, income and balance of payments analysis, and is also the basis for credit allocation of member countries (see, Polak (1997), Khan and Montiel (1989), Khan, Montiel, and Haque (1990), Bolnick (1999), IMF (1977), IMF (1987). Unlike the T-H model, the World Bank's "standard" model is roughly comparable to the IMF's financial programming framework as both these models are built on the same accounting framework. More importantly, both the Fund and Bank models explicitly address the important policy problem of maintaining a target level of foreign exchange reserves and the implications of that target to the monetary/credit variables in the given country. The monetary model of the balance of payments is the theoretical underpinning of the domestic credit ceilings (especially the credit to government sector) that are part of IMF conditionality. Unfortunately, the T-H model does not address these questions explicitly.

## Practical Application of Models in Macroeconomic Policy Work

Why the macroeconomic framework needs to be explicitly treated in an integrated manner can also be considered from a very practical point of view. In their work, donors, policy makers at country level, and country economists at international organizations have to be concerned with an integrated view of macroeconomic developments. That is, they consider the three gaps (the savings-investment, the foreign exchange and the fiscal balance) in a consistent manner. All the parties in a policy dialogue demand to see the basic information regarding growth, inflation, the balance of payments, the fiscal gap, the external debt indicators (the standard external exposure indicators as well as details about concessionary financing availabilities etc). Even if the T-H model is used, it would be necessary to present the implications of macroeconomic scenario in terms of all three gaps. More specifically, it would be necessary to translate the growth and financing gap arrived at by T-H to their private and public components of investment and savings. This is particularly important for tracing the implications of a balance of payments outcome on the public investment and budgetary financing situation of the country under consideration. This is a point missed by both Hussain and Easterly. In Hussain's case, it results in a mistaken claim that he has found an "alternative" model. Ignoring this real life process makes the T-H model more of an academic exercise.

In Easterly's case, it appears that he was carried away by the lack of rigor in the Harrod-Domar specification that underlies the World Bank's model and he missed the importance of the procedure that leads to the identification of the so-called "financing gap." The World Bank's model is not a rigorous tool, but rather a "back of envelope" calculation (as Easterly mentioned) that enables a dialogue among different partners: the country-specific policy makers, the country economists in the World Bank and/or IMF, and the donor countries' representatives. The World Bank and/or the IMF's models and projections provide a consistent framework within which a meaningful dialogue on the growth, inflation, balance of payments, and fiscal implications of several external sector developments and policy scenarios can be carried out. One such important instance is the Special Program for Africa (SPA) where the "financing gap" is a crucial indicator for the dialogue between the donors and the country officials. Another is the Country Assistance Strategy (CAS) of the World Bank. As mentioned before, a large volume of information is utilized to draw up "high", "most reasonable" and "low" case scenarios, which are presented for consideration. In identifying the relevant "financing gaps", country economists are not solely guided by the Harrod-Domar model as Easterly would want up to believe (Easterly (1999). As mentioned before, they take into account a large number of factors such as possibly lumpy investments, productivity, and emerging opportunities for export-diversification etc. The resulting growth model, however, may be cast in the Harrod-Domar framework, more as a convenient way to summarize the scenarios and results than to be "dogmatic". In his quest of rigor, Easterly seems to have overlooked this procedural aspect, which actually, in a sense, does not rely that much on the formal Harrod-Domar specification of growth.[9] In this sense, it is hard to see where the "ghost" is in the "financing gap."

As pointed out above, ignoring the saving-investment relation within the framework under consideration has resulted in the T-H model taking an incomplete view of the interrelations under consideration. Thus, the T-H model has not only fialed to address the investment-savings gap issue treated by Easterly but also has grossly underestimated the importance of the iterative procedure that is used in the World Bank and related organizations to arrive at "financing gaps." This iterative procedure essentially concerns the identification of balance of payments financing requirements and fiscal deficits that are mutually consistent in the "three gap" framework show above.

9 For a very pragmatic description of the use of the financial programming model of the IMF for stabilization policy, see Mussa and Savastano (1999).

Referring to the savings-investment gap, Hussain states that "...measuring the resource gap as the difference between planned investment and planned savings does not mean that capital inflows to fill the gap will automatically be invested or that they are predestined for investment. The T-H approach does not imply such presumptions." Neither do the World Bank/IMF models or their country economic work carry such presumptions. Besides, the World Bank and the IMF, after 50 years of experience, do not seem to carry any illusions about the implementation capacities in member countries. The question here is not so much about presumptions as about practical implications of capital inflows to finance public and private investment. In the World Bank/IMF frameworks, the relative magnitudes of resource flows have an important bearing on both the time path and the nature of the policy package that is designed for implementation. When shortfalls in implementation occur, the targets for resources flows as well as implementation schedules are revised. Given this iterative process of aid-related work at the international financial institutions, it is hard to believe Easterly's assertion that these institutions assume that "aid will go into investment one for one" (Easterly, 1999).

One important consideration worth mentioning in the policy dialogue in programs such as the SPA is the explicit treatment of the external indebtedness of a country. The external debt module (DM) attached to the "standard" model facilitates this analysis. External loan disbursements, repayments, and interest payments are considered from the point of view of donors as well as receivers. The donors are classified according to multilateral, bilateral, private-guaranteed, and private non-guaranteed while the borrowers are categorized by central government, monetary sector, or private sector (including public sector organizations). This enables a reasonably accurate mapping of resource supply and identification of specific resource needs within say a medium-term adjustment framework under consideration. As such, "financing" gaps are not just a matter of an estimate based on investment demand determined by an incremental-output ratio. Rather, they are the result of a common-sense dialogue, which takes into account all possible information available on expected external and domestic developments, the emerging resource needs and available finance.

Given the pragmatic way the World Bank/IMF models have been used in the recent past as tools for a policy dialogue with member countries, it is somewhat inappropriate to state that these models are used to "prescribe policies" for developing member countries (see Hussain, 2001). It is equally inaccurate to say that these models are used to "make growth projections..." Rather, the models are used essentially to explore resource implications of different macroeconomic scenarios.

These points have been brought into focus by Mussa and Savastano (1999) when they analyzed the IMF experience with stabilization programs. They observe that: "...the intellectual doctrine associated with IMF financial programming is primarily a recognition of basic accounting identities supplemented with a small number of behavioral relationships and forecasts of key economic variables, the latter two being subject to revision as new evidence becomes available. This is topped with a reasonable discretion in judging both the size of the required macroeconomic adjustment and the relative effectiveness of the policy instruments available to the authorities to undertake it."

## Data and Estimation Issues

Comparing the T-H and the Harrod-Domar models, Hussain refers to the problems of estimating the parameters and the "inaccuracy of the ICOR approach in measuring the financing gap and in predicting growth performances." He claims that "in contrast, the basic parameters of the T-H approach are the price and income elasticities of demand for exports and imports....these elasticities....are, therefore, fairly constant and largely exogenous, and hence more reliable to use for predictive purposes." Economists at the country level and in international organizations are well aware of the difficulties associated with economic data. There is no empirical evidence to show that trade data in developing countries are in anyway "better" or more "reliable" than investment or consumption data. Furthermore, Bairam and Ng (2001) who investigated the stability of export and income elasticities embodied in the T-H model found that the export and import demand functions for Canada and UK were unstable during the period 1973-95. The sample of countries studied by Bairam and Ng included Canada, New Zealand, and the UK, where statistics are better developed than in most developing countries. Thus, there seems to be no guarantee of the stability of the elasticities in question for most of the developing countries. If these parameters are not stable the, T-H model is bound to yield biased results.

**Concluding Remarks**

The brief examination of the World Bank and the T-H models reveals that the latter is a somewhat of a partial representation of the former. The T-H model lays emphasis on the balance of payments constraint only and has not taken into explicit consideration the aggregative saving-investment behavior that is implicit in the balance of payments picture. Thus, the exposition has missed the important point made by Easterly regarding the theoretical and empirical weaknesses of the investment/growth relationship underlying the World Bank model. Bank Easterly and Hussain, however, fail to realize the practical ways in which these theoretical and empirical weaknesses are overcome in practical applications of these models. The World Bank's model is only a starting point of a policy dialogue between donors and developing countries that eventually converges to agreements on the magnitude and time path of resource flows. In this sense, both Easterly and Hussain seem to be chasing after non-existing "ghosts."

It may be pertinent to quote what Paul Krugman said recently (Krugman, 2000) when he considered the question how complicated a model has to be: "...what we know pretty well, from decades of trying to give micro-foundations to macro, is that logical completeness and intellectual satisfaction are not necessarily indications that a model will actually do a better job of tracking what really happens. For many purposes, the small, ad-hoc models are as good as or better than the carefully specified, maximizing intertemporal model."

Considering Krugman's oservation, although made in another context, and what Mussa and Savastano have said about the pragmatic use of IMF' financial programming model, one might be tempted to conclude that the "ghost of the financing gap" after all may not be a bad ghost to lie with, until a credible alternative is found.

## APPENDIX 1

### Symbols used

| | | |
|---|---|---|
| Y | - | Gross domestic product at market prices. |
| C | - | Total consumption |
| I | - | Gross domestic fixed capital formation (investment) |
| X | - | Export of goods and services |
| IM | - | Imports of goods and services |
| NFY | - | Net factor income |
| NCT | - | Net current transfers |
| $KT_{fg}$ | - | Capital transfers to government from abroad |
| DFI | - | Direct foreign investment |
| POR | - | Portfolio investment |
| NLT | - | Net long-term borrowing |
| NST | - | Net short-term borrowing |
| dRES | - | Change in external reserves |
| GAPF | - | Financing requirements for closing the balance of payments gap.[10] |
| Td | - | Direct taxes |
| Ti | - | Indirect taxes |
| Sub | - | Subsidies |
| NCTfg | - | Net foreign current transfers to government |
| NTXpg | - | Non-tax revenue of government |
| NFfg | - | Net foreign factor payments by government |
| NCTgp | - | Net current transfers from government to private sector |

[10] For simplicity, government and private sectors flows have been aggregated to show NFY, NCT, NLT, NST on a net basis. Not also that the flow-of-funds matrix in table 2 contain more details than shown in the equations in the text.

| | | |
|---|---|---|
| NFgp | - | Net factor payments by government to private sector |
| NFgm | - | Net factor payments by government to monetary sector |
| Cg | - | Government consumption |
| Krev | - | Capital revenue |
| Ig | - | Government investment |
| NKTRgp | - | Net private capital transfers of government |
| Lmg | - | Government sector borrowing from the monetary sector. |
| NLTfg | - | Net long-term borrowing from abroad |
| NSTfg | - | Net short-term borrowing from abroad |
| KTfg | - | Net foreign capital transfers |
| Lpg | - | Net government borrowing from the private sector |
| Lmp | - | Private sector borrowing from the monetary sector: i.e. change in the stock of domestic credit to the private sector (DCp) |
| Lmg | - | Government sector borrowing from the monetary sector: i.e. change in the stock of domestic credit to the government sector (DCg) |
| dNOL | - | Change in net other liabilities of the monetary system |
| M | - | Broad money (M2) |
| dM | - | Change in broad money stock |
| P | - | Price level |
| y | - | Real GDP at market prices |
| v | - | Velocity of circulation of broad money. |

| | | |
|---|---|---|
| ICOR | - | Incremental capital-output ratio |
| c | - | Propensity to consume |
| NCTR | - | Net current transfers in real terms[11] received by the rest of the economy from the other sectors.[12] |
| Imi | - | Demand for ith import category;[13] |
| RERi | - | Real exchange rate for the ith import category.[14] |
| Xm | - | Exports of manufacturing goods. |
| Yf | - | Trading partners income level |
| RERm | - | Real exchange rate for manufactures |
| Gxi | - | Exogenously given growth rate of export category i. |

## Equations of the Thirlwall-Hussain Model (using T-H Equation Numbers)

$$m = \varepsilon (p_f - e - p_d) + \pi y \qquad (2)$$

$$x = \beta (p_d + e - p_f) + \sigma w \qquad (3)$$

$$\Theta = (p_d + e + x) + \tau k = p_f + m \qquad (4)$$

$$y = \frac{(1 + \Theta\beta + \varepsilon)(p_d + e - p_f) + \Theta\sigma w + \tau(k - p_d - e)}{\pi} \qquad (5)$$

---

[11] If a component specific deflator of net current transfers is not available the deflator used to deflate the specific item in net current transfers is the domestic absorption deflator.

[12] An example of transfers that contribute to a person's net disposable income is worker's remittances from abroad and pension payments by the government.

[13] The import components identified in the model are: food, consumer goods, intermediate raw materials, intermediate manufactured, capital goods and fuel and other petroleum based products.

[14] In the linear form of specific functions used, the user specifies the elasticities of demand with respect to income (y) and the real exchange rate (RER).

$$y = \frac{(1+\varepsilon)(p_d + e - p_f) + \Theta x + \tau(k - p_d - e)}{\pi} \quad (6)$$

$$y = \frac{\sigma w}{\pi} \text{ or } \frac{x}{\pi} \quad (7)$$

$$k^* = \frac{\pi y^* - (1+\Theta\beta+\varepsilon)(p_d + e - p_f) - \Theta\sigma w}{(1-\Theta)} + (p_d + e) \quad (8)$$

$$k^A = \frac{\pi y^* - (1+\varepsilon)(p_d + e - p_f) - \Theta x}{(1-\Theta)} + (p_d + e) \quad (9)$$

$m$ = rate of growth of real imports

$x$ = rate of growth of real exports

$y$ = rate of growth of real income

$w$ = rate of growth of world income

$p_f$ = rate of change in the foreign price of imports

$p_d$ = rate of change in domestic prices

$k$ = rate of change in nominal capital inflows

$e$ = rate of change in the exchange rate measured as the foreign price of domestic currency

$\varepsilon$ = price elasticity of demand for imports ($\varepsilon < 0$)

$\beta$ = price elasticity of demand for exports ($\beta < 0$)

$\pi$ = income elasticity of demand for imports ($\pi > 0$)

$\sigma$ = income elasticity of demand for exports ($\sigma > 0$)

$\Phi$ = proportion of the total import bill "financed" by export earnings

$\tau$ = proportion of the total import bill "financed" by capital flows

$y^*$ = target growth rate

$k^*$ = rate of growth of nominal capital inflows (measured in foreign currency) required to achieve the target growth rate $y^*$

## REFERENCES

Bacha, Edmar L., "A Three-Gap Model of Foreign Transfers and the GDP Growth Rate in Developing Countries," Journal of Development Economics, Vol. 32, 1990, pp. 279–296.

Bacha Edmar L., "Growth with Limited Supplies of Foreign Exchange: A Reappraisal of the Two-Gap Model," in M. Syrquin, L. Taylor and L. Westhphal (eds), Economic Structure and Performance: Essays in honor of Hollis Chenery, Academic Press, New York, 1984.

Bairam, Erkin, I, and Lawrence Ng, "Thirlwall's Law and the Stability of Export and Import Income Elasticities," International Review of Applied Economics, Vol. 15, No. 3, 2001.

Blitzer, Charles, Peter B. Clark, and Lance Taylor, Economy-Wide Models and Development Planning, Oxford University Press, 1975.

BolnicK, Bruce R., "The Role of Financial Programming in Macroeconomic Policy Management," Development Discussion Paper No. 720, Harvard Institute for International Development, September, 1999.

Burnside, Craig, and David Dollar, "Aid, Policies, and Growth," Policy Research Working Paper No. 1777, The World Bank, Washington DC, June, 1997.

Burnside, Craig, and David Dollar, "Aid, Policies, and Growth," American Economic Review, Vol. 90, No. 4, pp. 847–68.

Chenery, H.B, and A. Strout, "Foreign Assistance and Economic Development," American Economic Review, Vol. LVI, No. 4, Part I, September, 1966.

Collier, Paul and David Dollar, "Aid Allocation and Poverty Reduction," Policy Research Working Paper 2041, Washington DC, The World Bank, 1999.

Dalgaard, Carl-Johan and Henrik Hansen, "On Aid, Growth and Good Policies," The Journal of Development Studies, August, 2001.

Doornbos Martin, "Good Governance: The Rise and Decline of a Policy Metaphor?," The Journal of Development Studies, August, 2001.

Easterly, William, "The ghost of financing gap: testing the growth model used in the international financial institutions," Journal of Development Economics, Vol. 60, pp. 423–438, 1999.

Easterly, William, "The Ghost of Financing Gap: How the Harrod-Dmar Growth Model Still Haunts Development Economics," Policy Research Working Paper 1807. The World Bank, Washington DC, August, 1997.

Elliott, Dawn Richards, and Rupert Rhodd," Explaining growth rate differences in highly indebted countries: an extension to Thirlwall and Hussain," Applied Economics, 31, pp. 1145–1148, 1999.

Feyzioglu, T., V. Swaroop, and M. Zhu, "A Panel Data Analysis of the Fungibility of Aid," World Bank Economic Review, 12 (1), 1998.

Guillaumont, Patrick, and Lisa Chauvet, "Aid and Performance: A Reassessment," The Journal of Development Studies, August, 2001.

Hansen, Henrik, and Fin Tarp, "Aid Effectiveness Disputed," Journal of International Development, Vol. 12, No. 3, pp. 375–98, 2000.

Hermes, Niels and Robert Lensink, "Changing the Conditions for Development Aid: A New Paradigm?" The Journal of Development Studies, August, 2001.

Hoeven, Rolph van der, "Assessing Aid and Global Governance," The Journal of Development Studies, August, 2001.

Hussain, M. Nureldin, "Exorcising the ghost: An alternative model for measuring the financing gap in developing countries," Journal of Post Keynesian Economics, Armonk; Vol. 24, Iss. 1; pp. 89–125, Fall 2001.

International Monetary Fund, "The Monetary Approach to the Balance of Payments," IMF, Washington DC, 1977.

International Monetary Fund, "Theoretical aspects of the design of Fund-supported adjustment programs," Occasional paper, September, 1987.

Iqbal, Zafar, "Foreign Aid and Public Sector: A Model of Fiscal Behavior in Pakistan," The Pakistan Development Review, Vol. 36: 2 (Summer), 1997, pp. 115–129.

Iqbal, Zafar, Constraints to the Economic Growth of Pakistan: A Three-Gap Approach," Pakistan Development Review, Vol. 34, 1995, pp. 1119–1133.

Iqbal, Zafar, Jeffrey James, and Graham Pyatt, "Three-Gap Analysis of Structural Adjustment in Pakistan," Journal of Policy Modeling, 2000, 22 (1), pp. 117–138.

Khan, Mohsin, Peter J. Montiel, and Nadeem U. Haque, "Adjustment with growth: Relating the Analytical Approaches of the IMF and the World Bank" Journal of Development Economics, 32, 1990, pp. 155–179.

Khan, Mohsin, and Peter J. Montiel, "Growth-Oriented Adjustment Programs: A Conceptual Framework," IMF Staff Papers, Vol. 36, No. 2, June 1989, pp. 279–306.

Krugman, Paul, How Complicated Does the Model Have To Be? Oxford Review of Economic Policy, Vol. 16, No. 4, Winter 2000, pp. 33–42.

Lensink, Robert, and Howard White, "Aid Allocation, Poverty Reduction, and the Assessing Aid Report," Journal of International Development, Vol. 12, No. 3, pp. 399–412, 2000.

Masson, Paul R., Steven A. Symansky, and Guy Meredith, MULTIMOD Mark II: A Revised and Extended Model, IMF Occasional Paper, No. 71, International Monetary Fund, Washington, 1999.

McGillivray, Mark "Aid and Public Sector Fiscal Behavior in Developing Countries," Review of Development Economics, Vol. 44, No. 2, pp. 156–63, 2000.

Mussa, Michael, and Miguel Savastano, The IMF Approach to Economic Stabilization, IMF Working Paper, WP/99/104, July, 1999.

Nickell, Stephen, "The Supply Side and Macroeconomic Modeling," in Empirical Macroeconomics for Interdependent Economies, ed. By Ralph C. Bryant and others, Brookings Institution, Washington, 1988, pp. 202–21.

Jacques J. Polak, "The IMF Monetary Model at Forty," IMF Working Paper, WP/97/49, April, 1997.

Sepehri, A., S. Moshiri, and M, Doudongee, "The Foreign Exchange Constraints to Economic Adjustment: The Case of

Iran," International Review of Applied Economics, Vol. 14, No. 2, 2000, pp. 235–251.

Taylor, L., "A Three-Gap Model," in F.D. McCarthy (ed), Problems of Developing Countries in the 1990s, World Bank, Washington DC, 1990, pp. 55–90.

Taylor, L., "Gap Models," Journal of Development Economics, 45, pp. 17–34, 1994. The World Bank, Assessing Aid, What Works, What Doesn't and Why. The World Bank, Washington DC, 1998.

# 4

# Venture Capital - International Experience

*T. Satyanrayana Chary**

Venture capital is post-war phenomenon in the business world, mainly developed as a sideline activity of the rich in the USA. To connote the risk and adventure and some element of investment, the generic name of 'venture capital' was coined. The term venture capital comprises of two words viz., 'Venture' and 'Capital'. Venture means 'Chance' or 'Trails' hitting at speculation to try one's luck i.e. good or bad involving risk or hazard or exposure to insecurity or danger. The term 'Capital' means resources to start the enterprise. Therefore, venture capital is understood as capital that is available for financing new business venture. It is also often thought of as "the early stage financing of new and young enterprises seeking to grow rapidly".[1]

In a broad sense the venture capital refers to capital investment made in a business or industrial enterprise that carries elements of risk, insecurity and probability of business hazards. Capital investment may assume, the form

* Dr. T. Satyanrayana Chary; Assistant Professor, Institute of Public Enterprise (IPE), Osmania University Campus, Hyderabad-500007.

Pratt, Pratt's guide on venture capital 1983, USA.

of either equity or debt or both i.e. Derivative investment. The risk associates with the enterprise could be so high as to entail total loss or be so insignificant as to lead to high gains. However, venture capital finance is different from conventional finance i.e. money lending and bank finance, because venture capital financier takes keen interest in business performance of the investees' firm.

Venture capital has been primarily an American phenomenon, there has been significant growth in the 1980s in venture capital outside the United States. This began first in the United Kingdom in the late 1979s, and then spread to France and other Continental European countries in the 1980s. By the middle-to-late 1980s the expansion had spread to the Pacific Rim countries. However the overall success of venture capital in USA stimulated global countries to practice on venture capital.

This research paper is a unpretentious attempt to discuss on the emergence and the present status of the venture capital in global countries.

## Venture Capital in the USA

In the United States of America, venture capital has contributed immensely to the growth of the economy. It has made significant contribution to the development of the computer and semi-conductor industry. It has also helped in the implementation of very large scale integration technology. While venture capital was instrumental in the development of American economy, its institutionalization did not begin until after World War II. Prior to that, it was a common practice for wealthy individuals, syndicates organized by investment bankers or by a few families to make venture investment. The institutionalization process was facilitated by the formulation of American Research and Development Corporation (ARDC) in Boston in 1964, passing of Small Business Investment Company (SBIC) Act in 1958 as a vehicle of small business financing and the substantial tax incentives provided to those investing their funds in VCFs.

ARDC, started by General Doriot,[1] was the first successful venture capital firm. Its first investment worth $61,400 in 1957 was in the shares of Digital Equipment Corporation, a new company, which grew phenomenonally in terms of sales, number of employees and market worth of its shares. Doriot's philosophy was to build creative men and their companies. For him capital gains were the reward of this philosophy, not a business goal. The objective of his company was to seek out creative men with a vision of things to be done; help breathe life into new ideas and processes and products with capital – and with more than capital – with sensitive appreciation for creative drive.

The creation of small business investment companies (SBICs) as a means of small business financing in 1958 gave the real impetus to the development of the venture capital industry in the USA. The purpose of the SBIC Act was to establish government-controlled venture capital funds for developing new and early stage business and they proved to be very effective during the sixties and seventies. Even today, when the large venture capital organizations dominant the US venture industry, SBICs in their new and modified form, are the major source of its growth.

The venture industry in the USA has been growing ever since its inception. Its growth was, however, accentuated

---

[1] Venture capital, which has played a constructive role in the industrial development of the USA, owes its growth in that country to the initiative taken after World War II by a few wealthy American family groups. Among them were Rockefeller (Standard Oil), the Rosenwelbs (Sears), the Pitcairns (Pitsburgh Plate Glass) and the Whitneys (Vanderbilt Shipping). But in fact, the beginning of venture capital industry was made by George Doriot who, as a Harvard Business School Professor, Promoted small business development at Harvard and collaborated in establishing in 1964 the American Research and Development Corporation (AEDC), a Boston based investment fund. The fund's main objective was to finance a variety of new businesses based on university technology from institutions like Massachusetts Institute of Technology (MIT).

after 1978 when the capital gains tax was reduced from 49% to 28%. The rate was brought down to 20 per cent for individuals in 1981. These reductions resulted insubstantial returns to investors, and since the investors readily accepted their securities, the venture capital industry was able to attract capital without difficulty. This coincided with the emergence of the very large scale integration that substantially reduced the cost of computer chips and gave a boost to the computer industry.

Although the venture capital finance is made available to all enterprises in the USA, the high technology businesses have received large funds over the years. Most of the venture capital investments in the US are confined to high technology, high-risk and rapidly changing businesses. Substantially venture capital has been invested in the fields of information, communications, genetic engineering medical electronics, biotechnology and artificial intelligence. In volume terms, the USA dominated the venture capital business with a pool of about $30 billion in 1991, having increased from $16.3 billion at the end of 1984 (OCED, 1986). Three main reasons can be cited for the significant growth of venture capital in the US.[2]

1. Favorable Public Attitude
2. Dynamic financial system
3. Government Support

VCFs in the US can be categorized into four main groups (Clark, 1987) as follow:

**1. *Private Venture Capital Firms (PVCFs):*** PVCFs include family firms and institutionally funded independent private partnerships and are the most dominant source of venture capital. They account for about 60 per cent of the venture capital industry's capital and they are very experienced and sophisticated investors. Institutionally funded private firms are generally organized as limited

[2] OECD, 1986a.

partnership where venture capitalist, in his capacity as general partner, is responsible for the management of the partnership. For their management, general partners are compensated in the form of an annual management fee generally 2.5 to 3 per cent of the capital invested and a percentage, quite often 20 per cent of the net long-term capital gain.

**2. *Small Business Investment Companies (SBICs):*** SBICs, created nude the SBIC Act 1958, have access to government loans in addition to private committed capital. They are of two types: equity-oriented SBICs, which account for about 8 per cent of the venture capital and mostly provide equity capital, and debt-oriented SBICs. Subsidiaries of finance and non-finance corporations account for about 17 per cent of the venture capital.

**3. *Subsidiaries of Finance Corporations, and***

**4. *Subsidiaries of Non-Finance Corporations***

## Venture Capital in Europe

In Europe, venture capital started in the eighties. A number of European countries now have venture capital firms, which are members of the European Venture Capital Association (EVCA) founded in 1983. In spite of these developments, about three fourths of the venture capital investment in Europe is confined to three countries, namely, the UK, France and Netherlands.

The slow growth of venture capital in Europe in the initial years can be attributed to a number of factors. For example, it is suggested that, financial institutions, equity markets and company law have all evolved differently in these countries, equity markets and company law have all evolved differently in these countries, with the result that venture capital along United States, United Kingdom lines has scarcely developed (OECD, 1986). The government policy in the USA has been to create a climate conducive to risk-taking and entrepreneurship, and deregulating markets and reducing taxes rather than providing special incentives for the financing of Small and Medium Scale Enterprises (SMEs) as was the case in a number of European countries.

In the late eighties, Europe witnessed a fast growth of venture capital due to changes in public policy and the economic conditions. The creation of over-the counter (OTC) or secondary stock exchanges gave further impetus to the development of venture capital. For example, the venture capital pool increased from $8.95 billion in 1986 to $29 billion in 1990, slightly more than 80% of the size of the US venture capital.[3] Banks contribute about one-fifth of venture capitals in Europe. The other sources are the government, insurance, companies, pension funds, and corporate investors. Venture capitalists in Europe focus on industrial products, consumer products and electronics products. West European countries such as the UK, France and Germany place relatively more emphasis on technology and R&D activities than countries like Italy and the Netherlands.

A significant development vis-à-vis venture capital in Europe is the establishment of a Pan-European network of VCFs by twelve companies including Bosch, Fiat, Olivetti, Petrofina, Philips, Pirelli and Volvo. This network has created a holding company with US $30 million funds for investing in European VCFs.[4]

## The United Kingdom

The UK has the largest venture capital industry outside the USA and it accounts for about two-thirds of total VC investments in the European Community (OECD, 1986). In the past, the growth of the new businesses in Britain had been hampered by the "equity gap". The need has been for a steady and growing supply of venture capital to finance entrepreneurial talent.[5]

---

[3] Bygrave and Timmons, 1992.

[4] Schilit, 1992.

[5] Lorenz, 1985.

The venture capital industry had invested only £10 million in 1979 but the amount had increased to £284 million in 1984. It has made significant contribution in creating hundreds of new enterprises and in catalyzing the spirit of entrepreneurship. There are estimated to be well over a hundred venture capital firms in UK having provided venture funds to thousands of companies. In 1988, for example, funds worth Rs. 37,000 million to over 1,500 companies were provided by the UK venture capital industry (Cottrell, 1989). The following reasons are attributed for the rapid growth of the UK venture capital industry.[6]

1. The demonstration effect of the high profitability of venture capital in the USA (e.g. the flotation of Apple Computer).
2. The establishment o regional ventures capital organizations such as Investors in Industry (3i). Tax incentives to individuals investing in entrepreneurial companies.
3. The establishment of the Unlisted Securities Market (USM) and the Business Expansion Scheme (BES). BES is designed to motivate private investors through large tax exemptions, to invest in shares of private unquoted companies.
4. The growth in the number of management buyouts, which ahs created a demand for equity finance.
5. The increased involvement of merchant banks, providing venture capital to small, growing companies with a view to obtaining future fee-earning work from them.
6. The "bandwagon" effect.

Historically, the small firms in the UK have received equity finance from the investment trusts. But in the post-war periods, investment trusts started investing in large,

[6] Mason, 1987: Kitchen, 1988.

quoted companies at the cost of the small, risky companies. The most important source of equity finance for new firms during the 1960 and early 1970 was Investors in Industry or 3i. The Bank of England and the major clearing banks with the purpose of supplying long-term finance to growing firms established 3i in 1945. About two-thirds of 3i's financing goes to small firms. They provide finance in the form of loans and equity investments. In USA is not venture capital in the sense that it is understood. 3i depends on interest or dividend for its return rather than only on capital gains. 3i has an excellent pool of management and a large number of its managers have joined VCF.

It was in the latter part of the 1980's that a large number of private venture funds emerged in the UK. A number of factors, such as tax incentives, establishment of the Unlisted Securities Market (USM) and encouragement to investment rusts etc, contributed to this development.

The UK is an excellent example of a country where a number of tax incentives have been initiated specifically to give a fillip to the venture capital investment in fact, it has been found in the UK that investors are motivated more by the potential tax breaks than by the quality of investments. It is estimated that only 2 per cent of the BES total investments are invested in the high-tech sector, and 6 per cent in the young or very young start-up companies. *(OCED 1986).*

The UK's USM was established in 1980 with highly flexible rules to admit stat-ups. It operates on the same basis as the regular stock market, but with liberal regulations for trading the shares. For example, USM requires 10 per cent of a company's shares to offer in the primary issues before they can be traded; in the listed market the requirement is 25 per cent. The establishment of USM boosted venture activity since it made it much easier for entrepreneurs and venture capitalists to realize their capital gains. However the UK experience has shown that most businesses that obtained the USM listing were at the larger end of the SME scale. This necessitated the introduction of a third market in 1987 for smaller companies, and with even easier listing requirements than demanded by the USM. Yet another policy change in the UK giving encouragement to venture capital business.

**France**

In France, Societies Financiers Innovation (SFI), with the fiscal advantage of setting 50 per cent of their new investments against taxable income, was established in 1972. They were not highly successful. This lack of success could be attributed to the SFIs failing to attract the right sort of managers, and failing to appreciate the importance of a direct involvement in the management of the supported companies.[7] The French government introduced more tax incentives to revitalize the venture capital industry, which has led to the establishment of Fonds Common de Placement a Risqué in 1983. Investors' receive tax-exempt capital gains at the end of five years.

Venture capital is a fast developing concept in France, with a number of genuine venture capital funds now in existence, mostly owned or supported by banks. Three of these funds are long-standing with experience of over 10 years; there are about 40 other sources of small company risk capital.[8] The creation of the Second Marche in 1983 and development of financial instruments such as warrants and options have helped the growth of the French venture capital industry. Expansion capital dominates the French venture capital industry, accounting for as much as 65 per cent of investment in recent years.

**The Netherlands**

The Netherlands has a fast growing venture capital market, with some 25 private venture capital funds and

---

[7] Teixeria de Costa, 1983.

[8] Lorenz, 1985.

20 other small business risk finance funds in the eighties. As in.

France, a number of the funds are owned or supported by banks and the government provides a lot of encouragement to the venture capital industry. The government has established a number of Particuletic Participate Maatschapijen (PPM)[9], which are giving a great boost to the venture capital industry. The establishment by the Amsterdam Stock Exchange in 1982 of the Parallel Market has given a further boost to the venture capital.

## Germany

In Germany, company resources generally come in the form of loans. Companies are mostly privately owned, of which almost 75 per cent are family-owned. The family-owned companies are rather reluctant to raise equity capital from the market, hence the significance of equity as an instrument of finance has been limited. The growth of venture capital was quite slow until the mid-eighties, but this attitude of recession, may companies gave up their conservative attitude and raised equity capital. Since 1983-84, a number of companies have gone public, and a number of venture capital companies have also been established.[10] A new secondary market in 1987 provided an exit route.

## Australia

Public Institutions in Australia were supporting equity funding for new enterprises till 1980s. These institutions were: Australian Industry Development Corporation (AIDC), Advanced Technology Development Fund of New

---

[9] A special measure introduced by the government in 1981 to help provide risk capital for the small-business sector is the Particuletic Participatic Maatschappijen (PPM scheme). PPMs are small-company investment funds where up to half the risk is indemnified by the government. PPMs can invest upto 40 per cent of their total investments outside the rather complex rules of the scheme.

[10] Lorenz, 1985.

South Wales, Victorian Economic Development Corporation and Enterprise Investments (South Australia) Ltd. These institutions supplied equity and even today meet about 50 per cent of the equity capital pool for early-stage and development financing. There is a supportive business environment, which encourages entrepreneurs in more competitive industry, innovative and risk taking activities and provides tax incentive to investors who subscribe to venture capital firms.

The Management Investment Companies Act, 1984 has the following objectives:

1. The encourage the development of venture capital in Australia by creating a number of venture capital companies'.
2. To attract management and financial support for the start-up and early growth of Australian-based enterprises that has the potential to grow rapidly, are export-oriented and use innovative technology.

Venture capital companies established under this Act are called management and investment companies (MICs). They are staffed by multidisciplinary professionals possessing management, financial, marketing and technical skills. A high degree of returns is sought for funding the businesses. An MIC investment must meet at least three of the following criteria fulfill regulatory requirements. They must use innovative technology, be internationally competitive and have the potential for creating skilled employment in Australia. The portfolio business must operate in certain categories of business, including certain types of manufacturing, agriculture, forestry and fishing and service activities such as architecture, surveying, engineering and education, and they must carry out the activities in Australia. They must have average growth in sales projected over the first three year in excess of 20 per cent and must be less than ten years old.

## Growth of Venture Capital in Newly Industrialised Countries of Asia

Venture capital financing is well established in Asian countries particularly South Korea, Singapore, Hong Kong, Thailand and Malaysia, which drew on the venture capital experience of the USA in the early 1970s and 1980s.[11]

### South Korea

The role of the Korean government in fostering venture capital has been quite significant, particularly in the adoption of the American model (high technology/high risk) in South Korea, making significant fiscal and regulatory changes, and directly establishing venture capital funds and other related institutions. South Korea has set up the Korea Technology Advancement Corporation (KTAC) in 1974 for implementing R&D projects in public research institutes, Korea Technology Development Corporation (KTDC) in 1981 to encourage technology development and technical entrepreneurship through R&D project loans and venture capital financing and Korea Development Investment Corporation (KDIC) and Korea Technology Financing Corporation (KTFC) in 1983. Then after passed the Small and Medium Business Establishment Assistance Law in 1986 for equity investment by venture capitalists. Soon after developed the Technology Credit Guarantee System designed to assist venture business lacking in collateral to secure borrowings and set-up of Investment Partnership Fund, which invests the assets of either an investment company or venture capital financing company or its general investors in venture businesses. This fund also enjoys the same tax benefits as venture capital financing companies. Finally introduced in 1987 of Over the Counter (OTC) market for transacting in the shares of promising

---

[11] Venture Capital Economics Ltd., Venture Capital Year Book, 1986 and Graham Bannock and Grham Bannock and David Goacher; 'Bridging the Finance Gap', Quarterly Enterprise Digest, Vol. 3, March 1988.

venture business. The venture capital firms established under the relaxed legal system serve different needs of the entrepreneurial community. They are classified as investment companies and venture capital companies.

Investment companies provide classic venture capital assistance, viz. equity capital plus value-added management assistance. One the other hand Venture capital companies provide venture capital i.e. equity financing plus various forms of debt financing managerial and technical assistance. These companies require greater paid in capital.

5,000 million won as against 2,000 million won for investment companies and have a broader range of activities. Venture capital firms in South Korea enjoy a number of tax benefits, which as follows:

1. There is no tax on realized capital gains.
2. As long as reserves against losses are established, up to 50 per cent of total investment may be included in the loss account.
3. Divided income from investment companies or venture capital financing companies is subject to a 10 per cent withholding and final tax at source.
4. Shareholders are not subject to regulations pertaining to presumptive divided under the Income Tax Law when transferring shares or equity interest in investment companies or venture financing companies.
5. Companies are subject to five times the ordinary registration duty when incorporated in big cities, but the same does not apply to investment companies and venture capital financing companies.

**Taiwan**

Taiwan is poorly endowed in natural resources but rich in human resources, engineers, scientists, technically trained personnel having overseas experience and receptive to new ways of starting new businesses. Legislation in 1983 offered attractive incentives for investors in venture capital funds. The focus in Taiwan is on high technology. Until 1986 venture capital in Taiwan was handled primarily by three government associated institutions, namely Bank of Communications (BOC), Development Fund of Executive Yuan, and China Development Corporation (CDC).

The government's tax incentives includes a reduced maximum income tax rate (20 per cent), pass-through of tax-free capital gains to shareholders, tax holidays and foreign tax credit for overseas investments, investment tax credits with a tax carry-forward provision and tax deferment on stock dividends and retention of excess retained earnings. In Taiwan, a venture capital firm pays a maximum income tax of 20 per cent, whereas non-venture capital firm pay 25 per cent. When a venture capital firm invests in a high technology company, it can pass through tax-free capital gains to its shareholders. However, the pass-through applies only to capital gains and not to dividend income. In addition, it applies only when the technology company is publicly traded and when the shares are sold and transferred. To encourage overseas investments, additional tax incentives are provided to venture capital companies that included a five-year income tax holiday, on fulfilling certain conditions as laid down by the government from time to time to boost investment in technology-based companies. Investors holding stock in venture capital companies are also provided tax relief's on dividend income.

The government of Taiwan also changes the requirements of the Taiwan Stock Exchange to encourage high technology companies to list. Such companies can seek public listing by meting less stringent requirements. The changes in the regulatory and fiscal policies in Taiwan have been designed to promote technological development. In order to take full advantage of the regulations and tax concessions, the venture capital firms must invest in one or more of the following:

1. Energy Technology
2. Production automation
3. Biotechnology
4. Material Technology
5. Food Technology
6. Laser/Optical fiber technology
7. Prevention of hepatitis
8. Information Technology

The Bank of Communication (BOC) and the Development Fund (DF) jointly established an NT $800 million fund in 1985 to invest in venture capital companies in Taiwan. The BOC and DF fund make its first investment in a US$2 million fund with the New York based Steinberg Lyman Life Science Fund in 1986. In addition, the Han Tech Venture Capital Company received about US$ 10 million from the BOC and DF pool in 1986.

**Singapore**

Venture Capital funds in Singapore are structured under the Companies Act (Cap 185) as public companies with limited liability. They are closed-end investment companies and can acquire and hold investments in private start-up companies on a medium to long-term basis. The funds of the investment holding company are managed by a separate fund management company, which is paid a fee by the holding company for the services rendered. Fund managers are required to hold an investment adviser's license issued by the government of Singapore. Singapore's venture capital community is growing. Its venture capital association has 30 members and local entrepreneurs are encouraged to approach members directly with their business plans.

The government is determinedly fostering venture capital investments. It grants fiscal incentives and relaxation in tax procedures to both domestic and foreign venture capital companies and investors in venture capital funds. These exemptions are available to companies on fulfilling the following conditions:

1. They have reasonably sized funds;
2. They support local entrepreneurship and innovation;
3. They assist in developing local venture capital management expertise; and
4. They achieve transfer of technology and investments if they venture investments are made in overseas companies.

Investors based in Singapore, whether companies or individuals, participating in risky new technology activities are allowed to write off losses from the sale of shares in approved venture investments against other incomes, up to 100 per cent of the investment made. The Economic Development Board (EDB) of Singapore plays a significant role in the venture capital industry. EDB administers the S$100 million Venture Capital Fund established in 1995 by the government. The fund is available to Singapore-based Companies to acquire and diversify into new technologies, promote and support local innovation and entrepreneurship and persuade new technology companies from overseas to establish facilities for manufacturing or distributing in Singapore.

Besides the EDB coinvests with local corporations in risky, high technology projects in Singapore or overseas. The Board participates in national and international venture capital funds, in order to acquire new technologies. DBS bank is the other major player in venture capital financing in Singapore. The government currently offers pioneer services and incentives to encourage locally based venture capital firms. Exemption from corporate tax for such companies is possible for a period of 10 years. A second-tier stock market for smaller companies has been operating from early 1987, providing a route for 'exit'.

**Hong Kong**

In Hong Kong, venture capital companies have been used a base for technology transfer to China. China gets a lot of downstream engineering done on a cost-effective basis in Hong-Kong. Thus, venture capital funds in Hong Kong are more application-oriented. In December 1987 Hong Kong Venture Capital Association was formed with 20 companies as full members and $320 million in investment funds. More than half of these firms are engaged in risk capital investment in manufacturing in South China.

To facilitate transfer of technology from the USA and Europe the Hong Kong Venture Investment Trust (HKVIT) was established. HKVIT makes investments in the USA, Europe and Hong Kong. Investments in the USA and Europe are in companies whose technology can be transferred to Hong Kong. This is done through a subsidiary of HKVIT, Venture Manufacturing-HK, which arranges joint venture for Hong Kong based manufactures. A few of the recent developments in venture investments in Hong Kong are noted below:

1. AIA Capital, a Hong Kong based venture capital company, has taken up a 30 per cent interest in a Beijing government owned financial services company, FOTIC Capital. FOTIC Capital has assets of more than US$ 10 billion, assists Chinese companies to be listed overseas and attracts investors in burgeoning enterprises.
2. Carr Indosuez Asia announced its plants to raise US$ 200 million, and set up Carr Indosuez Communications Fund (CICF) with the focus on investing in China's telecommunications projects. The Chinese partner is the largest subsidiary of the Ministry of Post and Telecommunications. Carr Indosuez is currently reviewing 27 companies. CICF has an expected return of 25 per cent and exit is through trade sales instead of initial public offerings (IPOs).

3. ING Beijing Investment, which is listed on the Hong Kong Stock Exchange, has acquired a 35 per cent stake in an instrument manufacturing company with a capital injection of US$ 5.3 million. Due to the escalating inflation in China, ING Beijing is revising its return rate from 15 per cent to 20 per cent.
4. The Hong Kong office of the UK based Pantheon Group's Atlas Participations Asia Limited (APAL) is the first Asian fund in which European institutional investors have subscribed US$ 29.5 million. APAL has a total fund pool of US$ 70 million available for investment in Asian private equity funds.
5. Two other Hong Kong venture fund companies, Prudential Asia and Schroders Capital Asia raised US$ 276 million and US$ 100 million, respectively, with 17 committed investors.
6. Zhonghua Investment Management Partners (ZIM), A US$ 60 million fund sponsored by Oppenheimer and Odyssey Partners, have acquired majority stake in two mainland projects. ZIM, together with a Swiss partner, invested US$ 16 million in a printing in k factory, representing an acquisition of 70 per cent of this Chinese concern. The most recent acquisition involves taking a controlling equity stake in a chocolate factory. ZIM is planning to increase the current fund size from US$ 60 million to US$ 150 million.

## Thailand

In 1987 the Business Venture Promotion Company was promoted in Thailand by a consortium of six local commercial banks and United States Agency for International Development (USAID). US$ 6 million was provided as a soft loan by USAID and an equivalent amount was raised as equity from the six participating banks. In Thailand venture capital companies have to involve themselves even in the preparation of business plans for prospective clients. There is an apprehension with regard to existing legislation, which may treat a venture capital fund as an investment dealing company, leading to higher tax incidence.

Thai Development Capital Fund (TDCF) established in 1990 is active in venture financing. TDCF is managed by Hong Kong based Crosby Assets Management (CMA). Till 1994 TDCF had committed 11 investments in unlisted companies of which five had initial public offerings. Investments in unlisted portfolio offered 30 per cent IRR with no write-downs. Thailand's infrastructure suits the development of venture capital industry. Its GDP in 1992 was estimated to be US$1,420 with 12 per cent contribution from agriculture. The country has an open economy, and its stock markets have been working from over 20 years. However, in Thailand, venture capital industry is not regulated, i.e. anyone can start a venture capital concern if it is properly registered. But lack of experienced personnel is a definite hindrance.

The types of venture capital financing are start-up, first stage and second stage. Other types of venture financing are considered on case-to-case basis. Minimum investment is 5,00,000 burts. Industry preference for venture capital financing covers agro industry, agribusiness, export-oriented industry, tourism, electronics instrumentations, genetic engineering (agricultural), industrial products and equipments. South East Asia Venture Investment Programme (SEAVIP) is activity functioning in Thailand.

### Malaysia

In 1984 Malaysia Bhd Fund was set up under SEVAIP programme. There are incentives available to attract foreign direct investors, although recession over the past three years had been an inhibiting factor. Malaysian venture capital companies have been encountered many impediments as in other countries of Southeast Asia such as business is family controlled or oriented, market research is inadequate, no significant evaluation of service ventures, emphasis on collateral based financing and a dearth of adequate mechanism for 'exit'.

However, in Malaysia, Permodalan National Bank (PNB) has been established by the government in Malaysia to manage the ASEAN Fund worth US$ 40 million for investing in public offers and unlisted companies in the ASEAN region. PNB's venture capital arm is PNB Equity Resources.

## China

Political, Social and economic circumstances of China have not favored entrepreneurship, development of stock markets and private equity which are all required for the venture capital industry. But there appears to be a will and as such these are not inhibiting factors for the growth of venture industry in China. China's immediate aim is technology revolution for which it needs technical transformation, which in turn calls for special funding for venture technology projects. China is advancing towards open economy and striving to boost entrepreneurship along with technological advancement.

To achieve these objectives, China Venturetech Investment Corporation (CVIC) was established. CVIC is a financial institution run on commercial principles affiliated with PRC state, Science and Technology Commission and People's Bank of China. CVIC is the only venture capital company in China. It makes equity investments in technological ventures. It serves as a vehicle to combine the creative business ideas of an entrepreneur together with the sophisticated financial and management skill, and financial resources of the venture investors for economic success.

South China has business relations with Hong Kong Hong Kong manufacturers have access to an enormous pool of low-cost labour and vast areas of industrial real estate in China. Hong Kong provides vital technology and market expertise, and the financial infrastructure. Entrepreneurs from Taiwan and Japan are also utilizing these facilities and investing heavily in China. In addition to the above, China has recently shown remarkable progress in promoting private equity investments through various funds. However venture capital financing in China, while considerably different than in other Asian countries, provides risk capital, equity and management to small companies with sufficient collateral bases. The venture capital has to serve the purpose of creating new industries, new jobs and new wealth.

**Indonesia**

Efforts have been on since 1973 in Indonesia at government level as well as through private initiative, for promoting venture capital and private equity investments. The government owned PT Bahana Pembinaan Usaha Indonesia (PT Bahana) was established in 1973 to promote private equity investments. Development and financial institutions and several private companies were actively engaged till the 1980s in private equity investments. Apart from this, Hong Kong based financial institutions like Sun Hung Kai Fund Management etc, were also engaged in promoting venture investments. Important venture capital firms in Indonesia include, PT Eshaka Finance, Asian Oceanic Group and PTAOG Mitra Capital. In mid 1991 United Nations Development Programme formed a venture fund in Indonesia. In 1991 Nomura/JAFCO became the first foreign-owned organization to establish an office in Indonesia. In 1993 the Indonesian and Malaysian governments jointly created the Malindo Venture Capital Company (MVCA) as the first investment specific venture fund in Indonesia to serve medium and small enterprises. In Indonesia the local private sector plays a commanding role in all venture fund sources. World Bank, IFC and UK based CDC have extended support to the Indonesian private equity market. Despite these efforts investors are still cautious in making investments.

### New Zealand

The growth of venture capital industry in New Zealand can be traced to the early 1980s. Large corporations manage most of the venture capital companies' funds or government sponsored institutions like Development Finance Corporation of New Zealand (DFC). The stock market boom in New Zealand and Australia gave a boost to the venture capital industry in both countries. Many entrepreneurial groups raised risk capital for investment in start-up enterprises or in small companies. The stock market collapse in October 1987 caused a halt to this growth and the after effects were noticed in 1988 and 1989 as many management promoter group failed. During the 1990s there has been an improvement in the industry in both New Zealand and Australia.

### Conclusion

Venture capital has become the age of the finance that can play a significant role in the economic development of any country, because it promotes technocrat entrepreneurs having new and innovative business proposals, which can lead the economy in ultimate growth and solves the problems of unemployment as well as enables the country to meet global challenges in the present economic conditions. But to enjoy the fruits of the venture capital governments concerned should play the needed role in avoiding the problems and challenges of the venture capital industry in their countries and putting the venture capital on the right track to take-off.

## REFERENCES

Zider & Bob: How Venture Capital Works?; Harvard Business Review (Nov-Dec., 1998), pp. 131-139.

Pandey, I.M.: Venture Capital: The Indian Experience, Prentice Hal of India Pvt. Ltd., New Delhi, 1996.

Jeffrey Zygmont: The VC Way – Investment secrets from the wizards of venture capital.

T. Satyanarayana Chary: Venture Capital in India-An Overview, Management Researcher, 2000, Tiruvananthapuram.

T. Satyanarayana Chary: Venture Capital Industry-Issues and Measures for Development, Pratibimba, 2001.

T. Satyanarayana Chary: Venture Capital Industry, JIMS 8M, Nov-Dec., 2001.

J.C. Verma – Venture Capital Financing.

# 5

# Money and Real Economy Linkages in the Anchor of the Gold Standard : An Epistemological Approach

*Masudul Alam Choudhury**
*Mohammad Ziaul Hoque***

The experience of globalization to date has been riddled with extreme swings in uncertainty and volatility concerning the economies and financial markets. To respond to such uncertainties and crisis troubleshooting the IMF is searching for a new global financial architecture (1995) and Basle II (2003) has proposed a new capital accord. The causes underlying such economic and financial situations can be traced to several significant causes. Firstly, the conception and practice of money and the real economy are seen to create dichotomous and competing sectors, with each of these sectors giving different concepts of rates of returns to the individual. On the side of the financial sector the return is that of interest-bearing rates on bank savings, bonds and short-term financial papers. On the side of the real economy the dividends on equity are rates of returns.

* Professor of Economics, Sultan Qaboos University, Muscat, Sultanate of Oman and the School of Business, University College of Cape Breton, Sydney, Nova Scotia, Canada.

** Assistant Professor of Finance, Sultan Qaboos University.

Interest rates and rates of returns move oppositely as relative prices signifying competition rather than linkage between the two sectors. Secondly, the privatization agenda under globalization has led to an intensifying dichotomy between of the financial and real economy through competition between these sectors. Commercial banks have thus taken advantage of this type of transformation to gain from the low rates of interest in generating large supply of commercial papers and money without the intervention of the Central Bank both in the banking sector and the external sector, where exchange rates are allowed to float. Thirdly, household preferences are being increasingly swayed by the supply side of privatization in concert with the nature of the financial sector and real economy de-link.

The argument of this paper is that the presence of unstable economic relationships befogs the problem of discerning the endogenous function between money and economic activity. The presence of interest-bearing forces and their effects in the financial and real goods economy cause this instability. The result is a fundamental disequilibrium in the money and economic sectors. The adverse implication of the fundamental disequilibrium is seriously social in nature. The study of the interrelationships between money, economic activities and social issues governed by an epistemological rule that organizes the money-economy interrelationship as a circular causation in social and economic functions is the conceptual objective of this paper.

## Certain Definitions

*The money and real economy linkage* means sustainability of the circular causation interrelationship between money and real economy in the sense of the real economy being the domain of non-inflationary and development driven spending in market exchangeables. Such a definition comes close to Boulding's (1971) definition of the moral economy. Boulding defines the economy as that part of his three-parts total social system comprising the benevolent, the malevolent and the integrative sub-systems, which is organized through exchange and deals with exchangeables. But with the introduction of such a total social system with its particular sub-systems the nature of the exchangeable becomes a fuzzy mixture between tangibles and intangibles.

The real economy is such a total social system in which money and economy link cogently with the social question to determine the stable circular interrelationships between these. That part of the economy belonging to the malevolent sub-system that causes market exchange in speculation, volatile and unethical activities, is discounted from the definition of the real economy. This exclusion is not by way of imposition on the market. Rather, the consequences on ethical preferences and menus of the general economic relationships (Sen, 1990) arise from the endogenous nature of the circular interrelationships among these three sectors together with the fourth most crucially governing epistemology guiding and sustaining the full circular causation interrelationships. Only by way of this sustainability consequence but not as an imposed premise of definition, is a real economy one in which real output remains stable and establishes its stable relationship with money in the equation of exchange.

The *Universal Standard* in the money-real economy social harmonization, which is the complementary circular causation interrelationship between money, real economy, social and epistemological domains means the following two coterminous concepts in the choice of the monetary numeraire (anchor). Firstly, the most useful numeraire as a stable commodity standard for currency valuation is found to be the gold standard. Secondly, the re-establishment of the gold standard means institutional restructuring of the monetary, financial and economic systems governed by a regime of the 100 percent reserve requirement monetary system. Yet the quantity of the gold holding to support the currency circulation in the real economy governed by the

100 percent RRMS is minimal and of a special nature as will be explained.

*The epistemological background is unity of knowledge* [unified money-real economy system in our particular case] working endogenously in the circular causation interrelationships between and within two levels of systems together forming the socio-economic general equilibrium framework. Firstly, there is the Ontological Evidential System (OES). This provides the list of socio-economic variables and their ontological functions. Secondly, there is the Institutional System (IS) comprising the Central Bank, Commercial Banks, Financial and non-Financial Intermediaries and a national/global Department/Institute of Social and Economic Development Planning. The IS discourses within it in respect to the interrelationships observed or formulated for the OES. Thus the normative and positive evidences of unity of knowledge at the OES circularly recourses with the IS, while there are dynamic functions within and between these systems as there are similar circular feedbacks by discourse or interaction within the systems.

Because of the primacy of feedback premised on the axiom of unity of knowledge as the governing law of such circularly interrelating systems, three properties characterize these relations intra- and inter- systems. These are firstly pervasive interaction between evidential forms, institutional decisions and between them. We refer to this stage as the Interactive Stage (I). Secondly, such extensive interactions lead into participatory consensus or equilibrium convergences at the levels of OES and IS, respectively. We refer to such interactively resulting convergences or consensus as Integration (I).

Each sequence of interaction leading to integration ends with the evaluation of the interactive, integrative (II) relations between and within the OES and IS. The evaluative objective function is referred to as the Social Wellbeing Function (SWF). SWF measures the degree to which unity of knowledge is attained in the interactive, integrative process (II-process) as defined above. Evolution (E) thereafter follows evaluation of SWF into subsequent sequences of processes of similar types. The OES-IS interrelations are thus circularly generated and perpetuated across processes through the evaluation of the SWF in the light of the epistemology of unity of knowledge that is characterized by the Interactive, Integrative and Evolutionary process (IIE-process).

The sequences of the interaction, integration and evolutionary processes (IIE-process) signifying the circular causation interrelationships governed by the epistemology of unity of knowledge are shown in Figure 1.

**Figure 1: Circular Causation Interrelationships in IIE Processes**

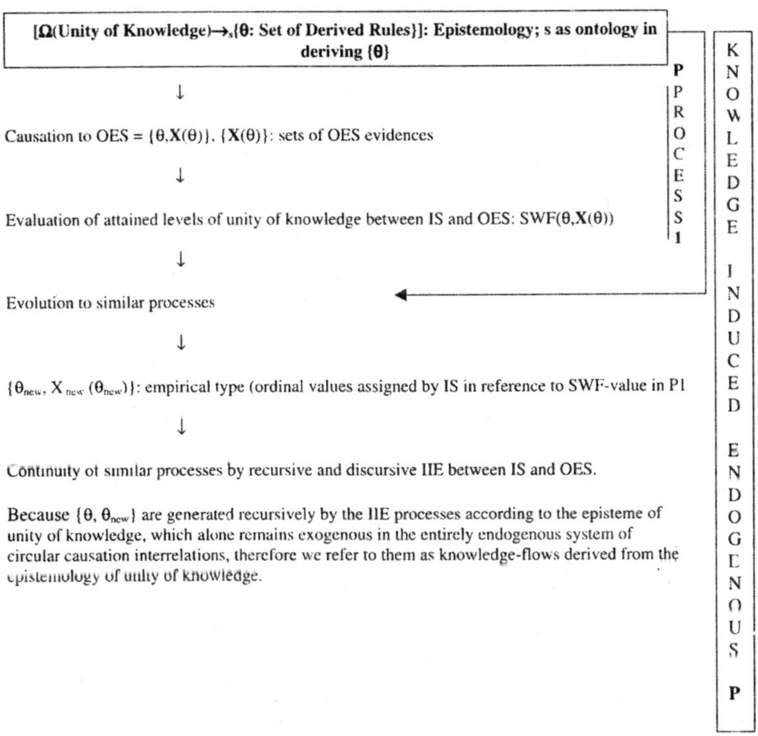

## Deriving the Money-Real Economy Social Interrelations tn the OES-IS Framework

The epistemological model of Figure 1 is now used to formulate the money-real economy circular causation social interrelations. We depict this first in Figure 2.

**Figure 2: Epistemological Induction in the Money-Real Economy Social Interrelations**

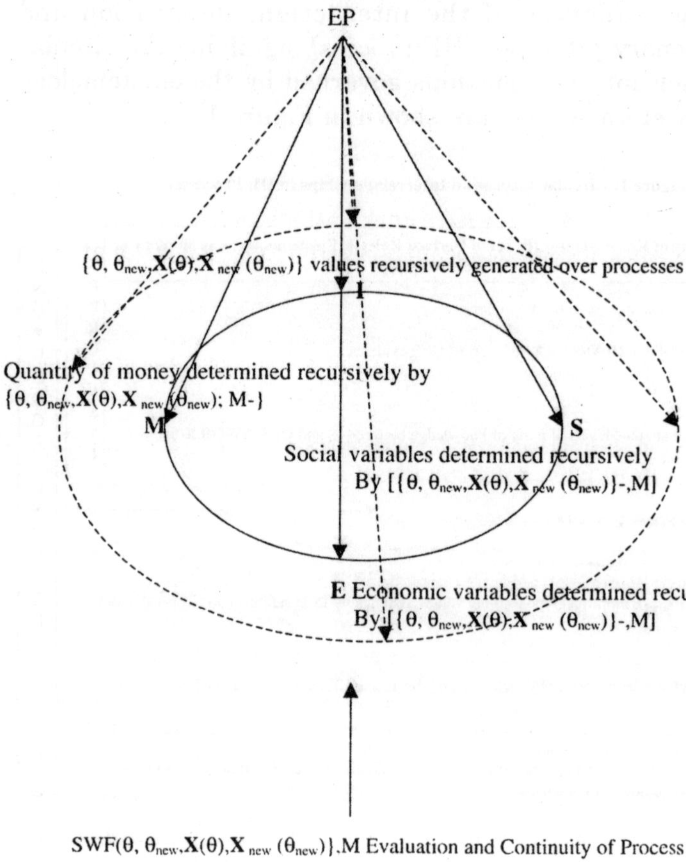

*Explanation of Figure 2*

EP is the epistemology of unity of knowledge at the IS level. M denotes quantity of money and is recursively determined in the sense of complementarities between $\{\theta^*, Q(\theta^*), p(\theta^*), (r(\theta^*)/i(\theta^*)), T(\theta^*), E(\theta^*), M(\theta^*)\}_t$, t denotes lagged recursion of θ*-values and its induced variables, beginning with the first process when t = 0.

For simplicity we have subsumed the knowledge-flow vector in the symbol θ*. Q(θ*) denotes θ*-induced output. p(θ*) denotes θ*-induced price level. r(θ*) denotes θ*-induced rate of return on equities. i(θ*) denotes θ*-induced reduction in interest rates. Thus (r(θ*)/i(θ*)) is a relative price of two mutually exclusive financial policy variables in the interest free money-economy relationship. T(θ*) denotes knowledge-induced total balance of payments (Current Accounts + Capital Accounts). E(θ*) denotes employment variable as a social indicator. M(θ*) denotes knowledge-induced quantity of money variable.

The variables shown are circularly interrelated according to the IIE framework of unity of knowledge. Therefore, the normative target is to derive and guide this system of circular causation interrelations into positive relationships between the variables, while evaluating the degree to which such progressive complementarities in the recursively evaluated social wellbeing function,

$$SWF(\{\theta^*, Q(\theta^*), p(\theta^*), (r(\theta^*)/i(\theta^*)), T(\theta^*), E(\theta^*), M(\theta^*)\})_t. \quad (1)$$

Consequently, in a positive direction of the money-real economy social transformation we ought to be looking for a progressively enhancing positive values of the elasticity coefficients between the variables interrelated and recursively estimated in the circular causation interrelationships.

What does this formalism mean? According to the money-real economy social interrelations as explained earlier, the quantity of money equals the spending in goods, financial assets and services determined by policy guidance and preference changes in the light of knowledge induction. Vice-versa in the cyclical round of processes, the lagged monetary, financial, real economy and social variables determine the new matching quantity of money. The indeterminacy of the money-price-output relationship of various versions of the quantity theory is thus removed by the lagged determination of the variables in the circular causation process. Money is thus fully endogenous in terms of the other variables and the lagged ones in the IIE process.

Now since the return on money is predetermined by the return of the real economy, which is productive and social in spending according to the policy and preference choices, therefore, the accumulation of capital and the growth of the economy is determined by an inverse relationship between r and i in accordance with the degree of impact of recursive $\theta^*$-values. Consequently, the IS and OES are now made to recursively respond to each other along the path of sustainability of the following expected relationship of normatively guided direction of money-real economy social transformation.

$$\theta^*\uparrow\rightarrow \{p(\theta^*).Q(\theta^*) = \text{spending}\} \uparrow\rightarrow r(\theta^*) \tag{2}$$

$$\uparrow\rightarrow i(\theta^*) \downarrow\rightarrow T(\theta^*) \uparrow\rightarrow e = \text{exchange rate}$$

$$\text{stabilizes} \uparrow\rightarrow E(\theta^*) \uparrow \rightarrow M\uparrow \rightarrow \ldots \text{SWF} \uparrow\rightarrow$$

repeated by sustainability of the IS-OES complementarities referring to the episteme of unity of knowledge and the policies, instruments and preferences so evolved. $\uparrow$ denotes increase; $\downarrow$ denotes decrease; $\rightarrow$ denotes implication.

Because of the productive and socially guided nature of spending matching with the quantity of money in a progressively eroding interest regime, the rate of growth of the quantity of money exceeds the rate of growth of prices, thereby causing a supply-side economics to emerge. From the Fisher (1911) version of the quantity theory we note that the rate of growth of real money (M/p) equals the rate of growth of output. Consequently, the rate of growth of price level is zero. Inflationary pressure is arrested by the money-real economy social conditions of the equation of exchange. Such a relationship is thereby a harbinger of social and economic progress and economic stabilization in a general social equilibrium framework.

Because of circular causation in the IIE processes the strict order of the money-real economy social relationships may not be necessary, as money-real economy social relations get reinforced and sustained.

### Money-Real Economy Social Relations is Realized by the 100 Percent Reserve Requirement Monetary System with the Gold Standard

We define the 100 percent reserve requirement monetary system in the light of the endogenous money-real economy social interrelations as both the 100 percent mobilization of bank deposits in commercial banks into productive assets, goods and services in exchange and also the holding of 100 percent of un-mobilized funds of depositors with the Central Bank. Consequently, the commercial bank has no scope to direct funds into interest-bearing savings and the return on money between the commercial bank and the real economy is perfectly shared between the depositors, the commercial bank and a diversified number of shareholders of the outlet into which funds are mobilized. Hence, the rate of return on money equals the rate of return on assets and exchangeables of the real economy in accordance with the effect of θ-values in the system of causal interrelationships.

The accumulated amount of excess funds after resource mobilization by the commercial banks is held at the central bank where it is supported by a stock of gold. But since such residual funds would be marginal in a vibrant money-real economy social interrelationship with r increasing along with socially productive spending, therefore, only a proportionate quantity of gold stock would be required to assign denomination to the currency held. But since two currencies cannot exist within the same economy, therefore the denomination of held funds in terms of the proportionate stock of gold would be applied to all the money in circulation in the real economy.

The seigniorage from the cost of production of a proportionate amount of gold to back up the residual un-mobilized funds forms a percentage charge on the residual reserve held with the central bank. The central bank collects this seigniorage from the commercial bank. The seigniorage cost overwrites the cost of managing the funds by the commercial banks. The clientele is protected from devaluation of the currency value by its gold backing. In this way the clientele benefits in two ways. Firstly, he is a shareholder with a proportionate profit share of his mobilized funds into socially productive spending through commercial banks. Secondly, his un-mobilized funds are protected from devaluation by the gold backing. In both of these cases money now becomes asset-backed money with the gold numeraire for valuation of the stock of money in circulation and held at the central bank. The commercial bank can at any time draw out of the accumulated reserves with the central bank to finance projects in tandem with the socially productive transformation of the real economy.

In the 100 percent RRMS commercial banks lose their ability to affect multiple credit creation and thereby accumulate large volumes of interest payments from inter-bank lending and other lending. Money is created out of nothing in the fractional reserve requirement system to the benefit of large savers, banks and corporations (Shakespeare, 2003). Besides this, commercial banks can also borrow from their reserves with the central bank to generate new loans and thus earn profits from the interest spread between the prime rate and the commercial rate.

In the 100 percent RRMS the absence of savings in liquid funds in commercial banks turns all inter-bank capital flows to be of the profit-sharing type in venture capital, trade financing and equity participation.

Consequently, the quantity of money in circulation matches with the existing project and spending value. Speculation is avoided by such a matching formula and volatility as well as uncertainty is avoided by the stability of relative prices in complementary money and financial and real goods and services. There can exist no incentive to save in liquidity in such a financial system. Indeed Keynes (1930) considered savings as a lure for money to be a withdrawal from productive economic activity when savings did not equal expected investment in the short run. The 100 percent RRMS is thus a monetary system that by its complementary systemic nature discourages savings as resource holdup and encourages and enhances resource mobilization. Resource mobilization and savings as withdrawal are opposite activities between the financial and real sectors, respectively.[1]

## Denominating Currency Value Backed by the Gold Standard

Central bank sets the value of the gold-backed currency by allocating a stock of gold, say G that is equivalent to the purchase of basic needs basket of goods, say X. Such basic needs are dynamic over time and learning in the IIE-processes governing IS-OES relationships. Thereby, $G = p.X$, value of spending in X at prices p (treat p.X as vector multiplication).

Next consider a quantity of money M being held at the central bank as residual holding that could not be mobilized but will be required later on by the commercial bank. Since $M = p.X$ (vector multiplication) therefore, $M = p.X = G$. M is backed by gold to the extent of spending in X at prices p (vectors). Since the dynamic basic needs basket is invoked in this gold valuation of money, therefore, all money in circulation in the real economy is backed by the same gold standard. Thereby, prices are stabilized by gold backing in terms of money growth being measured by the rate of growth of output.[2]

The central bank is responsible for overseeing the health of the economy by consulting with commercial banks on the allocation of funds in socially productive directions and fixing the gold-backing for the quantity of money in the economy. Note that the base of gold and money valuation is the basic needs basket, which is a dynamic category because of the presence of θ-values in all such variables according to the episteme of systemic unity of knowledge.

How much gold stock would be required to maintain the 100 percent RRMS? A minimal amount, for $\Delta M = M1 - M2$, where M1 denotes the potential quantity of money in circulation if the commercial bank deposit was fully mobilized at a point in time. M2 denotes the actual quantity of money in circulation through the commercial bank. The actual case would be that a certain amount of foreign debt will exist and the central bank must create a quantity of money to liquidate this if otherwise the private sector is unable to fully securitize the debt by debt-equity swap.

Hence[2] $\Delta M = M1 - M2 = (G1 - G2)(1 + g) = \Delta G.(1 + g)$ That is, $\Delta M/\Delta G = (1 + g)$. This is equivalent to $(\Delta M/M)/(\Delta G/G) = (1 + g)$. That is the rate of elasticity of money with respect to gold remains in a steady state and is determined by the growth rate of the economy.

In the ideal case when full mobilization of resources takes place through the commercial bank, then too $\Delta M \neq 0$; consequently, $\Delta G \neq 0$. That is because a stock of gold-backed money must always remain with the central bank for purposes of valuation and supply on short notice as needed in case of excess demand in a growing non-inflationary economy in the absence of interest rate and the presence of spending. Thus there is an inverse relationship between resource mobilization and the stock of gold. The function of the central bank is simply to oversee the health of the economy, maintain the gold standard and provide necessary guidance to the commercial bank and the development process.

## Conclusion

In the face of high uncertainty and volatility caused by the competing as opposed to the complementary nature of wealth creation in the midst of globalization, the money-real economy linkages would require pertinent policies. Such policies could be formulated and executed by national governments or by a global central bank, as is presently being proposed by some academicians (Single Global Currency Association, 9 July 2004).

Some of the kinds of policy instruments that the money-real economy gold-backed 100 percent reserve requirement monetary system will use are as follows:

Continuous discourse that is policy participatory for learning and guidance by institutional arrangement in the ever-spanning tripartite interrelationship involving the central bank, the commercial banks and the real economy.

Participatory instruments such as profit-sharing, equity participation, trade financing, joint ventures, cofinancing and other cooperative forms that help to (a) select socially and economically useful projects; (b) mobilize resources between the financial and real sectors.

Extension of the money-real economy complementary concept across the economy at large by means of the micro-money perspective causes the participatory dynamics to pervade throughout the economy.

The continuous monitoring of a social and economic objective in the tripartite relationship mentioned in (1), thus reflecting the general social and economic equilibrium.

## NOTES

| 1 | $t=0$ | $t-1$ | $t-2$ | $t=n$ |
|---|---|---|---|---|
| Output | $Q_0$ | $Q_1 = Q_0(1-s)(1+i)$ | $Q_2 = Q_0(1-s)^2(1+i)^2$ | $Q_n = Q_0(1-s)^n(1+i)^n$ |
| Returns on | | | | |
| Savings s denotes the constant savings rate | | | | |
| Savings | $Q_0(1-s)$ | $Q_1(1-s) = Q_0(1-s)^2(1+i)$ | | $Q_n = Q_0(1-s)^n(1+i)^{n-1}$ |
| Output | $Q_0$ | $Q_1' = Q_0(1+r)$ | $Q_2' = Q_0(1+r)^2$ | $Q_n' = Q_0(1+r)^n$ |

Returns on

Spending

If all of savings is mobilized into spending at any given point of time then the above two results will be the same. There is no savings deduction in the latter case because resource mobilization at any point of time enters the GDP accounting and forms aggregate output.

Now consider the following results:

At $t = n$,

$Q_n' > Q_n$, because of the withdrawal by way of savings, provided, $(1+r)^{n-1} > (1-s)^n(1+i)^{n-1}$

That is, $1 + r > (1-s)^{n/(n-1)}(1 + i)$

or, $1 + r > 1 - s + r$, to a linear approximation;

or, $r > i - s$. This is the leverage of rate of return over the net interest rate after savings, proving that savings, which depends upon interest rate, is always a withdrawal irrespective of the accumulation of funds over time.

[2] $\Delta M = p.X = \Delta G$, $\Delta$ and thereby $\Delta G$ denote the residual money and its gold-backing required following resource mobilization through commercial banks. This relation can be re-written as, $\Delta M = \Sigma p_i.X_i = \Delta G$ by taking individual prices of the corresponding goods. The same relation can be written as,

$$\Delta M = [\Sigma p_i.X_i/\Sigma p_{i0}.X_{i0}].[\Sigma p_{i0}.X_{i0}] = \Delta G,$$

$\Sigma p_{i0}.X_{i0}$ denotes base year spending in the basic needs basket; $[\Sigma p_i.X_i/\Sigma p_{i0}.X_{i0}]$ = CPI in a given year in reference to the base year.

$$\Delta M/CPI = (p_0.X_0) = \Delta G_0; \text{ or, } CPI = \Delta M/\Delta G_0 = [\Delta M_0/\Delta G_0](1 + g),$$

because $\Delta M_0$ is determined according to the rate of growth of output, g, in the money-real economy social relationship.

Thus, CPI changes proportionately to the rate of change in productivity. There cannot be inflationary pressure in such a case, a point that was pointed out earlier as well.

## REFERENCES

Basle II, Committee on Banking Supervision (31 July 2003), Overview of the Basle Capital Accord (Consultative Document), Basle, Switzerland: Bank of International Settlements.

Boulding, K.E. (1971), "Economics as a moral science", in F.R. Globe ed. Boulding: Collected Papers, Vol. 2. Boulder, CO: Association of University Press.

Fisher, I. (1911), The Purchasing Power of Money, New York: Macmillan.

IMF (1995), "Financing global governance", in Our Global Neighbourhood, the Report of the Commission on Global Governance, Oxford: Oxford University Press, pp. 217-221

Keynes, J.M. (1930), "Economic possibilities for our grandchildren", in his *Lectures in Persuasion*, New York: W.W. Norton, 1930.

Sen. A.K. (1990), On Ethics and Economics. Oxford, Eng: Basil Blackwell.

Shakespeare, R. (2003), Seven Steps to Justice. London, Eng: New European.

Single Global Currency Association (9 July 2004), Single Global Currency Conference, Bretton Woods, New Hampshire.

# 6

# Risk and Rewards in Asian Stock Markets : An Empirical Evidence

*B.S. Bodla* and M.S. Turan***

## Backdrop

Generally people invest with the motives of maximizing returns and minimizing risk. Constructing portfolios comprising of either several assets or a group of corporate securities could attain these motives. International diversification may also be used to achieve the objectives cited above. The rationale for international diversification of portfolios stems from the probability that stock returns within one country are highly correlated, but on account of inter-country variations in economic environments, industrial and business growth rates and inflationary conditions the correlations among the investment returns across countries is low (Madura, 1985).

The growing liberalisation and development of capital markets in a number of countries has increased the opportunity for diversifying portfolios internationally. The

* Reader, Department of Business Management, Guru Jambheshwar University, Hisar-125001, Haryana, INDIA.

** Dean & Chairman, Faculty of Management Studies, Guru Jambheshwar University, Hisar-125001, Haryana, INDIA.

interest in country funds in recent years, especially in Asia's emerging markets testifies to this growing awareness on the part of portfolio managers. The attraction towards emerging markets may be attributed to the fact that many of these markets have increasingly moved towards open-markets, and adoption of liberal guidelines with respect to both foreign direct investments and foreign institutional investments. Though Asian markets are more volatile as compared to their counterparts in the west, the volatility of these markets should be balanced against the fact that these markets exhibit very low or negative correlations with the developed markets (Sudhakar, 1996). The portfolio comprising of stocks from developed and emerging markets provides a very high potential for risk diversification.

International portfolio construction involves several aspects, which are unique and arise out of the need to compare return and risk in various countries and the benefits of international portfolio diversification. Further, there arise a need to measure the impact of foreign exchange rate fluctuations on return and risk. Obviously, the investor who intends to allocate funds in an internationally diversified portfolio must estimate the riskiness and return of the stock markets of his interest. However, according to the modern portfolio theory, the benefits of international diversification could arise only when the international stock markets are less than perfectly correlated. So, the correlation in the movement of rates of return on groups of stocks from two different countries needs to be computed while constructing international portfolio of securities. The present paper is an attempt in this direction. More specifically, the paper strives to achieve the following objectives:

(i) to make risk return analysis of analysis of investment in Asian equity markets;

(ii) to measure the impact of exchange rate fluctuations on stock returns; and

(iii) to determine correlation between the stock market indices of select Asian countries.

The paper has been divided into four sections, besides introduction. While, the first section analyses the methodology used herein, the second section presents the risk and return analysis of the select Asian markets. The third section brings out the relationship between the returns of the sample countries. The final section presents the summary and conclusion of the study.

## SECTION-1

### Research Methodology

The various stock markets considered in this study include three emerging economies (India, Taiwan and Singapore) and two developed markets (Japan and Hong Kong). Exhibit 1 shows the country-wise indices considered for the study.

**Exhibit 1**

| *Country* | *Exchange* | *Index* |
|---|---|---|
| India | Mumbai Stock Exchange | BSE Sensex |
| Japan | Tokyo Stock Exchange | Nikkei 225 |
| Taiwan | Taiwan Stock Exchange | TSEC Weighted Stock Price Index |
| Hong Kong | Stock Exchange of Hong Kong Ltd. | Hangseng |
| Singapore | Stock Exchange of Singapore Ltd. | SGX |

The data used for the present study are month end values of stock market indices and currency exchange rates for the sample countries. The reference period is January 1992 to December 2002. Most of the data have been collected through internet. Monthly data are used to calculate the stock returns which are expressed as logarithmic price relatives i.e. ln $(P_t/P_{t-1})* 100$ where $P_t$ and $P_{t-1}$ are the stock indices at time 't' and time 't-1' respectively. As the study utilizes monthly data, the shortest investment horizon is one month.

Almost as important as risk and return in investment decision-making is time horizon. Madhusoodanan (1997) emphasised that time needs to be taken as an important variable in the investment decision process. According to him long-term investments could reduce risk significantly and increase return. But the time diversification theory has been criticised by many researchers (Samuelson, 1994; Bodie, et al., 1996). In the present study, we have also tried to analyse the risk and returns pertaining to various investment horizons. For this objective, the investment horizons of one, two, three, six, twelve and twenty-four months have been considered. Hence, it is assumed that the investor would buy index fund in the end of a month and would realise returns by his exit from the fund at the end of subsequent month in case of one month holding period and would sell at the end of $2^{nd}$ month in case of two month holding period, and so an. Moreover, to get a better answer to the question whether the time diversification affect return and risk of equity investments, the return and risk statistics obtained as per various holding periods are being transformed into annualised statistics. For doing so, an assumption that stock prices follow random walk is taken. While the annualised returns have been calculated from the monthly, bimonthly, trimonthly, and six monthly stock returns by multiplying them with 12, 6, 4 and 2 respectively, the annualised volatility is estimated from holding period wise volatility by multiplying them with the square root of the numbers of holding periods in the year. The results obtained from various holding period returns and volatility, by simply multiplying by *n* and square root of *n* respectively, are presented in Table 5 and 6.

In calculating the return series for each holding period, non-overlapping periods are used. Obviously the number of observations decreases with every increase in the length of the holding period. Risk being the other side of investment coin, the local risk, exchange rate risk and total risk associated with the select Asian stock markets have been worked out and these statistics are presented in Table 2. The risk has been measured by standard deviation (σ) of return series as well as exchange rate series for respective countries.

The Karl Pearson's Product-moment formula has been applied to determine relationship amongst the returns series of select countries. However, the correlation coefficients based on time series data are valid only under the assumption of non autocorrelation (i.e. lag correlation of a given series with itself) an stationarity. The hypothesis of no serial correlation in the return series is tested by the Q statistic developed by L Jung-Box (1978). The Q statistic is approximately (i.e., in large samples) distributed as the chi-square distribution with m degree of freedom. In an application, if the computed Q exceeds the critical Q value from the chi-square table at the chosen level of significance, one can reject the null hypothesis that all $\rho_k$ are zero; at least some of them must be non zero (Note that for the present study $\rho_k$ stands for autocorrelation function (ACF) at stock returns series, with one month holding period). These coefficients are obtained from Easy Rag—a software designed to solve econometric models. We have computed the coefficients up to 24 lags.

To test whether the stock index series of various sample countries are stationary, a unit root test is performed using the Augmented Dickey-Fuller (1979) method. The augmented Dickey-Fuller (ADF) test has been applied to regression run in the following form:

$$\Delta Y_t = \beta_1 + \beta_2 t + \delta Y_{t-1} + \alpha_I \sum_{i=1}^{m} \Delta Y_{t-I} + \mu_t$$

Where, $Y_t = \ln (P_t)$ is the natural logarithm of the value of each stock index at time t, $\Delta$ is the difference operator, and t is for time.

In this model, the null hypothesis is that $\delta = 0$, that is, there is a unit root. The above model has been applied to log levels as well as at first difference i.e. return series for each sample country. The ADF test statistic has the same asymptotic distribution as the DF statistic, so the same critical values are used.

## SECTION-2

### Annual Return Pattern

This section presents analysis of the performance of select Asian stock markets in terms of annual returns in home currency and US dollar terms. The annual exchange gain/loss has also been worked out as portrayed in Table 1 along with returns. Before making the performance analysis, it is to clarify that the returns shown by Table 1 are purely index year-on-year growth and they don't include divided and bonus income. The annual return series have also been shown by graph 1.0.

Table 1 shows that the return in home currency as well as in dollars in case of Indian stock market was the maximum for the year 1999 (49.37 and 47.20% respectively) followed by the returns in 1993 (24.64%) and 1992 (29%). Contrarily, the years 1995, 1997, 2000 and 2001 brought more than 18 per cent negative returns (losses),. After putting a dent in the investments of global investors to the magnitude of 30.44 and 22.11 per cent in 2000 and 2001 respectively, the BSE Sensex yielded a return of merely 1 per cent during 2002. The attractive returns for the years 1999 may be attributed to the Union Budget of the year and political stability, which brought some cheers to the market and to the investors also. But the trend got reversed during 2000-01 as the tapes of senior political officials taking bribes created panic selling in the market. Market darling *Infosys Technology,* for example, lost 31 per cent of its market

**Table 1 : Annual Return of Select Asian Stock Markets**

| | *1992* | *1993* | *1994* | *1995* | *1996* | *1997* | *1998* | *1999* | *2000* | *2001* | *2002* | *Average* |
|---|---|---|---|---|---|---|---|---|---|---|---|---|
| **(A) India** | | | | | | | | | | | | |
| Return in Home Currency | 28.982 | 24.638 | 16.007 | –23.307 | –0.816 | 7.057 | –18.027 | 49.369 | –23.130 | –19.686 | 1.483 | 2.225 |
| Exchange Gain/Loss | –17.101 | –2.159 | -0.056 | –10.769 | –2.482 | –9.017 | –8.165 | –2.167 | –7.314 | –2.428 | 0.449 | –5.528 |
| Returns in US Dollars | 11.881 | 22.479 | 15.951 | –34.076 | –3.298 | 8.039 | –26.192 | 47.202 | –30.444 | –22.114 | 1.034 | –3.830 |
| **(B) Japan** | | | | | | | | | | | | |
| Return in Home Currency | –30.805 | 2.865 | 12.434 | 0.732 | –2.585 | –23.809 | –9.745 | 31.326 | –31.735 | –26.821 | –13.900 | –10.232 |
| Exchange Gain/Loss | 0.360 | 10.976 | 11.394 | –3.632 | –11.622 | –11.376 | 13.551 | 10.635 | –11.310 | –13.595 | 10.101 | 1.062 |
| Returns in US Dollars | –30.445 | 13.842 | 23.828 | –2.900 | –14.207 | –35.185 | 3.806 | 41.961 | –43.044 | –40.416 | –3.799 | –11.691 |
| **(C) Taiwan** | | | | | | | | | | | | |
| Return in Home Currency | –27.335 | 58.645 | 16.011 | –31.997 | 29.283 | 16.615 | –24.341 | 27.486 | –57.818 | 15.818 | –22.057 | –6.046 |

*(Table Contd...)*

**Table 1 : (Contd...)**

| | *1992* | *1993* | *1994* | *1995* | *1996* | *1997* | *1998* | *1999* | *2000* | *2001* | *2002* | *Average* |
|---|---|---|---|---|---|---|---|---|---|---|---|---|
| Exchange Gain/Loss | 0.936 | –5.343 | 2.141 | –3.799 | –0.656 | –16.283 | 0.031 | 2.121 | –4.198 | –4.261 | –1.123 | –2.652 |
| Returns in US Dollars | –26.398 | 53.302 | 18.152 | –35.796 | 28.628 | 0.332 | –24.310 | 29.607 | –52.017 | 11.557 | –23.180 | –9.038 |
| **(D) Hong Kong** | | | | | | | | | | | | |
| Return in Home Currency | 24.901 | 76.860 | –37.249 | 20.682 | 28.927 | –22.674 | –6.492 | 52.350 | –11.655 | –28.108 | –20.108 | 1.714 |
| Exchange Gain/Loss | 0.501 | 0.206 | 0.166 | 0.075 | –0.032 | –0.168 | 0.014 | –0.317 | –0.362 | 0.031 | –0.031 | –0.022 |
| Returns in US Dollars | 25.402 | 77.066 | –37.415 | 20.757 | 28.895 | –22.842 | –6.478 | 52.033 | –12.017 | –28.077 | –20.139 | 1.665 |
| **(E) Singapore** | | | | | | | | | | | | |
| Return in Home Currency | 2.102 | 52.021 | –11.826 | 3.352 | 3.813 | –27.843 | –7.928 | 57.682 | –25.221 | –17.123 | –19.118 | –2.336 |
| Exchange Gain/Loss | –1.027 | 2.269 | 9.608 | 3.228 | 1.031 | –17.978 | 0.899 | –0.331 | –3.856 | –6.674 | 6.385 | 0.356 |
| Returns in US Dollars | 1.075 | 54.290 | –2.219 | 6.580 | 4.843 | –45.821 | –7.029 | 57.352 | –29.078 | –23.797 | –12.732 | –4.018 |

*Note :* As the returns are based on stock indices, they don't include dividends income and bonus issues.

Chart 1 : Annual Stock Returns

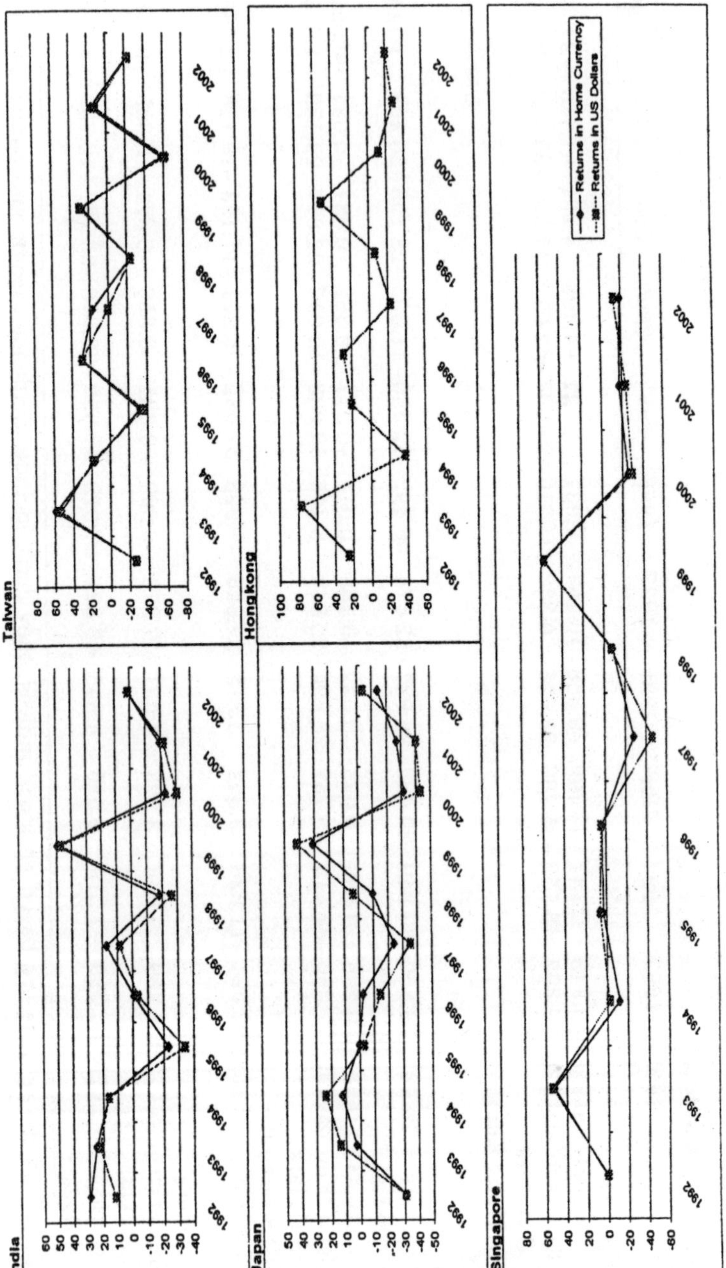

capitalization in a horror week of trading (HT, 4 March 2001). On the whole, the average return for a global investor has turned negative (-3.83%) as against the positive return (2.23%) for a local investor. Thus, due to the adverse movement of local currency against dollar the attractive returns in the Indian market disappear totally. On an average, there has been 5.53 per cent annual depreciation in Indian rupee against US dollar. The study conducted by Obaidullah (1994) for the five year period (1987-1992) had also shown similar results.

Section B of the Table 1, presents both annual stock return yielded by Nikkei 225 of Japan and annual exchange gain/loss of Yen against US dollar. It is obvious from the table that Nikkei stock average showed an alarming decline in 1992 (30.8%). But in next two years Nikkei provided appreciable return. After 1995, the Japanese securities market experienced steady decline continuously for three years. The poor performance of Japanese financial institutions and banks, poor corporate results, lack of political stability, continued recession in its economy are some of the factors responsible for negative returns from securities market. During 1999, Nikkei yielded a return of 31.32 per cent in home currency but thereafter the index suffered 31.74, 26.82 and 13.90 per cent losses in 2000, 2001 and 2002 respectively. On the whole, the Japanese investors have incurred a loss of 10.23 per cent annum over the study period. Fortunately, the average annual dividend (cash) yield on stocks (All First Section Stocks) in Japan works at 11.26 per cent approximately (Tokyo Stock Exchange Fact Book, 2003). So, considering dividend into account, the investments in Japanese equity provide around one per cent net return (i.e. dividend yield minus index loss). For a global investor the yield has most of the time been worse than that for a local investor.

Part-C of the table shows that the Taiwan's stock market (TSEC Weighted Stock Price Index) yielded significantly high return during 1993, both in home currency (58.65%) and US dollars (53.30%). However, the index rose by around

16 per cent in 1994. The TSEC Weighted Stock Price Index fell considerably (31.997%) during 1995. The market showed signs of improvement in the subsequent two years as the returns in home currency are worked out at 29.28 and 16.62 per cent during 1996 and 1997, respectively. But, the Taiwanese currency came under a severe pressure in 1997 as it depreciated to the tune of 16.28 per cent. It is evident from the table that the crisis triggered in Asia, in 1997-98, did not exempt Taiwanese investors as the index lost 24.34 per cent value during 1998. While the index followed the international trend during 1999 and bestowed the investors with 27.48 and 29.61 per cent returns in home currency and dollar terms, respectively, the year 2000 saw the highest fall out in the TSEC in its life since 1992. But, contrary to the many other countries of Asia, the investors of Taiwan remained a bit lucky for the year 2001 and enjoyed 15 per cent return, in home currency terms. However, again the index was observed at 22 per cent lower level in 2002 compared to the previous year. One the whole the market fetched negative annual returns of 6 per cent for a local investor and 9 per cent for a global investor. On an average, the Taiwanese currency has depreciated by 2.65 per cent every year in the reference period. It is worth mentioning that Taiwanese stocks have enjoyed annual dividend yield to the tune of 4.4 per cent approximately during the study period (Fact book Taiwan Stock Exchange, 2002).

The return performance of Hangseng index of Hong Kong may be glanced through part D of Table 1. It is obvious from the return statistics that Hong Kong stocks have outperformed the Asian markets during 1992 and 1993 as the cumulative return of this period works out more than 100 per cent both in home and foreign currency terms. After showing a negative return of above 37 per cent in 1994, the market offered positive returns of around 20 and 29 per cent during 1995 and 1996 respectively. Similar to other Asian tigers, Hong Kong stock index brought out heavy losses during 1997 and 1998. However, the Hong Kong investors zoomed during 1999 as they harvested a positive return of

52 per cent. The last three years came heavily on the fate of investors since they suffered a cumulative loss of around 60 per cent in this period. On the whole, the Hangseng provide the annual return of 1.71 and 1.665 per cent to local and global investors respectively. Moreover, the investors in equity stocks have enjoyed a dividend yield of 2.96 per cent per annum (HKEx Fact Book, 2002). Therefore, the overall return earned by Hong Kong investors turns the best amongst the five sample countries.

As indicated in Table 1-E, the pattern of occurrence of stock returns in Singapore seems in full consonance to that of Hong Kong (Hangseng). An inspection of the table shows that the investors earned the maximum return during 1999 followed, with small difference, by 1993. On the other hand, 1997 brought the highest loss (i.e. 27.84%) to the investors followed by 2000, 2002 and 2001, respectively. In other words, the period between 2000 and 2002 has been the worst for both local and the foreign investors in case of Singapore stock market.

Inter-country comparison of returns at the overall level, shows that the highest level of average return (home currency) has accrued in Indian stock market followed by Hong Kong. But from the point of view of a global investor, the Hong Kong market outperformed the other Asian countries. The Japanese markets have yielded the highest losses followed by Singapore and Taiwan where the negative return is minimum. The above pattern is also true for return in US dollars except the case of India.

## Risk Analysis

Any rational investor, before investing his or her investible wealth in the stocks, analyses the risk associated with them. The risk is expressed in terms of variability of return and therefore, the statistical tool often used to measure risk is the standard deviation. We have measured the risk in Asian stock markets by computing standard deviation of index based monthly returns. The exchange rate risk has also been computed on the same pattern. The net result is termed as total risk. The risk statistics so obtained are presented in Table 2.

It is clear from the table that both local risk and total risk are the highest in India amongst the sample countries during 1992. This may be attributed to the stock market scam in India, which came to light in April 1992. Even currency fluctuations in this year was the maximum in India followed by Japan and Taiwan. Taiwan's stock market faced the highest level of fluctuations in 1993. It is interesting to see that the stock markets in Asia remained relatively more stable between 1994 and 1996 as the standard deviation of returns in this duration is lower than other years for all countries except Japan in 1995. In the above duration, the exchange rate risk is found the maximum for Japan followed by India, Taiwan, Singapore and Hong Kong. During 1997, the Hong-Kong turned as the most volatile market followed, with wide margin, by Taiwan, Singapore, India and Japan. However, Singapore experienced the highest risk in 1998 followed, closely, by Hong Kong. The risk ranged between 9.021 and 4.011 in 1999 and 8.97 and 6.86 in 2000. The total as well as local risk during 2001 is found lower than that of the year 2000 and 2002, irrespective of the country involved. At the overall level, Taiwan turned as the most risky whereas Japan experienced the lowest level of risk. On looking index based returns and risk (Table 1 & 2) at a glance, we find that the hypothesis *higher the risk, higher the returns* stands accepted in all the countries except Taiwan where the risk is the maximum but the rewards are not in that proportion.

## Risk and Return Under Different Investment Horizons

Almost as important a risk and return in investment decision-making is time horizon. This is the investment-planning period for individuals. It is highly variable from individual to individual. Investors may adopt passive or active approaches to the management of their portfolios. A passive or buy-and-hold strategy essentially means purchasing and holding a security to maturity and then

**Table 2 : Annual Risk (Standard Deviation of Monthly Returns of Select Asian Stock Markets**

| | *1992* | *1993* | *1994* | *1995* | *1996* | *1997* | *1998* | *1999* | *2000* | *2001* | *2002* | *Average* |
|---|---|---|---|---|---|---|---|---|---|---|---|---|
| **(A) India** | | | | | | | | | | | | |
| Local Risk | 18.160 | 8.549 | 8.097 | 5.899 | 7.849 | 7.968 | 8.719 | 7.996 | 7.052 | 8.025 | 5.802 | 8.556 |
| Exchange Rate Risk | 3.971 | 1.989 | 0.019 | 1.744 | 2.301 | 1.660 | 1.438 | 0.329 | 0.662 | 0.419 | 0.498 | 1.366 |
| Total Risk | 16.471 | 8.255 | 8.100 | 5.734 | 8.138 | 8.365 | 9.507 | 8.050 | 6.792 | 8.227 | 5.788 | 8.493 |
| **(B) Japan** | | | | | | | | | | | | |
| Local Risk | 7.515 | 7.808 | 5.645 | 7.400 | 5.316 | 5.475 | 6.760 | 4.011 | 6.868 | 5.910 | 5.752 | 6.224 |
| Exchange Rate Risk | 2.574 | 2.477 | 2.510 | 4.780 | 2.273 | 3.780 | 6.197 | 2.566 | 2.735 | 3.591 | 2.311 | 3.254 |
| Total Risk | 8.859 | 3.927 | 5.982 | 6.496 | 5.087 | 7.585 | 7.919 | 4.502 | 8.501 | 5.713 | 6.475 | 6.913 |
| **(C) Taiwan** | | | | | | | | | | | | |
| Local Risk | 8.245 | 12.810 | 7.389 | 6.148 | 7.518 | 8.752 | 7.736 | 8.604 | 8.974 | 13.280 | 6.723 | 8.744 |
| Exchange Rate Risk | 1.058 | 0.730 | 0.931 | 1.578 | 0.606 | 2.391 | 2.083 | 0.926 | 1.345 | 1.269 | 1.273 | 1.290 |
| Total Risk | 8.541 | 12.855 | 7.415 | 6.089 | 7.633 | 8.583 | 8.374 | 8.248 | 9.636 | 13.659 | 6.377 | 8.855 |
| **(D) Hong Kong** | | | | | | | | | | | | |
| Local Risk | 6.817 | 9.003 | 7.365 | 6.406 | 4.640 | 12.526 | 13.099 | 9.021 | 7.609 | 7.877 | 5.491 | 8.169 |
| Exchange Rate Risk | 0.148 | 0.126 | 0.042 | 0.051 | 0.037 | 0.107 | 0.072 | 0.024 | 0.034 | 0.010 | 0.030 | 0.062 |
| Total Risk | 6.828 | 9.051 | 7.386 | 6.432 | 4.639 | 12.523 | 13.067 | 9.030 | 7.611 | 7.884 | 586 | 8.176 |

*(Table Contd...)*

**Table 2 : (Contd...)**

| | *1992* | *1993* | *1994* | *1995* | *1996* | *1997* | *1998* | *1999* | *2000* | *2001* | *2002* | *Average* |
|---|---|---|---|---|---|---|---|---|---|---|---|---|
| **(E) Singapore** | | | | | | | | | | | | |
| Local Risk | 4.194 | 6.218 | 5.742 | 4.525 | 4.897 | 8.240 | 14.577 | 7.588 | 7.842 | 8.839 | 5.127 | 7.072 |
| Exchange Rate Risk | 0.924 | 0.851 | 0.303 | 1.050 | 0.308 | 1.934 | 4.082 | 1.455 | 1.074 | 1.850 | 0.971 | 1.346 |
| Total Risk | 4.072 | 6.516 | 5.812 | 4.618 | 4.978 | 9.639 | 17.766 | 8.459 | 8.576 | 9.243 | 5.411 | 7.735 |

*Note* : 1. Local risk refers to the standard deviation of monthly returns in home currency.

2. Exchange rate risk refers to the standard deviation of exchange rates of domestic currency against US Dollar.

3. Total risk is the net effect of 1 and 2 above on the global investor.

reinvesting cash proceeds in similar securities. One technique for a passive strategy is an index fund. Index fund basically provide diversification along with minimum transaction costs. On the other, the active strategy aims at periodic realisation of returns. In this strategy portfolios typically have a shorter time horizons, varying from a few days to a year or so. Major emphasis is focused upon price appreciation.

In the present study, the investment horizons of one, two, three, six twelve and twenty-four months have been considered. The descriptive statistics including mean return, standard deviation, coefficient of variation, minimum and maximum returns and skewness are calculated for each time horizon of investments and the same are exhibited in tables 3 and 4 in terms of home currency and US dollar respectively.

It is evident from the aforesaid table that the average returns are the highest in case of Hong Kong followed by India, Singapore, Taiwan and Japan. Interestingly, this phenomenon holds good irrespective of nature of average as well as holding period. The table further pinpoints that the average returns have a tendency to rise with the rise in holding period. However, the position emerging about those stock markets, which resulted into negative return, for instance Japan and Taiwan, is different from the markets showing positive returns. In their case, the losses increased significantly with the increase in holding period.

The table shows very interesting results about the risk statistics, i.e. standard deviation and coefficient of variation (c.v.). While the standard deviation for various Asian markets exhibit rising trend with widening of holding period, the coefficient of variation, which is a relative measure of dispersion implies a decreasing trend. Considering the supremacy of coefficient of variation over standard deviation, it concludes that the risk reduces with the increase in holding period. The table further indicates that longer holding period offers the opportunity to earn a

**Table 3 : Summary Statistics for Stock Returns in Select Asian Stock Markets in Home Currency Terms (1992-2002)**

| Sr. | Country | Index | *Average Return* G.M. | A.M. | Std.Dev. | C.V. | Max. | Min. | *T-test* Sig.level | Skew-ness |
|---|---|---|---|---|---|---|---|---|---|---|
| **(a) Holding Period: 1 month** | | | | | | | | | | |
| 1 | India | BSE Sensex | 0.0039 | 0.3982 | 8.9845 | 2255.996 | 35.0600 | –25.7200 | | 0.429 |
| 2 | Japan | NIKKEI 225 | –0.8956 | –0.6973 | 6.2748 | –899.889 | 14.9700 | –18.3100 | 0.2519 | –0.081 |
| 3 | Taiwan | TSEC Weighted Stock Price Index | –0.3982 | 0.0023 | 9.0930 | 386938.660 | 33.2400 | –21.5000 | 0.7223 | 0.622 |
| 4 | Hong Kong | Hangseng Index | 0.2038 | 0.5866 | 8.7163 | 1485.817 | 26.4500 | –34.8200 | 0.8629 | –0.056 |
| 5 | Singapore | SGX | –0.2195 | 0.0751 | 7.6702 | 10216.779 | 24.8400 | –21.0700 | 0.7535 | 0.030 |
| **(b)** | | **Holding Period: 2 months** | | | | | | | | |
| 1 | India | BSE Sensex | 0.0357 | 0.7965 | 12.6395 | 1586.887 | 43.2900 | –23.2700 | | 0.579 |
| 2 | Japan | NIKKEI 225 | –1.7914 | –1.3946 | 8.9604 | –642.522 | 22.1500 | –20.4600 | 0.2529 | 0.340 |
| 3 | Taiwan | TSEC Weighted Stock Price Index | 0.8393 | 0.0047 | 13.2055 | 280970.798 | 38.4800 | –31.7600 | 0.7255 | 0.500 |
| 4 | Hong Kong | Hangseng Index | 0.4987 | 1.1733 | 11.8102 | 1006.609 | 33.3500 | –28.5500 | 0.8598 | 0.335 |
| 5 | Singapore | SGX | –0.3914 | 0.1501 | 10.5666 | 7037.434 | 34.1100 | –29.4000 | 0.7505 | 0.504 |
| **(c)** | | **Holding Period : 3 months** | | | | | | | | |
| 1 | India | BSE Sensex | –0.1302 | 1.1950 | 17.5535 | 1468.912 | 78.3500 | –33.0000 | | 1.810 |
| 2 | Japan | NIKKEI 225 | –2.7371 | –2.0920 | 11.2049 | –535.597 | 21.0200 | –28.2800 | 0.2986 | –0.244 |
| 3 | Taiwan | TSEC Weighted Stock Price Index | –1.5866 | 0.0070 | 18.3388 | 260292.132 | 45.9900 | –29.4700 | 0.7571 | 0.547 |
| 4 | Hong Kong | Hangseng Index | 0.5364 | 1.7593 | 15.6169 | 887.667 | 43.7400 | –33.8900 | 0.8736 | –0.087 |
| 5 | Singapore | SGX | –0.8676 | 0.2248 | 14.8545 | 6608.660 | 39.3500 | –38.5900 | 0.7804 | 0.240 |

*(Table Contd...)*

**Table 3 : (Contd...)**

| Sr. | Country | Index | Average Return G.M. | A.M. | Std.Dev. | C.V. | Max. | Min. | T-test Sig.level | Skew-ness |
|---|---|---|---|---|---|---|---|---|---|---|
| **(d) Holding Period : 6 months** | | | | | | | | | | |
| 1 | India | BSE Sensex | 0.5225 | 2.3886 | 20.7864 | 870.220 | 45.3500 | –21,1700 | | 0.822 |
| 2 | Japan | NIKKEI 225 | –5.8901 | –4.1836 | 18.2852 | –437.064 | 31.3800 | –36.7300 | 0.2719 | 0.053 |
| 3 | Taiwan | TSEC Weighted Stock Price Index | –2.6184 | 0.0145 | 21.8284 | 150070.006 | 41.8300 | –55.6200 | 0.7135 | –0.438 |
| 4 | Hong Kong | Hangseng Index | 1.2455 | 3.5191 | 22.1041 | 628.119 | 51.5600 | –34.8700 | 0.8621 | 0.241 |
| 5 | Singapore | SGX | –1.3868 | 0.4500 | 19.8092 | 4402.050 | 44.2400 | –40.1400 | 0.7530 | 0.565 |
| **(e)** | | **Holding Period: 12 months** | | | | | | | | |
| 1 | India | BSE Sensex | 2.2250 | 4.7782 | 24.4413 | 511.520 | 49.3700 | –23.3100 | | 0.363 |
| 2 | Japan | NIKKEI 225 | –10.2317 | –8.3655 | 19.7778 | –236.422 | 31.3300 | –31.7300 | 0.1814 | 0.627 |
| 3 | Taiwan | TSEC Weighted Stock Price Index | –6.0458 | 0.0282 | 34.6810 | 123061.436 | 58.6400 | –57.8200 | 0.7147 | –0.036 |
| 4 | Hong Kong | Hangseng Index | 1.7140 | 7.0400 | 36.4163 | 517.277 | 76.8600 | –37.2500 | 0.8662 | 0.675 |
| 5 | Singapore | SGX | –2.3357 | 0.9000 | 28.857 | 3206.373 | 57.6800 | –27.8400 | 0.7374 | 1.315 |
| **(f) Holding Period : 2 years** | | | | | | | | | | |
| 1 | India | BSE Sensex | 0.2805 | 5.4800 | 35.0965 | 640.447 | 53.6202 | –42.8160 | | 0.014 |
| 2 | Japan | NIKKEI 225 | –24.9079 | –19.8100 | 31.1400 | –157.194 | 21.5808 | –58.5551 | 0.2166 | 0.384 |
| 3 | Taiwan | TSEC Weighted Stock Price Index | –1.6897 | 2.6867 | 31.9752 | 1190.144 | 45.8987 | –42.0008 | 0.8883 | 0.070 |
| 4 | Hong Kong | Hangseng Index | –3.3760 | 8.2200 | 57.0478 | 694.012 | 101.7612 | –48.2160 | 0.9225 | 0.915 |
| 5 | Singapore | SGX | –8.4197 | –1.20.17 | 42.7826 | –3560.275 | 54.1228 | –42.3443 | 0.7737 | 0.677 |

*Note* . t-test has been applied to test the significance of difference between average return of India and other Asian countries.

**Table 4 : Risk and Return Statistics of Select Asian Stock Markets in US Dollar Terms (1992-2002)**

| Sr. | Country | Index | *Average Return* G.M. | *Average Return* A.M. | Std.Dev. | C.V. | Max. | Min. | T-test Sig.level | Skew-ness |
|---|---|---|---|---|---|---|---|---|---|---|
| (a) | | **Holding Period: 1 month** | | | | | | | | |
| 1 | India | BSE Sensex | –0.4575 | –0.0722 | 8.8159 | –12202.077 | 27.3771 | –23.8101 | | 0.199 |
| 2 | Japan | NIKKEI 225 | –0.9101 | –0.6558 | 7.1448 | –1089.552 | 17.3201 | –18.729 | 0.5552 | 0.174 |
| 3 | Taiwan | TSEC Weighted Stock Price Index | –0.6393 | –0.2282 | 9.2108 | –4036.133 | 33.3122 | –21.3011 | 0.8883 | 0.646 |
| 4 | Hong Kong | Hangseng Index | 0.2014 | 0.5847 | 8.7229 | 1491.743 | 26.4576 | –34.7524 | 0.5433 | –0.052 |
| 5 | Singapore | SGX | –0.3487 | 0.0262 | 8.6122 | 32817.463 | 28.6518 | –24.8528 | 0.9269 | –0.052 |
| (b) | | **Holding Period: 2 months** | | | | | | | | |
| 1 | India | BSE Sensex | –0.9073 | –0.1445 | 12.6162 | –8731.092 | 43.1984 | –27.2278 | | 0.622 |
| 2 | Japan | NIKKEI 225 | –1.8606 | –1.3115 | 10.5811 | –806.790 | 27.7952 | –23.6349 | 0.5658 | 0.416 |
| 3 | Taiwan | TSEC Weighted Stock Price Index | –1.3449 | –0.4564 | 13.5310 | –2964.609 | 38.5138 | –32.4992 | 0.8913 | 0.521 |
| 4 | Hong Kong | Hangseng Index | 0.4933 | 1.1695 | 11.8287 | 1011.441 | 33.3587 | –28.351 | 0.5382 | 0.342 |
| 5 | Singapore | SGX | –0.6623 | 0.0525 | 12.0009 | 22865.198 | 43.4100 | –36.8182 | 0.9269 | 0.350 |
| (c) | | **Holding Period : 3 months** | | | | | | | | |
| 1 | India | BSE Sensex | –1.5756 | –0.2167 | 17.1228 | –7899.927 | 65.3938 | –35.6185 | | 1.057 |
| 2 | Japan | NIKKEI 225 | –2.8239 | –1.9673 | 13.0118 | –661.416 | 21.3774 | –24.0117 | 0.5907 | –0.032 |
| 3 | Taiwan | TSEC Weighted Stock Price Index | –2.4643 | 0.6846 | 19.2147 | –2806.581 | 46.3223 | –32.6419 | 0.9043 | 0.456 |
| 4 | Hong Kong | Hangseng Index | 0.5252 | 1.7542 | 15.6531 | 892.302 | 43.8918 | –34.0147 | 0.5745 | –0.083 |
| 5 | Singapore | SGX | –1.1942 | 0.0787 | 15.7564 | 20013.720 | 40.8160 | –44.6727 | 0.9331 | 0.017 |

*(Table Contd...)*

**Table 4 : (Contd...)**

| Sr. | Country | Index | Average Return G.M. | A.M. | Std.Dev. | C.V. | Max. | Min. | T-test Sig.level | Skewness |
|---|---|---|---|---|---|---|---|---|---|---|
| **(d) Holding Period : 6 months** | | | | | | | | | | |
| 1 | India | BSE Sensex | –2.4235 | –0.4335 | 20.9855 | –4841.027 | 40.8045 | –24.2058 | | 0.649 |
| 2 | Japan | NIKKEI 225 | –6.2172 | –3.9345 | 20.8699 | –530.431 | 30.3335 | –42.9385 | 0.5819 | –0.099 |
| 3 | Taiwan | TSEC Weighted Stock Price Index | –4.5112 | –1.3693 | 22.9760 | –1677.992 | 39.1541 | –62.534 | 0.8885 | –0.646 |
| 4 | Hong Kong | Hangseng Index | 1.2223 | 3.5085 | 22.1777 | 632.118 | 51.8522 | –34.8836 | 0.5481 | 0.254 |
| 5 | Singapore | SGX | –2.1467 | 0.1575 | 21.5155 | 13664.428 | 41.8127 | –41.9904 | 0.9270 | 0.148 |
| **(e) Holding Period: 12 months** | | | | | | | | | | |
| 1 | India | BSE Sensex | –3.8300 | –0.8670 | 25.4170 | –2931.658 | 47.2022 | –34.0757 | | 0.320 |
| 2 | Japan | NIKKEI 225 | –11.6914 | –7.8690 | 27.8015 | –353.302 | 41,9605 | –43.0443 | 0.5446 | 0.327 |
| 3 | Taiwan | TSEC Weighted Stock Price Index | –9.0383 | –2.7385 | 34.4535 | –1258.108 | 53.3018 | –62.0165 | 0.8863 | –0.070 |
| 4 | Hong Kong | Hangseng Index | 1.6653 | 7.0169 | 36.4937 | 520.080 | 77.0658 | –37.4149 | 0.5639 | 0.672 |
| 5 | Singapore | SGX | –4.0175 | 0.3149 | 31.6722 | 10057.446 | 57.3517 | –45.8212 | 0.9241 | 0.781 |
| **(f) Holding Period : 2 years** | | | | | | | | | | |
| 1 | India | BSE Sensex | –10.2670 | –5.2752 | 31.6633 | –600.232 | 34.3603 | –52.5579 | | –0.287 |
| 2 | Japan | NIKKEI 225 | –36.0117 | –21.1626 | 47.9192 | –226.434 | 45.7664 | –83.4601 | 0.5157 | 0.267 |
| 3 | Taiwan | TSEC Weighted Stock Price Index | –7.6248 | –3.0945 | 30.0856 | –972.225 | 28.9602 | –50.4599 | 0.9051 | –0.545 |
| 4 | Hong Kong | Hangseng Index | –3.4898 | 8.1848 | 57.3053 | 700.139 | 102.4680 | –48.216 | 0.6285 | 0.929 |
| 5 | Singapore | SGX | –13.1119 | –3.3888 | 47.6593 | –1406.377 | 55.3650 | –52.8744 | 0.9375 | 0.409 |

*Note* : t-test has been applied to test the significance of difference between average return of India and other Asian countries.

**Table 5 : Annualised Return and Risk for Various Investment Horizons (Home Currency)**

| Country | Index | *Based on One Month H.P.* G.M. | A.M. | Std.Dev. | *Based on Two Month H.P.* G.M. | A.M. | Std.Dev. |
|---|---|---|---|---|---|---|---|
| India | BSE Sensex | 0.047 | 4.779 | 31.123 | 0.214 | 4.779 | 30.960 |
| Japan | NIKKEI 225 | –10.747 | –8.367 | 21.737 | –10.748 | –8.367 | 21.948 |
| Taiwan | TSEC Weighted Stock Price Index | –4.778 | 0.028 | 31.499 | –5.036 | 0.028 | 32.347 |
| Hon Kong | Hangseng Index | 2.446 | 7.040 | 30.194 | 2.992 | 7.040 | 28.929 |
| Singapore | SGX | –2.633 | 0.901 | 26.570 | –2.349 | 0.901 | 25.883 |

| Country | Index | *Based on Three Month H.P.* G.M. | A.M. | Std.Dev. | *Based on Six Month H.P.* G.M. | A.M. | Std.Dev. |
|---|---|---|---|---|---|---|---|
| India | BSE Sensex | –0.521 | 4.780 | 35.107 | 1.045 | 4.777 | 29.396 |
| Japan | NIKKEI 225 | –10.948 | –8.368 | 22.410 | –11.780 | –8.367 | 25.859 |
| Taiwan | TSEC Weighted Stock Price Index | –6.347 | 0.028 | 36.678 | –5.237 | 0.029 | 30.870 |
| Hong Kong | Hangseng Index | 2.145 | 7.037 | 31.234 | 2.491 | 7.038 | 31.260 |
| Singapore | SGX | –3.470 | 0.899 | 29.709 | –2.774 | 0.900 | 28.014 |

**Table 6 : Annualised Return and Risk for Various Investment Horizons (Dollar Terms)**

| | | *Based on One Month H.P.* | | | *Based on Two Month H.P.* | | |
|---|---|---|---|---|---|---|---|
| *Country* | *Index* | *G.M.* | *A.M.* | *Std.Dev.* | *G.M.* | *A.M.* | *Std.Dev.* |
| India | BSE Sensex | –5.490 | –0.867 | 30.539 | –5.444 | –0.867 | 30.903 |
| Japan | NIKKEI 225 | –10.921 | –7.869 | 24.750 | –11.163 | –7.869 | 25.918 |
| Taiwan | TSEC Weighted Stock Price Index | –7.672 | –2.739 | 31.907 | –8.069 | –2.739 | 33.144 |
| Hon Kong | Hangseng Index | 2.417 | 7.017 | 30.217 | 2.960 | 7.017 | 28.974 |
| Singapore | SGX | –4.184 | 0.315 | 29.834 | –3.974 | 0.315 | 29.396 |

| | | *Based on Three Month H.P.* | | | *Based on six Month H.P.* | | |
|---|---|---|---|---|---|---|---|
| *Country* | *Index* | *G.M.* | *A.M.* | *Std.Dev.* | *G.M.* | *A.M.* | *Std.Dev.* |
| India | BSE Sensex | –6.302 | –0.867 | 34.246 | –4.847 | –0.867 | 29.678 |
| Japan | NIKKEI 225 | –11.295 | –7.869 | 26.024 | –12.434 | –7.869 | 29.515 |
| Taiwan | TSEC Weighted Stock Price Index | –9.857 | –2.739 | 38.429 | –9.022 | –2.739 | 32.493 |
| Hong Kong | Hangseng Index | 2.101 | 7.017 | 31.306 | 2.445 | 7.017 | 31.364 |
| Singapore | SGX | –4.777 | 0.315 | 31.513 | –4.293 | 0.315 | 30.428 |

return higher than that is available in the shorter holding periods. Regarding nature of distribution of stock returns, it may be captured from the table that the returns are *positively skewed* in case of India and Singapore, irrespective of holding period. Vijaya and Vedpuriswal (2002), in their study also found that there is significant positive skewness in Indian stock returns. Studies in the US and Australian markets have also revealed that there is positive skewness in the distribution of stock returns (Beedles, 1986). But there appears no set pattern of distribution of returns in case of Japan, Taiwan and Hong Kong.

**Table 7 : Autocorrelation Coefficients of Stock Indices (Holding Period = 1 month)**

| Leg | India | Japan | Taiwan | Hongkong | Singapore |
|---|---|---|---|---|---|
| 1 | 0.0982 | 0.0099 | 0.0615 | 0.0087 | 0.0153 |
| 2 | 0.0269 | –0.096 | 0.0417 | –0.0163 | 0.0876 |
| 3 | –0.1496 | 0.0362 | –0.099 | –0.0941 | –0.0843 |
| 4 | –0.144 | 0.0265 | –0.0305 | –0.0659 | –0.0116 |
| 5 | 0.089 | 0.051 | –0.0034 | –0.031 | –0.0049 |
| 6 | 0.1818 | –0.0931 | –0.2016 | –0.0187 | –0.004 |
| 7 | –0.1668 | –0.123 | 0.0923 | 0.2119 | 0.126 |
| 8 | –0.1644 | 0.0663 | –0.0829 | 0.1292 | 0.1146 |
| 9 | –0.0694 | 0.0373 | 0.1045 | 0.0182 | –0.0605 |
| 10 | 0.043 | –0.0144 | 0.0792 | 0.0893 | –0.0431 |
| 11 | 0.0959 | –0.0407 | –0.0175 | –0.1592 | –0.1796 |
| 12 | 0.0156 | –0.0076 | –0.0317 | –0.1129 | 0.0069 |
| 13 | –0.2073 | –0.137 | –0.0827 | –0.1524 | –0.0537 |
| 14 | –0.1878 | 0.0951 | 0.0674 | 0.0372 | 0.0381 |
| 15 | –0.1107 | –0.0934 | –0.0314 | –0.039 | –0.1457 |
| 16 | –0.1482 | –0.0254 | –0.165 | 0.1334 | 0.0215 |
| 17 | 0.0723 | 0.0516 | –0.1055 | 0.0311 | –0.0017 |
| 18 | –0.0295 | –0.1482 | –0.2494 | –0.0978 | –0.1037 |
| 19 | –0.1483 | 0.0264 | –0.0741 | –0.0813 | –0.0658 |

*(Table Contd...)*

**Table 7 : (Contd...)**

| | | | | | |
|---|---|---|---|---|---|
| 20 | 0.0774 | 0.052 | –0.1407 | –0.0788 | –0.0522 |
| 21 | 0.0406 | 0.0115 | 0.1086 | 0.0902 | 0.0767 |
| 22 | 0.1745 | –0.1003 | 0.0839 | –0.0573 | –0.1342 |
| 23 | 0.2647 | –0.0618 | 0.1541 | –0.0629 | –0.0376 |
| 24 | 0.0324 | 0.0013 | 0.1066 | 0.0239 | –0.0025 |
| Q(1) | 1.24 | 0.01 | 0.48 | 0.01 | 0.03 |
| p-value | 0.2652 | 0.9098 | 0.4878 | 0.9211 | 0.8609 |
| Q(6) | 9.60 | 2.81 | 7.03 | 1.91 | 2.00 |
| p-value | 0.1426 | 0.8329 | 0.3182 | 0.9281 | 0.9201 |
| Q(12) | 15.91 | 5.40 | 11.06 | 15.16 | 10.42 |
| p-value | 0.1952 | 0.9432 | 0.5240 | 0.2330 | 0.5788 |
| Q(24) | 34.79 | 13.23 | 28.72 | 24.66 | 18.22 |
| p-value | 0.0715 | 0.9622 | 0.2309 | 0.4245 | 0.7923 |

An attempt has also been made to test a null hypothesis that there is no difference in returns offered by Indian stock market and the other selected Asian stock markets. The results of t-test applied for the purpose under various holding periods led to the acceptance of the above hypothesis at 5 per cent level of significance. The above is valid for both home currency and dollar form returns.

To get a better answer to the question whether the time diversification affect return and risk of equity investments, the return and risk statistics obtained as per various holding periods are being transformed into annualized statistics. The results obtained from various holding period returns and volatility are presented in tables 5 and 6 respectively. It is worth noting from the said tables that both annualized returns and risks are more or less same in case of each of the holding period under study. The above finding is true for each of the five Asian countries. Thus, the claim made by Kritzman (1994) that time diversification surely reduces risk, stands invalid in Asian countries. But in case one considers the coefficient of variation as a measure of volatility, the findings of Kritzman as well as Madhusoodanan (1997) are found to get the approval from present study too.

## SECTION-3

### Correlation Among Asian Stock Markets

Numerous studies have documented the potential portfolio diversification benefits of global investing (Levi and Sarnad, 1970; Baily and Stulz, 1990; Hunter and Coggin, 1990). The logic of the benefits of global diversification stems from the fact that international stock markets are less than perfectly correlated. However, there is a school of those analysts, who argue that the global stock markets have started showing signs of co-integration due to the more openness of the capital markets resulting from ongoing process of liberalisation and hence, potential for international diversification exists no longer. In view of the above debate, we have made an attempt to examine the correlation among the select Asian stock markets so as to comment whether these markets still have potential for global diversification.

However, the correlation coefficients based on time series data are valid only under the assumption of non-autocorrelation (i.e. lag correlation of a given series with itself) and stationarity. The hypothesis of no serial correlation in the return series is tested by the Q statistic developed by L Jung-Box (1978). The results show that the null hypothesis of no autocorrelation cannot be rejected at the 5 per cent level for all return series. It is also found that the stock returns are random walk in each and every country. Thus, all the selected markets are efficient markets.

The regression results concerning Augmented-Dickey-Fuller Test applied with the aim of examining stationarity of the index series and return series are presented in Table 8. All ADF statistics based on log levels provide support to the null hypothesis of a unit root at 5 per cent level of significance. But these statistic reject the null hypothesis of a unit root for the return series at 5 per cent level of significance. Hence, the stock price index series for each country have the element of non-stationarity but stock-return series are stationarity. That is, the first difference of a random walk time series are stationarity. Now, after evaluating the data for its stationarity and no serial correlation, we can dare to proceed towards the analysis of correlation coefficients between sample countries.

**Table 8 : Augmented-Dicky Fuller Unit Root Test**

| *Country* | *D.F. Statistic at level in* $(P_t)$ | | | *Unit Root of D.F. Statistics at 1st difference* $R_t = In(P_t) - In(P_{t-1})$ | | |
|---|---|---|---|---|---|---|
| | *D.F.* | *t* | $r^2$ | *D.F.* | *t* | $r^2$ |
| India | –0.2155 | –2.8239 | 0.2994 | –0.8129* | –3.7987 | 0.55172 |
| Japan | 0.0949 | 1.4527 | 0.1243 | 1.1118* | 6.0289 | 0.5261 |
| Taiwan | –0.0622 | –1.2417 | 0.1836 | –1.0172* | –5.9293 | 0.4877 |
| Hong Kong | –0.1263 | –1.8023 | 0.23352 | –1.2757* | –6.7277 | 0.51622 |
| Singapore | –800 | –0.7568 | 0.1755 | –1.0218* | –5.818 | 0.5051 |

*$H_0$ Rejected at 5% significance level.

*Note* : Table value for t-test at 5% level of significance is 2.89.

Table 9 depicts the correlation coefficients for the monthly returns of each pair of the indices of five Asian markets measured in local currency terms (Panel A) and dollar terms (Panel B). The table reveals some interesting points. First, these Asian stock markets behave quite differently from one another, that is the correlations of their returns tend to be substantially less than unity. Although the highest coefficients are 0.764 and 0.762 in home currency and dollar terms respectively between the Hong Kong and Singapore, rest all values are below 0.50. Thus, investors can diversify their holdings by spreading their portfolio across the various markets of Asia. The second notable point is that stock prices in Hong Kong and Singapore move more closely (r = 0.764) than do either the stock prices in Japan and Hong Kong (r = 0.286 in home currency) or the prices in India and Hong Kong (r = 0.286 in home currency). Consequently, investors seeking diversification must choose carefully from amongst the various markets.

**Table 9 : Correlation Coefficients of Selected Asian Stock Markets**

**(A)Home Currency Terms**

| | Hong Kong | India | Japan | Singapore | Taiwan |
|---|---|---|---|---|---|
| Hong Kong | 1.000 | | | | |
| India | 0.137 | 1.000 | | | |
| Japan | 0.286** | 0.038 | 1.000 | | |
| Singapore | 0.764** | 0.163 | 0.335** | 1.000 | |
| Taiwan | 0.470** | 0.191* | 0.257** | 0.430** | 1.000 |
| Average "r" | 0.414 | 0.132 | 0.229 | 0.423 | 0.337 |

**(B) US Dollar Terms**

| | Hong Kong | India | Japan | Singapore | Taiwan |
|---|---|---|---|---|---|
| Hong Kong | 1.000 | | | | |
| India | 0.139 | 1.000 | | | |
| Japan | 0.316** | 0.078 | 1.000 | | |
| Singapore | 0.762** | 0.190* | 0.367** | 1.000 | |
| Taiwan | 0.481** | 0.229** | 0.189* | 0.417** | 1.000 |
| Average "r" | 0.424 | 0.159 | 0.238 | 0.434 | 0.329 |

** Correlation is significant at the 0.01 level (2-tailed).

* Correlation is significant at the 0.05 level (2-tailed).

Note : All the above correlation coefficients are based on monthly returns for the period January 1992 to December 2002.

The third point emerging from the table is that all the correlations are positive and well above zero. Moreover, the majority correlation coefficients of Taiwan and two coefficients of Singapore are significant at 0.01 level. This implies the absence of complete dissimilarity in the movement of stock prices. The positive values indicate that the world's stock prices are, like their economies, some what integrated. Thus, the benefit of international diversification has limits. In other words, the markets of the world are members of a somewhat loosely connected system of economies, and allocating funds among the various economies provides some, but not complete, reduction of variability in returns on securities. Fourth, it is worth noting that the correlation coefficients of Indian stock prices are the lowest amongst the five Asian stock markets. On an average, the coefficients for Singapore are the highest followed, very closely, by Hong Kong and Taiwan. In contrast, average coefficients for India is the lowest (0.132) followed, in upside, by that of Japan (0.229). Thus, the Indian stock market offers extra ordinary benefits of risk reduction through diversification since it is a well established proposition that the lower the correlation between return of assets, the greater are the benefits of diversification in terms of risk reduction. While the Hong Kong market provided higher return (next to India), the opportunities for risk reduction are not significant because of its relatively high correlations with all of the sample countries (average correlation 0.414 in home currency terms).

Finally, it is interesting to note that the results pertaining to each of the above mentioned four points turn absolutely similar when correlation coefficients examined in US dollar terms. That is, for a global investor too India turns as the most favourable market for risk reduction through international portfolio diversification. Obaidullah (1994) in his study titled "Internationalisation of Equity Portfolios : Risk and Return in South Asian Security Markets" also found that the Indian stock market was the very promising one from the stand point of the global investor with its high returns and extremely low correlation with other markets. But he argued that the low correlations may be due to the fact that the Indian market remained independent from global influence for a long time due to artificial restrictions imposed by the government.

But, despite the continuing process of economic reforms since 1991, the Indian stock prices show a tendency to move quite independently. Interestingly, Japanese market

(Fabozzi, et al, 2002) has a relatively low level of correlation with developed markets such as US, France, UK, Canada and Australia. An another recent study on Stock Performance of Emerging Markets by Cohen (2001) also supports the above mentioned feature of Japanese stock market. Sudhakar Satyanarayan (1996) in his study also showed that Japanese market has a low degree of co-variability with emerging Asian Markets including Hong Kong, Thailand, Taiwan and Korea. The study also highlights that there is no significant divergence in the correlation for Taiwan and Japan.

## SECTION-4

### Summary and Conclusions

The study finds that the highest level of average return for a local investor has accrued in Indian stock market followed closely by Hong Kong. But for a global investor, Hong Kong stock markets proved the best and the Indian stock markets shifted to the second rank. This is attributed to the depreciation rate of Indian rupee against dollar, which is significantly higher as compared to that of Hong Kong and other Asian markets. Surprisingly, we find no attraction towards the Japanese stock markets for the global as well as local investors because it has shown the maximum loss since 1992. The period of last three years (2000 to 2002) has been most unlucky for the equity investors in Asia since the Index of every country underwent more than 50 per cent depreciation in the said period.

Further, no significance difference is observed between different investment horizons insofar as annualized returns are concerned. In other words, both active and passive investment strategies have yielded the similar level of return/risk irrespective of the country under consideration. Although the stock markets of Hong Kong and Singapore move more closely, the correlation between the returns of Asian countries is substantially less than unity. It implies that the Asian market offers a good opportunity for equity portfolio diversification. Further, the Indian stock market is judged as the most beneficial case for inclusion in the equity portfolio of a global investor. Two important reasons may be assigned to the above conclusion. One, stock returns in India have shown the lowest level of correlation with various countries in Asia. Second, the rewards of investment in equity securities are the highest for a local investor and the second highest for a global investor. At the overall level, Taiwanese market turned as the most volatile (risky), whereas, Japanese stocks experienced the lowest level of volatility. Interestingly, the general belief 'Higher the risk, higher the return' stands approved in all the countries except Taiwan where the risk is the maximum but the rewards are not in that proportion.

## REFERENCES

Baily, W. and Stulz, R.M. (1990), "Benefits of International Diversification: The case of Pacific Basin Stock Markets", *Journal of Portfolio Management,* 16.

Beedles, WL, (1986), "Asymmetry in Australian Equity Return's", *Australian Journal of Management,* 11, pp. 1-12.

Bodie, A., Kanl, A. and Marcus, A.J. (1996), Investments, Chicago.

Cohen, S.I. (2001), "Stock Performance of Emerging Markets", *The Developing Economies,* XXXIX-2, June, pp. 168-188.

Dickey, D.A., and Fuller, W.A. (1979), "Distribution of the estimates for autoregressive time series with unit root", *Journal of the American Statistical Association,* 74, pp. 427-32.

Fabozzi, Modigliani, Janes and Ferri (2002), Foundations of Financial Markets and Institutions, third edition, *Pearson Education Asia,* p. 359.

Fact Book 2003, Tokyo Stock Exchange, *Inc. http:/www.tsl.or.jp/ English/* printed in Japan, p. 24.

Hindustan Times, 4 March, 2001.

Hunter, J.E. and Coggin, T.D. (1990), "An Analysis of the diversification benefit from international equity investment", Journal of Portfolio Management, No. 16.

Kritzman, M. (1994), "What practioner's need to know....about time diversification", *Financial Analyst Journal.*

LJung, G.M. and Box, G.E.P. (1978), "On a measure of lack of fit in time series", *Biometrika,* 65, pp. 297-303.

Levy, H. and Sarnat, M. (1970), "International diversification of investment portfolios", American Economic Review, p. 60.

M. Obaidullah (1994), "Internationalisation of Equity Portfolios : Risk and Return in South Asian Security Markets", *Indian Journal of Finance and Research,* Vol. I, No. 2, July, pp. 1-6.

Madhusoodanan, T.P. (1997), "Time Diversification : The Indian Evidence", *Journal of Financial Management and Analysis,* Vol. 10, No. 2, July-Dec. pp. 11-22.

Madura, J. (1985), "International Portfolio Construction", *Journal of Business Research,* p. 93.

Morgan Stanley Capital International, *Red Book,* January, 2000.

Samuelson, P.A. (1994), "The long-term case for equities", *Journal of Portfolio Management.*

Sudhakar Satyanarayan (1996), "Are the Emerging Asian Markets Cointegrated with the Japanese Stock Market? Empirical research findings", *Journal of Financial Management and Analysis,* July-December, pp. 1-8.

Vijaya B. Marisetty and Vedpuriswar Alayur (2002), "Asymmetry in Indian Stock Returns : An Empirical Investigation", *TheICFAI Journal of Applied Finance,* Vol. 8, No. 3, May, pp. 14-19.

7

# Performance, Reforms and Prospects of Local Commercial Banks in Oman

*Mazhar M. Islam**

## Structure and Characteristics

Oman's financial sector comprises seven local commercial banks, nine foreign banks, four specialised banks (two each in the public and private sectors), three investment banks, two non-bank financial companies and 59 money changers and draft issuers. The following table 1 lists the financial institutions operating in the country.

Local banking history in Oman dates back to 1973 with the establishment of National Bank of Oman (NBO) and Oman Arab Bank (OAB) Prior to 1973 the baking business in the country was conducted entirely by foreign institutions. NBO was the first locally-incorporated bank. It was set up in 1973 with equity participation from the now defunct BCCI. The shares of BCCI were acquired by the government in 1992 and later divested in favour of local companies and pension funds. In 1973, OAB opened when local investors purchased the Omani branches of Jordan's Arab Bank.

* Alabama A&M University, USA.

**Table 1 :**

| **Local Commercial Banks** | **Established** |
|---|---|
| National Bank of Oman (NBO) | 1973 |
| Oman Arab Bank (OAB) | 1973 |
| Oman International Bank (OIB) | 1975 |
| Commercial Bank of Oman (COMBANK) | 1976 |
| Bank Muscat (BM) | 1981 |
| Bank Dhofar Al Omani Al Fransi (BDOF) | 1990 |
| Majan International Bank (MIB) | 1998 |
| **Specialised Banks** | |
| Oman Development Bank | 1977 |
| Oman Housing Bank | 1977 |
| Alliance Housing Bank | 1997 |
| Industrial Bank of Oman | 1998 |
| **Investment Bank** | |
| Oman International Development and Investment Company | 1983 |
| Oman Investment Services | 1990 |
| Oman Financial Services Company | 1990 |
| **Non-bank Financial Companies** | |
| Capital Leasing Company | 1987 |
| Muscat Finance Company | 1988 |

*Source:* Central Bank of Oman Quarterly Bulletin.

Omani banking sector has developed as a result of several mergers and acquisitions that took place throughout its 22-year history. In June 1998, Commerce Bank (COMBANK) merged with the well-regarded Bank of Oman, Bahrain and Kuwait. COMBANK's main shareholder (the Oman National Insurance Corporation) following sizeable losses in its investment portfolio last year eventually has merged with Bank Muscat in December 2000. Bank Muscat (the name was shortened from Bank Muscat International in 1999) was earlier known as Bank Muscat Al Ahli Al Omani, and was itself the product of a merger between Bank of Muscat and Al Bank Al Ahli Al Omani in 1993. Banque Paribas in Oman was converted into a local bank and renamed Bank Dhofar Al Omani Al Fransi (BDOF) in 1990. Majan International Bank (MIB) was set up in November 1998, after the Omani operations of Habib Bank Zurich were bought by a group of businessmen under the leadership of Ali Redha Darwish Al Lawati, who is also the chairman of the bank. Commerce bank signed a strategic alliance with the bank in May 1999, under which it has the option to buy up to 25% of MIB's shares in 2000. MIB and Bank Muscat were in merger talks with the Industrial Bank of Oman (IBO) in late 1999; the talks were later called off by IBO.

The specialised banks were established in the late 1970s, to serve the specific needs of different market segments. Public-sector specialised banks are small and rely heavily on government support. The Oman Housing Bank (OHB) provides housing loans at low rates to lower and middle-income Omanis. It is owned by the government of Oman, local pension funds, the General Organisation for Social Insurance and Oman Development Bank. OHB receives considerable support from the government by way of subsidies. Oman Development Bank (ODB) was merged with the Oman Bank for Agriculture & Fisheries in July 1997. It is wholly owned by the government. ODB's principal objective is to finance small projects of less than US$650,000. The bank also manages the government's soft loan programme under which medium-sized private sector projects are provided low-cost finance. Two other specialised banks, the Alliance Housing (mainly involved in financing homes) and the Industrial Bank of Oman (for industrial project) are very small in terms of their assets.

## Growth of Omani Banking Sector

Many local banks were formed or grew when foreign banks sold their operations to Omani interests. Table 2 shows the total assets and the principal shareholders of local commercial banks.

**Table 2 : Total Assets (US$mn) Principal Shareholders**

| *Banks* | *1999* | *1998* | *Change (%)* | |
|---|---|---|---|---|
| National Bank of Oman | 2,164 | 1,824 | 19 | W J Towell Group and various funds. |
| Oman International | 2,172 | 1,782 | 22 | Zawawi Group Bank |
| Bank Muscat* | 1,942 | 1,714 | 13 | Diwan of Royal Court and Societe Generale. |
| Commercial Bank of Oman | 1,335 | 1,518 | -12 | 45% held by ONIC and Nomura up for sale. |
| Oman Arab Bank | 685 | 680 | 1 | Oman invest and Arab Bank plc. |
| Bank Dhofar Al Omani Al Fransi Co. | 680 | 632 | 8 | Dhofar Int'l Development and Investment |
| Majan International Bank | 120 | | | Omani businessmen and Commerce Bank (as call option) |

*Note* : *previously known as Bank Muscat International)

*Source:* Central Bank of Oman Quarterly Bulletin.

## Bank Branches

Omani commercial banks have expanded their branch networks considerably, from 255 branches at end-1994 to 314 at end-September 1999 as is shown in table 3. However, the pace of expansion has slowed in recent times. Most networks are concentrated in the capital area, though the CBO encourages local banks to open branches in regions outside the capital area that are currently considered industrially backward. Three geographical zones have been identified by the central bank.[1]

## Overseas Operations

Foreign exchange transactions are tightly controlled.

[1] They are the "capital area," the "other capital area," (both sections of greater Muscat, although the capital area also includes Salalah City to the south of Oman) and "outside the capital area", which constitutes the rest of Oman.

Overseas operations are limited. Foreign exchange transactions are closely regulated by the central bank to ensure that local banks do not undertake speculative trading. Only a few Omani banks have branches overseas. All are located in the Middle East and the Indian sub-continent.

**Table 3 : Branches of Banks in Oman**

| *Banks* | *Operating 1999* | *Authorised 1999* |
|---|---|---|
| Oman International Bank | 81 | 81 |
| Commercial Bank of Oman | 60 | 66 |
| National Bank of Oman | 50 | 52 |
| Bank Muscat | 46 | 46 |
| Oman Arab Bank | 24 | 29 |
| Bank Dhofar Al Omani Al Fransi | 23 | 25 |
| Majan International Bank | 4 | 5 |
| Foreign Banks | 26 | 26 |
| Total | 314 | 330 |

*Source:* Central Bank of Oman Quarterly Bulletin.

## PERFORMANCE OF OMANI BANKS

### Technology

Technology levels are generally high. Banks have invested heavily in upgrading their existing computer systems. All banks are well automated, with back-up and disaster recovery system mostly in place. OIB is considered one of the best automated banks in the country. Except for a few rural branches, all outlets operate on-line in real-time. The bank uses an IBM AS/400 mainframe and has a back-up system installed. OIB uses the services of outside consultants to keep ahead in technology matters. NBO also uses the IMB/AS400, along with NCR UNIX and DEC VAX, and all branches are networked. BankMuscat is in the process of upgrading its information technology systems.

The bank currently uses the AT&T World Mark 4100S mainframe. BDOF upgraded its automation levels in 1997 to ACT Kindle's Bankmaster and Branch Power software. OAB uses IMB/AS400 hardware and all its branches are linked on-line. ATMs have become important extensions of the branch networks of all local banks.

## Management & Personnel Development

Local banks' boards have ensured that their banks are well managed and run by experienced personnel. Expatriates, usually from Europe, USA and the Indian sub-continent, hold most senior management positions in Omani banks. However, the number of Omanis in senior management positions is likely to increase as the government's Omanisation strategy takes shape. Most Omani managers have previous experience with one or more foreign banks in the region. All banks place strong emphasis on training, not only to upgrade the skills of their staff, but to develop a pool of high-quality Omani banking professionals. Banks in Oman have to ensure that 90% of bank staff comprises Omani nationals by end-2000. By this date at least 75% of top and middle management, 95% of clerical and 100% of non-clerical staff should be Omanis.[2]

## Audits and Reporting

Under a 1986 Royal Decreé, Auditors are required to follow IAS when preparing the balance sheets and final accounts of companies and banks. The application of IAS ensures that banks maintain high disclosure standards in their financial statements and notes, particularly with regard to related-party transactions. The central bank closely supervises the accounting policies followed by banks. From time to time, the central bank may contract an audit

---

2 For several years now the central bank has been urging banks to employ more Omanis in their workforce. In 1984 the central bank established the Oman Institute of Bankers as a national training center for Omanis. The institute caters to the growing requirement for professional staff in the financial sector.

firm to conduct feasibility studies on certain regulations it may want to implement. The central bank occasionally uses an external auditor to inspect the books of a certain bank on its behalf. These inspections are lengthy and detailed and may last up to two months. Oman's bank auditors are affiliated with the large international accountancy firms. The central bank examiners have the right to direct banks to increase their provisions. A bank's provisions must be acceptable to the central bank before the bank may declare dividends or make remittances to a head office abroad.

**Deposit Insurance Scheme**

The central bank runs a Bank Deposit Insurance Scheme. The central bank and the commercial banks have jointly subscribed to the scheme's US$26mn capital. Member banks are required to pay annual insurance premiums ranging from 0.01% to 0.03% of the total value of deposits. The CBO will also pay an insurance premium equivalent to 50% of the total annual premiums paid by the member banks. The amounts payable to any depositor cannot exceed OMR20,000 (US$52,000) or 75% of the net deposit, whichever is less. The scheme aims to encourage savings, boost the confidence of the public in the financial soundness of the banking system, minimise the inpact of inherited risks in the operations of the baking system, and assist banks in financial difficulties.

**Asset Quality of Local Banks**

Table 4 exhibits the key asset quality ratios of local commercial banks in Oman. The overall asset quality of Omani banks is moderately good as is indicated in table 4. High level of concentration in consumer loans. Mild deterioration in asset quality due to the economic downturn. Asset classification and provisioning norms are close to internationally accepted standards. The judicial system is fair, and banks stand a good chance of recovering their bad debts.

Loans and advances constitute a substantial portion of the asset base (varying from about 60% to 80%). Credit administration and supervision is satisfactory and is by and large adequately backed by sophisticated MIS. Most banks use modern risk management techniques, and a strict central bank ensures that provisioning levels are prudent. The asset quality of the domestic banks has improved significantly over the last five or six years. In 1999, the credit environment deteriorated and the non-performing portfolios of many banks rose. Cutbacks in government spending, lower exports and reduced demand adversely impacted the private sector. Stock market conditions remained weak and some corporate entities have suffered portfolio losses. While the larger conglomerates have been able to withstand the downturn in the economy, several smaller companies and some start-up projects have been hit, pushing up the NPL portfolios of the banks in the country. However, due to the moderate growth in gross credit, there was only a slight increase in the NPLs to gross loans ratios of the three largest banks. BDOF maintained its asset quality at the previous year's level, while OAB marginally reduced its NPL ratio.

**Table 4 : Key Asset Quality Ratios of Banks**

| *Banks* | *Growth in NPLs %* | *NPL / Gross Loans (%)* | | *Reserves / NPLs %* | | *Prov. Charge / Gross Loans (%)* | |
|---|---|---|---|---|---|---|---|
| | *1999* | *1999* | *1998* | *1999* | *1998* | *1999* | *1998* |
| National Bank of Oman | 21 | 6.0 | 5.5 | 88.7 | 101.3 | 1.18 | 0.58 |
| OmanInter-national Bank | 29 | 7.5 | 7.3 | 56.2 | 49.7 | 1.38 | 1.02 |
| Bank Muscat | 24 | 3.7 | 3.6 | 69.9 | 62.9 | 0.72 | 0.68 |
| Commercial Bank of Oman | 10 | 5.3 | 5.2 | 36.5 | 44.9 | 0.56 | 0.68 |
| Bank Dhofar Al Omani Al Fransi | 18 | 2.6 | 2.6 | 124.6 | 127.9 | 0.62 | 0.68 |
| Oman Arab Bank | 3 | 4.4 | 4.6 | 55.2 | 54.5 | 0.10 | 0.02 |

*Note* : NPL—non-performing loan; Prov.—provision; NPLs and gross loans exclude suspended interest.

*Source* : Complied from financial statements by Capital Intelligence.

Provisioning norms were generally tightened in 1998 in view of the economic slowdown in the country. Overall, provisioning levels are believed to be adequate. The provision charge to gross loans ratios of four banks rose in 1999, indicating some deterioration in asset quality. The ratios of NBO and OIB exceeded 1% and were significantly higher than those of other banks.[3]

Many bank have old NPLs dating back to the 1980s when recessionary condition in the country took a heavy toll on local institutions. The old debts are fully provided for, but banks continue to hold them on their books in the hope of recovering at least a part of them. Over the last few years, the CBO has encouraged banks to write off old NPLs on which no recoveries have been made for more than ten years. NBO has outstanding exposures to BCCI that are now fully covered by non-distributable capital reserves. BDOF acquired some old NPLs when it took over the branches of BCCI in 1992. These are under a remedial programme and the bank is not ready to write them off as yet. COMBANK cleaned out its portfolio by writing off and recovering much of its old bad debt. Unlike other banks, OAB does not have substantial amounts of inherited bad debts of deal with.

## Distribution of Loan Portfolio

Table 5 shows that the loan portfolios of local banks grew at a robust pace between 1995 and 1998. However, the pace slowed in 1999, and total credit expanded by just 10.2% in 1999 (9.5% up to end September 1999) due to the combined effects of the economic slowdown and severe restrictions on the expansion of consumer loans. The slowdown in attributed to lower levels of economic activity in the country, particularly in the services and the wholesale and retail trade sectors. Bank credit to the

---

3 NBO provided for its exposure to three new industrial projects that ran into difficulties last year, while OIB's foreign operations have needed higher provisioning in both 1998 and 1999.

wholesale and retail trade dropped by 12% in the first three quarters of the year, while the share of the services sector fell by 14%. Lower exposures to these two major sectors were offset by a substantial 37% growth in lending to the manufacturing sector, partly reflecting the progress made by the Oman LNG project, which was completed in early 2000.

**Table 5 : Sectoral Distribution of Bank Credit (% of total credit)**

| *Sectors* | *1999* | *1998* | *1997* | *1996* | *1995* |
|---|---|---|---|---|---|
| Personal Loans | 38.9 | 35.3 | 35.8 | 33.2 | 30.5 |
| Import/Export Trade | 12.4 | 11.7 | 14.0 | 15.7 | 17.6 |
| Manufacturing | 8.3 | 6.5 | 5.6 | 5.2 | 4.6 |
| Financial Institutions | 7.0 | 6.3 | 5.9 | 6.3 | |
| Construction | 6.5 | 6.1 | 6.8 | 8.2 | 8.9 |
| Wholesale and Retail Trade | 5.4 | 6.6 | 7.1 | 7.1 | 9.0 |
| Services | 5.0 | 6.1 | 5.9 | 4.1 | 4.9 |
| Government | 1.9 | 1.5 | 2.1 | 4.1 | 1.9 |
| Others | 14.6 | 19.9 | 16.8 | 16.1 | 21.6 |
| Total | 100.0 | 100.0 | 100.0 | 100.0 | 100.0 |
| Total Loans Outstanding (US$mn) | 7,488 | 6,840 | 5,832 | 4,327 | 3,659 |
| Rate of Growth of Loans (%) | 9.5 | 17.3 | 34.8 | 18.3 | 11.7 |

*Source:* Central Bank of Oman Statistical Bulletin: 2001.

The lack of lending opportunities in the country and the narrowing spreads on good quality corporate loans have led banks to focus increasingly on consumer lending in recent years.[4] Consumer loans rose by a huge 45% in

[4] Consumer loans are generally extended to nationals who are employed by the government and good private-sector entities. The repayments are made directly by the organization to the banks by deduction from employee salaries. All banks state that their consumer loan portfolios are performing well and that delinquencies have been remarkably low.

1997 and by 18% in 1998, prompting the central bank to impose loan concentration limits. Commercial banks were first required to reduced their personal loan portfolios to 25% of their portfolio, and a 13% ceiling on consumer loan interest rates was removed. The limit was later changed to 30% and banks were given up to end-2000 to meet this regulation. However, consumer lending continued to grow—by about 18% in the first nine months of 1999, and the exposure formed 38.9% of total credit at end-September. The slow pace of economic growth in other sectors and the deregulation of interest rates encouraged banks to promote their consumer lending products last year. The central bank therefore imposed further brakes on consumer lending. Banks were forced to trim the excess over the limit by one-third by end-1999 and another third had to go by mid-2000. The CBO also re-imposed the 13% ceiling on the interest rate charged on consumer loans (banks were charging between 14% and 18% on these loans in the first half of 1999). These measures dampened consumer loan growth in the last quarter of 1999 and many banks reported almost nil activity in this area.[5]

## Capitalization

Table 6 shows all local banks are well capitalised, although the BIS ratios of BankMuscat and OIB are running close to the 12% minimum requirement imposed by the central bank.

---

5 Related-party exposures are strictly regulated by the central bank, and banks have to ensure that their aggregate exposures to related parties do not exceed 35% of net worth. Several leading Omani businessmen sit on the boards of many local banks, making it difficult for banks to contain their related-party exposures to the limits prescribed by the central bank BDOF, OIB and COMBANK have high levels of related-party exposure.

**Table 6 : BIS Ratios and Equity of Local Banks**

| *Banks* | *BIS ratio %* | | *Total capital (US$mn)* | | *Tier 2 Capital (US$mn)* | |
|---|---|---|---|---|---|---|
| | *1999* | *1998* | *1999* | *1998* | *1999* | *1998* |
| National Bank of Oman | 17.3 | 18.5 | 338 | 334 | 21 | 21 |
| Bank Muscat | 13.4 | 14.7 | 218 | 203 | 28 | 25 |
| Oman International Bank | 13.8 | 15.8 | 220 | 217 | – | – |
| Commercial Bank of Oman | 18.9 | 17.4 | 189 | 183 | – | – |
| Oman Arab Bank | 18.3 | 16.4 | 93 | 87 | – | – |
| Bank Dhofar Al Omani Al Fransi | 16.5 | 18.2 | 89 | 88 | – | – |

*Source:* Compiled from financial statements by Capital Intelligence.

Bank Muscat intends to issue global depository receipts in 2000 to boost its capital adequacy ratio. It is not clear how OIB will raise its capital adequacy ratio. The bank has the highest paid-up capital base (US$163mn) among local banks but low retained earnings, as most of its distributable reserves have been capitalised through stock dividends over the years. Moreover, servicing the capital base has been a strain. Though the bank strives to pay good dividends—it paid 15% in 1999—this is still lower than NBO's (25% cash and stock) and Bank Muscat's (20%) dividend payout. Besides, dividend payments have eaten into reserve accretion and overall capital growth has been very low. Other banks are unlikely to require new capital, at least for the medium term. However, with profitability under pressure, banks may be unable to grow their reserves at the pace they have become accustomed to, and many will need to raise more equity from domestic or international markets after a few years. COMBANK's BIS ratio was the highest among local banks at end-1999.

### Liquidity

Table 7 shows that the liquidity ratios remain stretched for most banks. Customer deposit growth was modest in

1999. The smaller banks appear to have lost market share to the two largest banks. Customer deposits are the primary source of funding for banks in the country. Deposits from the private sector (individuals and corporate entities) form more than 80% of customer funds. However, the customer deposit base as a proportion of the total liabilities of banks has declined steadily in recent years. It fell from a high 58.1% of total liabilities at end-1995 to 49.7 at end-1999. Banks have found other sources of funding mainly from overseas banks. Bank borrowings grew substantially, from 7.2% of total liabilities at end-1995 to peak at 15.8% at end-1998. Strong measures taken by the central banks in 1998 and 1999 shrank overseas borrowings by 4% in 1999; these funds formed 14% of the balance sheet at the end of the year. One of the problems of the Omani financial system is that liquidity is still very much driven by oil revenues and government activity, and the rate of growth of customer deposits is unsteady and swings wildly from year to year.

**Table 7 : Sources of Bank Funding**
**(% of Total Liabilities)**

| *Sources* | *1999* | *1998* | *1997* | *1996* | *1995* |
|---|---|---|---|---|---|
| Government and Public Sector Deposits | 11.4 | 10.9 | 11.3 | 12.1 | 11.2 |
| Private Sector Deposits | 49.7 | 50.4 | 50.9 | 56.4 | 58.1 |
| Due to Banks | 14.0 | 15.8 | 14.1 | 9.3 | 7.2 |
| Due to Head Office/ Branches | 2.0 | 0.9 | 2.6 | 1.5 | 1.3 |
| Capital and Reserves | 11.8 | 11.9 | 9.0 | 8.2 | 8.5 |
| Other Liabilities | 11.1 | 10.1 | 12.1 | 12.5 | 13.7 |
| Rate of Growth of Deposits(%) | 7 | 5 | 30 | 14 | 9 |
| Rate of Growth of Balances due to Non-resident Banks (%) | –4 | 33 | 94 | 57 | 115 |
| Rate of Growth of Balances due fromNon-resident Banks | 38 | 58 | 106 | –10 | 11 |

*Source:* Capital Intelligence 2001.

Table 8 shows the key liquidity ratios of local banks. Deposit growth was fairly robust prior to 1998 (peaking at 30% in 1997) but the rate of growth slowed to just 5% in 1998, and improved slightly to 7% in 1999. Liquidity conditions have stabilised since November 1999. Increased government spending has pumped in more liquidity, and local banks have reined in their consumer credit growth to meet the central bank's strict regulations by year-end. However, overall, liquidity at end-1999 was still tight and it worsened for some banks. While the key liquidity ratios of NBO and OIB have improved, the ratios of the other four banks actually deteriorated, as seen in the table 8. NBO's robust 18% asset growth last year was funded by a strong 27% increase in customer deposits, thereby improving the bank's overall liquidity. The bank has the best liquidity ratios among local banks. Bank Muscat's total assets rose by a moderate 13% last year, but customer deposit growth was a modest 5%, forcing the bank to borrow short-term from overseas. COMBANK, on the other hand, shrank its asset base by 12% in 1999. Consequently, both bank borrowings and placements dropped sharply, and customer funds fell by 14%. As net loans rose by 7.5% last year, this led to a worsening of the main liquidity ratios.

**Table 8 : Key Liquidity Ratios of Local Banks (%)**

| *Banks* | *Net Loans / Customer Deposits* | | *Net Loans / Total Deposits* | | *Liquid Asset Ratio* | |
|---|---|---|---|---|---|---|
| | *1999* | *1998* | *1999* | *1998* | *1999* | *1998* |
| National Bank of Oman | 150 | 172 | 94 | 104 | 19 | 12 |
| Oman International Bank | 88 | 109 | 77 | 87 | 30 | 23 |
| Bank Muscat | 121 | 116 | 96 | 99 | 20 | 17 |
| Commercial Bank of Oman | 125 | 99 | 91 | 73 | 21 | 35 |
| Oman Arab Bank | 113 | 93 | 96 | 88 | 15 | 22 |
| Bank Dhofar Al Bank Al Fransi | 101 | 96 | 92 | 85 | 21 | 27 |

*Source* : Compiled from financial statements by Capital Intelligence.

BDOF's 17% credit growth was funded through an 11% increase in customer deposits and a reduction in bank placements, however the bank's overall liquidity tightened at year-end. OAB's asset growth was flat last year. The bank's net loans, however, rose by a moderate 10%. Liquidity management at local banks is of high quality. All banks have good MIS to aid their decision-making process, and risk management systems are being beefed up.

## Profitability

Omani banks continued to be profitable in 1999, despite the difficult economic conditions in the country. Table 9 shows that all banks but one reported lower net profits, mainly due to depressed non-interest revenues and higher provisioning charges on the loan and investment portfolios.

**Table 9 : Key Profitability Ratios of Local Banks (%)**

| *Bank* | *Return on Average Assets* | | *Net Interest Income / Average Assets* | | *Expenses / Average Assets* | |
|---|---|---|---|---|---|---|
| | *1999* | *1998* | *1999* | *1998* | *1999* | *1998* |
| National Bank of Oman | 1.39 | 2.35 | 4.17 | 3.93 | 1.99 | 2.17 |
| Oman International Bank | 1.39 | 1.87 | 3.45 | 3.89 | 2.33 | 2.83 |
| Bank Muscat International | 1.72 | 2.04 | 3.73 | 3.67 | 1.99 | 2.09 |
| Commercial Bank of Oman | 1.67 | 2.04 | 3.84 | 3.55 | 2.31 | 2.28 |
| Oman Arab Bank | 2.39 | 3.03 | 3.67 | 3.53 | 2.71 | 2.55 |
| Bank Dhofar Al Omani Al Fransi | 2.13 | 2.11 | 4.14 | 4.01 | 2.42 | 2.49 |

*Source:* Compiled from financial statements by Capital Intelligence.

Interest margins improved in 1999, but remained under pressure, particularly towards the end of the year when the

CBO re-introduced the 13% interest ceiling on consumer loans. The average interest spread (on Omani rial activity) rose from 4.3% in 1998 to 4.4% in December 1999, but is likely to fall in 2000. The average funding cost has risen substantially, by almost 200 basis points, between end-1996 and end 1999, due to severe competitive pressures. Depressed stock market conditions last year robbed local banks of the opportunity to grow their investment banking activities. Unfavourable trade conditions also reduced commissions and foreign exchange trading profits. Non-interest revenue growth therefore slowed last year. Higher provision charges on the loan portfolio and the CBO's insistence that all banks provide fully for investment losses on the MSM (in line with IAS) resulted in reduced earnings. The pressure on earnings forced most banks to cut back on expenses, and operating costs have grown only moderately compared to previous years.

All banks except BDOF reported lower net profits and return on average assets (AROA) ratios. The steepest fall in net profit was at NBO, where there was a 30% drop in earnings last year. For several years, NBO's profitability had remained very high, and the bank had maintained its average ROA above 2%. Higher average loan volumes, improved net interest margins, robust non-interest revenues and good cost control had contributed to the bank's overall profitability. The bank's core operations remained extremely profitable in 1999, however higher provisioning costs on loans and on the bank's exposures to the MSM affected its net earnings. The interest ceiling on consumer loans imposed by the central bank in the third quarter of 1999 will reduce the profitability of all banks in 2000, but NBO, which had a significant proportion of high-earning loans in its portfolio, will be the hardest hit.

OIB's core operations remain profitable, but its interest margin continued to fall in 1999 due to higher funding costs. Its non-interest revenue growth was also modest last year. High provision charges on the loan portfolio substantially reduced the bank's ROAA. Bank

Muscat's lower profitability in 1999 is attribute to taxation charges that the bank had to pay last year after the expiry of a five-year tax holiday granted to the bank at the time of its 1993 merger with Al Bank Al Ahli Al Omani. On a profit-before-tax basis, the bank's profitability was higher than in the previous year. COMBANK's overall profitability fell in 1999, due to lower non-interest revenues and extraordinary income (sale of property) and substantially higher provisions on the investment portfolio. OAB's ROAA dropped to 2.39% in 1999, but remained the highest among local banks. OAB is currently enjoying a tax holiday granted to it at the time of its merger with Omani European Bank. This expires in July 2000, after which the bank's ROAA is likely to come down. The bank reported substantially reduced non-interest revenues due to lower foreign exchange trading profits, lower gains on the sale of investments and some provisioning on the investment portfolio. BDOF's profitability improved in 1999. The bank's margins widened and non-interest income rose, while operating expenses were kept under control. Despite higher provisioning costs the bank increased its net profit by 7.6%.

## Ratings of Local Commercial Banks of Oman

Capital Intelligence ratings is summarized in table 10. The ratings show the probability that a bank will require external assistance to overcome adversities.[6] All banks in Oman show robust performance in all areas and the short term outlook looks stable.

---

[6] Appendix A provides detailed explanations for the ratings.

**Table 10 : Summary of Ratings of Local Commercial Banks Soverign Ceiling: Long Term: BBB**

| *Banks* | *Foreign Currency LT* | *ST* | *Domestic Strength* | *Support* | *Short Term Outlook* |
|---|---|---|---|---|---|
| National Bank of Oman | BBB- | A3 | BBB | 2 | Stable |
| Oman Arab Bank | BBB- | A3 | BBB | 2 | Stable |
| Oman International Bank | BBB- | A3 | BBB | 3 | Stable |
| Commercial Bank of Oman | BBB- | A3 | BBB | 2 | Stable |
| Bank Muscat | BBB- | A3 | BBB | 2 | Stable |
| Bank Dofar Al Omani Al Farnsi | BBB- | A3 | BBB | 3 | Stable |
| Oman Development Bank | BBB- | A3 | BBB | 2 | Stable |

*Note :* See table k-9 for definitions of ranks.

## Prospects

Oman's financial system is well regulated. Oman has proactive central bank with strong regulatory and supervisory functions. The principal role of the central bank is the effective management of the monetary and banking system. Since the establishment of the central bank in 1975, the financial sector has expanded considerably in line with Oman's economic development. The CBO's monetary policy aims to maintain price stability, keep confidence in the local currency at a high level and ensure adequate credit flows to the private and public sectors. Inflation was kept in check in 1999, and in fact there was a marginal decline in the consumer price index. Money supply rose by 6.4% in 1999, from 4.8% in the previous year. In June 1999, the government ruled out the possibility of devaluing the rial despite pressures on the external front. The US dollar and Omani Rial parity has remained unchanged for several years. A strong central bank has encouraged local banks to merge over the years, considerably strengthening the banking sector. Merger activity is continuing in 2000. In 1998 and 1999 a number of measures were introduced to curb excessive credit growth in personal loans and to reduce the banking sector's growing dependence on short-term borrowings from abroad. The CBO has strengthened prudential norms in recent years, and assest classification and provisioning norms have moved closer to international standards. Banks are required to maintain capital to risk weighted assets ratios of at least 12%, well above the 8% required by the BIS. Local banks use international Accounting Standards. Overall, the CBO is regarded as a strong and competent regulator.

All commercial banks are well managed with professional teams in place, and their operations have been extensively restructured in recent years. Capitalisation standards are high and all banks have strong net worth. The asset quality of local banks has improved over the 1990s, despite tough business conditions over the last two years, overall asset quality remains moderately good. There are large concentrations of credit in consumer loans, partly reflecting the limited opportunities for corporate lending in the country. Provisioning standards were raised two years ago and the central bank has forced local banks to provide fully on their exposures to the local stock market, which remains depressed. Higher provision charges on loans and investments and higher taxes have adversely impacted the net earnings of most banks in 1999, but the overall profitability of the banking sector remains high. The central bank has also instituted measures to limit local banks' dependence on short-term foreign currency borrowings. Liquidity ratios of most banks remained stretched at end-1999. However, higher levels of government spending and curbs on consumer lending will improve the situation this year.

The upturn in oil prices last year brought some good cheer to the Omani economy, which had contracted by a significant 10.2% in 1998 on the back of a prolonged weakness in oil prices. The GDP expanded by a cautions 2.9% in 1999, and is expected to improved further in the current year. The government intends to increase its spending in 2000. This will inject new liquidity to domestic financial markets and nudge economic activity to a higher level. The fiscal deficit is expected to climb down from its previous level. Fiscal operations are generally well managed; the government was quick to raise state revenues through higher customs and income taxes, and to curb official spending when the fiscal situation looked grim in 1998. Improved oil prices have eased the strain on government finances this year. The government is investing in several projects aimed at diversifying the local economy. However, major structural reforms are still required to ensure that Oman's foundations are strong when it runs out of oil in about 17 years' time. The state's revenue base needs to be further widened and the government machinery requires substantial trimming. Encouraging private-sector investment is a priority for the government. Despite fairly liberal investment rules, foreign investment inflows remain low. Competition from neighbouring countries has intensified and the government may need to further modify the rules to attract new capital into the country.

**Favorable Factors**

- Economic prospects have improved following the upturn in oil prices last year.
- Investments in several industrial projects currently underway will aid future economic growth.
- Financial institutions are well regulated. The central bank is proactive.
- Local banks are well managed, strongly capitalised and profitable.

**Unfavorable Factors**

- The economy is not sufficiently diversified and remains dependent on the energy sector.

- Loan portfolios of banks are concentrated in consumer credit.
- Liquidity ratios of local banks are stretched.
- The weak stock market has forced banks to make provisions affecting 1999 earnings.
- Investments in liquefied natural gas (LNG) and related industries will aid future economic growth.
- Banks are well regulated. Strong central bank support for the financial sector.
- Local banks are well managed, strongly capitalised and profitable.
- LNG exports are becoming a strong feature of Qatar's foreign trade.

## Unfavorable Factors

- As income flows from the LNG, banks will need to find alternative sectors to finance since government financing needs will be reduced.
- Banks are subject to interest group and political pressures.

## Appendix A : Definitions of CI's Ratings

Foreign currency long-term (LT): "A" indicates high credit quality while "BBB" indicates good credit quality (Both are investment grades). Plus(+) or Minus (–) sign indicates that the strength of a particular institution is slightly greater or less than that of similar rated peers. Foreign currency short term(ST): "A3" indicates strong capacity for timely repayment but may be affected by unexpected adversities while "A2" indicates very strong capacity for timely repayment but may be affected slightly by unexpected adversities (both are investment grades). "B" is speculative grade that indicates capacity for timely repayment that could be seriously affected by unexpected adversities. Domestic strength: "AA" indicates financially in very strong condition and significant strengths in other non-financial areas. Operating environment likely to be very attractive and stable. "A" indicates strong financial fundamentals and very favourable non-financial consideration. Operating environment may be unstable but institution's market position and/or financial strength more than compensate. Rating BBB" indicates basically sound overall; slight weaknesses in financial or other factors could be remedied fairly easily. May be limited by unstable operating environment. While "BB" indicates one or two significant weaknesses in the bank's financial makeup could cause problems and unstable operating environment likely. Support ratings: "3" indicates owners of very good reputation and resources, and which can provide clear support. Rating "2" indicates government support extremely likely despite absence of written guarantee. There may be some uncertainty regarding the government's willingness or ability to provide support. A private bank which has extremely strong ownership. "4" indicates support is likely but not certain. Outlook: "stable"–no change or deterioration in rating over the 12 months following its publication.

## REFERENCES

Barth, M.,W. Beaver, and M. Wolfson, "Components of Earnings and the Structure of Bank Share Prices," Financial Analysis Journal, May/June, 1990, pp. 52-60.

Bhattacharya, Biswa N. "Trends of Financial Deepening in GCC Countries and Future Policy Directions." Arab Bank and Finance Directory, Tele-Gulf-Directory, Manama, Bahrain, 1994-95, pp. 373-38.

Bencivenge, Valerie R. and Smith, Bruce D. "Financial Intermediation and Endogenous Growth," Review of Economic Studies, April, 1991, 58 (2), pp. 195-209.

Beatty, R., A. Santomero, and M. Smirlock, Bank Merger Premiums: Analysis and Evidence, Salomon Brothers Center for the Study of Financial Institutions Monograph Series in Finance and Economic, Monograph, 1987-3, 1987.

Bovenzi, John F., James A. Morino, and Frank E. McFadden. "Commercial Bank failure Prediction Models," Federal Reserve Bank of Atlanta, Economic Review, November 1983, pp. 14-26.

Cooper, Kerry, and Donald Fraser, The Financial Marketplace, 4th Edition, Addison-Wesley Publishing Co., 1993.

Capital Intelligence, Bank Scope CD Rom Databases 2002.

Central Bank of Oman, Statistical Bulletin, various issues.

Central Bank of Kuwait, Statistical Bulletin, various issues.

DeGregorio, Jose and Gudotti, Pablo E. "Financial Development and Economic Growth." World Development. March, 1995. 23 (3), pp. 433-48.

Fraser, Donald, and Lyn Fraser, Evaluating Commercial Bank Performance, Rolling Meadows, III.: Bankers Publishing Company, 1990.

Goldsmith, Raymond W. Financial Structure and Development. New Haven, CT: Yale University Press, 1969.

Islam, Mazhar M., "Development and Performance of Domestic and Foreign Banks in GCC Countries." *Managerial Finance,* Vol. 29, No. 2/3, pp. 42-72, 2003.

Islam, Mazhar M., "Regulations and Supervision of Financial Institutions in GCC Countries." *Managerial Finance,* Vol. 29, No. 7, pp. 17-42, 2003.

Kaufman, G., "Measuring and Managing Interest Rate Risk: A Primer", Federal Reserve Bank of Chicago, Economic Perspective, January, 1984, pp. 16-29.

King, Robert G. and Levine, Ross, "Finance and Growth: Schumpeter Might Be Right". Quarterly Journal of Economics, August 1993a, 108 (3), pp. 717-38

Litan, Robert, "What Should Banks Do?" Washington, D.C.: The Brookings Institution, 1987.

McKinnon, Ronald, Money and Capital in Economic Development. Washington DcC: The Brookings Institution, 1973.

Mickdady, Riad, "Gulf Banks Prepare to take Merger Medicine." Gulf Business, December, 1998.

Rajan G. Raghuram, and Luigi Zingales, "Financial Dependence and Growth," American Economic Review (June 1998), pp. 559-586.

Rose, Peter, James Kolari, and Donald Fraser, Financial Institutions: Understanding and Managing Financial Services, 4th Edition, Richard D. Irwin, 1993.

Saunders, Anthony, Financial Institutions Management, Burr Ridge, Illinois, Richard D. Irwin, Inc. 1994.

Shaw, Edward. Financial Deepening in Economic Development, New York: Oxford University Press, 1973.

# 8

# An Empirical Study of Determinants of Savings During 1980–2000 in India

*Ganesh S. Mani* and Srivyal Vuyyuri**

## Introduction

In India, in the post independence period we have seen a consistent increase in the national saving rate, though with considerable fluctuations from year to year (Table 1). The national saving rate increased from about 10 per cent in the early 1950s to 17 per cent in the early 1970s and then to over 25 per cent by the mid-1990s.

During this period, we saw private saving accounting for the major share of total domestic savings, with public savings showing a decline from the early eighties onwards. The private saving rate increased from 8.6 per cent in 1950-55 to 17.3 per cent in 1970-75 and then to 24.2 per cent in 1990-98. The annual increase in the private saving rate was much faster in the 1950s and 1960s compared to the period from the late 1960s to early 1980s. From then on, there has been significant increase in the saving rate well into the 1990s.

* Fellowship Students of ICFAI Institute for Management Teachers, Hyderabad, India.

**Table 1 : Gross Domestic Savings (At Current Prices)**

| *Year* | *House hold Sector* | | *Private Corporate Sector* | | *Public Sector* | | *Total (2+3+4)* | |
|---|---|---|---|---|---|---|---|---|
| *1* | *2* | | *3* | | *4* | | *5* | |
| 1950-51 | 612 | 6.2 | 93 | 0.9 | 182 | 1.8 | 887 | 8.9 |
| 1955-56 | 1046 | 9.6 | 134 | 1.2 | 190 | 1.7 | 1370 | 12.6 |
| 1960-61 | 1254 | 7.3 | 281 | 1.6 | 454 | 2.6 | 1989 | 11.6 |
| 1965-66 | 2602 | 9.4 | 405 | 1.5 | 863 | 3.1 | 3870 | 14.0 |
| 1970-71 | 4634 | 10.1 | 672 | 1.5 | 1343 | 2.9 | 6649 | 14.6 |
| 1975-76 | 9743 | 11.7 | 1083 | 1.3 | 3520 | 4.2 | 14346 | 17.2 |
| 1980-81 | 19868 | 13.8 | 2339 | 1.6 | 4929 | 3.4 | 27136 | 18.9 |
| 1981-82 | 21225 | 12.6 | 2560 | 1.5 | 7570 | 4.5 | 31355 | 18.6 |
| 1982-83 | 23216 | 12.3 | 2980 | 1.6 | 8172 | 4.3 | 34368 | 18.3 |
| 1983-84 | 28165 | 12.8 | 3254 | 1.5 | 7168 | 3.3 | 38587 | 17.6 |
| 1984-85 | 35067 | 14.3 | 4040 | 1.6 | 6956 | 2.8 | 46063 | 18.8 |
| 1985-86 | 39795 | 14.3 | 5426 | 2.0 | 8946 | 3.2 | 54167 | 19.5 |
| 1986-87 | 45072 | 14.5 | 5336 | 1.7 | 8543 | 2.7 | 58951 | 18.9 |
| 1987-88 | 59157 | 16.7 | 5932 | 1.7 | 7819 | 2.2 | 72908 | 20.6 |
| 1988-89 | 70657 | 16.8 | 8486 | 2.0 | 8770 | 2.1 | 87913 | 20.9 |
| 1989-90 | 86955 | 17.9 | 11845 | 2.4 | 8179 | 1.7 | 106979 | 20.0 |
| 1990-91 | 109897 | 19.3 | 15164 | 2.7 | 6279 | 1.1 | 131340 | 23.1 |
| 1991-92 | 110736 | 17.0 | 20304 | 3.1 | 12868 | 2.0 | 143908 | 22.0 |
| 1992-93 | 131073 | 17.5 | 19968 | 2.7 | 11865 | 1.6 | 162906 | 21.8 |
| 1993-94 | 158310 | 18.4 | 29866 | 3.5 | 5445 | 0.6 | 193621 | 22.5 |
| 1994-95 | 199358 | 19.7 | 35260 | 3.5 | 16845 | 1.7 | 251463 | 24.8 |
| 1995-96 | 215588 | 18.1 | 58542 | 4.9 | 24065 | 2.0 | 298195 | 25.1 |
| 1996-97 | 232914 | 17.0 | 61092 | 4.5 | 22917 | 1.7 | 316923 | 23.2 |
| 1997-98 | 271383 | 17.8 | 63468 | 4.2 | 23381 | 1.5 | 358250 | 23.5 |
| 1998-99 | 336469 | 19.1 | 64608 | 3.7 | -14345 | -0.8 | 386732 | 22.0 |
| 1999-00 | 386913 | 19.8 | 71879 | 3.7 | -23220 | -1.2 | 435572 | 22.3 |

Q : Quick Estimates.

*Source:* Economic Survey 2000-2001.

(i) Ratio of savings and capital formation of information of individual sectors may not add to total because of rounding.

In international perspective, India has had a high saving rate compared to many other countries, except those in East Asia as can be seen from Table 2. Interestingly India's saving rate in the 1960s (16.7 per cent) was much higher than that of Korea, Taiwan and Singapore, and only slightly lower than that of Thailand and Malaysia. From about the early 1970s the India's saving rate continued to lag behind that of all these 'High Performing East Asian Economies (HPEAs). By the mid-1990s, India's saving rate (22 per cent) amounted to a little over a half of the average rate for the HPEAs. Among the South Asian countries, India's performance has continued to be impressive, apart from some notable catching-up by Sri Lanka following market-oriented policy reforms introduced in the late 1970s. In Latin America, Chile and Costa Rica-were the countries having consistently superior saving records compared to India during this period. Countries like Brazil, Peru, Argentina and Mexico which had higher saving rates than India in the 1960s, ended up with lower or comparable rates in the mid-1990s. In general, India's saving performance has been consistently superior to that of the overall Latin American record from after about the first oil shock in the early 1970s. Between 1999-2000, the savings rate in India has remained steady at about 20-25% without deviating significantly from the earlier trend.

Until the 1970s interest rate policy in these countries was primarily guided by the Keynesian view that interest rates should be kept low in order to promote investment.[1]

With lowering of the interest rates in the past few years it has become vital to understand the response of personal saving to changes in interest rates. This understanding could contribute to designing of appropriate economic policies in the future. The fact that we have been running a high fiscal deficit with high interest rates prevailing has resulted in a substantial part of the revenues being used to

---

[1] Keynes, J.M. (1936), The General Theory o Employment, Interest and Money, Chapter 24.

pay interest. The huge fiscal deficit pushes up the rates of interest. A reduction in the budget deficit would probably cause interest rates to decline. If personal saving declined as a result, the overall increase in national saving would be less than the reduction in the budget deficit. Alternatively, contractionary monetary policy generally causes interest rates to rise. If personal saving increases as a result, the corresponding fall in consumer spending helps to slow the economy. As a final example, changes in the tax rates can raise or lower the net-of-tax return to saving. The effect of these changes on the amount of saving may play an important role in tax policymaking.

**Table 2 : National Savings Rates, India and Selected Developing Countries, 1960-1998**

| Countries | 1960-64 | 1965-69 | 1970-74 | 1975-79 | 1980-84 | 1985-89 | 1990-98 |
|---|---|---|---|---|---|---|---|
| ***South Asia*** | | | | | | | |
| India | 14.3 | 15.0 | 17.4 | 20.8 | 19.3 | 20.8 | 24.2 |
| Pakistan | 10.5 | 11.8 | 8.7 | 7.3 | 7.9 | 9.6 | 15.8 |
| Sri Lanka | 11.9 | 10.4 | 13.5 | 13.8 | 13.7 | 11.9 | 14.6 |
| Bangladesh | – | – | – | 1.5 | 1.9 | 2.9 | 6.3 |
| ***East Asia*** | | | | | | | |
| Taiwan | 21.2 | 22.2 | 30.5 | 31.8 | 32.0 | 36.0 | 28.2 |
| China | – | – | – | 32.6 | 34.3 | 35.2 | 39.5 |
| China Hong Kong | 20.9 | 25.8 | 29.3 | 32.3 | 31.7 | 35.0 | 34.1 |
| Singapore | 4.3 | 14.9 | 24.0 | 33.2 | 42.7 | 41.0 | 23.6 |
| Korea, Rep of | 4.4 | 13.0 | 17.5 | 25.3 | 26.9 | 35.6 | 35.9 |
| Thailand | 16.4 | 21.3 | 22.6 | 21.9 | 23.8 | 29.1 | 35.6 |
| Indonesia | 10.0 | 5.6 | 20.7 | 28.1 | 31.6 | 29.3 | 33.1 |
| Malaysia | 23.8 | 24.4 | 26.9 | 32.5 | 31.6 | 34.6 | 35.7 |
| ***Latin America*** | | | | | | | |
| Paraguay | 12.6 | 12.8 | 15.8 | 21.6 | 18.8 | 20.6 | 12.0 |
| Venezuela | 35.2 | 33.7 | 39.6 | 36.0 | 27.4 | 23.9 | 22.5 |

*(Table Contd...)*

**Table 2 : (Contd...)**

| | | | | | | | |
|---|---|---|---|---|---|---|---|
| Costa Rica | 14.4 | 13.0 | 14.6 | 16.1 | 22.9 | 23.7 | 22.9 |
| Brazil | 19.8 | 20.3 | 20.1 | 21.5 | 20.9 | 25.5 | 22.3 |
| Mexico | 16.1 | 18.2 | 18.1 | 20.3 | 27.1 | 23.6 | 19.5 |
| Peru | 38.0 | 29.2 | 17.1 | 18.0 | 28.5 | 21.5 | 14.3 |
| Colombia | 16.8 | 17.5 | 18.2 | 20.6 | 17.7 | 23.6 | 19.4 |
| Chile | 15.2 | 20.0 | 16.3 | 17.3 | 14.3 | 25.3 | 28.4 |
| Dominican Rep | 13.6 | 7.9 | 13.3 | 18.2 | 16.7 | 19.9 | 15.8 |
| Argentina | 22.1 | 23.7 | 23.7 | 30.6 | 23.5 | 21.2 | 17.3 |
| Ecuador | 10.9 | 12.3 | 18.8 | 23.0 | 23.6 | 20.0 | 22.7 |
| Jamaica | 26.0 | 28.1 | 21.5 | 15.0 | 14.0 | 19.7 | 16.5 |
| Honduras | 13.3 | 16.4 | 16.1 | 17.4 | 12.6 | 13.5 | 17.6 |
| El Salvador | 12.4 | 11.0 | 14.3 | 18.8 | 8.2 | 5.7 | 3.3 |
| Panama | 14.8 | 20.4 | – | – | – | 12.3 | 22.6 |
| Uruguay | 18.2 | 19.4 | 18.0 | 18.9 | 16.0 | 17.3 | 14.4 |
| Bolivia | 10.7 | 19.1 | 26.2 | 23.0 | 14.0 | 6.8 | 7.8 |
| Guatemala | 8.5 | 11.3 | 13.8 | 15.6 | 10.6 | 9.2 | 9.5 |
| Nicaragua | 15.1 | 15.8 | 16.5 | 15.5 | 6.3 | 4.6 | –8.5 |
| Haiti | 5.2 | 3.1 | 9.0 | 7.3 | 6.2 | 4.9 | –6.1 |

*Source:* Compiled from World Bank, World Tables Database and Republic of China, Council for Planning and Development, Taiwan Statistical Data Book (various issues) for Taiwan.

*Note* : Data not available.

This paper examines the interest rate-saving interrelations in the Indian economy using annual data for the period 1980-2000. The paper has been structured in the following manner. Section 2 gives the theoretical literature, explains the reasons for undertaking such a study and gives an idea of the superiority of data available in India. Section 3 gives the data, model specification and methodology. Section 4 and Section 5 are about results and economic evaluation and the conclusions respectively.

## Theoretical Literature

Irving Fisher considered saving as involving a choice between present and future consumption, which is influenced by one's rate of time preference vis-à-vis the rate of interest. For the economy as a whole, saving and investment are brought into equilibrium by movements in the interest rate.[2]

Keynes (1936) propounded an alternative view that current consumption moves with current income and saving is the residual. The Keynesian view proved to be too simple and unsatisfactory to explain the reality and gave way to a number of alternative hypotheses on saving behaviour incorporating the inter-temporal nature of consumption which was implied in the earlier Fisherian approach.

The most important contributions in this regard are the "Permanent Income Hypothesis" of Friedman (1957) and the "life-cycle hypothesis" of Modigliani and Brumberg (1954) both of which consider anticipated life-income and consequently the smoothing out of consumption over time.

There have been numerous studies on the savings behaviour in developed and developing countries. Deaton and Paxson (1998) studied the relationship between savings and growth using cohort evidence. They found evidence of large effects of growth on saving, at least at some rates of population growth. The study was done with Taiwanese data. Morisset and Revoredo (1995) analyze how education contributes to savings. After a study of a panel of 74 countries over the period 1960-90 the authors found education to positively influence savings in the long run. For each percentage point increase in education stock, the savings rate increases 0.37 per cent. The lagged effect (five years) of a change in the stock of education appears positive in all regions except Latin America. Monadjemi and Kearney (1991) and Cebula and Belton (1993) conclude that government deficits reduce savings but do not raise interest rates because of the foreign capital inflow to the

2 Dr. Joseph, Mathew (1997), India's Savings Rate : Analysis and Policy Prescriptions, A study done for SCICI.

United States.[3] Berhneim (1987) examines intermediate-term (six-year and twelve year) average data across countries and finds that government deficits reduce savings.[4] Snyder (1974) has reviewed the literature of econometric studies, which cover more than one economy at a time. Further he finds that savings studies in developing countries are limited. He concludes that with the exception of India there has not been sufficient research in any one country to draw firm conclusions about its saving determinants.

Warman and Thirlwall (1994) have tested the theory of financial liberalization over the period 1960-90 for Mexico making the distinction between financial saving and total saving. They find that financial saving is positively related to real interest rates, but total savings is invariant with respect to real interest rates. They also quote a study by two World Bank economists (Cho and Khatkhate, 1990), which says that the relationship between savings and real interest rates is ambiguous for five Asian countries.

Dayal-Gulati and Thimann (1997) compared the saving in Southeast Asia and Latin America over the period 1975-95. Using panel estimation they have tried to establish relationships between private saving rates and a range of policy and non-policy variables. The finding show that fiscal policy, particularly social security arrangement, influence private saving; also macroeconomic stability and financial deepening appear to have been important in accounting for differences in saving behaviour between the two regions. The paper uses cross country regressions to establish empirical relationships between the variables.

Schmidt-Hebbel and Serven (1996) empirically review and analyze the link between income distribution and

---

3 Ni, Shawn (1999), National debt, savings and real interest rates in a neoclassical model with endogenous labour supply and knowledge-based growth, Canadian Journal of Economics, Vol. 32, No. 5, November, Page 1239.

4 Ibid, Page 1239.

aggregate savings. The results provide no evidence that income equality affects aggregate saving across countries. The authors have used a large cross-country sample to study the linkage.

Bandiera et. al (1998) studies the effect of financial liberalization on eight developing countries.[5] The liberalization has had a significant positive direct effect on saving in Ghana and Turkey, and a negative effect in Korea and Mexico. No clear effect is discernible in the other countries. There is no evidence of significant, positive and sizeable interest rate effects.

The Indian studies have used econometric models to identify the determinants of the Indian saving rate.[6] Ordinary least squares method have been used to derive results some of which have been listed below:

- GDP growth has had no significant impact on the saving rate.
- Per-capita income has a weak positive effect on private saving.
- A high real interest rate has increased saving.
- Terms of trade has a significant effect on saving.
- Savings has been negatively related to the age dependency ratio.

These studies are without using the recent econometric tools. The statistical significance of the estimates is generally weak.

Existing work has been affected by the lack of detailed reliable data, and has offered limited help to policy makers that ask how saving rates can increase (Edwards, 1995).

**Motivation for the Study**

There are two fundamental limitations that make results from any cross-country study on this subject rather dubious. First, cross-country regression analysis is based on the

---

[5] Chile, Ghana, Indonesia, Korea, Malaysia, Mexico, Turkey and Zimbabwe.

[6] Krishnamurty et al. (1987), Lahiri (1989), Salgado (1995).

implicit assumption of "homogeneity" in the observed relationship across countries. This is a very restrictive assumption. It is common knowledge that there are considerable variations among developing countries in relation to various structural features and institutional aspects, which have a direct bearing upon the impact of financial factors on the growth process. Second, given vast differences among countries with respect to the nature and quality of data, cross-country comparison is fraught with danger.[7] Not only the statistical procedures for measuring saving and investment, but also the magnitude of errors in data in the implementation of these procedures, vary significantly among countries.

These considerations point to the need for undertaking econometric analysis of saving behaviour within individual countries over time in order to build a sound empirical foundation for informing the policy debate. Unfortunately, systematic country studies of this nature are few and far between. There are only few country specific studies available like Athukorala & Jayasuriya (1994), Onis & Riedel (1993), Collins (1994), Warman & Thirlwall (1994) and De Melo & Tybout (1986).[8] Interestingly, some of the available country studies have, in fact, produced large and quite significant interest elasticities with respect to saving (and investment). At the same time there are significant variations in the magnitude of measured elasticities among countries, suggesting that data should not be pooled without considerable caution.[9]

---

7 Deaton, A. (1989), *Saving in Developing Countries; Theory and Review,* Proceedings of the World Bank Annual Conference on Development Economics (Washington DC: World Bank, 1980), 61-108; T.N. Srinivasan (1994), *Data Base for development Analysis: An Overview,* Journal of Development Economics, pp. 44 3-27.

8 Athukorala, P. (1998), *Interest Rates, Savings and Investment: Evidence from India,* (Oxford Development Studies, 13600818, Jun Vol. 26, Issue 2.

9 Athukorala P. (1998), *Interest Rates, Savings and Investment: Evidence from India,* (Oxford Development Studies, 13600818, Jun Vol. 26, Issue 2.

## Why India?

First, the Indian saving (and investment) database is considered relatively good by developing country standards, and data are available on a comparable basis for a period of time, which is adequate for systematic econometric investigation.[10] Second, saving/investment performance is a key emphasis in the policy debate in India following the structural adjustment reforms initiated in 1991[11]; but, there is no hard empirical evidence to inform this policy debate.[12] Also there have been no sufficient studies done in any one country to draw firm conclusions about its savings determinants with the possible exception of India.[13]

## Model Specification, Data and Methodology

The saving function is estimated for private saving (PS). Most of the previous studies of saving behaviour in developing countries have focused solely on total saving as the dependent variable. This is unsatisfactory because the positive response of private savings to interest rates stipulated by the financial repressionist theory may be obscured in the typical developing country context where public sector saving is a significant element in total saving. There is another reason for not using total saving, which includes public saving. The results of Athukorala's studies (1998) reveal that use of total saving including the public

---

[10] T.N. Srinivasan, *Data Base for Development Analysis: An Overview,* Journal of Development Economics, 44 (1994), pp. 3-27.

[11] Athukorala, P. & Sen K. (1995) *Economic Reforms and the Rate of Saving in India: some observations,* Economic and Political Weekly, 30, pp. 2184-2190 and EPWRF (Economic and Political Weekly Research Foundation) (1995) *Economic Reforms and Rate of Saving,* Economic and Political Weekly, 30, pp. 1021-1041.

[12] T.N. Srinivasan (1994), *Data Base for Development Analysis: An Overview,* Journal of Development Economics, 44, pp. 3-27.

[13] Snyder, Donald W., *Econometric Studies of Household Saving Behaviour in Developing Countries: A Survey,* Journal of Development Studies, Page 150, pp. 139-153.

sector saving is likely to infuse a downward bias into the estimates of interest elasticity of saving.[14]

## The Life-Cycle Model

The life cycle model has been used where accumulation for retirement is the prime motive for saving. The model is built around the consumption/saving behaviour of a representative agent. The theory of saving behaviour focused first on a representative agent and then extended the analysis to the national level using the household as the point of focus. Thus, it could be argued from a theoretical standpoint that the most appropriate dependent variable for empirical analysis is household saving, and *not* private saving which comprises both household and corporate saving). However, the conventional view in this is that, because households own business firms, household saving behaviour basically determines private saving. Thus, if firms save more, households, may save less, because they will regard the firms as doing the saving for them (that is, in their expenditure decisions, households 'pierce the corporate veil').[15] This view justifies the use of private saving rate as the dependent variable of the analysis.

As Poterba's (1987) seminal paper explains, if households "pierce the corporate veil," aggregate private saving becomes the variable of interest, with little informational gain from further breaking it down into household and corporate saving. On the other hand, if household and corporate saving decisions are independently obtained, then they must be studied separately, for it is likely that they have different determinants. As an illustration, consider the example of corporate saving not being neutral

[14] Athukorala, P (1998) Interest Rates, Saving And Investment: Evidence From India, Oxford Development Studies, 13600818, Jun, Vol. 26, Issue 2.

[15] Modigliani Franco, The Life Cycle Hypothesis of Saving and Inter-country Differences in the Saving Ratio, Modigliani Franco (1986), Life Cycle, Individual Thrift, and the Wealth of Nations, American Economic Review, 76, pp. 297-313.

with respect to private saving. If corporate dividends increase at the expense of undistributed profits, generating an increase in private disposable income, and a decrease in share prices, total private saving will fall if the marginal propensity to consume out of disposable income exceeds that from wealth. "The results are we believe consistent with the hypothesis that households pierce the corporate veil (or at least, see through it) to a sufficient extent for us to focus on the behavior of aggregate private saving." (Loayza and Shanker, 1998). Private Saving (PS = Private Household Savings + Corporate Savings at constant prices) is specified as a function of GDP Growth Rate, Real Interest Rate and Inflation Rate (Base Year 93-94). Corporate saving is defined as excess of profits over dividends as was defined by Loayza & Shankar (1998).

Equation Used for estimating the regression for Savings Function

$$\ln(PS/GDP) = \alpha + \beta_2 \ln(GDPGR) + \beta_3 \ln(IR) + \beta_4 \ln(RID) + \beta_5 \ln(LBD_1) + u_i$$

**Table of Variables used in Regression for Private Savings Function**

| | *Dependent Variable* | *Independent Variable* |
|---|---|---|
| Savings Function | Private Savings/GDP (PSGDP) [Private Savings (PS) = Household Savings + Corporate Savings] | GDP Growth Rate (GDPGR)<br>Inflation Rate (IR)<br>Real Interest on Deposits (RID)<br>Dummy Variable ($LBD_1$) |

1. Real Rate of Interest is average of 1 to 3 years deposit rates less inflation.
2. GDP Growth Rate is expressed in natural logarithms

and log (1 + x) for Inflation and Real Rate of Interest. The variables are expressed in logarithmic form so that the first differences give us the growth rates.

3. Private Savings are measured at constant prices. Private Savings has been deflated using the rate of inflation (Base: 1993-94).
4. $u_i$ is the error tem in the regression equation.

The savings rate, rather than the absolute level of saving, is used as the dependent variable for three reasons. First, there is no adequate deflator for saving that can be used to constant-price savings series. Second, by using ratios, instead of levels, cross-country comparisons can be made without having to choose appropriate exchange rates. Third, savings rates tend to be stationary, whereas absolute savings flow grow over time, so that, by using rates, spurious correlation with time-trended explanation variables can be minimized (Morisset and Revoredo, 1995).

With the application of the basic life-cycle model we need to look at the key premise of the life-cycle hypothesis that the saving rate is related to the growth of per capita income, *not* the level of per capita income. As Modigliani himself has noted.

*"For at least that portion of the population that lives at, or near, the starvation level, may find it impossible or too burdensome to set aside resources now in order to provide for later consumption. People in that predicament may tend to live more from hand-to-mouth, skipping retirement or being supported by the extended family. It is thus conceivable that, for a sufficiently low value of per capita income,...the saving-income ratio for given growth would...tend to rise with income."*[16]

For these considerations, the growth rate is included as

[16] Modigliani Franco, Recent Declines in the Savings Rate: A Life Cycle Perspective, M. Baldassarri, L. Paganetto and E.S. Phelps (eds.), World Saving, Prosperity and Growth (London: Macmillan, 1993), pp. 249-286.

explanatory variable in the saving function. From the argument of Modigliani it is expected that growth rate would have a positive coefficient.

According to the Keynesian view on saving behaviour, the income and substitution effects of a change in the real interest rate may work in opposite directions, rendering the net effect ambiguous. Thus, the interest rate effect on saving is considered "secondary and relatively unimportant, except where unusually large changes are in question"[17]. The financial repression paradigm of McKinnon (1973) and Shaw (1973), however, postulates the impact of a change in real interest rate on saving in the typical developing economy to be positive.[18] The reason for this phenomenon can be explained this way. In the typical developing economy where portfolio choices are rather limited, the saving process tends to be highly money intensive. Given this peculiarity of saving behaviour, plus the fact that the bulk of saving comes from small savers, the substitutions effect generally tends to be much larger than the income effect of an interest rate change.

Williamson (1968) has studied the influence of interest-rate changes on savings using panel data for six developing Asian countries. The coefficient is significant for about half of the countries tested, and strongly negative.[19]

The combination of theory and empirical evidence suggest on balance that the aggregate interest elasticity of saving is unlikely to be negative, may be substantially positive. (Elmendorf, 1996). Inflation is assumed to have an impact on saving only through its role in the determination of Real

---

[17] Keynes J.M. (1936), The General Theory of Employment, Interest and Money http://www.marxists.org/reference/subject/economics/keyness/general-theory/ch09.htm.

[18] McKinnon Ronald I. (1973), Money and Capital in Economic Development, (Washington DC. Brooking Institute,) and Shaw Edward (1973), Financial Deepening in Economic Development (Oxford University Press).

[19] Snyder, Donald W. (1974) Econometric Studies of Household Savings Behaviour in Developing Countries: A Survey, Journal of Development Studies.

Interest on Deposits. Quite apart from its influence on real returns to saving, inflation may influence saving through its impact on real wealth. If consumers attempt to maintain a target rate of consumption to wealth or of liquid assets to income, saving will rise with anticipated inflation. Also, consumer response to unexpected changes in inflation can result in involuntary saving (Deaton, 1977). On the other hand, in an inflationary situation, a switch from financial assets to real assets can result in a decline in savings. For these reasons, Rate of Inflation as an additional variable has been included. The coefficient for inflation would therefore be positive also as stated in a study by Deaton in the American Economic Review in 1977.

This paper does not take the institutional development as one of the variables of savings. Athukorala has attempted it in his paper in 2001. Defining appropriate proxies for the degree of financial development is indeed, one of the challenges faced by empirical researchers (Edwards, 1995). Also financial market development is difficult to quantify. (Gulati and Thimann, 1997).

Apart from the explanatory variables discussed above, an intercept dummy variable ("liberalization dummy," LBD) is included in the equation, in order to test whether the market-oriented policy reforms initiated in 1991 per se have had a specific influence (over and above their impact operating through the other variables explicitly allowed for in regression specifications) on saving behaviour in the Indian economy. The value of the dummy variable has been kept at zero for the period from 1980-81 to 1990-91 and one from 1991-92 to 1999-2000.

## Data

Data on the different variables has been obtained from the Hand Book of Statistics of Reserve Bank of India 2000, Economic Survey 2000-2001, various issues of Report on Currency and Finance, National Account Statistics, Government of India provided by MacroScan Database.

## Methodology

Augmented Dickey Fuller test has been used to test the stationarity of the data. If the data is found to be non-stationary then the cointegration test needs to be performed. With that we proceed to apply OLS based multiple regression model for Savings.

## Results

The Augmented Dickey Fuller Test has been conducted for all the variables included in the regression function. The ADF test results are given in Table 3.

**Table 3 : (Test for Unit Root in Level)**

| Variables | Test Statistic | Critical Value at 5% |
|---|---|---|
| Pvt. Savings | 2.212992 | -3.7119 |
| Real Int. Rates | -1.704844 | -3.7119 |
| Exp. Inflation | -1.315751 | -3.7119 |
| GDP Growth rate | -3.580198 | -37119 |

In all the cases considered, the test statistic is greater than the critical value, hence the null hypothesis of stationary can be accepted.

As the data is stationary, the regression has been run without the cointegration test. Throughout the period under study up to 1991, the nominal interest rate was an administered price, changed at infrequent intervals. However, there were no persistent adverse movements in real deposit rates; macroeconomic policy had an anti-inflationary stance, and high inflation and sharply negative real deposit rates were not allowed to continue for long. At the same time, the spread of banking facilities played a useful supplementary role in increasing financial (and hence total) saving. The summary of the results of the variables is given in the Table 4.

For the Savings Function significant variables are GDP Growth Rate, Real Interest Rate and Inflation for the period between 1980-2000. Also the dummy variable $LBD_1$ has a

**Table 4 : Estimates of Co-efficients for Savings Function and t-statistics**

| | $\alpha$ | $\beta_2$ (GDPGR) | t-value | $\beta_3$ (IR) | t-value | $\beta_4$ (RID) | t-value | $\beta_5$ ($LBD_1$) | t-value | $R^2$ |
|---|---|---|---|---|---|---|---|---|---|---|
| Savings Function | 0.271 | 0.350 | 1.983** | | 1.403* | 13.080 | 2.132** | 0.387 | 4.950*** | 0.861 |
| | (0.336) | (0.176) | | 9.929 (7.079) | | (6.134) | | (6.134) | | |

* significant at 10%

** significant at 5%

*** significant at 1%

*Note* : The number in brackets is the standard error.

significant value. From the value of $R^2$, it can be said that about 86% of the phenomenon of private savings is explained by the included variables.

## Economic Evaluation

## The Savings Function for Private Savings

General economic performance measured in terms of growth of GDP and real interest rates and inflation have proved to be significant variables.

India has been financial liberalization now for the past one-decade or so. With financial liberalization national savings rate can decline as households move from being constrained under financially repressed regime to freer conditions. This lessens the need for more savings in the present, as borrowing could be resorted to tide over financially tight situations. "Financial liberalisation also relaxes liquidity constraints of households and opens up access to borrowing, thereby obviating the need for saving to make large down payments for purchase of house and expensive consumer durables (Mathew, 1997). This could go to reduce the saving rate.

In this study, the variable RID is significant at 5% level of significance indicating strong relationship between private savings and rate of interest. The high interest rate affects the savings behaviour as total private savings is made up of financial savings to the extent of 45%. The significant results for Real Interest Rate (RID) therefore substantiate the Mckinnon-Shaw proposition that, in an economy where the saving behaviour is highly intensive in financial assets, high real interest rates promote financial saving (and total saving).

The results for inflation returned by the regression run for savings function is that inflation is statistically significant. Results of a study done by Norman Loayza and Rashmi Shanker (1998) find inflation to be insignificant. But in the period under consideration the inflation rates have been pushing savings. The real interest rates have started coming down only in the last few years. In the major part of the period studied here real interest rates were high. Inflation above 6-8% pushes the nominal interest rates higher into double digits naturally encouraging savings behaviour.

After nationalization of the banks in the seventies we have seen an increase in the number of branches of these nationalized banks. This had a significant impact on the saving rates.[20] But the Chart 1 shows that the impact of bank density in the past two decades has decreased.

**Chart - 1**
**Bank Branch Density**

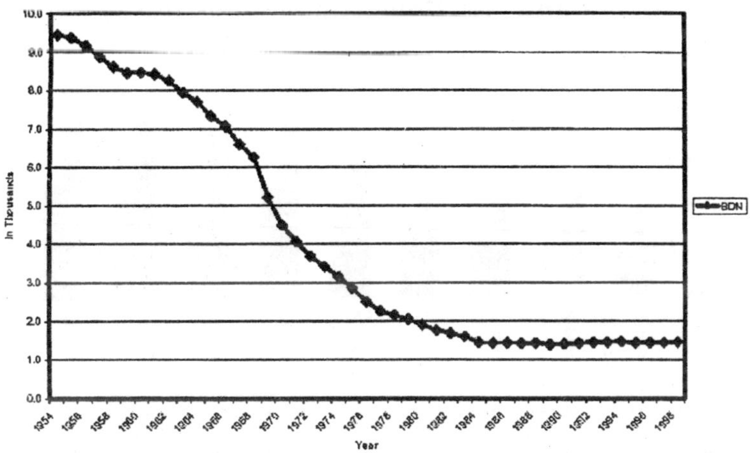


*Source:* "The Determinants of Private Saving In India" by Prema-Chandra Athukorala and Kunal Sen in December 2001, Forthcoming in *Economic Development and Cultural Change.*

## Significance of Interest Rate as a Determinant

A sizeable body of empirical literature has attempted to quantify the impact of interest rates on saving. Given the nature of data availability, many of these studies have been

[20] Athukorala P. & Sen K. (2001) The Determinants of Private Saving In India, Forthcoming in Economic Development and Cultural Change Page 19 and 20.

conducted using cross-country time-series data, focusing largely on the total domestic saving-interest rate nexus. The results of these studies are at best ambiguous; while some studies come down against any interest rate effect on savings, others find a positive but rather small interest elasticity (around 0.1) which is "not large enough to warrant much policy significance" (Fry, 1995, p. 42). If the banks can create credit without having to rely on initial deposits, an increase in financial saving through higher real deposit rates makes no difference to the amount to total credit given to the private sector.[21]

**Chart-2**
**Gross and Net Domestic Savings Rates**

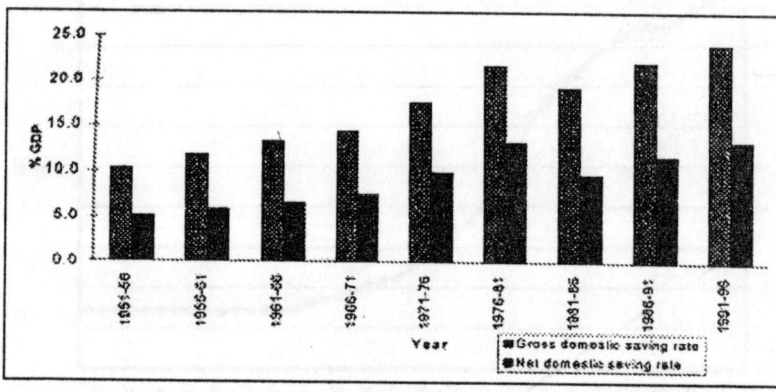


**Source :** Joseph, Mathew (1997), India's Saving Rate : Analysis And Policy Prescriptions, April, Study done for SCICI. http://www.icici.com/cb_resan/

For raising rate in the future would involve the preservation of the dynamism of the private corporate sector, reinvigoration of the households and a substantial boosting of the saving behaviour of the public sector. However

[21] Davidson, P. (1986), Finance, funding, saving, and investment, Journal of Post-Keynesian Economics, 9, pp. 101-110. Thirlwall, A.P. (1976), Financing Economic Development (London, Macmillan).

evidence from a score of countries – including the East Asian miracle nations – suggests that the increase in private domestic savings ratios is a rather slow process.[22]

In addition to the variables included in the savings function it has been found that a drastic increase of private savings has usually been affected by an important factor not captured in the regression analysis: the creation of an institutional environment that instills confidence on small savers - the case of postal savings in East Asia is a good example of this type of institution.[23]

## Conclusion

The paper using the life cycle framework has studied the saving behaviour in India for the past two decades. Further advanced econometric techniques have been used to test the data. The study reports that saving is largely driven by inflation rates, growth rates of GDP, real interest rates. India has been a savings oriented economy with savings habits of people deeply entrenched in Indian. The winds of liberalisation have seen the interest rates fall across the board for all types of savings options. The administered interest rate mechanism has been dismantled to a great extent. But the high real interest rates are driving the saving habits of Indians.

---

22 World Bank; The East Asian Miracle: Economic Growth and Public Policy New York, Oxford University Press.

23 Edwards Sebastian (1995), Why are Savings Rates so Different Across Countries? An International Comparative Analysis, Working Paper No. 5097, April, National Bureau of Economic Research. Page 38.

## REFERENCES

Athukorala, Prema-Chandra and Sen Kunal (2001), The Determinants of Private Saving In India, Forthcoming in Economic Development and Cultural Change.

Athukorala, Prema-Chandra (1998), Interest Rates, Saving And Investment Evidence From India, Oxford Development Studies, 13600818, Jun, Vol. 26, Issue 2.

Athukoral, Prema-Chandra and Sen, Kunal (1996), Liberalisation and Business Investment in India, August.

Athukorala, Prema-Chandra and Sen, Kunal (2001), Reforms and Investment in India. http://rspas.anu.edu.au/economics/publish/papers/workingpapers.htm.

Athukorala P. & Sen K. (1995), Economic Reforms and the Rate of Saving in India; some observations, Economic and Political Weekly, 30, pp. 2184-2190 and EPWRF (Economic and Political Weekly Research Foundation) (1995), Economic Reforms and Rate of Saving, Economic and Political Weekly, 30, pp. 1021-1041.

Bandiera, O., Caprio Jr., G., Honohan, P., and Schiantarelli, F. (1998), Does financial reform raise or reduce savings? Boston College Working, p. 413.

Bernstein, P.L. (1992), Savings and Investment and other Myths, Public Interest, 00333557, Spring 1992, Issue 107.

Davidson, P. (1986), Finance, funding, saving and investment, Journal of Post-Keynesian Economics, 9, pp. 101-110.

Deaton, Angus and Paxson, Christina (1998), Saving and growth: another look at the cohort evidence, Research Program in Development Studies, Princeton University, Feb.

Edwards, Sebastian (1995), Why are Savings Rates so Different Across Countries? An International Comparative Analysis, Working Paper No. 5097, April, National Bureau of Economic Research, pp. 1-46.

Elmendorf, D.W. (1996), The effect of Interest-Rate Changes On Household Saving And Consumption : A Survey (Federal Reserve Board), June.

Friedman, Milton, A theory of consumption function, Princeton 1957.

Gale, William G. and Sabelhaus, John (1999), Perspectives on the Household Saving Rate. http://www.brook.edu/es/commentary/journals/bpea_macro/1999_1.htm.

Global Savings And Investment, Economic Trends (Federal Reserve Bank of Cleveland), 07482922, Nov. 1995, p. 18, 2p.

Gulati, Anuradha D. and Thimann, Christian (1997), Saving in Southeast Asia and Latin America Compared: Searching For Policy Lessons, September © 1997 International Monetary Fund, WP/97/110.

Joseph, Mathew (1997), India's Saving Rate: Analysis And Policy Prescriptions, April, Study done for SCICI. http://www.icici.com/cb_resanl/.

Johansen, Soren (1991), "Estimation and Hypothesis Testing of Cointegration Vectors in Gaussian Vector Autoregressive Models," Econometrica, 59, pp. 1551-1580.

Johansen, Soren (1995), Likelihood-based Inference in Cointegrated Vector Autoregressive Models, Oxford University Press.

Krishnamurty, K., K.S. Krishnaswamy, and P.D. Sharma (1987), Determinants of Saving Rates in India, Journal of Quantitative Economics, 3, pp. 335-57.

Keynes, J.M. (1936), The General Theory of Employment, Interest and Money.

Lahiri, Ashok (1989), Dynamics of Asian Saving: the Role of Growth and Age Structure, Staff Papers, International Monetary Fund, Vol. 36 (March), pp. 228-61.

Loayza, Norman (World Bank) and Shankar, Rashmi (U.C. Santa Cruz) (1998), Private Saving In India, World Bank Economic Review, Vol. 14, No. 3, September, pp. 571-94.

Mallick, Sushanta K. (2002), Determinants of Long Term Growth in India: A Keynesian Approach Progress In Development Studies 2,4 pp. 306-324.

McKinnon, Ronald I. (1973), Money and Capital in Economic Development, (Washington DC. Brooking Institute).

Modigliani Franco, The Life Cycle Hypothesis of Saving and Inter-country Differences in the Saving Ratio.

Modigliani Franco (1986), Life Cycle, Individual Thrift, and the Wealth of Nations, American Economic Review, 76, pp. 297-313.

Modigliani Franco, Recent Declines in the Savings Rate: A Life Cycle Perspective, M. Baldassarri, L. Paganetto and E.S. Phelps (eds.), World Saving, Prosperity and Growth (London: Mcmillan, 1993), pp. 249-286.

Modigliani, F. & Brumberg, R. (1954), Utility analysis and the consumption function: An interpretation of cross-section data. In Kurihara, K.K (ed.): Post-Keynesian Economics. New Brunswick, NJ: Rutgers University Press.

Morisset, Jacques and Revoredo, Cesar (1995), Savings and Education: A life-cycle model applied to a Panel of 74 countries, The World Bank LA1CO: Policy Research Working Paper No. 1504, August.

Ni, Shawn (1999), National debt, savings and real interest rates in a neoclassical model with endogenous labour supply and knowledge-based growth, Canadian Journal or Economics, Vol. 32, No. 5, November, pp. 1227-44.

Orazio, P. Attanasio, Lucio Picci, Antonello Scorcu (1997), Saving Growth and Investment: A macroeconomic analysis using a panel of countries (originally published in December 1997, version referred to of September 1999). Vol. 82 (2), pp. 182-211.

Salgado, R. (1995), Saving Trends in India: Long-Run Determinants, Short-Run Dynamics and Recent Developments, IMF.

Shaw, Edward (1973), Financial Deepening in Economic Development (Oxford: Oxford University Press).

Schmidt-Hebbel, Klaus and Serven Luis (1996), Income equality and aggregate saving: The cross-country evidence, The World Bank, Policy Research Working Paper 1561, January.

Snyder, Donald W. (1974) Econometric Studies of Household Savings Behaviour in Developing Countries: A Survey, Journal of Development Studies, Vol. 12, pp. 139-153.

T.N. Srinivasan (1994), Data Base for development Analysis: An Overview, Journal of Development Economics, pp. 44 3-27.

Thirlwall, A.P. (1976), Financing Economic Development (London, Macmillan).

Warman, Fanny and Thirlwall, A.P. (1994), Interest Rates, Saving, Investment and Growth in Mexico 1960-90: Tests of the Financial Liberalisation Hypothesis, The Journal of Development Studies, Vol. 30 No. 3, 1994, pp. 629-649, Published By Frank Cass, London.

World Bank; The East Asian Miracle: Economic Growth and Public Policy New York, Oxford University Press.

# 9

# Impact of Growth and Performance on Market Capitalization: A Case Study

*M.M. Metwally**

## Introduction

Qatar is a small open economy that depends heavily on exportation of oil and natural gas. The relative contribution of other sectors to GDP fluctuates with changes in oil prices. The growth and stability in both the primary and non-primary sectors have some important impact on the performance of the companies listed on Doha Stock Exchange.

There are three distinguishing features of Doha Securities market. First it is a very young market. It was established in accordance with the Law No. 14 of 1996 and started operating in May 1997. Secondly, it is a very small market. The number of companies listed on it has reached 23 in 2001. Two of these companies were listed less than 18 months ago. Thirdly, Doha securities market is semi-closed in the sense that only Qatar citizens and citizens of the Gulf Cooperation Council (consisting of Bahrian, Kuwait, Oman,

* University of Wollongong in Dubai
e-mail: mokhtarmetwally@uowdubai.ac.ae

Qatar, Saudi Arabia and the United Arab Emirates) are allowed to buy and sell shares on Doha Securities.

The main objectives of Doha Securities Market are to find opportunities to invest savings in stock trading; carry out studies and collect data and information on securities exchanged in the market and confirms the professional code of conduct among the brokers and staff of the market in service of the national economy (Higazy, 2002). The market works to encourage the introduction and organization of investment funds, which are considered effective instruments for investors with poor experience. Other objectives of the market include curtailing the flight of funds outside the country, attracting funds to the country and providing the opportunity to sell some of the public companies to the private sector. One could expect that the market will play an important role in enhancing the national economy and creating the suitable conditions in which to establish, finance and improve joint stock companies.

This paper is financial study of the 18 Qatar companies listed on Doha Stock Exchange in the year 2001, for which data are available. These companies are classified into four sectors, namely, the Banks Sector (consisting of 5 banks), the Insurance Sector (consisting of 4 companies), the Service Sector (covering 6 companies) and the Industrial Sector (consisting of 3 companies). A study of the structure and performance of these companies help to verify the ideas taught in microeconomic theory relative to the various market models and their performance, both in term of profitability and financial behvior (Asch, 1967).

The paper is divided into three sections. Section one outlines the main financial characteristics of the studied companies. Section two develops and tests a simultaneous-equation model to examine the relationship between the performance of the company and the value of its shares on the market. Finally, section three summarizes the main findings of the study.

## Main Characteristics of the Sample Companies

The Qatar companies listed on Doha Stock Exchange differ substantially in terms of their structure and performance. Table 1 gives information on the volume of assets, value of equity and total profitability of 18 companies out of the listed 23 companies in 2001. The table also gives the rate of return on assets and equity as well as the current ratio. The data in Table 1 suggest that:

1. The largest company listed in the stock market has assets value at US$7776.2m; while the smallest company has assets valued at US$10.3m.
2. Equity of most listed companies constitutes a high proportion of assets. This proportion is as high as 91.84 per cent in some companies.
3. The companies vary a great deal in their performance. The highest rate of return on equity was 52.1 per cent, while the lowest rate was 4.31 per cent.

Spearman's rank correlation coefficient was used to test if there is any association between size and profitability. The results, given in Table 2 suggest the following:

1. There is a significant negative correlation between size, measured in terms of assets, and the rate of return on assets. Spreaman's rank correlation coefficient is –0.474, which is statistically signifi-cant at the 5 per cent level of significance. This suggests that smaller companies score high rates of return on their assets.
2. There is a significant positive correlation between size, measure in terms of Assets, and the rate of return on equity. The Spearman's rank correlation coefficient between the two variables (0.589) is statistically significant at the 1 per cent level of significance.

The above two results suggest that a number of large companies listed on Doha Securities Market have a smaller equity/assets ratio.

**Table 1 : Financial Characteristics of the Qatar Stock Exchange Listed Companies in 2001. (Million QR)**

| *Name of Company* | *Assets US$M* | *Liability US$M* | *Equity Net US$M* | *Profit US$M* |
|---|---|---|---|---|
| **Banking** | | | | |
| Qatar National Bank | 7775.2 | 6598.4 | 1176.8 | 144.5 |
| Commercial Bank of Qatar | 1427.0 | 1259.2 | 167.8 | 27.7 |
| Doha Bank | 1782.3 | 1610.4 | 171.0 | 19.4 |
| Qatar Islamic Bank | 1209.6 | 1121.7 | 87.8 | 18.4 |
| Qatar International Islamic Bank | 739.7 | 687.4 | 52.3 | 11.4 |
| **Insurance** | | | | |
| Qatar Insurance Co. | 232.9 | 59.2 | 173.7 | 19.3 |
| General Insurance Co. | 110.8 | 44.8 | 60.0 | 2.9 |
| Al-Khaleej Insurance Co. | 32.4 | 6.6 | 25.8 | 2.1 |
| Islamic Insurance Co. | 17.9 | 10.9 | 7.0 | 0.56 |
| **Services** | | | | |
| Qatar National Navigation Co. | 386.7 | 56.9 | 329.7 | 32.1 |
| Qatar Cinema Co. | 10.3 | 0.893 | 9.4 | 0.96 |
| Qatar Water and Electricity Co. | 1115.1 | 709.3 | 405.8 | 73.6 |
| Qatar Shipping Co. | 355.7 | 174.5 | 161.2 | 28.2 |
| Qatar Real Estate Co. | 148.5 | 74.3 | 74.3 | 12.6 |
| Q-Tel | 803.3 | 350.2 | 453.1 | 236.5 |
| **Manufacturing** | | | | |
| Cement Co. | 224.6 | 31.1 | 193.5 | 30.9 |
| Flower Mills Co. | 91.1 | 37.7 | 53.3 | 2.3 |
| Qatar Industrial Manufacturing Co. | 74.6 | 16.6 | 58.0 | 6.7 |

*Source:* Doha Securities Market, Qatar, 2002.

3. The statistical results suggest that there is no significant correlation between size and the rate of return on assets or the rate of return on equity, when size is measured in terms of equity. This implies that

companies with high levels of equity do not necessarily achieve a higher ratio of profitability than companies with small levels of equity.

**Table 2 : Rank Correlation Between Size and Measures of Profitability**

| | *Relationships* | *Coefficient* |
|---|---|---|
| 1. | Correlation between size, measured by total assets, and rate of return on assets | –0.474* |
| 2. | Correlation between size, measured by total assets, and rate of return on equity | 0.589* |
| 3. | Correlation between size, measured by equity and rate by return on assets | 0.102 |
| 4. | Correlation between size, measured by equity and rate of return on equity | 0.424 |
| 5. | Correlation between size, measured by total assets and the current ratio | 0.395 |
| 6. | Correlation between size, measured by equity and the current ratio | –0.366 |

*Notes* : The Coefficients are calculated using the formula : $r = 1- \{\Sigma d^2/n(n^2 - 1)\}$, where d is the difference between ranks. The test significance is given by : $t = r (\sqrt{n-2}) / (\sqrt{1-r^2})$ with $d.f = n - 2$.

4. There is no significant correlation between size, measured in terms or assets and the current ratio (i.e. the ratio of current assets to current liabilities). This suggests that the company's ability in meeting its short-term obligations or current liabilities does not depend on the company's size. The same conclusion holds when size is measured in terms of equity.

## A Simultaneous Equation Model of Share Values and Company Financial Structure and Performance

This section develops and tests a simultaneous equation model to examine the relationship between the market value of shares and the performance of the relevant companies. The following simultaneous relationships, known as structural equations, has been developed:

**Structural Equations**

$$(MC/AC) = ao + a_0 (E\ S) + a_2 (R_{P/BV}) + a_3 R_R + u_1$$

$$(E\ S) = b_o + b_1 (PL/E) + b_2 (L/A) + u_2$$

$$(PL/E) = c_o + c_1 (C/I) + c_2 (R_R) + c_3 (MC/AC) + u_3$$

**Endogenous Variables**

MC/AC = Market capitalization as a ratio of authorized and paid capital

E S = Earnings per share

PL/E = Profit/Loss equity ratio

**Predetermined Variables**

$R_{P/BV}$ = Average rate of change in the price book value ratio

L /A = Ratio of external liabilities to assets

C /I = Cost to income ratio

$R_R$ = Average rate of growth of revenue

The first equation shows that the ratio of market capitalization to authorized and issued capital in the company depends on earnings per share, the rate of change in the price of book value ratio and the average rate of growth of revenue. It is hypothesized that market capitalization improves with the increase in demand for shares of the specific company and with the acceleration of revenue are motivated by the earnings per share while speculators care more about the prospects of growth in share prices relative to book value (Chen Roll and Ross, 1986). Thus, we would expect all coefficients in that equation to have positive signs.

The second equation indicates that earnings per share depend on net profits to equity, and on the ratio of total external liability to equity. It is hypothesized that the earnings per share will increase with the rise in the share of net profits to equity. On the other hand, earning per share would be smaller for companies that have a high ratio of external liabilities to equity (Fama, 1970, and Martin 1983). Thus, we would expect the sign of the coefficient ($b_1$) to be positive while the sign of the coefficient ($b_2$) to be negative.

The third equation suggests that the profit/loss equity ratio would depend on the cost to income ratio, the average rate of growth of revenue and market capitalization as a ratio of authorized and paid capital. It is hypothesized that the profitability of the company would increase if costs incurred in deriving the company's income were reduced and the company's revenue enjoy growth. It is also assumed that companies who achieve greater market capitalization are likely to make more profit through reduction in cost of borrowing (Brealey and Myers, 1988). Thus, we would expect the sign of the coefficient ($c_1$) to be negative while the signs of the coefficients ($c_2$) and ($c_3$) to be positive.

The above system is mathematically complete in the sense that it contains as many equations as it contains endogenous variables. Applying the order and the rank conditions of identification, we find that the first equation is just identified. We may therefore use the method of two-stage least squares to estimate the system (Greene 2000). The estimation was applied to 18 Doha stock exchange listed companies in 2001, for which the complete set of relevant data was available.

The 2SLS results for the three equations of the model are presented in Table 3. The equations were also estimated by Ordinary Least Squares (OLS), as a sensitivity analysis[1]; these results are presented in Table 4. Overall the OLS results strongly support the 2SLS results. However, the 2SLS results are better than those given by OLS, which suggests presence of simultaneous bias.

---

[1] This is because the properties of the sampling distributions of 2SLS estimates in small samples are unknown; OLS produces biased estimates but which nevertheless have finite sampling distributions (Hayashi 2000). Both sets of estimations were performed with the RATS program.

## Table 3 : Simultaneous-Equation Regression Results 2 SLS Estimates

$(MC/AC) = 0.779 + 2.53\ (E\ S) + .0364\ (R_{P/BV}) + .248\ (R_R)$

(2.438) (2.491) (3.186) (3.266)

$R^{-2} = 0.658$; F = 39.3; D.W. = 1.687

$(E\ S) = 4.982 + 7.495\ (PL/E) - 6.213\ )\ (L/A)$

(3.119) (3.041) (–3.463)

$R^{-2} = 0.568$; F = 19.784; D.W. = 2.096

$(PL/E) = .0672 - .00112\ (C/I) + .0139\ (R_R) + .00479\ (MC/AC)$

(01.021) (–4.001) (5.997) (3.819)

$R^{-2} = 0.665$; F = 54.6; D.W. = 1.831

## Table 4 : Simultaneous Equation Regression Results OLS Estimates

$(MC/AC) = 1.113 + .269\ (E\ S) + 0.379\ (R_{P/BV}) + .222\ (R_R)$

(3.315) (2.423) (2.987) (2.842)

$R^{-2} = 0.626$; F = 30.1; D.W. = 1.789

$(E\ S) = 3.778 + 11.874\ (PL/E) - 6.555\ (L/A)$

(4.325) (2.632) (–3.103)

$R^{-2} = 0.544$; F = 14.304; D.W. = 1.874

$(PL/E) = .1014 - .00122\ (C/I) + .0147\ (R_R) + .00633\ (MC/AC)$

(1.989) (–3.847) (4.616) (3.302)

$R^{-2} = 0.621$; F = 49.90; D.W. = 1.908

The $R^2$ and F statistics of the fitted equations suggest that the model is a good fit. Also the estimated Durbin-Watson (DW) support the view that the residuals about the fitted equations were independent (Davidson, 2000)[2].

The regression results would seem to suggest that:

(i) There seems to be a significant positive correlation between market capitalization as a ratio of authorized and paid capital and each of earnings per share and the rate of change in the price book value ratio. The coefficients of the variables (ES) and ($R_{P/BV}$) are statistically significant at the 1 per cent level of significance.

(ii) There seems to be significant positive relationship between the earnings per share and the net profit/loss equity ratio. The coefficient of the variable (PL/E) is statistically significant at the 1 per cent level of significance. On the other hand, there seems to be significant negative relationship between the earnings per share and the ratio of external liabilities to assets. The coefficient of the variable (L/A) is negative and statistically significant at the 1 per cent level of significance.

(iii) The results of the third equation suggest that the ratio of net profits to equity is strongly influenced by the cost/income ratio and the rate of growth of revenue. The profit/loss equity ratio seems also to be

---

2 In the light of the comments in footnote 1, the values of $R^2$, t, F, DW and Durbin's h statistics in Table 3 and 4 are given for what they are worth. In addition to the test for serial correlation, inspection of the residuals about the fitted equations did not suggest any obvious violations of the homoscedasticity of error terms assumption. The equations were also analysed for multicollinearity and these tests gave no undue cause for concern; this is further confirmed by a comparison of the t statistics with the F statistics of the fitted equations. For further discussion, including the robustness of Least Squares methods in the presence of minor violations of the error term assumptions, see Mittelhammer, 2000 and Judge and Miller, 2000.

influenced by market capitalization as a ratio of authorized and paid capital. As expected, there is a strong negative relationship between the company's profitability and its cost/income ratio. The coefficient of the variable (C/I) is negative and statistically significant at the 1 per cent level of significance. On the other hand, the coefficients of the variables ($R_R$) and (MC/AC) are positive and statistically significant at the 1 per cent of significance.

## Conclusions

The main findings of this paper may be summarized in the following:

1. The companies listed on Doha Stock Exchange vary a great deal in their performance. The rate of return on equity varied from a high of 52.1 per cent to a low of 4.31 per cent.
2. There is a significant negative correlation between size of the company, measured in terms of assets, and the rate of return on assets. This suggests that smaller companies score high rates of return on their assets. On the other hand, there is a significant positive correlation between size, measured in terms of assets, and the rate of return on equity.
3. There is no significant correlation between size of the company, measured in terms of equity, and each of the rate of return on assets and the rate of return on equity. This implies that companies with high levels of equity do not necessarily achieve a higher ratio of profitability than companies with small levels of equity.
4. The company's ability to meet its short-term obligations or current liabilities does not depend on the company's size. There is no significant correlation between size (measured by assets or equity) and the current ratio.

5. The simultaneous equation model results suggest that

   (i) Earnings per share, revenue growth and the rate of change in the price book value ratio seem to have a strong positive effect on market capitalization.

   (ii) There seems to be significant positive relationship between the earnings per share and the net profit/loss equity ratio. On the other hand, earnings per share are negatively related to ratio of external liabilities to assets.

   (iii) The ratio of net profits to equity is strongly influenced by the cost/income ratio and the rate of growth of revenue. The profit/loss equity ratio also seems to be influenced by market capitalization as a ratio of authorized and paid capital. There is a strong negative relationship between the company's profitability and its cost-income ratio and a strong positive relationship between profitability growth and market capitalization.

## REFERENCES

Asch, P. (1967), "Industry Structure and Performance: Some Empirical Evidence" *Review of Social Economy,* Vol. 25, No. 2, September, pp. 167-182.

Blume, M.E. (1071), "On the Assessment of Risk" *Journal of Finance,* Vol. 26, No. 1, March, pp. 1-10.

Brealey R.A. and S.C. Myers (1988), *Principles of Corporate Finance,* 3rd ed., New York, McGraw-Hill.

Chen, N.R. Roll and S.A. Ross (1986), "Economic Forces and the Stock Market" *Journal of Business,* Vol. 59, No. 3, pp. 383-403.

Davidson, J. (2000), *Econometric Theory,* Oxford, Blackwell Publishers.

Fama, E.F., (1970), "Efficient Capital Markets: A Review of Theory and Empirical Work", *Journal of Finance,* Vol. 25, No. 2, May, pp. 383-417.

Fama, E.F., (1976), *Foundations of Finance,* New York, Basic Books.

Greene, W.H. (2000), *Econometric Analysis.* 4th ed. Englewood Cliffs, Prentice Hall.

Hayashi, M. (2000), *Econometric,* Princeton, N.J., Princeton University Press.

Hegazy, Z.S. (2002), *Structure and Performance of GCC Capital Markets,* Doha, National Center for Economic Research, UQ.

Martin, S. (1983), *Market,Firm and Economic Performance, An Empirical Analysis,* 2nd ed., Chicago, Rand McNally & Co.

Mittelhammer, R.C., G.G. Judge and D.J. Miller (2000), *Econometric Foundations,* Cambridge, Cambridge University Press.

Wood, W., and R. Porter (1979), *Analysis of Bank Financial Statements,* Van New York, Nostrand-Peinhold Company.

# 10

# Investment Preferences of Retail Equity Investors : An Empirical Study

*B.S. Bodla* and M.S. Turan***

## Backdrop

Individual investors occupy a prominent place in the economic development of a nation. Their savings and investment pattern needs considerable attention. Their role in serving as a major source of risk capital can hardly be overemphasized. Portfolio managers only shuffle around the holdings in existing scrips in their basket based on their subjective evaluation of various scrips, but do not inject much needed risk capital to upcoming enterprises to undertake new industrial activity (Gupta, R: 1998). Even foreign institutional investors (FIIs) generally bring capital in the country to acquire shares in existing profitable companies but do not provide risk capital to the corporate world.

Individuals invest their savings in different ways. The investment preferences in risky assets like equity shares is

* Department of Business Management, Guru Jambheshwar University, Hisar-125 001, Haryana, INDIA.
email : bsgju@yahoo.co.in

** Dean & Chairman, Faculty of Management Studies, Guru Jambheshwar University, Hisar-125001, Haryana, INDIA.

influenced by many factors, such as family size, number of earning members in the family, nature of family (nuclear/ joint), stages in life cycle, experience of investing, education level, family income size, nature of occupation, life styles and personality characteristics. The perception of the retail investors about risk and return of various investment alternatives has been the important issue for discussion and analysis in the subject of behavioural finance.

Because of the role played by retail equity investors in the development of stock market, the Finance Ministry, SEBI, capital market reformists, seminar/conference speakers, media commentators, all have been emphasizing on the need to bring them to the market back. Though, according to NSDL database, there has been an appreciable increase in the number of retail equity investors in 2003, net household savings and investment in shares and debentures are just 1.3 per cent in total savings (ET. 3 March 2004).

The study of retail equity investor, which is the only surplus sector of the economy, has implications for the financial development of the economy, fund managers, issuing companies and the marketers.

We have very little information on the profile of retail investors, not only on their sheer numbers, but also of their share in total number of trades and in total volume as also the frequency of trading. The data even on their population is misleading. According to the last SEBI-NCAER survey, there were 2.10 crore investors. However, the maximum number of active investors, as represented by the depository accounts, stands at a mere 48 lakhs and even the real number here would be lower as there are innumerable multiple/inactive accounts, says Haldea (Public Opinion, April 2004).

When we ask the CEO of a company how well he knows about the top 20 investors of his company, he could claim to spend enough time in knowing about them. But, what about small investors. The CEOs would probably fail to tell precisely about the preference and risk-perception of the small investors about their company. Certainly, the sketchy knowledge companies typically have about their investors contrasts strikingly with the close relationships they usually have with their customers. In case of established companies, the senior managers are very familiar with the needs and preferences of their leading clients. Indeed, these managers employ armies of researchers and national- account sales teams to investigate and explain the purchasing patterns of top customers (Kelvin et al: 2002). Managers make even minor decisions about product changes after conducting a detailed, quantitative analysis of their customers' likely reactions. We believe that managers need to adopt the same philosophy towards investors. However, the managers can try to have regular contact and relation with the big investors only. As the smaller investors are large in number and scattered over a large geographical area, it is not so easy for the managers to keep in regular touch with them. Accordingly, this puts the onus on the researchers and consultancy firms to conduct the detailed survey of investors.

In nutshell, without authentic data on retail participation in the equity market, the picture would continue to remain only hazy. This is dangerous not only because policies get vitiated but, because even a small loss to the large body of retail investors may cause unwarranted panic. It is time that data on retail investors is made public, and this should now be easy as all trades are now electronic.

This is under the above background that the present survey of retail equity investors has been conducted with the aim of analysing their investment-behaviour. More specifically, the study strives to achieve the following objectives:

- to prepare a profile of retail equity investors;
- to work out the amount of investment by retail investors in various instruments;

- to identify the order of preference given to various investment alternatives by the retail investors;
- to bring out the impact of demographic factors such as age and income on the investment behaviour of retail investors;
- to study the sector-wise, country-wise, industry-wise and period of investment wise preferences of individual investors; and

## Data and Methodology

The study is based on primary data, which have been collected through a detailed, well-designed questionnaire. The scope of the survey is limited to Delhi, Haryana and Chandigarh regions. A sample of 525 retail equity investors has been selected covering different age, income, experience and educational groups. To begin with, a list of retail investors (with full addresses) was prepared with the help of sub-brokers and brokers of various stock exchanges, operating in various cities of the area under study and then sample was selected by using simple random sampling technique. The survey was conducted from April 2003 to September 2003 through face-to-face interview method. The information has been collected only from those investing a part of their savings in equity shares and those willing to co-operate. For the present survey, anyone who is not an institutional investor (FIIs, mutual funds, etc.) is a retail investor.

The various statistical tools utilized herein include frequency tables, percentages, cumulative percentages, arithmetic mean, correlation coefficient and test of its significance, analysis of variance (ANOVA), scaling techniques and chi-square test. The data have been processed and analysed by using SPSS software.

An investor's investment in financial assets in general, and in risky assets in particular is exceedingly influenced, among other things, by their income size, stages in life cycle/ age, life styles and personality characteristics. Among these variables, age and income being the most important characteristics of sample (V. Rajarajan, 1998, Furquan Qumar-2003) have been considered as the basis for studying the investment preferences and behaviour of the retail equity investors.

## Results and Discussion

*Profile of Sample Investors* : A profile of sample investors is given in Table 1. The demographic features of the sample respondents clearly indicate that the retail equity investor in North India is a mature person (average age being 41 years approx.). A bit higher to one-third of them are in the age group of 36 to 46 and one-third are in their second stage of life (26 to 36 years). The majority of the retail investors belong to nuclear family. Around 69 per cent own inherited wealth. The sample is dominated by the middle income group households (Rs. 1.5 to 3.0 lakh) followed by low income group (37.14%) and the large income group (20.95%). While the average annual income of the sample is worked out as Rs. 2,34,163, average size of family is 4.7 person. Among the family members, major proportion (56.07 per cent) is of non-earning members.

### Table 1 : Profile of Sample Investors

**(A) Age Profile**

| *Stage of Life Cycle* | *Age Group (Years)* | *Frequency* | *Percent* | *Cumulative Percent* |
|---|---|---|---|---|
| I | Below 26 | 32 | 6.10 | 6.10 |
| II | 26-36 | 141 | 26.86 | 32.95 |
| III | 36-46 | 185 | 35.24 | 68.19 |
| IV | 46-56 | 103 | 19.62 | 87.81 |
| V | 56 and above | 64 | 12.19 | 100.00 |
| | Total | 525 | 100 | |
| | Average Age = 40.98 Years | | | |

*(Table Contd...)*

**Table 1 : (Contd...)**

**(B) Type of Family**

| Family | Frequency | Percent | Cumulative Percent |
|---|---|---|---|
| Joint | 180 | 34.29 | 34.29 |
| Nuclear | 345 | 65.71 | 100.00 |
| Total | 525 | 100.00 | 100.00 |

**(C) Investors with Inherited Wealth**

| | *Frequency* | *Percent* | *Cumulative Percent* |
|---|---|---|---|
| No | 161 | 30.67 | 30.67 |
| Yes | 364 | 69.33 | 100.00 |
| Total | 525 | 100.00 | 100.00 |

**(D) Income Profile**

| | *Income Group* | *Frequency* | *Percent* | *Cumulative Percent* |
|---|---|---|---|---|
| I | Below 1.5 Lakhs | 195 | 37.14 | 37.14 |
| II | 1.5-3.0 Lakhs | 220 | 41.90 | 79.05 |
| III | Above 3.0 Lakhs | 110 | 20.95 | 100.00 |
| | Total | 525 | 100.00 | 100.00 |
| | Average Income = Rs. 234163 | | | |

**(E) Earning Status of Family Members**

| | *Frequency* | *Percent* | *Cumulative Percent* | *Average no. per Household* |
|---|---|---|---|---|
| Earning Family Members | 1085 | 43.93 | 43.93 | 2.07 |
| Non-Earning Family Members | 1385 | 56.07 | 100.00 | 2.64 |
| Total | 2470 | 100.00 | 100.00 | 4.70 |

*(Table Contd...)*

**Table 1 : (Contd...)**

**F) Education Profile**

| *Education* | *Frequency* | *Percent* | *Cumulative Percent* |
|---|---|---|---|
| Matric | 40 | 7.62 | 7.62 |
| Graduate | 211 | 40.19 | 47.81 |
| Post Graduate | 149 | 28.38 | 76.19 |
| Any Other Professional Degree | 125 | 23.81 | 100.00 |

**G) Occupational Profile**

| *Prime Occupation* | *Frequency* | *Percent* | *Cumulative Percent* |
|---|---|---|---|
| Industry & Business | 145 | 27.62 | 27.62 |
| Agriculture | 35 | 6.67 | 34.29 |
| Salaried Class | 220 | 41.90 | 76.19 |
| Professional | 125 | 23.81 | 100.00 |
| Total | 525 | 100.00 | 100.00 |

**H) Investment Experience of Investors**

| *Years of Experience* | *Frequency* | *Percent* | *Cumulative Percent* |
|---|---|---|---|
| Below 2 | 155 | 29.52 | 29.52 |
| 2 to 6 | 125 | 23.81 | 53.33 |
| 6 to 10 | 105 | 20.00 | 73.33 |
| Above 10 | 140 | 26.67 | 100.00 |
| Total | 525 | 100.00 | 100.00 |

In terms of educational qualifications, the retail investors are placed satisfactorily as around 70 per cent of them are either graduate or post-graduate. The sample covers 41.90 per cent salaried investors, 23.81 professionals and 27.62 per cent businessmen. Agriculture is the primary occupation of only 6.67 per cent of the sample investors. Another point emerging from the under reference is that around 30 and 27 per cent of the retail investors are the new entrants and these belonging to the oldest group, respectively. The cumulative percentage shows that approximately 47 per cent of the investors are with long experience in the line. As high as 73.33 per cent have started investing in equity shares during the last one decade. This shows that SEBI and other regulators have somewhat succeeded in bringing back the retail investors to the equity market.

***Source of Acquiring Equity Shares :*** The retail equity investors can acquire the shares from two markets: primary market and secondary market. Table 2 exhibits that the retail equity investors have acquired around 26.02 per cent of their holdings by applying in the primary market and the rest 73.98 per cent through brokers from the secondary market. Thus, a major share of their equity investments comes through secondary market.

**Table 2 : Source of Acquiring Equity Share**

| *Source* | *No. of Observations* | *Average %age* | *Std. Deviation* |
|---|---|---|---|
| Primary Market | 525 | 26.02 | 32.64 |
| Secondary Market | 525 | 73.98 | 33.96 |

***Dematerialisation of Securities:*** Another important question asked from the sample investors encompasses the acceptability of dematerialisation of shares. It is evidenced by Table 3 that dematerialisation of securities has been happily accepted by the small investors. The percentage of those who have more than 75 per cent of their holdings in demat form is as high as 77.14 per cent. In contrast, only 12.38 per cent of the investors have less than half of their shareholdings in demat form. Those who still have 100 per cent of their holdings in physical form is merely 7.62 per cent. Thus, the doubts expressed about the success of dematerialisation have proved invalid in case of small investors category.

**Table 3 : Equity Holding in Demat Form**

| Range (%) | Frequency | Percent | Cumulative Percent |
|---|---|---|---|
| Nil | 40 | 7.62 | 7.62 |
| Upto 25 | 20 | 3.81 | 11.43 |
| 25 to 50 | 5 | 0.95 | 12.38 |
| 50 to 75 | 55 | 10.48 | 22.86 |
| 75 and Above | 405 | 77.14 | 100.00 |
| Total | 525 | 100 | 154.29 |

**Objectives of Investments:** Generally, the investment objective differs from person to person and one may invest with more than one objective in mind. However, we can classify the investors in various categories according to the prime objective of their investment, irrespective of the nature of investment. In the present study, the different investment objectives are classified as safety of investment, liquidity, regular income, capital gain and tax-saving. The respondents were asked to give points to the above objectives in order of their importance for them. The points were to be awarded in such a manner that total does not exceed 100 points. The responses obtained are organised in Tables 4 and 5 according to age-groups and income-groups, respectively.

Table 4 indicates that, at the overall level, the highest weight (26.66) is assigned to 'capital gain', followed by safety of investment (22.73). The objectives of maintaining liquidity and tax-savings are awarded the lowest points by the retail equity investors.

The analysis across the age-groups, concerning importance of various investment objectives, reveals no significant difference amongst the average points awarded to 'safety of investment'. But, the pattern of points assigned to the remaining objectives shows that their importance differs with the age. The importance of 'regular income' objective increases with the increase in age. In contrast, 'capital gain' objective loses its importance with the growing age of the investors. The tax-saving objective is given more importance by the middle income group investors. To determine the validity of the above conclusions, the analysis of variance (ANOVA) has been applied (Table 4 A). The F-values indicate clearly that there is significant variation across the different age-groups, in so far as the importance of various investment objectives, except 'safety of investment', is concerned.

**Table 4 : Age-wise Importance of Various Objectives of Investments in Terms of Weights**

| Objective | *Below 26 Years* | *26-36 Years* | *36-46 Years* | *46-56 Years* | *56 Years & above* | *Total* |
|---|---|---|---|---|---|---|
| | *Avg. Weight* | *Avg. Weight* | *Avg. Weight* | *Avg. Weight* | *Avg. Weight* | *Avg. Weight* |
| Safety of Investment | 24.09 | 20.92 | 20.49 | 23.08 | 25.08 | 22.73 |
| Liquidity | 18.13 | 18.00 | 10.20 | 16.50 | 17.34 | 16.03 |
| Regular Income | 12.97 | 12.48 | 16.80 | 18.53 | 29.53 | 18.06 |
| Capital Gain | 39.81 | 28.40 | 24.87 | 20.70 | 19.53 | 26.66 |
| Tax Saving | 5.00 | 20.20 | 27.64 | 21.19 | 8.52 | 16.51 |

**A. ANOVA**

| Objective | | Sum of Squares | df | Mean Square | F | Sig. |
|---|---|---|---|---|---|---|
| Safety of Investment | Between Groups | 2146.73 | 4.00 | 536.68 | 1.65 | 0.16 |
| | Within Groups | 168777.84 | 520.00 | 324.57 | | |
| | Total | 170924.57 | 524.00 | | | |
| Liquidity | Between Groups | 4755.33 | 4.00 | 1188.83 | 4.08 | 0.00 |
| | Within Groups | 151625.62 | 520.00 | 291.59 | | |
| | Total | 156380.95 | 524.00 | | | |

*(Table Contd...)*

**Table 4 : (Contd...)**

| | | | | | | |
|---|---|---|---|---|---|---|
| Regular Income | Between Groups | 5497.36 | 4.00 | 1374.34 | 3.03 | 0.02 |
| | Within Groups | 236069.31 | 520.00 | 453.98 | | |
| | Total | 241566.67 | 524.00 | | | |
| Capital Gain | Between Groups | 10576.62 | 4.00 | 2644.16 | 3.72 | 0.01 |
| | Within Groups | 369284.62 | 520.00 | 710.16 | | |
| | Total | 379861.24 | 524.00 | | | |
| Tax Saving | Between Groups | 4860.15 | 4.00 | 1215.04 | 3.91 | 0.01 |
| | Within Groups | 161625.62 | 520.00 | 310.82 | | |
| | Total | 166485.77 | 524.00 | | | |

After analysing the association between the age and investment objectives, we now turn to examine whether annual income of the investor has any bearing on the choice of objective of investment. Table 5 which discerns the average score awarded to various objectives by the investors belonging to various income groups, shows that 'safety of investment' obtains the highest score in case of low income group. Contrarily, 'capital gain objective' has got the highest score in case of both medium and high income groups.

**Table 5 : Income-wise Importance of Various Objectives of Investments in Terms of Weights**

| *Objective* | *Below 1.5 lakhs* | *1.5 to 3.0 lakhs* | *Above 3 lakhs* | *Total* |
|---|---|---|---|---|
| | *Avg. Weight* | *Avg. Weight* | *Avg. Weight* | *Avg. Weight* |
| Safety of Investment | 33.63 | 21.82 | 12.77 | 22.73 |
| Liquidity | 14.48 | 17.93 | 15.68 | 16.03 |
| Regular Income | 28.33 | 13.58 | 12.27 | 18.06 |
| Capital Gain | 18.51 | 25.33 | 36.14 | 26.66 |
| Tax Saving | 5.05 | 21.34 | 23.14 | 16.51 |

*(Table Contd...)*

**Table 5 : (Contd...)**

**A. ANOVA**

| *Objective* | | *Sum of Squares* | *df* | *Mean Square* | *F* | *Sig.* |
|---|---|---|---|---|---|---|
| Safety of Investment | Between Groups | 2214.70 | 2.00 | 1107.35 | 3.43 | 0.03 |
| | Within Groups | 168709.87 | 522.00 | 323.20 | | |
| | Total | 170924.57 | 524.00 | | | |
| Liquidity | Between Groups | 1214.65 | 2.00 | 607.32 | 2.57 | 0.08 |
| | Within Groups | 123166.30 | 522.00 | 235.95 | | |
| | Total | 156380.95 | 524.00 | | | |
| Regular Income | Between Groups | 7062.88 | 2.00 | 3531.44 | 7.86 | 0.00 |
| | Within Groups | 234503.79 | 522.00 | 449.24 | | |
| | Total | 241566.67 | 524.00 | | | |
| Capital Gain | Between Groups | 4490.13 | 2.00 | 2245.07 | 3.12 | 0.05 |
| | Within Groups | 375671.10 | 522.00 | 719.68 | | |
| | Total | 379861.24 | 524.00 | | | |
| Tax Saving | Between Groups | 3235.55 | 2.00 | 1617.78 | 5.47 | 0.00 |
| | Within Groups | 154166.30 | 522.00 | 295.34 | | |
| | Total | 157401.85 | 524.00 | | | |

While the average score shows a positive association with the income of investors in case of both capital gain and tax saving objectives, there is an inverse relationship between income and the objective of investment. To make an in-depth analysis, an attempt has been made to test the significance of income group wise variation by applying

ANOVA. The results of the tests also confirm the fact that the importance of various objectives of investing differs significantly across the income of the investors except one objective, i.e. liquidity.

***Time Horizon for Investments :*** Like institutional investors, retail investors can be differentiated in terms of time horizon and content. But here it is useful to add a third dimension: trading velocity. *Low velocity shareholders* hold shares for many years-often because they have inherited them or are using them for retirement investments. They are unlikely to buy, sell, or make any decisions unless forced to do so by the circumstances. At the other end of the spectrum, *day traders* are high-velocity traders who turnover entire portfolios every few days or weeks. The third, but most important group is the *event betters* who trade at a medium velocity, generally holding stocks for a few months or even a few years. The responses obtained during the present survey of retail equity investors concerning the time horizon of investment are presented through Tables 6 to 8.

It is obvious from Table 6 that, at the overall level, as high as 59.05 per cent of the respondents are in the category of medium velocity shareholders since they generally hold stocks for a few months or even a few years. Around one-fifth of the sample investors are high velocity or active investors and almost a similar proportion comprise low velocity investors. The high and low velocity investors are also known as *even betters* and *fundamental analysts*, respectively. The analysis across the various age-groups of the investors shows that the highest percentage of the investors, irrespective of age, hold the shares for few months or years. However, the percentage of those holding shares for many years is indicative of the positive association with age. Further, the hypothesis that there is no difference in the holding period amongst various age-groups stands rejected by chi-square test when applied at 1 per cent level of significance.

**Table 6 : Age-wise Analysis of Investor Preferences for Holding Period of Investments**

| *Holding Period* | *Below 26 Years* | *26-36 Years* | *36-46 Years* | *46-56 Years* | *56 Years and above* | *Total* |
|---|---|---|---|---|---|---|
| Few Days or weeks | 12 (37.50) | 18 (12.77) | 38 (20.54) | 37 (35.92) | 5 (7.81) | 110 (20.95) |
| Few Months or Years | 19 (59.38) | 104 (73.76) | 111 (60.00) | 44 (42.72) | 32 (50.00) | 310 (59.05) |
| Many Years | 1 (3.12) | 19 (13.47) | 36 (19.46) | 22 (21.36) | 27 (42.19) | 105 (20.00) |
| Total | 32 (100) | 141 (100) | 185 (100) | 103 (100) | 64 (100) | 525 (100) |

Chi-Square Tests

| | *Value* | *Df* | *Asymp. Sig. (2-sided)* |
|---|---|---|---|
| Pearson Chi-Square | 59.1657 | 8 | 0.00 |
| Likelihood Ratio | 58.0623 | 8 | 0.00 |
| N of Valid Cases | 525 | | |

0 cells (.0%) have expected count less than 5. The minimum expected count is 6.40.

*Note* : Figures in parentheses indicate percentages.

Table 7 presents the investors preferences for holding period of equity investments according to income-groups. In contrast to the age, income does not seem to have effect on the holding period as the pattern of time horizon is more or less similar in each group. This is also confirmed by the Pearson Chi-square test.

**Table 7 : Income-wise Analysis of Investor Preferences for Holding Period of Investments**

| *Holding Period* | *Below 1.5 Lakhs* | *1.5 -3.0 Lakhs* | *Above 3.0 Lakhs* | *Total* |
|---|---|---|---|---|
| Few Days or weeks | 45 (23.08) | 40 (18.18) | 25 (22.72) | 110 (20.95) |

*(Table Contd...)*

**Table 7 : (Contd...)**

| | | | | |
|---|---|---|---|---|
| Few Months or | 115 | 130 | 65 | 310 |
| Years | (58.97) | (59.09) | (59.09) | (59.05) |
| Many Years | 35 | 50 | 20 | 105 |
| | (17.95) | (22.73) | (18.18) | (20.00) |
| Total | 195 | 220 | 110 | 525 |
| | (100) | (100) | (100) | (100) |

Chi-Square Tests

| | *Value* | *df* | *Asymp. Sig. (2-sided)* |
|---|---|---|---|
| Pearson Chi-Square | 2.80 | 4 | 0.59 |
| Likelihood Ratio | 2.81 | 4 | 0.59 |

*Note :* Figures in parentheses indicate percentages.

But, the occupation of the investor plays an important role in determining the holding period preference. It can be seen from the Table 8 that the percentage of low velocity investors is lower among businessmen and professionals than those of salaried class and agriculturists. The percentage of medium velocity (i.e. few months or years) investors is the highest (71.42) in case of agriculturists followed by industry and business, professionals and salaried class. Chi-square test applied at 1 per cent level of significance rejects the hypothesis that occupation does not affect holding period.

**Table 8 : Occupation-wise Analysis of Investor Preferences for Holding Period of Investments**

| *Holding Period* | *Industry & Business* | *Agriculture* | *Salaried* | *Professional* | *Total* |
|---|---|---|---|---|---|
| Few Days | 30 | 0 | 50 | 30 | 110 |
| or weeks | (20.69) | (0.00) | (22.72) | (24.00) | (20.95) |
| Few Months | 90 | 25 | 119 | 76 | 310 |
| or Years | (62.07) | (71.42) | (54.09) | (60.80) | (59.05) |
| Many Years | 25 | 10 | 45 | 19 | 105 |

*(Table Contd...)*

**Table 8 : (Contd...)**

| | | | | | |
|---|---|---|---|---|---|
| | (17.24) | (28.57) | (23.18) | (15.20) | (20.00) |
| Total | 145 | 35 | 220 | 125 | 525 |
| (100) | (100) | (100) | (100) | (100) | |

Chi-Square Tests

| | *Value* | *df* | *Asymp. Sig. (2-sided)* |
|---|---|---|---|
| Pearson Chi-Square | 32.73 | 6 | 0.00 |
| Likelihood Ratio | 45.06 | 6 | 0.00 |

*Note* : Figures in parentheses indicate percentages.

***Instrument-wise Investment Preferences :*** Keeping in view the objective of identifying investment preferences of the retail equity investors, an enquiry was made to bring out the level of preference shown towards various financial investment alternatives. The survey results in this regard are presented and analysed across the securities selected for investment, income and age dimensions. Besides, the quantum of investments channelised in different instruments during last one year have been ascertained. While the instrument wise number of investors and magnitude of investments is shown in Table 9, the order of preferences according to instrument, age and income are brought out through Tables 10, 11 and 12, respectively.

About the investment pattern, it needs mention that our sample of 525 investors has been drawn from the population of those who have already gained some experience of investment in equity shares. Table 9, which reveals the number and percentage of the retail investors investing in various alternative instruments along with amount invested, offers the following points:

(a) 80.38 per cent invest in life insurance policies;

(b) 52.38 per cent invest in bank fixed deposits;

(c) 54.67 per cent invest in NSC/PPF and other saving schemes of post offices;

(d) 33.52 per cent invest in bonds/debentures;

(e) one-fifth invest in mutual funds;

(f) only 5.71 and 2.28 per cent invest in preference shares and derivatives respectively; and

(g) the average amount invested per investor in last one year is the highest in case of bank fixed deposits followed by equity shares and NSC/PPF/POS.

**Table 9 : Investment Alternatives Opted and Amount Invested in Last One Year by Sample Respondents**

| Investment Alternatives | No. of investors | %age of Investors | Average Amount Invested in Last One Year (Rs.) |
|---|---|---|---|
| Equity Shares | 525 | 100 | 34500 |
| Preference Shares | 30 | 5.71 | 2400 |
| Debentures / Bonds | 176 | 33.52 | 15000 |
| Derivatives | 12 | 2.28 | N.A. |
| Mutual Funds | 105 | 20.00 | 12500 |
| NSC / PPF / POS | 287 | 54.67 | 28400 |
| Bank FDs | 275 | 52.38 | 42500 |
| Life Insurance Policies | 422 | 80.38 | 21300 |

It is obvious from Table 10 that the retail equity investor has attached the highest importance to Blue Chip stocks. To be precise, 65.71 per cent of the sample investors attach high or very high preference to Blue Chip stocks. NSC/PPF/POS, the low risk alternatives, obtain second preference as around 45 per cent of the investors reveal high or very high preference towards them. The insurance policies, debentures/bonds and fixed deposit with banks enjoy high/very high preference in case of as many as 40, 36 and 33 per cent retail investors. The stocks of small companies and preference shares are the high/very high preference of merely 16 per cent investors. The table further shows that the financial derivatives are of very low preference and moderate preference for 62 and 25 per cent respondents, respectively.

**Table 10 : Preference for Various Investment Alternatives (%age)**

| *Investment Alternative* | *Very Low Pre-ference* | *Low Pre-ference* | *Moderate Pre-ference* | *High Pre ference* | *Very High Pre-ference* | *Total* |
|---|---|---|---|---|---|---|
| Blue Chip Stocks | 10.48 | 5.71 | 18.10 | 29.52 | 36.19 | 100.00 |
| Small Company Stocks | 29.52 | 25.71 | 28.57 | 12.38 | 3.81 | 100.00 |
| Preference Shares | 38.10 | 19.05 | 26.67 | 15.24 | 0.95 | 100.00 |
| Debentures/ Bonds | 17.14 | 14.29 | 32.38 | 32.38 | 3.81 | 100.00 |
| Stock Futures & Options | 40.00 | 21.90 | 24.76 | 8.57 | 4.76 | 100.00 |
| Mutual Funds | 12.38 | 26.67 | 37.14 | 19.05 | 4.76 | 100.00 |
| NSC / PPF/POS | 3.81 | 11.43 | 40.00 | 31.43 | 13.33 | 100.00 |
| Fixed Deposits | 12.38 | 20.00 | 34.29 | 26.67 | 6.67 | 100.00 |
| Insurance Policies | 4.76 | 18.10 | 37.14 | 26.67 | 13.33 | 100.00 |
| Real Estate | 28.57 | 31.43 | 11.43 | 16.19 | 12.38 | 100.00 |
| Gold / Silver | 28.57 | 40.00 | 13.33 | 11.43 | 6.67 | 100.00 |

The investment preference according to age structure of the retail equity investors (Table 11) also goes in accordance with the above analysis. Among the securities under reference, stocks of blue chip companies are most preferred, irrespective of age-group. While insurance policies turned the second high/highly preferred investment alternative in case of the investors below the age of 36 years, NSC/PPF/POS get top preference order in case of the investors above 36 years age. The coefficients of Karl Pearson's correlation clearly indicate that the preference for blue chip stocks declines with the increase in age, whereas vice-versa is obtained with respect to the preference of small company stocks. Similar to blue chip stock, the preference for insurance policies declines with the growing age. In contrast to the above, the preference for NSC/PPF, and real estate has increased with the increase in age.

**Table 11 : Investors Revealing High/Very High Preference Towards Various Investment Alternatives Across Different Age Groups (%age)**

| *Investment Alternative* | *Below 25 Years* | *26-36 Years* | *36-46 Years* | *46-56 Years* | *56 Years and above* | *Correlation (r)* | *Significance Level* |
|---|---|---|---|---|---|---|---|
| Blue Chip Stocks | 71.88 | 71.77 | 69.73 | 50.45 | 50.25 | -0.85 | 0.07 |
| Small Company Stocks | 6.25 | 17.73 | 15.14 | 11.65 | 28.13 | 0.75 | 0.14 |
| Preference Shares | 15.63 | 30.50 | 10.81 | 13.59 | 4.69 | -0.55 | 0.33 |
| Debentures / Bonds | 28.13 | 41.13 | 35.68 | 35.92 | 31.25 | 0.17 | 0.79 |
| Stock Futures & Options | 21.88 | 14.18 | 17.84 | 6.80 | 4.69 | -0.91 | 0.03 |
| Mutual Funds | 20.63 | 24.04 | 17.30 | 20.39 | 27.19 | 0.37 | 0.54 |
| NSC / PPF / POS | 30.00 | 38.30 | 42.70 | 49.51 | 54.69 | 1.00 | 0.00 |
| Fixed Deposits | 21.88 | 33.33 | 39.46 | 35.92 | 27.19 | 0.40 | 0.50 |
| Insurance Policies | 40.63 | 47.97 | 36.22 | 35.63 | 32.81 | -0.67 | 0.21 |
| Real Estate | 15.63 | 34.75 | 21.62 | 33.01 | 34.38 | 0.70 | 0.18 |
| Gold / Silver | 15.63 | 31.21 | 5.41 | 26.21 | 14.06 | -0.08 | 0.90 |

The pattern of preferences attached with various alternatives does not seem much different across the various income categories except the preferences for debentures/ bonds, and stock-futures and options. The values of correlation coefficients also confirm the above analysis (Table 12).

**Table 12 : Investors Revealing High/Very High Preference Towards Various Investment Alternatives Across Different Income Groups (%age)**

| *Investment Alternative* | *Below 1.5 lakhs* | *1.5-3.0 lakhs* | *Above 3.0 lakh* | *Correlation (r)* | *Significance Level* |
|---|---|---|---|---|---|
| Blue Chip Stocks | 58.97 | 72.73 | 63.64 | 0.33 | 0.78 |
| Small Company Stocks | 10.26 | 25.00 | 9.09 | -0.07 | 0.96 |
| Preference Shares | 15.38 | 15.91 | 18.18 | 0.94 | 0.22 |
| Debentures/ Bonds | 33.33 | 27.27 | 59.09 | 0.76 | 0.45 |
| Stock Futures & Options | 20.51 | 9.09 | 9.09 | -0.87 | 0.33 |
| Mutual Funds | 43.59 | 15.91 | 4.55 | -0.97 | 0.15 |
| NSC / PPF / POS | 46.15 | 45.45 | 40.91 | -0.92 | 0.25 |
| Fixed Deposits | 43.59 | 29.55 | 22.73 | -0.98 | 0.13 |
| Insurance Policies | 48.72 | 31.82 | 40.91 | -0.46 | 0.69 |
| Real Estate | 38.46 | 18.18 | 31.82 | -0.32 | 0.79 |
| Gold / Silver | 30.77 | 6.82 | 18.18 | -0.53 | 0.65 |

**Sectoral Preference:** Keeping in view the advent of private and public sectors simultaneously, it has been considered imperative to capture retail equity investors' sectoral preferences. The responses obtained in this regard are represented in Tables 13 and 14.

Table 13 which presents sectoral preference at the overall level and according to age-groups exhibits that the highest percentage (41.71%) of respondents have revealed equal preference both for public and private sector instruments, followed, with a wide margin by private sector (33.7%) and public sector (24.57%) preferences. This is averse to the general belief that the public sector securities enjoy investors' confidence in a much larger measure than do the private sector instruments/securities. It seems, therefore, that the increased emphasis on the concept of liberalised economy and privatisation of public enterprises have started to disenchant the investors from the public sector investments. The above finding is in contrast to the results of a primary survey of mutual fund investors seeking to bring out their sectoral preference. According to that study as high as 80 per cent of the mutual fund investors prefer public sector mutual fund schemes including those of UTI (Turan and Bodla, 2001). But, according to Rajas Kelker study (ET, Aug. 2002), institutional investors prefer to invest their funds in private sector securities while retail investors continue to hold a sizeable part of their investment with public sector funds/institutions/instruments.

**Table 13 : Age-wise Analysis of Sectoral Preference of Sample Investors**

| *Sector* | *Below 26 Years* | *26-36 Years* | *36-46 Years* | *46-56 Years* | *56 Years and above* | *Total* |
|---|---|---|---|---|---|---|
| Private Sector | 12 | 50 | 71 | 35 | 9 | 177 |
| | (37.5) | (35.71) | (38.38) | (33.98) | (14.06) | (33.72) |
| Public Sector | 5 | 29 | 45 | 20 | 30 | 129 |
| | (15.63) | (20.57) | (24.32) | (29.42) | (46.88) | (24.57) |
| Equally | 15 | 62 | 69 | 48 | 25 | 219 |
| Preferable | (46.87) | (43.72) | (37.30) | (40.60) | (39.06) | (41.71) |
| Total | 32 | 141 | 185 | 103 | 64 | 525 |

Chi-Square Tests

| | *Value* | *df* | *Asymp. Sig. (2-sided)* |
|---|---|---|---|
| Pearson Chi-Square | 34.63 | 8 | 0.00 |
| Likelihood Ratio | 38.71 | 8 | 0.00 |

*Note* : Figures in parentheses indicate percentages.

Age-wise analysis shows clearly that private sector investments are more preferred over public sector investments by the investors having age upto 46 years. On the other hand, the investors belonging to relatively older age-groups (i.e. above 46 years) are found to have their tilt towards public sector securities. The percentage of the investors showing equal preference for both public and private sector investments is slightly higher in first two age-groups. The application of Chi-square test at 100 per cent confidence level evidences that choice of sector for investment depends significantly on the age of investors.

The position obtained according to income groups, presented in Table 14, shows that the preference for private sector investments increases with the increase in income of the sample investor. Conversely, public sector preference is higher among low-income group. The percentage of those investors who have equal preference for both sectors is the highest (53.85%) among low-income investors followed by medium income and high-income groups. The above relationship has also been confirmed by the results of Chi-square test, which shows that choice of a sector regarding investment is by and large a function of income size.

**Table 14 : Income-wise Analysis of Sectoral Preference of Sample Investors**

| *Sector* | *Below 1.5 lakhs* | *1.5-3.0 lakhs* | *Above 3.0 lakh* | *Total* |
|---|---|---|---|---|
| Private Sector | 40 | 85 | 52 | 177 |
| | (20.51) | (38.64) | (47.27) | (33.71) |
| Public Sector | 50 | 55 | 24 | 129 |
| | (25.64) | (25.00) | (21.82) | (24.57) |
| Equally Preferable | 105 | 80 | 34 | 219 |
| | (53.85) | (36.36) | (30.91) | (41.71) |
| Total | 195 | 220 | 110 | 525 |

*(Table Contd...)*

**Table 14 : (Contd...)**

Chi-Square Tests

| | *Value* | *df* | *Asymp. Sig. (2-sided)* |
|---|---|---|---|
| Pearson Chi-Square | 25.04 | 4 | 0.00 |
| Likelihood Ratio | 26.39 | 4 | 0.00 |

*Note* : Figures in parentheses indicate percentages.

***Industry Preference:*** While conducting the survey, the respondents were asked to disclose their preference amongst fourteen broad industry groups on a five point scale, following the rule higher the rank, higher the preference. The mean rank and the overall ranking pattern according to age and income groups resulting from the survey are highlighted in Tables 15 and 16 respectively.

A glance through these tables offers a number of interesting points. First, communication/ computer/ electronics industry obtains the highest average rank at the overall level, followed closely by banking and insurance, pharmaceuticals and petroleum and gas industry groups. Second, electrical, textiles, chemicals and agro industries obtain the bottom four ranks (i.e. 14, 13, 12 and 11). Third, no significant variation is observed regarding industry preference across the various age groups. Fourth, while the first preference goes to pharma industry in case of lowest income group, banking and insurance industry claim the same in case of middle income group and petroleum and gas industries in case of highest income group. Thus, it is obvious that banking and insurance, petroleum and gas, and pharma industries have higher preference than others.

***Preference Among Asian Countries:*** Capital market liberalisation among emerging economies provides an opportunity to individual investors to invest in foreign markets also. Keeping this in view, the sample investors were asked to reveal their first preference amongst the select Asian countries. The responses so obtained are

**Table 15 : Age-wise Industry Preference of Sample Investors**

| *Industry* | *Below 26 Years* | | *26-36 Years* | | *36-46 Years* | | *46-56 Years and above* | | *56 Years* | | *Overall* | |
|---|---|---|---|---|---|---|---|---|---|---|---|---|
| | *Avg. Score* | *Rank-ing* | *Avg. Score* | *Rank-ing* | *Avg. Score* | *Rank-ing* | *Avg. Score* | *Rank-ing* | *Avg. Score* | *Rank ing* | *Avg. Score* | *Rank-ing* |
| Cement | 2.72 | 9 | 2.02 | 12 | 2.81 | 8 | 2.33 | 12 | 2.23 | 10 | 2.42 | 11 |
| Steel | 2.83 | 8 | 2.67 | 8 | 2.51 | 10 | 3.06 | 5 | 2.50 | 9 | 2.71 | 7 |
| Pharmaceutical | 3.29 | 4 | 3.83 | 1 | 3.25 | 3 | 2.91 | 8 | 3.52 | 4 | 3.36 | 3 |
| Textile/Garments | 1.43 | 13 | 2.29 | 9 | 1.82 | 14 | 2.41 | 11 | 1.73 | 13 | 1.94 | 13 |
| Chemicals | 1.69 | 12 | 2.81 | 6 | 3.15 | 5 | 2.72 | 10 | 1.81 | 12 | 2.44 | 10 |
| Fast Moving Consumer Goods | 3.00 | 5.5 | 3.49 | 2 | 2.98 | 6 | 2.94 | 7 | 2.95 | 6 | 3.07 | 6 |
| Agro Industries | 3.00 | 5.5 | 2.00 | 13.5 | 2.50 | 11 | 3.00 | 6 | 2.00 | 11 | 2.50 | 8 |
| Petroleum & Gas | 3.57 | 2 | 3.37 | 4 | 3.22 | 4 | 3.19 | 2 | 3.40 | 5 | 3.35 | 4 |
| Engineering | 2.50 | 11 | 2.22 | 10 | 2.08 | 12.5 | 3.10 | 4 | 2.54 | 7 | 2.49 | 9 |
| Comm./Computer Elect. Ent. | 2.89 | 7 | 3.42 | 3 | 3.63 | 1 | 3.58 | 1 | 3.90 | 1 | 3.48 | 1 |
| Electrical | 1.00 | 14 | 2.13 | 11 | 2.08 | 12.5 | 1.94 | 14 | 1.50 | 14 | 1.73 | 14 |
| Food & Beverages | 3.38 | 3 | 2.72 | 7 | 2.96 | 7 | 2.86 | 9 | 3.58 | 2 | 3.10 | 5 |
| Metal & Metal Products | 2.40 | 10 | 2.00 | 13.5 | 2.80 | 9 | 2.00 | 13 | 2.51 | 8 | 2.34 | 12 |
| Banking/Insurance | 3.92 | 1 | 3.12 | 5 | 3.62 | 2 | 3.17 | 3 | 3.46 | 3 | 3.46 | 2 |

exhibited in Tables 17 and 18 according to age-groups and income-groups respectively.

**Table 16 : Income-wise Industry Preference of Sample Investors**

| *Industry* | *Below 1.5 Lakhs* | | *1.5 -3.0 Lakhs* | | *Above 3.0 Lakhs* | |
|---|---|---|---|---|---|---|
| | *Avg. Score* | *Rank-ing* | *Avg. Score* | *Rank-ing* | *Avg. Score* | *Rank-ing* |
| Cement | 2.21 | 10 | 2.89 | 9 | 2.16 | 11 |
| Steel | 2.88 | 6 | 2.37 | 11 | 2.88 | 6 |
| Pharmaceutical | 3.74 | 1 | 3.19 | 5 | 3.15 | 4 |
| Textile/Garments | 2.10 | 12 | 2.14 | 13 | 2.00 | 13 |
| Chemicals | 2.00 | 13.5 | 3.00 | 6.5 | 3.14 | 5 |
| Fast Moving Consume Goods | 2.60 | 7 | 3.49 | 3 | 2.73 | 10 |
| Agro Industries | 2.20 | 11 | 2.50 | 10 | 2.80 | 9 |
| Petroleum & Gas | 3.30 | 4 | 3.44 | 4 | 3.72 | 1 |
| Engineering | 2.40 | 8 | 2.20 | 12 | 2.86 | 7 |
| Comm./Computer/ Elect. Ent. | 3.60 | 2 | 3.50 | 2 | 3.34 | 3 |
| Electrical | 2.36 | 9 | 1.83 | 14 | 2.00 | 14 |
| Food & Beverages | 3.50 | 3 | 2.96 | 8 | 2.84 | 8 |
| Metal & Metal Products | 2.00 | 13.5 | 3.00 | 6.5 | 2.02 | 12 |
| Banking/ Insurance | 3.28 | 5 | 3.70 | 1 | 3.40 | 2 |

Table 17 indicates that, at the overall level, the highest percentage (33.98) of the respondents gives first preference to India followed by China (20.39%), Japan (14.56%) and Hong Kong (13.59%). The lowest preference is revealed towards Taiwan and Pakistan. The above pattern of preference also holds true to a great extent when analysed across age and income of sample respondents. A glance at the table under reference offers that country preference does not vary with variation in age group. Analogously, the country specific preference does not seen depending on the income level (Table 18).

**Table 17 : Age-wise Preference Towards Asian Countries**

| *Country* | *Below 26 Years* | *26-36 Years* | *36-46 Years* | *46-56 Years* | *56 Years and above* | *Overall* |
|---|---|---|---|---|---|---|
| China | 7 | 33 | 35 | 20 | 10 | 105 |
| | (21.88) | (23.40) | (18.92) | (20.41) | (25.42) | (20.39) |
| Japan | 11 | 17 | 19 | 21 | 8 | 75 |
| | (34.38) | (12.06) | (10.27) | (21.43) | (13.56) | (14.56) |
| Hong Kong | 5 | 9 | 25 | 10 | 21 | 70 |
| | (15.63) | (6.38) | (13.51) | (10.20) | (35.59) | (13.59) |
| Taiwan | 0 | 5 | 0 | 0 | 0 | 5 |
| | (0.00) | (3.55) | (0.00) | (0.00) | (0.00) | (0.97) |
| Singapore | 0 | 25 | 15 | 20 | 5 | 65 |
| | (0.00) | (17.73) | (8.11) | (20.41) | (8.47) | (12.62) |
| India | 6 | 52 | 84 | 22 | 10 | 175 |
| | (18.75) | (36.88) | (45.41) | (22.45) | (16.95) | (33.98) |
| Pakistan | 3 | 0 | 7 | 5 | 5 | 20 |
| | (9.38) | (0.00) | (3.78) | (5.10) | (8.47) | (3.88) |
| Total | 32 | 141 | 185 | 98 | 59 | 515 |
| | (100) | (100) | (100) | (100) | (100) | (100) |

*Note* : Figures in parentheses indicate percentages.

**Table 18 : Income-wise Preference Towards Asian Countries**

| Country | Below 1.5 lakhs | 1.5-3.0 lakhs | Above 3.0 lakh | Total |
|---|---|---|---|---|
| China | 30 | 50 | 25 | 105 |
| | (15.38) | (23.81) | (22.73) | (20.39) |
| Japan | 35 | 17 | 23 | 75 |
| | (17.95) | (8.09) | (20.91) | (14.56) |
| Hong Kong | 25 | 35 | 10 | 70 |
| | (12.82) | (16.67) | (9.09) | (13.59) |
| Taiwan | 0 | 5 | 0 | 5 |
| | (0.00) | (2.38) | (0.00) | (0.97) |
| Singapore | 20 | 23 | 21 | 65 |
| | (10.26) | (10.95) | (19.09) | (12.62) |
| India | 75 | 70 | 30 | 175 |
| | (38.46) | (33.33) | (27.27) | (33.98) |

*(Table Contd...)*

**Table 18 : (Contd...)**

| | | | | |
|---|---|---|---|---|
| Pakistan | 10<br>(5.13) | 10<br>(4.76) | 0<br>(0.00) | 20<br>(3.88) |
| Total | 195<br>(100) | 210<br>(100) | 110<br>(100) | 515<br>(100) |

*Note* : Figures in parentheses indicate percentages.

## Conclusion

The demographic features of the sample respondents clearly indicate that the retail equity investor in North India is a mature person of 41 years age. The majority of them belong to nuclear family and middle income group. More than two-third of the retail investors are either graduate or postgraduate. More than 73 per cent of them started investing in equity shares during the last one decade. This shows that SEBI and other regulators have somewhat succeeded in bringing back the retail investors to the equity market.

Majority of the shareholdings of retail investors are in dematerialised form and a major share of them comes through secondary market. Among the retail investors, majority are in the category of medium velocity shareholders. The tendency to hold securities for many years is higher among the respondents in upper age-groups than their counterpart, the lower age-groups. Capital gain is found as the most important objective of investment followed, in down side, by safety of investment and regularity of income.

They have a heavier tilt towards the Blue Chip stocks. The companies belonging to new economy segment such as information technology, communication and computers obtained the highest rank followed closely by banking, insurance, pharmaceutical, and petroleum and gas industry groups. Contrarily, electric, textile, chemical and agro industries have turned least preferred sectors. In spite of phenomenal growth in equity market, the retail investors show higher preference towards less risky investments namely, PF, NSC, life insurance policies and FDs with public sector banks. Demographics like income and age are observed to have significant affect on choice of objective, industry and instrument of investment.

The retail investor has become a sort of a slogan that is raised in various quarters from time to time and this creature's extinction from the jungle of the stock markets is lamented. There is no need for this. There is really no need for retail investors to participate directly in the stock markets. Our opinion is that the retail investors should not enter the markets directly.

Mutual funds should be the preferred route for retail investors to participate in equities, but the study clearly suggests that this has not happened. Our survey reveals that merely 20 per cent of the retail equity investors put money in equity market through mutual funds. The same is also confirmed by official secondary data. In 2000, equity funds saw net inflows of Rs. 5,414 crore. In 2003 this number was just Rs. 2,103 crore, the two intervening years saw an outflow of Rs. 476 crore (2002). Compare this to the FIIs' inflow of Rs. 30,420 crore in 2003 (HT Businesses, Feb. 6, 2004). What is needed is more enthusiasm from the mutual funds to create an environment where equity investors come in through them for the long term.

In sum, it can be concluded from the results of the present study that the modern retail investor is a relatively mature and adequately groomed person. He is definitely participating in a big way in the primary market. A few more good IPOs may rekindle the interest of more retail investors. PSU divestment through the IPO route may in fact hold the key.

Retail investors are now being attracted to the market based on sentiments. Actually, a disturbing fact is the huge price rises that are not explainable easily by fundamentals are being attributed to sentiments. Hence, the retail investor might get caught in the herd mentality. This is evident in the huge price increase in scores of 'not-so-strong' as well as penny stocks, without any corresponding change in fundamentals. Data of BSE on increasing volumes in 'T' and 'Z' category stocks confirms this. Moreover, the political parties which are part and parcel of the ruling alliance needs to show an increased sense of responsibility and avoid irresponsible public statements on the subject of financial sector reforms. *Massacre on dalal street on* Monday, the 17th May, 2004 was mainly caused by irresponsible statements by community party politicians.

Clearly, the stock price rally in past more than a year has attracted many new retail investors. However, we still do not have a rich culture of long-term equity investing in this country. For this to happen we will also require long-term stability in terms of market regulation and governance so that a sustained equity culture is built based on fundamentals of economy.

## REFERENCES

Furqan Qumar (2003), "Saving Behaviour and Investment Preferences Among Average Urban Households", *The Indian Journal of Commerce,* Vol. 56, No. 1 (Jan.-March), pp. 36-49.

Gupta, Ramesh (1998), "Retail Investor-A lost species", *Chartered Secretary,* (August), pp. 164-167.

Kevin P. Coyne and Jonathan W. Witter (2002), "Taking the mystery out of Investor Behaviour", *Harward Business Review* (September), p. 73.

Madhusudan Karmakar (2001), "Investment Behaviour of Household Sector: A Study of a Rural Block in West Bengal", *Indian Journal of Commerce,* Vol. 54, No. 12.

Monthly Public Opinion Surveys, Vol. XLIX, No. 7, April, 2004, pp. 8-11.

Prasanna Chandra (2002), *Security Analysis and Portfolio Management,* Tata McGraw Hills, New Delhi.

Rajas Kelker, The Economic Times, Aug. 2002.

Sandeep Bamzai and Arun Kumar (2004), "Indian Homes' equity holding declining", *IIT Business,* 6th Feb.

The Economic Times, 18 May, 2004, p. 1.

The Economic Times, 3 March 2004, p. 7.

The Economic Times, Retail Investor Survey, Jan. 16, 2004.

Turan, M.S. and Bodla, B.S. (2001), *Performance of Mutual Funds in India,* Excel Books, New Delhi. www.hindustantimes.com/businesses.

# 11

# Cooperative Banking and Financial Sector Reforms in India

*Mohd. Izhar Ahmad**

## A Historical Perspective

The Indian cooperative movement, like its counterparts in other countries of the world has been essentially a child of distress. The Cooperative Societies Act of 1912 recognized the formation of non-credit societies and the central cooperative organizations. The state patronage to the cooperative movement continued even after 1947, the year in which India attained freedom. The independent India accepted the concept of planned economy and cooperative organizations were assigned an important role.

Since 1950s, the cooperatives in India have made remarkable progress in the various segments of Indian economy. During the last century, the cooperative movement has entered several sectors like credit, banking, production, processing, distribution/marketing, housing, warehousing, irrigation transport, textiles and even industries. In fact, dairy and sugar cooperatives have made India a major nation in the world with regard to milk

* Department of Economics, Aligarh Muslim University, Aligarh (U.P.) India. e-mail: izhar_eco@hotmail.com

and sugar production. Today, India can claim to have the largest network of cooperatives in the world numbering more than half a million, with a membership of more than 200 million. Of the primary (village) level cooperatives, around 28 per cent with 137 million memberships are agricultural cooperatives, dealing directly or indirectly with agricultural sector. The cooperative network in the country is rather strong covering all the villages in the country and more than 67 per cent of the households have been brought under the cooperative hold. Cooperatives supply about 46 per cent of the total rural credit (including agricultural credit), account for 36 per cent of the total distribution of fertilizers, produce about 55 per cent of the total sugar and constitute for 28 per cent of the rural fair shops.

Though cooperative movement has made remarkable progress in several areas, certain glaring defects have also developed in the movement, which have been, in a way, defeating the very objectives of these institutions. The following are the unique features of Indian cooperation movement.

1. Government and policy markets have paid more attention to agricultural cooperatives and thus, the growth and development of the India cooperative movement is heavily titled in favour agricultural cooperatives in general and in particular, credit cooperatives. In some areas like dairy, urban banking and sugar, the cooperatives have achieved success to an extent but there are larger areas where they have not been so successful.
2. The cooperative credit movement in modern India, curiously, is a state initiated movement. The state partnership is, perhaps, the unique feature of the Indian cooperative movement. Government contribution to the share capital of primary agricultural cooperatives accounts for about 7.5 per cent of the total.

3. The state partnership which was conceived as a measure for strengthening the cooperative institutions has paved the way for ever-increasing state control over cooperatives, their increasing officialization and politicization culminating in virtually depriving the cooperatives of their vitality as well as their democratic and autonomous character.
4. Dormant membership, lack of active participation of the members in the management, lack of professionalism, undue political and bureaucratic intervention, have made majority of the cooperatives at the primary level. This has resulted in weakening of the cooperatives. The upwardly transmission of the weaknesses of the primary societies have affected the capabilities of the higher level cooperative federations in so far as their usefulness to the former is concerned.
5. With regard to agricultural cooperative credit structure, although the quantitative expansion has been somewhat satisfactory, the movement continues to suffer from structural defects and operational deficiencies. The acknowledged operational deficiencies of the cooperative credit structure have been (i) weak recycling of credit, (ii) poor resource mobilization, (iii) ineffective lending and (iv) poor recovery.
6. The agricultural credit cooperative system in general has become rather over dependent on external support in terms of participation in share capital by Government and refinance from Government owned Financial Institutions.

## Cooperative Banking in India

Credit cooperatives are the oldest and most numerous of all the types of cooperatives in India. The cooperative credit institutions in the country may be broadly classified into urban credit cooperatives and rural credit cooperatives. Urban credit cooperatives societies constitute for about 10 per cent of the aggregate banking business and therefore regarded as an important segment of the banking system. The urban credit cooperatives are also popularly known as Urban Cooperative Banks.

The rural credit cooperatives may be further divided into short-term credit cooperative and long-term credit cooperatives. With regard to short-term credit cooperatives, at the grass-root level the Primary Agricultural Credit Societies (PACS) dealing directly with the individual borrowers. At the central level District Central Cooperative Banks (DCCB) function as a link between primary societies and State Cooperative Banks (SCB). It may be mentioned that DCCB and SCB are the federal cooperatives and thus the objective is to serve the member cooperatives. As against three-tier structure of short-term credit cooperatives, the long-term cooperative credit structure has two tiers in many states with Primary Cooperative Agriculture and Rural Development Banks (PCARDB) at the primary level and State Cooperative Agriculture and Rural Development Bank at the state level. However, some states in the country have unitary structure with state level cooperative operating with through their own branches and in one state an integrated structure prevails. Interestingly, under the Banking Regulation Act 1949, only State Cooperative Banks, District Central Cooperative Banks and select Urban Credit Cooperatives are qualified to be called as banks in the cooperative sector. In other words, only these banks are licensed to conduct full-fledged banking business.

## Financial Sector Reforms and Credit Cooperatives

The process of economic and financial sector reforms were initiated in 1991, as a step towards a broader process of international economic integration and globalization of financial markets. The objectives of the reform program have been to remove the structural constraints in the factor and product markets, allowing market forces to improve efficiency and ensuring outward orientation to the economy for bringing about a higher degree of integration of the Indian economy with the rest of the world. It may be mentioned that the structural reforms in the trade regime and industrial and financial policies have been given utmost priority in order to ensure macro-economic stability. A healthy financial system being the principal pre-requisite for the globalization process, the banking sector being an important component thereof came into sharper focus.

The financial system in India has built up a vast network of financial institutions and markets over time, and the sector is dominated by the banking sector which accounts for about two-thirds of the assets of the organized financial sector. The first phase of the current reform of the financial sector was initiated in 1992 based on the recommendations of the Committee on Financial System (CFS, 1992). The progress that has been made in a substantial, yet non-disruptive manner has given the confidence to launch what has been described as the second generation or second phase of reforms especially for the banking sector. The report of the Committee on Banking Sector Reforms (CBSR, 1998) provides a framework for the second phase of reforms in the banking system. The broad features of the on going banking reforms have been; gradual removal of pre-emptions (reduction in CRR and SLR), deregulation of interest rates, tightening of prudential standards, competition and transparency, improving the quality of supervision, partial removal of selective credit controls, assistance to banks in debt recovery and reforms in money and forex markets. This apart, needless to mention, the succinct objective of the banking sector reforms has been to improve the efficiency in the system by introducing an element of competition.

The extension of reforms, particularly prudential standards to cooperative banking institutions, an important component of the banking system was a natural corollary as the weaknesses in cooperative segment could pose risks. Though cooperative banks operate at the district and state level, the urgency and importance for extension of the reforms need hardly be emphasized keeping in view of their reach and scale of operations. Therefore, the banking sector reforms could be treated as complete only if it encompasses the cooperative segment, enabling the latter to function on sound lines at par with other banking institutions. Accordingly, prudential standards covering capital adequacy, income recognition, asset classification and provisioning norms were made applicable to cooperative banks in the phased manner. However, cooperative reforms encompassing legal and administrative aspects have not taken place in India. This is on account of multiplicity of controls. The impact of the extension of prudential standards to cooperative banks has resulted in an increased intervention by the regulator and the Government in the name of the financial regulation/supervision.

### Thematic Analyses

As far as the impact of reforms on the cooperative character of the cooperatives is concerned, be it in credit or non-credit segment, one may safely say that neither the policy makers nor the researchers have shown any serious interest. And this is particularly true in India. We are more concerned with the assessment and measurement of the impact of reforms on the performance of cooperatives using definite and quantifiable parameters. While the difficulties in examining the impact of reforms on the cooperative character of cooperatives are quite understandable, it does not mean the same cannot be attempted meaningfully. What is required perhaps is a normative analytical framework, which is different from the one usually used for capturing the impact of reforms on cooperatives.

Given the diversity that prevails today in the cooperative sector and the levels of reforms thereof, a general discussion on the impact of reforms on cooperative character would be almost impossible. For the sake of research, even if one attempt is made to evolve a conceptual framework of Urban Cooperative Banks (UCBs) in India against the backdrop of banking sector reforms. The analytical framework based on three basic assumptions:

(i) Banking sector reforms essentially refers to the guidelines/directions from the regulator and the Government during the last ten years.

(ii) Urban Cooperatives are more influenced by banking sector reforms in the short-run than other credit cooperatives.

(iii) Cooperative character of urban cooperative banks can be captured in terms of the adherence to cooperative principles.

## Urban Cooperative Banks in India

India inspired by the success of urban cooperative movement in Germany and Italy, in the early part of the last century, urban cooperative credit societies were organized on community basis and their lending operations were confined to meeting the consumption oriented credit needs of their members. Many urban cooperative banks, which were organized initially, were essentially credit societies but later converted themselves into urban cooperative banks. Interestingly, many urban cooperative credit societies, which were not engaged in any banking functions, also used the world Bank. There was no well-defined concept of urban cooperative bank till 1996, when banking laws (provisions of section 5 (CCV) of Banking Regulation Act 1949) were made applicable to cooperative banks. Accordingly, an urban cooperative bank was defined as a Primary Cooperative Bank other than a primary agricultural credit society; (i) the primary object of which is the transaction of banking business, (ii) the paid up share capital and reserves of which are not less than Rs. 1 lakh (01. Mn) and (iii) the by-laws of which do not permit admission of any other cooperative society as a member. The word primary is used to denote that the urban cooperative banks perform the role of a primary unit in a 3-tier cooperative credit structure. Following are the features of urban cooperative credit banks in India.

1. Urban cooperative banks are registered under Cooperation Societies Act of the respective state Governments. The Reserve Bank of India is the regulatory and supervisory authority for UCBs for their banking related operations.
2. The important feature of UCB structure is its heterogeneity. Nearly 50 per cent of the banks are unitary in nature (with single branch banking). Heterogeneity in their size is another facet of the UCB structure.
3. UCB structure is based on the needs of small men and micro credit sector. The average size of the loan also works out to be relatively low and an overwhelming segment of UCBs have been able to comply with the priority sector lending targets set by the central bank of the country.
4. Urban cooperative credit movement in general, and the number of UCBs in particular is concentrated in few states.
5. A noticeable feature of urban banking sector is its financial independence. Unlike the agricultural cooperative credit structure, the urban cooperative banks are not surviving on external assistance such as refinance support. In fact, UCBs have been supporting federal units (District Central Cooperative Banks and State Cooperative Banks) by keeping their surplus resources in the form of deposits.

## Reforms and Cooperative Banks

The reform measures as applicable to UCB sector may be classified into three broad categories.

First, while recognizing the differences between commercial and urban cooperative banks, a majority of the prudential norms introduced for commercial banks are being extended to UCBs, in a phased manner.

Second, policy initiatives have been introduced (through Monetary & Credit Policies) to contain the systemic risk emanating from cooperative sector.

Lastly, multiplicity of control has been recognized as an effective regulation and supervision. Although, the focal point of the reforms has been prudential norms, steps are also being initiated to professionalize the management and manpower of UCBs.

The influence of the reforms on the functioning as well as the cooperative character of UCBs is discussed below.

**Prudential Standards**

To begin with, in 1993, RBI introduced Income Recognition and Asset Classification Norms to UCBs. In 1995, the prudential exposure norms to single/group borrowers were also made applicable to them. Subsequently, in a phased time frame, the capital adequacy norms were also made applicable to UCBs. While the promotion of prudent financial practices has become a *since quo non* in the highly competitive globalized environment to safeguarding the financial health of the system, in particular of the UCB sector, it should not be forgotten that such standards were contrived essentially for commercial banks.

Although, the notion of a code of good practices is intuitively appealing, the temptation to prescribe universally valid model codes which do not allow for differences in institutional development, legislative frame work and more broadly, different stages of development must be avoided. To put it differently, while there is no dispute that UCBs should be subjected to prudential standards, it is not yet clear, whether the prudential standards prescribed for commercial banks would work without distorting the cooperative character of UCBs. For instance, capital is widely regarded as a measure of the risk taking ability of a financial intermediary and therefore, prescription of a minimum capital the urban cooperative bank mayseem to be justified from the viewpoint of ensuring stability n the financial system. If one looks at a cooperative credit society/bank, as a typical cooperative created on the basis self help and mutual help, then possibly the members may not be able to raise the required capital. It capital base is to be strengthened, as it is happening in India, these banks will have to start dealing with non-members or nominal members on a large scale and perhaps may have to shift from surplus to profit. The need to increase the deposit base as also to gainfully employ the funds generated have made it necessary to have a large number of customers who are not the members. It is worth mentioning that in India, urban cooperative banks though on par with commercial banks with regard to prudential standards, are not permitted to boost their capital base through sub-ordinate debts. Further, there are ceilings on the value individual share holdings have not been revised since long.

Secondly, in order to ensure the adherence to the prudential standards by cooperative credit societies/banks, the regulator's frequency of intervention increases thereby affecting the cooperative character. In this regard, in India regulator's intervention has indirectly infringed upon the functional autonomy covering areas like share-linkage, credit, investment, deposit and so on.

Thirdly, in the name of protecting the interests of the depositors are not only prudential standards are extended but even the professional content in the management committee of the urban cooperation credit societies/banks is also stipulated in India by the regulator/Government. While one cannot remain ignorant of the role of the Government in the promotion of and development of cooperation in India, prescribing the number and qualification of the nominee directors would not doubt impair the cooperative character.

Fourthly, the strict entry norms in terms of minimum capital, membership prescription as it prevails in India, prevents the birth of new credit cooperatives and constrain the existing societies in so far as the expansion is concerned.

Fifthly, with the introduction of same prudential standards the difference between urban credit cooperatives/banks and commercial banks get blurred and possibly, the former may have to progressively imbibe the character of the latter.

There could be several such dimensions as discussed above. Nonetheless, it appears that the benefits of the prudential standards to urban credit cooperatives/banks come at a cost. The cost, needless to mention, is the dilution in the cooperative character.

In view of the above discussion, four major issues are listed below which needs the consideration of the cooperative thinkers.

(a) How relevant are the prudential standards (norms of Basle Committee accepted and implemented by most countries) to cooperative credit societies/banks?

(b) In countries where prudential standards have been extended to urban credit societies/banks, whether desired result has been obtained? Could urban credit societies/banks adhere fully to prudential practices?

(c) What are the implications of extending prudential standards to urban credit societies/banks on their cooperative character?

(d) Is it possible to derive a set of prudential norms especially for urban credit cooperative societies/ banks from the Basle Standards?

## Professional Management and Governance

Good corporate governance is critical to efficient functioning of an entity and more so for a banking entity. Thus, the need for professional management and healthy governance practices in urban credit cooperative societies/ banks in the present competitive environment needs no emphasis. Thus, for managing a financial intermediary, whether a cooperative or a commercial bank (irrespective of its size), the human resource comprising of paid staff and elected management has to be highly competent. The framework for good governance and professional management in cooperative sector should essentially emanate from the guiding principles and the given legal framework in different countries. However, in India it is not uncommon that the cooperative banks are superseded and

Government officials are posted to head or nominated on the board and unfortunately this trend is increasing in the post reform period. Quite often the reason quoted is that there is lack of qualified and competent directors and the protection of depositors. Interests (majority of them are not the members) in the case of urban cooperative banks. While this is to some extent true, the solution to this problem certainly is not Government intervention, as it would seriously impair the cooperative character. It is disheartening to note that the elected management of 41% of State Cooperative Banks, 37 % of State Cooperative Agricultural and Rural Development Banks, 21% of the District Central Cooperative Banks and 8% of Primary Cooperative Agricultural and Rural Development Banks stood superseded as on March 2000. More than 200 urban cooperative banks are identified as weak/sick banks by the regulator as at the end of March 2002.

As per the prevailing act (and according to the cooperative philosophy/principles) and individual member can get himself/herself elected to the management committee of a cooperative bank. It is this management committee which is entrusted with the responsibilities like risk management-policy/strategy, credit and NPA management investment management, marketing plan/ strategy, Asset-Liability Management and so on. It should also be noted that the very concept of banking (financial inter-mediation) is undergoing change in the present competitive environment and the conventional framework for management with which cooperative banks are comfortable may not be sufficient. Given this, it is doubtful whether the elected management (as per the existing provisions of cooperative act and principles the individuals without sufficient knowledge/experience in financial markets or management can be at the helm of affairs of a cooperative bank) would be able to take on the emerging challenges. Perhaps, the need is to ensure that in cooperative organizations, the system of governance including the size and composition of the board of directors is driven by the purpose and objectives of the business.

## Supervision and Regulation

At present in India, urban credit cooperative/banks are subjected to duality of control, meaning that the administration related aspects are being supervised and regulated by State Government and the banking operations are supervised and regulated by the central bank of the country. This has, understandably resulted in overlapping jurisdiction of the state Government and the central bank of the country. Moreover, a clear-cut demarcation of the financial and administrative areas for regulation is almost impossible and even if it is possible it surely acts as an impediment in effective supervision. While the central bank of the country has the wherewithal under the Banking Regulation Act for dealing with crucial aspects of functioning of commercial banks, in the case of co-operative banks it requires the number of urban credit cooperatives/banks, the central bank of the country is not in a position to effectively supervising them. Thus, the duality of control not only affects the quality of supervision and regulations, but also the functioning of the urban cooperative banking sector. Needless to mention, under this regime of duality of control the urban cooperative banks may turn out to be neither cooperatives nor commercial banks.

## Conclusion

The progress of the cooperative movement in India in general, and the cooperative banking in particular has been rather appreciable, the movement can not be termed as a vibrant one in regard to cooperative values and philosophy of cooperative principles. With regard to the extension of reforms to cooperative banking segment, it is yet not clear as to whether the same would ensure soundness and stability in the cooperative banking segment. It must not be forgotten that the notion of a code of good practices though intuitively appealing, the temptation to prescribe universally valid model codes which do not allow for differences in institutional development, legislative framework and more broadly, different stages of development must be avoided. It seems the extension of reforms/prudential standards to urban cooperative banking has provided substantial scope for the external intervention and in the process, affecting the cooperative character in terms of adherence to the cooperative principles. Logically, if the prudential standards, and supervision and regulation for cooperative banks were same as that of commercial banks, then there would not be any difference worth mentioning between these entities.

## REFERENCES

Ramesha K. (1996), Self-Help Groups: Emerging Cooperatives, paper presented at the National Seminar on Rediscovering Cooperation, November 19-21, 1996. Paper subsequently published in Rajagopalan R edited Rediscovering Cooperation (Volume II), Institute of Rural Management Anand, 1996.

Ramesha K. (2001), Monetary and Credit Policy 2001-2002: Implications for Urban Cooperative Banking Sector, paper presented at Seminar on New Policy of RBI and Cooperative Credit Management, July 19, 2001, Department of Economics, Shivaji University, Kolhapur, India.

Ramesha K. (2001), Credit Risk Management in Agricultural Cooperative Banks, National Seminar on Cooperative Reforms, January 24-25, 2001, National Bank for Agriculture and Rural Development and Vaikunth Mehta National Institute of Cooperative Management, Pune, India

Reserve Bank of India (2002), Report on Trend and Progress of Banking in India 2001-2002, RBI, Mumbai.

Reserve Bank of India (1989), Report of the Agricultural Credit Review Committee, RBI, Mumbai.

Reserve Bank of India (1999), Report of the High Power Committee on Urban Cooperative Banks, RBI, Mumbai.

Reserve Bank of India (1991), Report of the Committee on Financial System, RBI, Mumbai.

Government of India (1998), Report of the Committee on Banking Sector Reforms, RBI, Mumbai.

Acharya, S. (2001), "India's Macroeconomic Management in the Nineties", Discussion Paper, India Council for Research in International Economic Relations, New Delhi.

Bajaj, R., Chairman, (1977), *Draft code on corporate governance,* Confederation of Indian Industry.

Barua, S.K., V. Raghunathan, J.R. Varma and N. Venkiteswaran (1994), "Analysis of the Indian Security Industry: Market for Debt", *Vikalpa,* 19 (3), pp. 3-22.

12

# Financial Risk Management in China: The Roles of Derivatives and Some Implications for Multinational Corporations

*Steven Li*, Simon S. Gao** and Jane Zhang****

## Introduction

Derivatives debacles have provided some of the past decade's most devastating headlines. Names such as Long Term Capital Management (LTC), Orange Country and Baring Brothers bring to mind where derivatives failed—often miserably. Several losses were enormous—an estimated $2 billion for Orange Country and $4 billion for LTC. Other incident resulted in highly publicized lawsuits between derivatives buyers and sellers, such as Procter & Gamble's lengthy dispute with Bankers Trust (see e.g., Dowd, 1998).

These well-published disasters had intensified the ongoing debate about risk management practice and the use of derivatives (e.g., Bauer and Ryser, 2004; Guay and

* School of Economics & Finance, Queensland University of Technology, Brisbane QLD4001, Australia, Email: s.li@qut.edu.au

** School of Accounting & Economics, Napier University Business School, Edinburgh, EH 11 4BN, UK, Email: s.gao@napier.ac.uk

***Sunderland Business School, University of Sunderland, St. Peter's Way Sunderland SR6 0DD, UK, Email: jane.zhang@sunderland.ac.uk

Kothari, 2003, Bodnar et al., 2003; Allayannis and Weston, 2001; Brown, 2001; Hentschel and Kothari, 2001; Guay, 1999). Consequently, many risk control measures and concepts such as "Value-at-Risk" (see, e.g. Chance, 2001) and corporate risk management strategies (see, Yu, 2002; Noy and Ellis, 2003; Theil and Ferguson, 2003) were introduced to prevent such disasters. In the mean time, these disasters due to the misuse of derivatives can also offer great lessons for the financial risk management of corporations.

In this paper, we are concerned with China's derivatives markets and their implications for the financial risk management of multinational corporations (MNCs) in China. A multinational corporation is a business firm incorporated in one country that has production and sales operations in several market and financial capital from another, producing goods with labour and capital equipment in a third country, and selling the finished product in yet other national markets. Indeed, some MNCs have operations in dozens of different countries. MNCs obtain financing from major money centres around the world in many different currencies to finance their operations. Global operations force the treasurer's office to establish international banking relationships, place short-term funds in several currency denominations, and effectively manage foreign exchange risk (Eun and Resnick, 2001).

The number of MNCs has grown steadily in the past decade. According to a UN report, there are about 60,000 MNCs in the world with over 50000 foreign affiliates (Eun and Resnick, 2001). Throughout the 1990s, foreign direct investments by MNCs grew at the annual rate of about 10 per cent. In addition to international trade, foreign direct investment by MNCs is a major force driving globalization of the world economy.

Since the end of the Cultural Revolution in China in 1978, economic reforms have moved the Chinese economy from a centrally planned, socialist model to socialist market economy. State-owned, collective, private and foreign firms now co-exist and compete with each other. China has successfully joined the WTO in 2001. Since the reform and opening up of China in the world, many MNCs have been attracted to China. China is now on the track to be fully merged into the global economy after its WTO entry.

However, the Chinese financial markets, especial the derivatives markets are still at a developing stage. The general financial circumstances in China are also very different from the West. All these imply that the MNCs in China could face enormous challenges in their financial risk management. On the other hand, publications of financial risk management in China are very limited, as far as we know. This paper reviews the status of China's financial and derivatives markets. We attempt to shed some light on the financial risk management of MNCs in China.

## Derivatives Markets and Their Roles

Derivatives markets have grown enormously in the past several decades. According to the Bank of International Settlement, at the end of 1998, the notional principle of outstanding of financial derivatives approached $88 trillion. In comparison, gross domestic product in the United States in 1999 was about $9 trillion (cf. Chance, 2001). Derivatives markets contribute to the development of the financial infrastructure of a country by providing the links among cash markets, hedgers, and speculators. At the corporate level, there has been a tremendous proliferation in the use of derivatives as a type of investment instrument or as a risk exposure management tool in recent years (Chen, 2003).

A wide variety of derivatives products exist in both the exchange traded and OTC markets. The different types of derivatives include options, forwards, futures, options on futures, swaps and hybrids. The number of hybrids is growing rapidly as a result of the financial innovation. The process of creating new financial products is sometimes referred as financial engineering.

It is widely accepted (e.g., Chen, 2003; Guay and Kothari, 2003) that the primary function of the derivatives market is to facilitate the transfer of risk among economic agents by offering mechanisms for liquidity and price discovery. In a well-designed derivatives market resources are efficiently allocated and risk sharing arrangements are optimal. For further discussions regarding to the future trends and challenges of financial risk management, we refer to Li (2002).

Financial innovation has significantly expanded the range of investment alternatives for investors of all types. There are essentially four roles that derivatives can play for investors (see e.g. Collins and Faozii, 1999):

- To modify the risk characteristics of an investment portfolio
- To enhance the expected return of a portfolio.
- To reduce transaction costs associated with managing a portfolio.
- To circumvent regulatory obstacles.

Though derivatives markets perform the same function, organizational arrangements necessary to perform this function are not the same across markets. In a recent study by Tsetsekos and Varnagis (1997), it is found that most of the older exchanges started with commodity derivatives (mainly agricultural commodities), newer exchanges first introduce financial derivative products. They also claim that higher potential for success have derivatives based on a domestic stock index, followed by derivatives based on local interest rates and currencies. Their research also supports the proposition developed by Merton and Bodie (1995): while the performance of core functions in the financial system are the same across time and place, the institutional arrangement are not.

In fact, van der Bijl (1996) claim that derivatives markets in emerging economies have developed via a variety of different routes. One source of the key difficulties in the developments of derivatives markets across emerging economies is due to poor infrastructure, particularly in clearing and settlement.

Derivatives are highly efficient instruments that can be used to manage risk. Nonetheless, part of this price people pay for such instruments is that they are highly leveraged and can be easily misused. Since every derivative generates a gain that is matched by a loss on the other side of the transaction, someone must lose the money. In some cases, those losses have been large and surprising to those who incurred the losses. Large losses tend to make for good headlines (cf. Chance, 2001).

## The Chinese Financial System and Derivatives Markets

### *Types of investment in China*

To assess China's domestic capital market, let us think about the limited options facing an individual saver. How can an individual saver deploy his or her savings? There are currently about five options:

- Invest in the equity (A shares) of some of the state owned enterprises (SOEs) listed on the Shanghai and Shenzhen stock exchanges;
- Deposit money with a state-owned bank and earn a moderate interest rate;
- Invest in government bonds;
- Purchase a life insurance contract;
- Purchase a home, usually with the help of a loan from a bank.

Viewed from the demand side, there is a vast array of investment opportunities in China seeking capital. But savings will not flow to them unless radical steps are taken to open the market (see Greenwood, 2001).

By definition, a derivative product is based on an underlying asset or variable such as stock index. Thus derivative market is closely linked to stock market and debt markets. For example, it is impossible to have a very efficient derivative market based on an inefficient stock market. On the other hand, an efficient derivative market would also enhance the efficiency of a stock market. Thus, to assess the future development of China's derivative market, one would also need to assess the equity and stock markets of China.

*The Equity Markets*

In the past decade, China's stock market capitalization and daily turnover has grown from nothing to 5 trillion RMB (609 billion U.S. dollars) and 25 trillion RMB (3 trillion U.S. dollars) respectively in March 2001, making the Chinese stock markets the third largest in Asia after Tokyo and Hong Kong. Table 1 below shows China's share offering from 1987-1998.

**Table 1 : China's Shares Offering from 1987-1998**

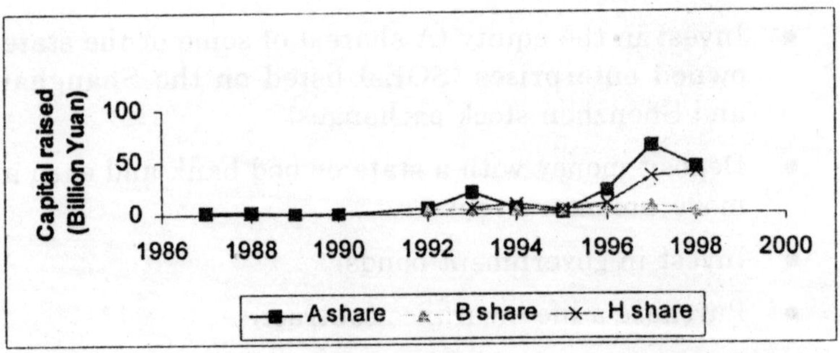


*Source :* China Securities Regulatory Commission (CSRC).

From the early days of the economic reform in the 1980s until the recent past, the stock exchange were viewed as a supplementary way for SOEs to raise funds. The SOEs were deemed the desirable model of future growth and development of conglomerates, based on the chaebols of South Korea. The listed SOEs were viewed as the major vehicles for raising capital and generating output, but being largely state-owned they have run into huge problems of bad governance, which is turn has meant large-scale misallocation of capital and wasted output.

China's progress in its economic reform as it affects the listed equity markets can be categorized into four main stages. Stage 1 was characterized by FDI in the coastal regions and later in the special economic zones (SEZs) by compatriot investors, primarily from Hong Kong and Taiwan. Later, joint ventures were started and wholly-owned investments were made by investors from developed countries such as Japan, USA, and European countries, Stage 2 in the development of equity markets was the flotation of A shares in Shanghai and Shenzhen to raise funds from the domestic market, and B share to raise funds from overseas. Stage 3 saw the listing of H shares in Hong Kong and N shares in New York. By and large, the performance of companies and shares on these markets was with few exceptions, a major disappointment.

Stage 4 will see a series of privatizations (listings) that is planned for some of China's major strategic industries. What will exact happen remain to be seen. For further discussion, see Greenwood (2001).

The key factors in developing equity markets anywhere in the world are liquidity and transparency. China's current equity market is no exception. Because there are two sets of listings (A and B shares) on the equity market, China's markets have effectively split the available liquidity and have created valuation distortions between the markets. Due to the lack of proper regulations, China's stock markets still suffer significantly from the transparency problem of trading. To attract large amount of capital from more quality markets, further reforms would be needed to eradicate these problems.

### *The Debt Market*

The debt markets in China are principally the markets for bank loans and central and provincial government debts. The corporate bond market remains virtually undeveloped. Since the start of issuing debts in 1981, China's debt market, though still underdeveloped, is playing an increasingly important role in the national economy.

Debt is not only an abundant source of funds for the growth of China's economy, but an important part of the fiscal policy used by the central authorities to exercise macro-control. The Chinese government has adopted a pro-active fiscal policy for four conservative years to meet the needs of the economy. Following the issuing of 100 billion RMB (12 billion U.S. dollars) of long-term debts for infrastructure development in 1998, the government issued 110 billion RMB (13 billion U.S. dollars) in 1999, 150 billion RMB (18 billion U.S. dollars) in 2000 and 2001 respectively. The pro-active fiscal policy has played an important role in the economic restructuring, deflation control, and maintenance of the sustainable rapid and robust growth of the economy.

Like banks elsewhere in Asia, China's banks have made loans to companies (mainly SOEs) that now cannot be repaid. Half of these non-performing loans on the books of banks have been placed in the hands of asset management companies (AMCs). However, the success of these reforms remains to be seen.

There is virtually no notable corporate bond market and no present opportunities for investors that might represent substantial returns. The current bond market is highly inefficient. To further develop China's debt market, more diversified investment instruments need to be introduced and some interest rate deregulation may be needed.

### *The Futures Market*

China's futures market originated from Henan Province's Zhengzhou grain wholesale market in 1990, with ups and downs since then, but it appears to be now on track to a steady and healthy growth. This momentum should be maintained.

After 10 years of development, China's futures market has played an important part in setting price standards, shedding risks and distributing resources in China's economy. As a growing economy, China has many products that lead the world in output. It should engage itself more actively in the pricing of products in the international market, instead of passively accepting prices formulated in the international market. Therefore, it should accelerate the development of the futures market and actively participate in futures transactions in the international market. Its participate will make pricing more accurate, which can truly reflect the supply and demand of certain products. In particular, the futures market can provide an efficient and effective mechanism for the management of price risks. Its establishment will help domestic enterprises, especially those whose products are victims of drastic price changes in the overseas market, have a clearer judge of price trends.

China has the second largest soybean and copper futures markets in Dalian, Northeast China's Liaoning Province and Shanghai respectively. But its futures markets for others products have not fared so well. The overall futures transaction volume in the domestic market is very poor, standing at only about 3 trillion Yuan (US$360 billion).

The varieties of traded commodities, especially those vital for the national economy, need to be amplified. Some commodities such as steel, rice, cotton and petroleum were once traded in the market, but were banned for market disorder. The trading of those products should be resumed with enhanced management and supervision. Financial futures should also be launched to help stabilize the financial market. As finance becomes more and more important in the national economy, financial futures are expected to play a larger role in the economy than the commodity futures will.

China's financial market has grown rapidly and internal risks increase accordingly. Meanwhile, the increased financial exchanges with overseas markets bring higher risks to the domestic market. The launch of stock indices futures will provide an instrument for investors to prevent risks.

Besides, there are more and more open-ended funds in domestic market. They will outnumber close-ended funds in the future. Without stock indices futures, the open-ended funds will loose money when the stock prices go down. Therefore, China should re-establish the stock indices futures market and resume the treasury bond futures market, which is the requirement of a market mechanism. According to some recent reports, the Shanghai Futures Exchange has applied to the China Securities Regulatory Commission to open a stock index futures market. Besides stock index futures, the Shanghai futures exchange is also considering other derivatives, such as interest rate futures and foreign exchange rate futures. Shanghai is aiming to be one of the major derivatives markets in the Asia Pacific region.

However, there are some obstacles to the launch of the futures market in China. A majority of people have little understanding of the significance of the market and even resent it. So the relevant laws and regulations should be strictly enforced to ensure a healthy market. People's resentment comes mainly from market irregularities. The immaturity of China's market-oriental economy is another obstacle.

*The Options Market*

Currently, there is virtually no options market in China. But the situation would not last long. The entry to the WTO will enable many foreign financial institutions to enter into the Chinese market. These institutions will bring their know-how and financial expertise into China. Thus the demand for options and more complicated hybrid securities will lead to the establishment of options markets in China.

*Financial Reform in China*

To meet the needs of its economic development, China has been reforming its financial system in recent years. A detailed analysis of China's financial reform and comparison with that of Vietnam can be found in O'Connor (2000). Jingu (2002) addresses the perspective of the China's capital market reform after China joins the WTO.

The first set of the banking sector reforms began in China in the early 1980s, when the government created four specialized banks separate from the central bank the People's Bank of China (the PBC). Since the banks acted as virtual monopoly lenders to their respective sectors, the main area of competition was in attracting depositors. On the one hand, the banks did not expect to be held accountable for bad loans, while on the other local branches expected to retain a share of any profit generated; both facts have encouraged excessive risk-taking, contributing to a sharp deteriorations in asset quality and contributed to inflationary credit expansion (O'Connor, 2000).

In late 1993, China initiated a second phase of financial reforms with the aims of transforming the specialized state bank into genuine commercial entities, thus reducing systemic risk by strengthening the regulatory supervision of the PBC and its capacity to conduct effective monetary policy. Since early 1998, China has begun to tackle in earnest the massive non-performing loan (NPL) problem of the state-owned commercial banks (SOCBs). The acceleration of the financial sector reform has been stimulated in part by the bid for and eventual entry to the WTO. One of the key measures taken is the debt-equity swaps with the target of SOEs. By mid-2000, the four AMCs were expected by government authorities to have concluded some 600 debt-equity swap agreement worth more than RMB400 billion. In theory, this places the onus on AMC management to take a hand in engineering the financial turn arounds for those SOEs, but in practice, they have taken equity stakes without actually taking control of the businesses (O'Connor 2000).

After China's WTO entry, the Chinese economy expects to be more closely integrated into the worldwide economy. At the same time, Chinese enterprises will be forced to compete under the global standards. Since 2000, China has been moving forward solving various problems in its capital market, as a well-functioning capital market will strengthen China's industries and enterprises. China will soon become an important capital market for international companies to raise and place funds.

In a keynote speech, Chao (2002) has outlined five great trends of change in China's financial market:

- China's banking system and the NPL problem.
- The growth of China's equity market.
- Diversification of investors and investment instruments.
- Cross-border capital flows.
- WTO and foreign financial institutions in China.

In summary, China's capital markets have made great progress in recent years, and now attract the attention of investors worldwide. China has reached the point where it cannot revert to the past or halt the globalization of its economy. Therefore reforms in the capital markets, which can leverage other reform plans, are expected to continue to move forward at the current rapid pace. Yet virtually every aspect of the financial markets, from the equity markets to the debt markets, has a long way to go before they will compel international investors to commit significant amount of capital.

## Financial Risk Management and MNCS in China

### *Financial Risk Management of MNCS is Advanced Markets*

All businesses face two types of risks: business risks and financial risks (Hunter and Smith, 2002; Froot et al., 1993). Business risks are related to the underlying nature of the business and deals with such matter as uncertainty sales or the cost of inputs, while financial risks are associated with the uncertainty of such factors as interest rate, exchange rates, stock prices, and commodity prices. In coping with growing financial risks, various derivatives have been developed in the past twenty years and they are now widely used (Guay and Kothari, 2003). For example, Grant and Marshall (1997) found that derivatives like swaps, forwards and options were widely used among large UK companies and the primary reasons were to manage interest rate and currency risk.

Although foreign exchange risk is one of the many business risks faced by MNCs, its management has become one of the key factors in overall financial management. Marshall (2000) surveyed foreign exchange risk management in large MNCs in the United Kingdom, the United States, and Asia Pacific, investigating their use of derivatives and their emphasis on different types of currency risks. He found that the most popular risk management tool was the over-the-counter forward contract. Exchange traded derivatives were less popular.

There are various ways of organizing a risk management department. A primary consideration in establishing the appropriate risk management structure goals is the extent to which the functions should be centralized. There are two extremes—fully centralized and fully decentralized. In a study by Lee et al. (2001), the practice of financial risk management is addressed through an international comparison. It is shown that the vast majority of MNCs in the UK, USA and the Asia Pacific organize themselves on a centralized basis. Furthermore, it was claimed that there were differences internationally in the concerns in choosing derivatives, driven to some extent by differences in the accounting treatment internationally. A recent study by Bodnar et al. (2003) documents several differences in the firms' uses and attitudes towards derivatives between the USA and the Netherlands, and these differences attribute to the differences in the institutional environments of these countries.

*Financial Risks Faced by MNCs in China*

Given the special market conditions in China, MNCs in China face considerable financial risks. First of all, as in the developed economy, MNCs in China face considerable foreign exchange risks. Though the Chinese RMB is pegged to the US$, but the pegging rate can be adjusted by the government from time to time. The rates between RMB and other major currencies fluctuate constantly. The pressure to the Chinese government to appreciate the value of RMB could add additional uncertainty to foreign exchanges.

There are three main types of foreign exchange exposure of MNCs in China as in other countries: transaction, operating (or economic), and accounting (or translation) (Shapiro, 1998). The transaction exposure measures changes in the value of outstanding financial obligations incurred prior to change in exchange rates but not due to settled until after the exchange rates change. Thus it deals with changes in cash flows that result from existing contractual obligations. Operating exposure, measures the changes in the present value of the firm resulting from any change in future operating cash flows of the firm caused by an unexpected change in exchange rates. Accounting exposure, also called translation exposure, is the potential for accounting-derived changes in owner's equity to occur because of the need to translate foreign currency financial statements of foreign affiliates into a reporting currency for worldwide consolidated financial statements.

Many MNCs also face the commodity price risks. For example, a car manufacturer faces the risk of steel price, which may be closely linked to the international market steel price.

*Some Thoughts for the Financial Risk Management of MNCs in China*

Firms can adopt several attitudes with respect to risk: avoid risk, limit risk, diversify risk, transfer risk, manage risk itself and insure risk. Here we are concerned with the management of risks. Managing risk does not necessarily mean eliminating risks. Firms can decide which risks are part of their core activities and should be retained, and which ones should be transferred or insured to third parties. Through financial engineering, risks can be unbundled and reallocated in a highly calibrated manner among people that are interested in bearing them. Nevertheless, it is important to recall the law of the "conservation of risk": financial engineering (derivatives) does not alter the underlying risk. The risk remains present, but in someone else's hands.

Due to the underdeveloped status of the derivatives markets, many hedges that are standard in developed economies may not be possible in China. However, given the relatively stable exchange rates between US$ and RMB, the US$ can be used as a substitute for hedging the short-term foreign exchange risk exposures of MNCs in China.

China's futures markets are now reasonably well established. Thus many commodity price risks may be hedged or cross-hedged by using the futures contracts available in the futures exchanges in China. Alternatively, one can also use futures contract available in the US to hedge the commodity price risk exposures given the pegged RMB.

For the time being, managing financial risks is difficult for many MNCs in China due to the lack of many derivatives products, on both exchange traded and over the counter markets. After China's WTO entry, the financial industry is changing fast and an efficient derivatives market will likely emerge in the near future. Thus the financial risk management practice of MNCs in China will soon be similar to the practice in countries where there are well-developed financial markets.

## Conclusion

As China's economic reform deepens, there will be a strong need for a complete derivatives market in China. Eventually China would need to become a leading financial centre as China's economy becomes more and more important in the world economy. As part of the financial system, derivatives markets are especially important in risk management for firms, investors and individuals. It is argued that a well-established derivatives market would be beneficial to the financial risk management of MNCs in China, given the current status of the capital markets and the derivatives market. At the present, it is difficult for many MNCs to manage their financial risks including foreign exchange exposures because of the underdeveloped derivatives markets in China. However, it also needs some cautions when China develops its derivatives market. The complexity of derivatives products and transactions along with potentially inherent risks would require such a development to be step-by-step and properly regulated.

## REFERENCES

Allyannis, Y. & Weston, J. (2001), The use of foreign currency derivatives and firm market value, *Review of Financial Studies,* Vol. 14, pp. 243-276.

Bauer, W. & Ryser, M. (2004), Risk Management Strategies for Banks. *Journal of Banking & Finance,* Vol. 28, pp. 331-352.

Bodnar, G.M., Jong, A.D. & Macrae, V. (2003), The impact of institutional differences on derivatives usage; a comparative study of US and Dutch firms. *European Financial Management,* Vol. 9 (3), pp. 271-297.

Brown, G. (2001), Managing foreign exchange risk with derivatives, *Journal of Financial Economics,* Vol. 60, pp. 401-448.

Chance, D.M. (2001), An introduction to derivatives and risk management, 5th edition, *Harcourt.*

Chao, H. (2002), Five great trends of change in Change in China's financial markets, keynote speech at *Asia Society Conference,* May 9.

Chen, R.S. (2003), Accounting practices for interest rate swap derivatives, *Journal of American Academy of Business,* Vol. 2(2), pp. 339-342.

Collins B.M. & Fabozzi, F.J. (1999), Derivatives and risk management, *Journal of Portfolio management,* pp. 16-27.

Dowd, K. (1998), *Beyond value at risk,* John Wiley & Sons.

Eun, C.S. & Resnick, B.G. (2001), International Financial Management, McGraw-Hill.

Froot, K.A., Scharfstein, D.S. & Stein, J.C. (1993), Risk management: coordinating corporate investment and financing policies. *Journal of Finance,* Vol. 48, pp. 1629-1658.

Grant, K. & Marshall, A.P. (1997), Large UK companies and derivatives. *European Financial Management,* 3 (2), pp. 191-08.

Greenwood J. (2001), The impact of China's WTO accession on capital freedom, *Cato Journal,* Vol. 21, No. 1, pp. 91-100.

Guay, W. (1999), The impact of derivatives on firm risk; an empirical examination of new derivatives users. *Journal of Accounting & Economics,* Vol. 26, pp. 319-351.

Guay, W. & Kothari, S.P. (2003), How much do firms hedge with derivatives? *Journal of Financial Economics,* Vol. 70, pp. 423-461.

Hentschel, L. & Kothari, S. (2001), Are corporations reducing or taking risks with derivatives? *Journal of Financial and Quantitative Analysis,* Vol. 36, pp. 93-116.

Hunter, W.C. and Smith, S.D. (2002), Risk management in the global economy: a review essay. *Journal of Banking & Finance,* Vol. 26, pp. 205-221.

Jailvand, A., Switzer, J. & Tang, C. (2000), A Global perspective on the use of derivatives for corporate risk management decisions, *Management Finance,* Vol. 26, No. 3, pp. 29-38.

Jingu, T. (2002), Moving forward in reforming China's capital market, *NRI papers,* No. 40, January.

Lee, F.M., Marshall, A., Szto, Y.K. & Tang, J. (2001), The Practice of financial Risk Management: An International Comparison, Thunderbird International Business Review, Vol. 43 (3), pp. 365-375.

Li, S. (2002), Future trend and challenges of financial risk management in the digital economy, *Management Finance,* Vol. 29, 5/6, pp. 111-125.

Marshall A.P. (2000), Foreign exchange risk management in the UK, USA and Asia Pacific Multinational Companies. Journal of Multinational Financial Management, 10(1), pp. 185-11.

Merton, R. & Bodie, Z. (1995), The global financial system: A functional perspective. *Harvard Business School Press.*

Noy, E. & Ellis S. (2003), Corporate risk strategy: does it vary across business activities? *European Management Journal,* Vol. 21(1), pp. 119-128.

O'Connor, D. (2000), Financial sector reform in China and Vietnam: a comparative perspective, *Comparative Economic Studies,* XLII, No.4, pp. 45-66.

Philips, A.L. (1995), Derivatives practices and instrument survey. *Financial Management,* 24, pp. 115-15.

Shapiro, A.C. (1998), Foundations of multinational financial management. Englewood Cliffs, NJ, Prentice Hall Inc.

Theil, M. & Ferguson, W.L. (2003), Risk management as a process: an international perspective. *Review of Business,* Vol. 24(3), pp. 30-35.

Tsetsekos G., & Varangis P. (2000), Lessons in structuring derivatives exchanges, *The World Bank Research Observer,* Vol. 15, No. 1, pp. 85-98.

Van der Bijl, R. (1996), Exchange traded derivatives in emerging markets: an overview, Technical report, IFC, Washington.

Yu, L. (2002), Risk management in practice, *MIT Sloon Management Review,* Vol. 44 (1), pp. 9-10.

# 13

# A Study on the Impacts of Globalization on Financial Markets-A Global Approach

*S. Vijayakumar** and *N. Namasivayam***

## Introduction

Every country is depending the other for one reason or another, because no country in the world is self-sufficient with its requirements fully met. As a result, countries having surplus resources exporting and the needy country importing the goods and services. Each country in the world realizes that it cannot depend on its internal trade. What is applied to goods and services, is equally applicable to transfer of capital from one country to another for investment purposes. India is not an exception to these trends. It cannot remain in isolation, especially after signing the "World Trade Organisation Treaty" (WTO). It has liberalized its economy from the year 1991. It has brought in lot of reforms in financial markets. These reforms not only activated Indian financial markets and also permitted foreign financial institutions to participate in Indian capital and money markets.

* Lecture Department of Commerce, M.K.U. College, Madurai-625002.

** Prof. & Head Department of Commerce, DDE Madurai Kamaraj University, Madurai-625021.

## Impacts on Financial Markets

The following are the major impacts of globalisation in the financial markets. They are:

## Availability of Huge Amount of Capital

Most of the Indian industries are always starved of capital and also paucity of funds. Their own investment as well as financial assistance from both commercial and development banks are found to be inadequate. But the process of globalisation permits movement of capital from one country to another country.

## Raising of Capital Directly in Foreign Countries

The industries in the course of doing business, need foreign currencies especially dollars for the purpose of importing materials, machineries, etc. The globalisation process have brought the investors in different countries under one roof as the whole world now becomes one global village. In India, many big business houses, raise dollars directly by way of issuing Global Deposit Receipt (GDR) instead of depending on some of the development banks.

## Profit Advantage

International business could be more profitable than domestic. Some companies earn even more than 100 per cent profit through foreign markets. International business enables the firm to achieve optimum capacity utilization on economies of scale. Foreign investment motivates to reduce cost of production by taking the advantage of the cheaper labour.

## Opportunities for Growth

The enormous growth potential of many foreign markets is a very strong attraction for foreign companies. Due to globalisation, developing countries and the newly industrializing countries grow much faster than developed countries.

## Domestic Market Constraints

Many countries expand markets beyond the national border due to domestic demand constraints. The market for a number of products have ended to saturate or decline in the advanced countries. This after happens when the market potential has been almost fully tapped. The technological advances have increased the size of the optimum scale of operation substantially in many industries making it necessary to have foreign markets, in addition to the domestic market to take advantages of the large scale economies.

## Expansion of Financial Markets

Financial institutions can have wide markets as they can operate in any part of the world. If they operate within a particular country, their growth will become stagnant at one stage. Thus globalisation permits them to increase their level of operations further and further.

## Low Cost of Capital

As the financial institutions are many the size of the financial markets is very wide. Such wide markets facilitate the industrial houses to procure the required capital at low cost and without any delay.

## Self Development

Globalisation was detrimental to some countries and profitable to others and that some fundamental changes needed to be made in existing accords and perspectives to deal with this problem. The developing countries must enhance their capacity to develop their economy, science and technology and financial markets. After all, their development will depend on continuously strengthening their capacity of self development.

## Possibility of Ethical Developments

Due to competition in the financial markets, there is a possibility of ethical developments within the financial markets in turn enhancing their good services to members.

**Other Benefits**

1. Competitions have become a driving force behind internationalisation.
2. Government policies and regulations also motivate internationalisation.
3. There are both positive and negative factors which could cause globalisation.
4. International business improves domestic business and the image of any company.
5. Foreign exchange earnings enable to import capital goods, technology, etc.

## Conclusion

Indian International business has been confined only to exports. The new economic policy of India is expected to encourage the internationalization of Indian business. Constant increase in domestic competition compels companies to pursue globalisation vigorously. The liberalisation expands foreign markets.

## REFERENCES

Liberal Times, Vol.VIII, 2000, Published by Friederich Naumann – Stiftung – Regional Office, New Delhi.

Maria John, Financial Markets and Institutions, Paramount Publication, Palani, Tamil Nadu.

# 14

# Financial Sector Reforms and Primary Agriculture Co-operative Credit Societies in India

*J.P. Bhosale*, H.D. Thorat***
*and Anil C. Bhavsar****

## Introduction

Indian agriculture has a vital stake in the success of co-operative movement because there is no better or more responsive and cost effective credit system than the co-operative to service the ever growing and diversifying needs of agriculture. The co-operative credit system, though federal in its organizational structure, is functional responsibilities of various components of the system.

Primary Agriculture Credit Societies as economic institution play a very important role at the grass roots level in the development of local areas.

* Co-ordinator Faculty of Commerce Arts, Commerce & Science College, Narayangaon Tal: Junnar, Dist : Pune, Maharashtra, India.

** Reader in Commerce Mahatma Phule College, Pimpri-Pune, Dist : Pune, Maharashtra, India.

*** ChairmanB.O.S. In Co-operation & Rural Development, Pune University, Pune, Maharashtra, India.

They are not only multipurpose organizations catering to the needs of diverse sections of society, but they are also multi functional organizations performing a host of activities like banking, input supplies, marketing produce and trading in consumer goods.

Hence effective performance of PACS would be crucial for satisfying the needs of mambas in particular and the needs of the general public in their respective area in general.

Success of a co-operative is dependent on sub-factors such as self-reliance, optimal development of available funds extent of member satisfaction & patronage and economic viability.

Agriculture sector needs finances, short-term, medium-term and long-term to get better production both in items of quantity and quality. Primary agricultural Co-operative societies are set up for financing the short-term and medium-term needs of the farmers. The basic purpose to encourage Co-operatives in agricultural share was to get rid of the exploitation or farmers by indigenous bankers or money leaders who charge high rate of interest and takes various types of charges in money as well as in kind from farmers.

Farmers need finances for purchasing high yield varieties of seeds, fertilizers, pesticides and agricultural implements. These agricultural inputs are also made available through Co-operative societies which are functioning at Gram Panchayat level.

Primary agricultural Co-operative societies are set up under the Co-operative Act and their members get the limited finance from these societies in the month of June–July every years so that are able to purchase the various inputs to be used in agricultural sector.

The primary Co-operative societies provide short-term finance to the farmers. They very back-bone of our economy is agricultural sector which should be developed on strong and efficient lines.

## Objectives of Primary Agriculture—Co-operative Credit Societies

The main objectives of Raiffeisen Model Societies were as under:

1. To borrow funds from members or to be utilized for loans to members for

   Loans to members for useful purpose:
2. To act as the agent for the joint purchase of the agricultural, domestic and other requirements of its members and for joint sale of their produce;
3. To purchase and own implements, machinery or animals for hire to its members;
4. To disseminate knowledge of the latest improvements in agricultural, handicrafts and weaving and encourage its member to adopt them; and
5. Generally to encourage thrift, self help and Co-operation among the members.

Subsequently, higher financing institution such as central

Co-operative banks at the district level and state Co-operative banks at the state level were also organized with a view to provide financial support and guidance to village primaries organized on the raiffeisen Model. Thus the three-tier Co-operative agricultural credit structure was brought in to existence for the institutionalizing farm credit.

## Functions of Primary Agriculture Co-operative Credit Societies

In pursuance of the above-mentioned objective of improving agricultural yields and aiding production, the service/primary agricultural co-operatives have to perform the following functions:

1. To arrange the supply of farm requirements, such as improved seeds, fertilizers and insecticides. Societies

should also stock for sale small implements such as sickles, grass-reapers, pick-axes, ploughs, chaff-cutters and other small improved implements which are generally required by every farmer. For procuring these implements societies the may establish a link with some industrial society.

2. To provide short-term credit required for the purchase of farm requirements and also medium-term loans for agricultural purpose such as reclamation of land, sinking of ordinary wells, purchase of bullocks and carts, etc.
3. To maintain the supply on hire light agricultural machinery. The range of this machinery will depend upon local requirements subject to which the society may possess such things as plant protection equipment like sprayers and dusters, incubators threshers, winnowers and cane crashers.
4. To provide household requirements. It is not intend that the societies should open full-fledged general stores. Only essential commodities in short supply such as sugar, kerosene oil, food grains, etc, may be stocked for distribution.
5. To raise funds for meeting the above mentioned requirements mainly by catering to the saving of members.

The functions of including the habits of thrift and saving among members are very important in order to make the people as much self-sufficient as possible.

The functions entrusted to service societies were, to a certain extent, being performed by the earlier credit for short an medium terms; they were at places, supplying farm and household requirements also and the encouragement of deposits from members had been one of their important objectives. The difference, however, lies mainly in the emphasis. The credit societies had a much simple task to perform. They mostly confined their activity to the grant of loans. Other functions, if at all performed, received a secondary attention and seldom were the two-credit and production programmers of the farmers-linked together. In the service co-operatives, the center of gravity has shifted from the counter in the society's office to the fields of the Cultivators. Increase in production rather than the mere removal of indebtedness is the core of the problems to be solved by them. The objectives of these new types of societies are thus circumscribed by a more dynamic philosophy, which revolves round the field of the cultivator and the overall problem of low yields and farming inadequacies.

In pursuance of the above objectives the societies should assess the farming needs and take measures to fulfill them. So far as possible the societies should even create demands for better seed, more fertilizers, better implements, etc., by educating the people about their advantages. Further, it is the duty of the society to propagate the best method of using the fertilizers and provide farm guidance service.

## Role of Primary Agricultural Co-operative Credit Societies

The primary agricultural credit societies (PACSs) are providing vital credit support along with a variety of service to the farming community for quite along. Their coverage extrendent to remotest part of the district. They have been playing a very signification role in marking institutional credit accessible to farmers since the beginning of the co-operative movement. Even today they continue play a lending role in the sphere of production finance, despite the very strong presence of the Commercial banks which have now come to acquire pre-eminence in the rural areas with there vastly larger resources. Nevertheless, while recognizing the role played by the co-operative to the cause of the agricultural community, one cannot remain oblivious of their functional drawbacks which might in course of time prove fatal to them in a severely competitive environment.

## Progress of Primary Agricultural Co-operative Credit Societies

**Table 1**

| S. No. | Year | 1951-52 | 1960-61 | 1971-72 | 1981-82 | 1991-92 | 1995-96 | 2000-01 |
|---|---|---|---|---|---|---|---|---|
| 1 | No. of Societies/ Bank (,000) | 108 | 212 | 157 | 94 | 83 | 93 | 100 |
| 2 | Membership (,000) | 48 | 170 | 32009 | 60999 | 86759 | 96600 | 10000 |
| 3 | Deposit (Rs.Crore) | 4 | 15 | 75 | 314 | 1605 | 3604 | 13431 |
| 4 | Loans outstanding (Rs.Crore) | 34 | 218 | 858 | 2966 | 7539 | 14246 | 34522 |

*Source:* RBI: Report of the all India rural credit review committee (1969)

*RBI* : Report on trend and progress of banking in India 2000-2001.

Above Table presents data pertaining the progress of PACCSs in the country during the period 1951-52 to 2000-01.

The data shows that the number of PACCSs which stood at 2.12 lakh in 1960-61, was 94 thousand in 1981-82 was further roused to 100 thousand in 2000-01. The membership in these societies steadily increased in the country from 32009 thousand in 1971-72, to 86759 thousand in 1991-92 and to 10,000 thousand in 2000-2001.

This steady increase in the number of membership and decrease in the number of societies are on account of the policy of the government of recognizing the primary agricultural credit societies on a strong and viable basis. The deposits increased from Rs. 314 crore in 1981-82 to

Rs. 3604 crore in 1995-96 and huge increment to Rs. 13,481 crore in 2000-01. The outstanding loans advanced by the societies recorded an increase from Rs. 7539 core in 1991-92 to Rs. 34522 crore in 2000-01.

## Problems before Primary Co-operative Credit Societies in Globalized Regime

Primary Agriculture Co-operative societies which are meant for the upliftment of the poor present who are lacking short-term and medium-term finance suffer from the following problems:

1. The PACs have paucity of funds. They hardly fulfill the short-term and medium term need of farmers in our and medium. It adversely affect the input needs of the farmers.
2. Outside leadership is the very basis of these societies. Outside leaders do not know the problems of the members. They always exploit its members for their political motives.
3. Most of the members in these societies belong to the so called progressive farmers and the small as well as marginal farmers are given their representation in these societies. It has led to the inequalities of income and wealth even in rural areas, which is against the very objective of our five year plans.
4. Lack of well – educated and well trained employees is another problem face with these societies. It leads to inefficient functioning of the societies. Timely supervision and inspection of the societies do not take place to political inference and efficient supervision and inspecting officials.
5. The offices of the government appointed for inspecting these societies and recovery of loans from the farmers do not take human relations approach in dealing with the officials and members of the societies.

6. Employees engaged in these societies are paid low salary and other fringe benefits which adversely affect their efficiency and there is no incentive fir renderings their services. Low salary also force them to involve themselves in the messes of the government funds and taking bribes from farmers while disbursing and recovering the loans.
7. Delay in the disbursement of loans by these societies to the farmers. The farmers who are to be benefited by these societies can not plan about the purchase of HYV, pesticides, fertilizers and other inputs of agriculture. The finances are not utilized to the maximum extent due to delay in the disbursement.
8. Rich farmers also become the members of these societies and they use sanctioned amount for exploiting the small and poor farmers by sharing high rate or interest. It has encouraged all the evils of money.

**Financial Problems of Co-operative Societies**

Almost all co-operative societies in the country, whether Agricultural or non agricultural, whether old or new whether located in urban or rural areas have been in financial crisis of various degrees. The crisis will continue unabated for some time at least in the near future.

The crisis of co-operative societies generally faced like lack of professional management, weak base of financial resources, co-operative laws and taxation laws does not conductive to the growth of co-operative sector etc. In fact was no clear-cut policy perspective for various segments of the co-operative sector.

The crisis faced by overall co-operative sector. Out of these some of the crisis are also experienced in NACCS. In regards to heir business, are as follows:

1. Cut throat competition.
2. Lack of training in banking, accounting, co-operative law for directors and employees.

3. High rate of bad debts.
4. In adequate finances.
5. Improper planning and forecasting.
6. Lack of proper Assets mgt.
7. Lack of proper and Regular Auditing system.
8. Inadequate recovery of loans.

## Measures for Problems Faced by Primary Agriculture Credit Co-operative Societies

The following remedial measures can be used for solving the various problems faced with these primary agricultural Co-operative societies in our money.

1. The funds of the primary Agricultural Co-operative societies should be augmented raising the institutional, membership increasing the share of the state and central government in the finance of these societies so that the medium and short-term needs can be met.
2. The leadership of these societies should be from with in society. Farmers should be given membership and the official of these societies should be restricted through the amendment in the co-operative societies active.
3. The membership in these societies should be given to small and marginal farmers in the majority of cases and rest should be allotted to the progressive or rich farmers. The Registrar of Co-operative societies should see this in practice.
4. Educational qualifications should be revised while recruiting and selecting the different categories of personal in these societies. They should also be imparted training while in service and refresher should also be introduced for the better functioning of these societies.
5. Government officers who are directly related with the functional of these societies should adopt human

relations approach while dealing with the sanction, disbursement and recovery of loans.

They should think that the members of these societies are human being and they are also part and parcel of the Co-operative movement in our country.

6. Employees engaged in these societies are being paid low salary and other remuneration's. Their pay scale should be revised and they should be made equivalent to other departments. This would encourage them to work honesty and sincerely.
7. The loan should be disbursed well in time to the members of these societies so that they can utilize these funds for augmenting the production of the agricultural sector. The machinery engaged in the disbursement should be geared with efficiency.
8. A calling on becoming the members of these societies should be linked according to the annual income of the farmers, the purpose, use and direction of the sanctioned loan would be inspected by the officer of the co-operative department and follow up action should be introduced so that the funds are not misutilized by the influential person for unproductive uses.

The moral character of the members who are able to be benefited and the officers engaged in the process-from sanctioning of loan to recovery of loans should be canalized in right direction by taking some corrective measures and boosting moral by providing financial and non-financial incentives.

## One Window Concept and Primary Agriculture Co-operative Credit Societies

This arrangement has now come to be known as "One window" system which promises to offer following advantage.

(i) It Achieves objective of integration at the village level without disturbing the existing two structure's.

(ii) The farmer member has to contact only one agency for his production and investment credit which is nearer to him.

(iii) It secures for him adequate and timely credit in a coordinated manner.

(iv) Duplication of work involving verification of document certificates, and statements by different agencies, separately is now availed.

(v) The PACS will be enabled to supplement their income for additional services rendered and will help them to become viable.

(vi) Effective supervision over use of credit would be beneficial to both the cultivator and the lending organization.

(vii) The costs of retailing credit to the farmers can be considerably reduced.

Incidentally, extension work, identification of prospects and development area, guidance and assistance to the borrowing members in fulfilling the formalities and securing quicker credit through one contact point as also the subsequent follow up the loaning process will be greatly facilitated as a result of this functional coordination at the village level.

## Conclusion

The Indian saying "Yatha Raja Thatha Praja" and the oft-quoted saying that if the leader is good and effective, everything will go smoothly are no exaggeration. But, offer all that has been said it is not easy to bring professionalism in management. At the same time, organizational development in the sense is not possible without professionalisation of management. This is essential for every type of business organizational for Human Resource Management.

"The insituational Structure and arrangement of PACCS at the village level would have to be developed so as to build capacities to offer technical guidance to supervise utilization of the loans for the purpose for which there are advanced and to recover them on due dates."

Finance being the brain of the body economy, is generously accepted as a FUAL to the machine of development.

"Perfection Does not Means Doing Extra Ordinary Work. But it Means Doing Work in Extra Ordinary Way." So 'Human Resource Development' is also important in the Primary Agriculture Credit Co-operative Societies, in the Globalized regime.

## REFERENCES

Dr. Niranjan Urs., Some Analytical Tools for Effective Management of PACS, "Co-operative Perspective Journal of Co-operative Management", July-Sept. Vol. 33, No. 2.

Dr. C.M. Chaudhary, "Primary Agriculture Co-operative Societies—Problems & Their Remedies Theory & Practice of Co-operation, Printwell", Jaipur-302004.

G.S. Kamat, New Dimensions of co-operative Management. Himalaya Publishing House (2001).

Dr. S. Ravi Varma, Dr. B. Bhagvan Reddy, "Performance of PACCS in Chittoor District" Co-operative perspective, Journal & Co-operative Management. April-June 1998, Vol. 33, No. 1.

S.S. Parulekar, "H.R.M. in SCBS, DCCBS, and PACS-Challenges & innovations, p. 25. The Maharashtra Co-operative Quarterly Oct-Dec., 1999.

V. Shrada, The Theory of Co-operation, Himalaya Publishing House, 1999.

D.K. Desai, Management in Rural Development, Oxford and IBH Publishing Company, New Delhi, 1983.

M. Srinivas, Organization in Management of Co-operation Bank, Printwell Publishers, Jaipur India, 1990.

Dr. B.S. Mathur, Co-operation in India Sahitya Bhavan Agra, 1985.

Dr. R.D. Bedi, Theory History & Practice of Co-operation, International Publishing House, Meerut, (UP), 1983.

# 15

# Banking Sector Reforms in India

*K. Rani and M. Manickam**

## Introduction

The financial reforms as also the globalization and liberalization measures have brought in a completely new operating environment to the banks, which had earlier, worked in a very protected environment. Emergence of new public, private and foreign banks on the scenario has made survival tough and challenging. The banking system has to necessarily join in the stream of reformation. Globalization of Indian economy has put more stress on the need for banking reforms

## Second Phase of Narasimham Committee: 1998

The Government appointed a second high level on "Committee on banking sector reforms" headed by Shri. M.Narasimham, to review the implementation of the reforms recommended by the earlier committee and to look ahead and chat the reforms necessary in the year ahead to make Indian banking system and better equipped to compete effectively in a fast changing environment.

The Committee in its report submitted in April 1978 made wide-ranging recommendations covering various

* Department of Commerce, Bharathiar University, Coimbatore-46.

aspects of banking policy, institutional, supervisory and legislative dimension. The Committee came out with recommendations with referred to capital adequacy, asset quality, non-performing assets, directed credit prudential norms, disclosure requirements, asset liability management, earnings and profitability systems and methods in banks restructuring including mergers and amalgamations and Voluntary Disclosure Scheme (VRS), reduction of cost and RBI share holding 33% in the Public sector banks as devising effective regulatory norms and review of banking sector laws. These recommendations are being progressively implemented.

## Major Components of Reforms

The basis for banking reforms was provided by the committee on financial Systems (Narasimham Committee) which made recommendations in November 1991 and these recommendations are land mark in the evolution of banking policy in the country. The major components of banking reforms are:

1. Modifying the policy frame work.
2. Improving the financial soundness of bank.
3. Strengthening the institutional frame work.
4. Strengthening of supervisory mechanism.

## Banking Sector Reforms

Consequent upon the liberalization move and basing on the Narasimham Committee report in recent years a number of reform measures have been introduced in the commercial banking sector to make them efficient and productive. These measures include;

(a) The administered interest rate structure is now made flexible, rationale and simple. Deposit rates have been deregulated subject to a ceiling and number of lending rates has been reduced from six to three with a floor rate for all advances above Rs. 2 lakh.

(b) With a view to substantially increasing the lend-able resources at the disposal of the banks, the cash reserve ratio and statutory liquidity ratio are being reduced/ proposed to be reduced in a phased manner from 15 to 10 per cent and from 38.5 to 25 per cent respectively.

(c) The international standard of capital adequacy norm (minimum 8 per cent has been implemented. The budget for 1993-94 has already announced Rs. 5,7000 crores as capital provision for the nationalized banks to help them meet the requirements of the new norms for capital adequacy.

In order to minimize the burden on Government recapitalizing the banks, the State Bank of India and other nationalized banks which are in a position to do so, are allowed to approach the capital market directly to moblise funds from the public. Of course the Government will retain 51 per cent equity to exercise control as before.

(d) The new accounting and prudential norms related to income recognition, asset classification and provisioning for impaired assets has been implemented to make the bank balance sheets more transparent. It is expected that the books of the banks will reflect their true financial position which is a prerequisite for effective monitoring and improving performance.

(e) With a view to improving the sale of non-perfor-ming advances, it has been decided to set up tribunals for expeditious adjudication and recovery of debts.

(f) Guidelines for entry of new private sector banks have been pronounced.

(g) Foreign banks are allowed to open their shops, as a result of liberalization, with a view to infusing competition in the sector.

(h) Merger of banks/branches is allowed and simultaneously branch licensing policy has been liberalized.

(i) For effective supervision of banks a new board, Board for Financial Bank Supervision, is established with in the Reserve Bank of India.

(j) Steps have been taken to increase the interest yield Government securities as per the market rate.

## Impact and Implications

By introduction of reform measures the Indian Banking System has witnessed a significant change. The introduction of new accounting and prudential norms related to income recognition and provisioning for impaired assets has upset the applecart of the banks, particularly of those in the public sector, as reflected in their balance sheets.

The balance sheets of the banks have reflected their financial strength, revealing the true extent of the deterioration in their profitability. Apart from the SBI group, only 7 other public sector banks have declared profit. While the net profit of the SBI group amounted to Rs.280.03 crores the net loss of the public sector banks was to the tune of Rs. 3, 648.91 crores. But during the year 1992-93 all the private sector banks and foreign banks in India except Benaras State Bank and Standard Chaetred Bank have declared profit and they could withstand the new accounting and prudential norms. The bleeding of the balance sheets of public sector banks would continue and possibly all the banks may turn red in the balance sheet of 1993-94, as the balance 70 per cent provision has to be compulsorily made in addition to the provision for 1994.

The RBI has asked the banks to reach the capital adequacy norm of minimum 8 per cent by 31st March 1996, in relation to risk weighted assets. The risk weights attached to investment in Government securities is zero while the risk weight given to other types of advances is significantly high. Since yield rate Government securities is around 13 per cent, now banks prefer to invest in gilt-edged securities rather than investing in other advances having high risk, both in recovery of principal and interest. This shift of investment may hamper the pace of economic development.

According to new norms of income recognition, interest will be taken into account only when it is received in cash. Banks will not be able to show the accrued interest not collected as income as before, while they incur expenses on payment of interest on deposits. Interest earned on advances should always be more than interest paid on deposits as a sound banking principle. Unless the banks recover sunstantial interest, they are likely to show operating loss which will portray a very bad signal of sickness. Therefore what becomes more urgent today for the banks is speedy recovery of advances, both principal and interest.

## Reforms

Reforms formed a significant part of financial sector reforms in India. The banking sector reforms can be divided into following broad areas:

(i) Policy Framework

(ii) Improvement in Financial Health

(iii) Institutional Strengthening

## Policy Framework

### *A. Structured of the Interest Rates*

In reforming the interest rates structure, a gradual approach has been adopted. It has been ensured that banks and financial intermediaries do not have incentives which tempt them to lend at high rates of interest assuming high risk. Prudential norms relating to provisioning and capital adequacy have been prescribed. For this purpose, recommendations of BASLE COMMITTEE in 1993 have been compiled with. Capital adequacy has been raised to 9%. For the purpose of provisioning, the banks and the financial institutions have been asked to classify their assets by compressing the health code into following broad groups:

1. Standard,
2. Sub-standard,

3. Doubtful, and
4. Loss.

In accordance with international practices, loans in arrears for three months or more are classified as sub-standard or below and loans in arrears of one to three month as precautionary loans.

*B. Pre-Emption of Deposits*

In order to reduce fiscal and monetized deficits or to contain deficit, reductions in reserve requirements, i.e. CRR and SLR, is being effected. It will help to increase the lendable resources available with the banking industry. CRR continues to be used flexibly depending upon the monetary situations. Reduction in CRR and SLR has taken place in phased manner. CRR has been reduced to 10% in May, 1999. RBI is likely to reduce CRR requirements further in April 2000 to 8%. It could be spread across a period of two months.

*C. Directed Credit*

There is a prescription that 40% of the net bank credit should go to certain sectors. It has become necessary. So, two concessional rates of interest have been prescribed. Targets regarding directed lending were fixed at a time when the reserve requirements of CRR and SLR combined were as high as 60%. The picture is not same for present. The lending based has more than doubled in last few years. So the lending must make a sense as banks fall short of their targets.

**Improvement in Financial Health**

The introduction of prudential norms and regulations is aimed at ensuring the safety and soundness of the financial system. It is also required to impart greater transparency and accountability in operations and restoring the credibility of and confidence in the financial system. Purposes are solved in this way-

1. The true position of a bank's loan portfolio is brought out.

2. It helps in arresting its deterioration prudential norms in India relate to·
   (a) income recognition
   (b) asset classification
   (c) provisioning of bad and doubtful debts, and
   (d) capital adequacy norms.

Major challenge for banks is the management of assets. Non-performing assets (NPAs) of banks are considered to be at higher levels than those are in other countries. It has attracted the attention of public and also of International Financial Institutions. It has gained further prominence in the wake of Transparency and disclosure measures initiated by the RBI. NPAs of public sector banks, instead of declining on account of the measures initiated by banks such as better follow up, recovery, write-offs, compromise proposals, have considerably increased in absolute terms. Prescription of a given percentage lending/credit to priority sector has also led to higher level of NPAs for Indian banks.

### Debt Recovery

For debt recovery, the objectives of the existing debt recovery Tribunals and the settlement advisory boards can be combined. The Narasimham Committee has reiterated its suggestion on the creation of a separate debt recovery institution, i.e. an Asset Recovery Corporation, a government body. But it was not done as the idea could have sent wrong signals. During the tenure of Sh. P. Chidambaram as the finance minister, banks were encouraged to set-up settlement advisory boards headed by a judge.

### Institutional Strengthening

Appropriate institution building measures are required to strengthen the banking sector in general and public sector banks in particular. These are·

### Recapitalization

The Narasimham Committee recommended that the government should reduce it's equity holding to below 51%

in all banks. Banks are facing competition from NBFCs as well as from within and from the need to improve their profitability. Banks with strong balance sheet are now going to the capital market and raising funds.

The Narasimham Committee recommended has asked public sector banks with consistent record of profitability to tap the capital market. It will make them accountable to a wider base of shareholders and thereby resulting in better performance.

## Improving the Quality of Loan Portfolio

Public sector banks were able to perform better in retaining market share in advances, mainly because new generation banks were facing constraints in rapid expansion,

(a) their limited resources base, and

(b) stringent capital adequacy norms.

Further private sector banks were required to maintain CRR of prescribed percentage from the day one whereas phased manner was prescribed for public sector banks to achieve a particular level. Moreover, private sector banks must have a profitable track for at least three years for the Initial Public Offerings as per RBI guidelines. After such time period, primary market conditions may not be conducive for mobilizing capital at attractive price.

## Strengthening of the Supervisory Process

For a sound banking system, a strong system is essential. Alert mechanism for monitoring compliance with prudential regulations and the directives of the RBI and other regulatory agencies is needed. The system of external supervision has been revamped with the setting up of a separate board for financial supervision (BFS) within RBI concentrating exclusively on supervisory issues. The compliance with regulations and guidelines in the areas of:

(a) credit management

(b) asset classification

(c) income recognition

(d) capital adequacy

(e) provisioning, and

(f) treasury operations will be ensured by the board.

## Reform Measures and Outlook

### *Pre-emptions*

Major problem faced by the banking system was on account of constraints, mainly in terms of massive pre-emption of banks' resources to finance Government's budgetary needs and administered interest rates. Removal of these constraints meant a planned reduction in statutory pre-emption and a gradual deregulation of interest rate prescriptions. Since FSR, total effective pre-emption has been brought down from 54 per cent to less than 35 per cent. The effective CRR which was as high as 16.5 per cent has been brought down to 9.75 per cent. CRR in excess of 3 per cent is currently remunerated at 4 per cent per annum. Given that the CRR is a tax on the banking system, it is better to gradually reduce the CRR rather than maintain a much higher CRR with a relatively higher remuneration on these balances. The medium-term objective of reducing CRR has to take account of money supply considerations and also the objectives of exchange rate stabilizations. Furthermore, reduction of the CRR would depend on maneuverability on money supply impact presently constrained by degree of monetization of fiscal deficit and uncertainties in forex markets.

Statutory Liquidity Ratio (SLR) has been gradually brought down from an average effective rate of 37.4 in 1992 to the statutory minimum of 25 per cent, though at present, many banks hold SLR well in excess of statutory prescription. Further reduction in SLR, though desirable, would have to await reductions in fiscal deficit apart from needed improvements in prudential standards including internal risk management systems. Of course, enabling legislative changes would also be needed.

## Interest Rates

Structure of administered interest rates has been almost totally dismantled. Prescriptions of rates on all term deposits, including conditions of premature withdrawal, and offering uniform rate irrespective of size of deposits have been dispensed with. Currently, there is a prescribed rate of 4.5 per cent for savings bank accounts, which are used by individuals virtually as current accounts and as the cost of servicing these accounts is high, the remuneration on these accounts has necessarily got to be low. There is yet to emerge a consensus on further deregulation of interest rate on savings deposits. There is understandably a differentiated interest rate ceiling prescribed for foreign currency denominated deposits from non-resident Indians, and such ceiling will have to continue as part of managing external debt flows, especially short-term flows till fuller liberalization of capital account. Lending rates for different categories, which were earlier prescribed, have been gradually abolished but transparency is insisted upon. Each Bank is required to announce Prime Lending Rates (PLR) and the maximum spread that it charges. However, there are three exceptions. Currently interest rate on smaller advances (i.e., up to Rs.200, 000) should not exceed PLR. The element of concessionality of very small loans below Rs.200, 000 has to be seen in the context of very small loans. As the figure up to Rs.200, 000 has not been adjusted since 1990; the real effective protection for small loans has been gradually reduced by the inflation drift. Lending rates for exports are still prescribed. The prescription of interest rates for exports linked to the period of availment is to some extent used as an instrument to influence leads and lags in repatriation of export proceeds. Finally, ceilings are prescribed in respect of certain.

## Prudential Norms

Prudential norms are being introduced gradually to meet the international standards. Consequent upon CBSR recommendations, action has already been initiated to increase the capital adequacy ratio; assign risk weights to Government approved securities; to take care of the market risks; and also assign risk weights to open position in forex and gold. In most of these, a time table has been indicated for the first phase only, so that banks are on notice for the first phase while the RBI has retained the freedom to decide on the timing of the second phase. Given the normal growth of 17 to 18 per cent in credit, and the required level of capital adequacy after implementing CBSR recommendations, a substantial infusion of capital into the banking system will be warranted. This is likely to have significant implications for public sector. Government has to weigh the desirability of further budgetary support *vis-à-vis* substantial reduction in share of Government ownership of banks. Incidentally, as long as capital markets are sluggish, and their view on banks, bearish, a high proportion of divestment may be needed to raise the resources required, since share premia may be low.

Similarly, internationally accepted norms of income recognition have been introduced except that income on asset is not recognized if it is not received within two quarters after it is past due, i.e., due date plus thirty days. The international norm is 90 days. Tighter standards, though desirable, have to be introduced gradually so that both banks and borrowers have notice to adjust their operations, and there is no serious disruption in the normal banking activity or erosion in public confidence in the banking system due to balance sheet impact. Also, a sharp tightening of the norms would pose an unbearable burden on banks and would serve no substantive purpose unless corresponding changes are made in credit appraisal systems and debt recovery mechanisms.

Asset classification, which was introduced as per internationally acceptable practices early in the reform process is sought to be further strengthened gradually, as per CBSR. A significant decision taken relates to treatment of assets guaranteed by the State Government as non-performing under certain circumstances. This is a somewhat exceptional provision to take care of the temporary delays observed in respect of a few State Governments in honouring their guarantee obligations when invoked.

**Competition and Transparency**

Competition is sought to be fostered by permitting new private sector banks, and more liberal entry of branches of foreign banks. The share of public sector banks in the bank-ing business is going down, particularly in metropolitan areas. Competition is sought to be fostered in rural and semi-urban areas also by encouraging Local Area Banks. Some diversification of ownership in select public sector banks has helped the process of autonomy and thus some response to competitive pressures. The RBI's efforts to enhance competition do, however, take into account the response of public sector banks and their principal, i.e., the Government. There are some banking institutions such as co-operatives, regional rural banks and local area banks, which are yet to be brought fully into the discipline of reform process. The transparency and disclosure standards have been enhanced to meet international standards, though there are a few areas where we are lagging. These relate to maturity pattern of assets and liabilities, movements in provision account and NPAs and progress needs to be made in all these areas. To provide an authentic comparative information on the performance of banks, the RBI's annual publication, 'Trend and Progress of Banking in India' presents, since the last two years, detailed information on individual banks enabling public assessment of the working of banks.

**Supervision**

An independent Board for Financial Supervision under aegis of the RBI has been established, and consistent with international practice, focus is also on offsite inspections and on control systems internal to the banks.

Status of implementation of Core Principles of Banking Supervision (Annex II) shows that of 46 principles, 33 have been implemented, 11 are partially implemented, while only two are yet to be implemented. These two relate to the critical aspect of adequacy of reserves against country risk and transfer risk; and consolidated reporting. While the former is not a major issue at this juncture in view of limited cross border exposure, the latter is of significance warranting early action. Even in respect of the Core Principles, which have been implemented, the RBI is making constant efforts to improve the quality of supervision and the skills of supervisors.

## Credit Controls

Selective credit controls have been dispensed with. Micro-regulation of credit-delivery has been given up, and there is a greater freedom to both banks and borrowers in matters relating to credit. However, there are apprehensions on two counts, viz., the discipline of priority sector lending and flow of credit to the needy and deserving, on a timely basis. The advances eligible for priority sector lending have been enlarged, interest rates deregulated and alternate avenues of investment permitted, thus making the priority lending far more flexible than before. No doubt, banks are averse to sub-ceilings in priority sector,and have some problems with procedural requirements. The major area of serious concern relates to Government sponsored programmes involving subsidies, where there are serious problems of both co-ordination and recovery. CBSR has made some recommendations and these are still under consideration.

There was a general consensus that the real issue in credit-delivery is more availability of credit than cost. Consequent upon the deregulation of interest rates, there was an expectation that credit flow to the needy will be enhanced, but there is some disappointment about the credit-delivery especially to small industry. Procedural simplifications have been advised by the RBI for rural credit, credit to small industry and more recently the RBI is working on procedural streamlining for export credit.

## Incentives and Legal Reforms

The most critical issue in financial sector reform relates to consequences of the extent of public ownership and special laws governing publicly owned banks. CBSR has devoted a significant part of its report to reform of public sector banks, on which Government, as the principal, needs to act. At present, public ownership has adverse effects on level playing field among banks, capacity and willingness to compete in the market place, incentives to perform, and binding work practices/methods that inhibit efficiency. The issue of efficiency in public sector banks has several dimensions, and legal is one of them. Again, issues of optimal efficiency, autonomy and ownership are intertwined and need to be resolved. Reduction of public ownership below the majority level prescribed would need an amendment to the three different laws that govern public sector banks. Sale of shares already held by Government also needs amendments to law.

## Debt Recovery

Progress in establishing and operationalising debt-recovery systems has been painfully slow, partly due to judicial review. CBSR suggested several legislative measures that would facilitate debt-recovery, securiti-zation, electronic systems, etc. A serious consequence of tightening prudential norms and pressurizing banks to reduce NPA without strengthening the debt-recovery system is the choking of credit. While large corporates may be partly spared by recourse to alternate sources such as debentures or commercial paper, the rest, especially medium and smaller corporates could face credit choke and hence the pace of introduction of measures needs to be carefully modulated.

## Accounting Standards

There is an apprehension in some quarters that the Indian Accounting Standards as followed by the Indian banks are not in line with International Accounting Standards. Annexure III gives a comparative position of some of the significant standards relevant to banking sector and comparative Indian standards/regulations. It will be seen that on accounting and valuation, Indian standards and *de facto* practices are comparable with international standards. The major area of divergence in accounting is in respect of group accounting and consolidation. In India, currently consolidation is not required and investments in associated companies are not accounted for under equity method. In regard to disclosure, Indian banks do not, at present, disclose maturity pattern of assets/ liabilities, concentrations of assets/ liabilities and off-balance sheet items, net foreign currency exposure, movement in provisions account, and gross non-performing assets and related party transactions in the financial statements. However, as regards disclosure of related party transactions, banks are prohibited from granting advances to firms in which a Director is interested. The Reserve Bank has formally stated that instructions on further disclosures will be announced in due course. Meanwhile, many banks are also taking steps to build appropriate information systems, which some disclosures entail.

## Banks

It is clear that actions of RBI and initiatives of Government provide enabling environment, incentive framework and to some extent punitive measures. The outcome will depend on the response of banks, i.e., boards of banks, management, officers and staff. There are, in particular, four broad areas of internal systems which may need thorough overhauling and which need to be facilitated by Government and the RBI.

First, the internal control systems in the banks, especially Public Sector Banks.

Second, the placement, work practices etc., which inhibit incentives for efficiency and improved customer service.

Third, flexibility in obtaining and enhancing highly skilled or talented people.

Fourth, introduction and effective use of technology in banks, especially public sector banks.

## Conclusion

Effective regulation and supervision must be based on a transparent set of rules as close as possible to the international standards combined with free and timely availability of information and strong proactive action against their breaking the rules. Close attention to the way, the regulating agencies are structured and empowered, has to be paid. Jurisdiction and the responsibility have to be clearly defined and the organization must be held accountable. There is undoubtedly a trade-off between having strict regulations oriented to protecting the interests of ordinary investors and allowing greater freedom to the market players.

## REFERENCES

IBA Bulletin.

RBI Bulletin.

# 16

# Marketing of Banking Services : Yesteday, Today and Tomorrow

*Baby M.D**

## Introduction

Indian banking is at cross roads today. With the de regulation and liberalization process in full swing, the consequent policy changes introduced in the Indian financial system in general and banking in particular are effecting unprecedented changes in its functioning. With the emerging changes did spring up new challenges of commercial viability, cost effectiveness, effective marketing strategy, etc. Market oriented policies also gave birth to new players like foreign and private sector banks and subsidiaries offering varied high-tech and cost effective Service. There was an absolute shift from sellers into buyers' market, establishing the 'consumer' as the key factor in the market. The dictum " as the bank exists because of its customers, has become more pronounced and relevant in the present context". Thus, marketing constitutes the key strategy for banks to retain good customers and also anticipate their future demands. Marketing of their liability products as well as credit are the areas in which the

* Reader in Commerce, Director Research and Post Graduate Department of Commerce, St. Dominic's College, Kanjirappally, Kerala.

banks have to bestow greater attentions. Instead of complaining about low competitive markets, narrowing down areas of business and profits, banks should device strategies for exploiting opportunities that the markets are going to open up and mechanisms to satisfy the needs and expectations of various segments of customers for their survival.

Against; this backdrop this paper attempts to discuss the bank marketing, reasons for bank marketing, their features, evolution and mix in bank marketing.

**What is Bank Marketing?**

Various definitions have been given for the term bank marketing. Bank marketing is the sum total of business activities, directed at providing services to satisfy 'customers financial needs and wants, more effectively and efficiently than competitors do, keeping in view the organizational activities of the bank. Deryk Weyer of Barclays Bank call it "a process, consisting of identifying the most profitable markets now and in future; assessing the present and the future needs of the customers; setting business development goals and making plans to meet them; and managing various services and promoting them to achieve the plans – all in the context of a changing environment in the market".

When we go deeper in to the concept, we can see that the basic objective of bank marketing is to sell the institution itself.

**Why Bank Marketing?**

*Awareness Among Customers*

Modern technology has made customers aware of the developments in the economic environment, which includes the financial system. Financial needs of the customers have grown multifold into various forms like quick cash accessibility, money transfer, asset security, increased return on surplus funds, financial advice, deferred payments etc. With a wide network of branches, even in a dissimilar banking scenario, customers expect the banks to offer more and better services to match their demands and this has compelled banks to take up marketing in right earnest.

### Quality as a Key Factor

With the opening up of the economy, fast change has been experienced in every activity, and banking has been no exemption. Quality is the watchword in the competitive world, which is market driven and banks have had to face up to this emerging scenario. In fact, it may not be out of place to reiterate that quality will in future be the sole determinant of successful banking ventures and marketing has to focus on this most crucial need of the hour.

### Profit Orientation

Until recently the performance of commercial bank was gauged on the scale of growth of deposits. A paradigm shift has come about towards other parameters like profit generation, health of asset portfolio etc. and this has compelled the banks to turn their attention to increased profits and higher income earnings.

With the decline in lending rates and introduction of new norms of prudential accounting, the profitability of intermediation business has begun to dwindle. As a result, banks are forced to look out for new and yet unheralded pastures to compensate for the apparent stability in growth in the past, which perhaps contributed to the burgeoning non-linheralded, pastures, and performing assets portfolio.

With many banks planning to tap the capital market sooner or later, the increased expectations of the investors need to be satisfied and this will be yet another factor compelling the banks to improve profits. This will, besides necessitating banks to innovate and devise new income oriented schemes, also entail improved marketing efforts to sell the different products so as to yield the planned results.

## Growing Competition

Increased completion is being faced by the Indian banking industry from within the system with other agencies both, local and foreign, offering value added services. Competition is no more confined to resource mobilization but also to lending and other areas of banking activity. The foreign commercial bank with their superior technology, speed in operations and imaginative positioning of their services has also provided the necessary impetus to the Indian banks to innovate and complete in the market place.

## Technological Advances

The influence and impact of information technology on banking and the financial sector is immense. Home banking and tele- banking have started making in roads in the country. Technological innovation has resulted in financial product development especially in the international and investment banking areas. The western experience has demonstrated that technology has not only made execution of work faster but has also resulted in greater availability of manpower for customer contact.

## Marketing Approach in Banks

With the need for marketing in banks having evolved out of the changing environment and constant interplay of various interdependent factors, the importance of a systematic approach to marketing cannot be overstressed. The application of a marketing approach in banks will therefore involve:

(a) Identifying customers' financial needs and wants;

(b) Developing appropriate banking services to meet these needs;

(c) Pricing for the services so developed;

(d) Setting up suitable outsells/ banks branches;

(e) Advertising to promote the services to the existing as well as prospective customers.

## Special Features of Bank Marketing

- Banking product cannot be seen or touched like manufactured products (intangibility)
- In marketing banking products, the product and the seller are in separable; they together define the banking product (inseparability)
- Banking products are produced and delivered at the same time; they cannot be stored and inspected before delivering' (perishability)
- Standardisation of banking product is difficult (variability)

## Saga of Bank Marketing

The origin of bank marketing dates back to the succeeding years of World War II when it was related its public relations, advertising and promotional efforts, popularly known as 'business development'. It was only during the 1960s that the concept of marketing began to catch up in the banks in England and in the U.S.A. The compulsion to understand the needs and preferences of the customers and impact of various markets led to the growth of market research and other sophisticated and disciplined marketing efforts. The development in US banks was not only confined to large and medium banks but also to small banks.

## Evolution of Bank Marketing in India

For the present discussion; the evolution of Bank Marketing in Post–independence India can be broadly classified in four phases via : (i) Pre-nationalization period (preceeding 1969), (ii) Post nationalization period (after 1969 and up to the mid- eighties) modern period (after the mid eighties but before liberalization, privalization and Globalization in 1991) and post modern period (after liberalization in 1991. Reflecting the marketing stands of Indian banks during their four phases they have been named the "traditional banking period", the development bank period, and innovative or electronic bank-marketing period respectively and the bank-marketing period. These names are reflective of only the major trends in the marketing orientation of Indian Banks.

**Traditional Banking Period ( Pre- nationalization Era up to 1969)**

"The hall marks of the period was a strong accounting orientation of bankers down the line, as distinct from a marketing" orientation. In other words it meant meticulous maintenance of account books and an inward, looking approach in transacting business with the customers, which emphasized strict adherence. To lay down rules and regulations, be it deposit business or loaning activity. The foremost point of emphasis was the bank. In loaning, howmuch funds the prospective borrower needed to run his business was less important than how much security he could provide to safe guard bank's financial interest (i.e. security oriented approach). The customer was presented with a set of pre-determined options of banking products with an air which implied" "Take it or leave it". Before mid 1950s banks had no understanding of marketing.

**Development Banking Period**

*(Post–nationalization Period from 1969 to mid 1980s)*

In so far as the revolution of bank marketing is concerned, after the nationalization of the 14 major commercial banks in 1969, approach of banks towards customers underwent a change and the focus was gradually shifted to marketing their products. Banks become products oriented by offering a range of product and service. A large number of deposits and loan schemes were devised during the period for different sections of society, frequently at the instance of the government in furtherance and of national priorities.

From 1969-70 onwards, the emphasis of bank was on social lending schemes, which resulted in market segmentation of the various beneficiary groups, which signified the emergence of social marketing.

The first major steps in the direction of marketing was initiated by the State Bank of India in 1972. When it recognized itself on the basis of major market segments, dividing the customers on the basis of activity and carved out four major market segments namely institutional, small industries and small business, agricultural, personal service segments. Again State Bank of India came out with its market segmentation scheme and innovative loan products like IRDP, DIR (Differential Interest Rate), crop loan etc. was extensively marketed. Thus, the discipline of bank marketing did travel some distance in as much as marketing tools like market segmentation product diversification and expansion were experimented.

By 1974 the environment become more demanding and during this period banks picked up the word "marketing". A few marketing practices replace the earlier practices which were found to be inadequate to cater to the needs of the diverse market segments.

## Bank Marketing Period

*(The Modern Period After the Mid 1980, but before 1991)*

The fantastic pace of branch expansion and credit disbursement during this period reflected in a proliferation of loss making branches, problems of communication, rising customer dissatisfaction with banking services. The bank management and some extent the rank and file in banks could visualize the risks inherent in continuing to do business as before. So there was a growing awareness that marketing was an essential tool in the kitty of a banker, an inescapable necessity without which perhaps survival itself might become difficult in the foreseeable future. To that extent this period is marked by a quantum jump in the evolution of the discipline of Bank Marketing in India.

*Innovative or Electronic Bank Marketing Period (After 1991)*

As a result of new deregulated banking environment resultant to liberalization privatization and globalization in the year 1991, Commercial banks already operating on the thin margins are trying to develop appropriate system to respond suitably to market compulsions quickly in the form of frequent adjustments of the interest rate changes both on deposits and advances.

The emerging market for the Indian banks will be in the non- traditional areas like investment banking portfolio counseling, factoring, venturing, merchant banking, consumer durables, export, import business, commercial papers securitisation of debits etc. which will yield return in the form of commission, exchange, brokerage etc.

Since income from traditional services mainly borrowing and lending is shrinking due to competition, in this area the banks are trying to improve service basis income, which need less for earning similar amount of income through fundbased activities. For these banks are trying to develop new segments, niche market, skill oriented specialist cadere to face the market competition, evolving strategic alliance and building core competence in technology.

## Marketing Mix in Bank Marketing

Marketing mix implies a firm's total marketing program. In other words it refers to the blend of ideas, and novel features which marketing management puts together to appeal to their target market segment. It requires decision-making with regard to; product, place, promotion and price. Mc Carthy has called these four marketing decision variables as the "Four Ps" of the marketing mix. The marketing mix has both strategic and tactical dimensions. The strategic dimension of the marketing mix is primarily concerned with decisions about the relative importance of the mix elements for a particular product- market combination. The tactical dimension of the marketing mix works within the framework created by decision regarding the balance of the mix and is concerned primarily with the specification of precise details for each element in the mix.

The traditional marketing mix of 'Four Ps' which was developed for marketing goods is not suitable for bank marketing since they deal with services. The service marketing mix (including bank marketing) is different from the traditional mix for goods.

Neil Borden, while quoting from an article of James Culletion, written that a marketer is viewed as a 'decider' or 'artist' or a 'mixer of ingredients' who plans various means of competition. "He may follow a recipe prepared by others, or prepare his own as he goes along or adopt a recipe to the ingredients immediately available, or experiment with or invent ingredients no one else has tried". If a marketer is a "mixer of ingredients", what he designed is a marketing mix.

Hence, marketing mix in bank marketing comprises 7Ps namely product, Price, Promotion, Place, people, Physical evidence and process.

## *Product*

It is defined as the benefit or benefits that a customer purchases when he or she pays for a supplied product. This embraces both tangible and intangible products.

The products offered by banks are divided into five principal dimensions reflecting to the day-to-day need of the customers. The dimensions are finance, money, advisory, foreign exchange and auxiliary dimensions.

- Finance Dimensions: It consists of services, funding a company's present and future assets. The dimension also involves acquisition of different types of credit, leasing, money market and bond market finance etc.
- Money Dimension: It consists of service which are used in day to day transactions.
- Advisory Dimension : It consists of products and services which are of an advisory nature and guiding the customers to utilize and implement those in the right manner.

- Foreign Exchange Dimension: This dimension is often connected to finance and money dimensions, but here product and service offered are in terms of foreign exchange currency flow.
- Auxiliary Dimension: The exchange between banks and their customers also includes several other items. These include tax planning, personal loans, insurance et. which are auxiliary service provided to customers by banks.

### *Price*

In formulating the marketing mix, price also plays a very important role. Price in banks relate to interest and fees. The prices is regulated by RBI and Indian Banking Association.

Pricing for banks takes a number of forms:

- Charge for different types of transaction e.g., debits, cheque clearance, standing orders.
- Charge rates for overdrafts/ loans.
- Fees for services.
- Interest rates on current / deposits and savings accounts.

### *Promotion*

Banks undertake major advertising campaigns continuously. The main purpose of advertising is to create awareness of services available to the customers. Today, many banks are developing promotional activities using sophisticated database to target direct mail campaigns at market segments by using publicity, sponsorship and other promotional means.

Due to the continuous technological advancement, banks have extended their services even to remote areas by means of network i.e. ATM's, EFTPOS (Electronic Fund Transfer Point of Sale).

### *Place*

Place or location plays a very critical role in the financial service. The service is mainly provided through branches. Even though service can be offered through telephone, it has proved that bank without branch is possible, but customer still need access to the ATM outlets, where appropriate place is considered. Some customers prefer personal, face-to-face contact. Change in distribution systems, technology and consumer demands are key influences on the evolution of the 'place' component of the marketing mix.

### *People*

Customer care is very important to bank employee. Both quality and differentiation in the financial industry is looked up on very seriously. The bank should participate in a number of internal strategic marketing activities, which focus on the role of employee in the delivery of financial services.

Banks are developing and implementing customer care/ quality programmes. This is the pre-requisite for success in the organization from top management down the line with effective leadership creating an effective customer–orien-ted culture.

### *Physical Evidence*

Physical evidence is one more marketing mix available to service providers. The service firms must consciously make efforts to manage the physical evidence associated with the services. The need for physical evidence within the marketing mix arises directly from the typically intangible nature of the service.

Product in service itself being intangible, there is a need to tangibilise it as for as possible. Physical entities can be successfully employed to describe the service product and its distinguishing qualities. The potential customers form impressions about the service organizations on the basis of physical evidence like brochures, stationary, equipment, furniture, building etc. It helps the organization to reinforce the proposed position and image of the organization.

### *Process*

This is the seventh component of marketing mix. In a service organization, the system by which the target audience receives delivery of the service constitutes the process. In other words, the process by which the service is produced and delivered to the ultimate customer in critical to the success of service operation. The process of a delivery function which can be compared with that of operations management implies the conversion of input into output. But in service organizations there is no clear-cut input or output. Rather is the process of adding 'value' or 'utility' to system inputs to create output which are useful to the customers.

## Bank Marketing- Never a Full Stop!

In conclusion, it is submitted that the banking system is on the threshold of a momentous era of change and continuity in growth and development, of individual customer needs and corporate practices, technology and competitions. The role of marketing in the banking industry continues to change. For many years the primary focus of bank marketing was public returns. Then the focus shifted to advertising and sales promotion. That was followed by a focus on the development of a sales culture. Now the focus is on the individual customer meeting and even anticipating his or needs and developing trusting, long-term relationships by delivering high quality personalized service. Marketing both as a philosophy and an activity; is expected to contribute immensely to the realization of goals both immediate and future. All though all the elements of the marketing concept- customer satisfaction, profit integrated framework, and social responsibility must receive the greatest emphasis in the years a head. They must be guided by the dictum of Mahatma Gandhi

"A customer is the most important visitor in our promises. He is most dependent on us. We are depending on him. He is not an interruption on our work. He is the purpose of it. He is not an outsider on our business. He is part of it. We are not doing him a favour by serving him. He is doing as a favour by giving as an opportunity".

## REFERENCES

Chidambram, Dr.R.M. 'Marketing approch must for bankers', Indian Banking, Today and Tomorrow, September, 1994, pp. 9-10.

Cavey, T.P.A, Banks and marketing 'The International Journal of Bank Marketing', Vol. 7, No.3, 1989, pp. 8-13

Rajeev K. Seth, Marketing of Banking Services. Mac Millan Indian LTD, 1997. Chapter I, The why of Bank Marketing? pp. 1-13.

P.N. Reddy et al. 'Services Marketing', Himalaya publishing house 2000. Chapter 16 Marketing Services, pp. 307-311.

# 17

# Financial Sector Reforms

*Thakor Devendrasingh Vijaysingh* *

## Introduction

The Indian financial sector consists of an impressive network of banks and financial institution in the economy and growth of financial flows in relation to economic activity. It consists of the financial markets, financial institutions and financial instruments. The banking and finance system of a country plays a significant role in its development. It mobilises savings and allocates credit. The acts as an intersmediary between savers and investors and undertakes the transformation of their different maturities. It provides payment services. It provides liquidity to financial assets of households, business and governments. Ability to increase efficiency and to serve the public interest are the two corner stones of financial system's contribution to growth and development in a country.

## Financial Intermediaries

Financial intermediaries are the institutions which collect savings from others issuing in return claims against themselves, and use the funds thus acquired to purchase ownership or debt claims. They are interposed between ultimate borrowers and lenders to acquire the primary

* Reader, Department of Commerce, M.S.G. College, Malegaon—Camp, Dist.-Nasik (Maharashtra).

securities of borrowers and provide other securities for the portfolios of lenders. Their out standing feature is that they issue to savers claims whose characteristics are quite different from those that they buy and hold. They do not merely intermediate, but in the process they also create higher degree of safety and liquidity. Their basic function is to satisfy simultaneously the portfolio preferences of lenders and borrowers. Financial intermediaries play a very important role in the saving-investment process by raising the level of saving and investment and allocating more efficiently scarce savings among most productive investments.

A satisfactory classification of financial intermediaries will vary from place to place, and time to time. Generally, they are grouped under five different categories as follows—

1. The banking system (Central bank, Commercial banks, Co-operative banks, etc.)
2. Other depository organisations (mutual funds, saving and loan associations, credit unions etc.)
3. Insurance organisations (Life insurance, general insurance, postal insurance, pension funds, provident funds etc.)
4. Development banks, and
5. Other financial intermediaries (investment and finance companies, stock exchanges, and other related intermediaries).

## Objective and Goals of Reforms

The reform objective in our country is largely to promote a diversified, efficient and competitive financial system. It aims at raising the allocative efficiency of available savings, increasing the return on investments and development of the real sector. Specific goals of the programme include:

(i) To correct and improve the macro-economic policy setting within which banks operate. This involves monetary control reforms, Including rationalisation of interest rate, redesigning direct credit programmes, and bringing down the levels of red source pre-emptions.

(ii) To improve the financial health and condition of banks, by recapitalising banks, restructuring the weaker ones and improving the incentives under which banks function.

(iii) To build financial institutions and infrastructure relating to supervision, audit, technology, and legal framework.

(iv) To improve the level of managerial competence and the quality of human resources by reviewing the policies relating to recruitment, training, placements etc.

(v) To improve access to financial savings.

(vi) To reduce intermediation costs and distortous in the banking system.

(vii) To promote competition through a level playing field and freer entry and exit in the financial sector.

(viii) To develop transparent and efficient capital and money markets.

**Reform Measures**

In Indian financial system the following reform measures were introduced prior to 1991 based on the recommendation of Chakravarty Committee, 1985 and Vaghul Committee, 1987.

1. The maximum coupon rate was raised from 6.5 per cent to 11.5 per cent in 1985-86 and the maximum maturity was reduced from 30 years to 20 years.
2. The rates in the money market related with call money, notice money, interbank deposits and bills rediscounting were freed in 1989.
3. Non–banking institution were allowed to participate as lenders in the money–market.

4. New–instruments were introduced in money–market. They were 182–day treasury bill, certificates of deposits, commercial paper and inter Bank participation at the initiative of the RBI.
5. A Discount and Finance House of India (DFHI) was set up in 1988 as a reserve bank subsidiary to facilitate smoothening of short term liquidity imbalance and to impart greater flexibility to the money market.
6. The term structure of interest rates was rationalised.

## Narasimham Committee Report, 1991

The report of the committee on the financial system popularly known as the Narasimham committee report, 1991 is a bold agenda for action. The committee has recommen-ded the following measures to improve the efficiency, productivity and profitability of the financial system in the country – which can be attained on the basis of operational flexibility and functional autonomy.

1. The state inference in the working of financial system should be reduced and the role of the market should be revised.
2. Proper level playing field for the operation of the various segments of financial system should be provided.
3. The public sector banks and financial institution should be given more operation flexibility and functional autonomy.
4. A part of the financial system should be privatised wherever possible so that the competition can be encouraged in the sector.

## The Reform Measures After – 1991

The important reform measures after 1991 were introduced in the following ways on the recommendations of the Narasimham committee – 1991.

1. In 1991 – the ceiling on interest rate on the Government securities was 11.5% while the minimum lending rate of the banks for larger advances was as high as 20%. In order to bring these rates into better alignment the coupon rate for a 10 years maturity was raised by as much as 2.75% between 1991 and 1993. The maximum maturity has been reduced from 20 years to 10 years. At present the ceiling on the government securities interest rate is 10.5% while the minimum lending rate of banks is 12%.

2. Banks, bank subsidiaries and financial institutions have been allowed by the RBI to set up money market mutual funds. Although the response so far is lukewarm in the absence of an active secondary market for money market instrument.

   The medium – terms goals of our monetary policy are market determined, greater integration of the Indian financial system with international flows and reliance on direct methods of monetary control.

3. The SLR (Statutory Liquidity Ratio) and CRR (Cash Reserve Ratio) were reduced from an unprecedented and unsubtanable level of 63.5% or demand and time liabilities to 39%.

4. An instrument of repurchase agreement (repos) between the RBI and commercial banks has been introduced in December 1992 aiming at even out liquidity within the reserves make-up fornight and to reduce the volatility in the call money-market. The RBI has only use this instrument to drain reserves from the banks and not to supply reserves. It has significantly reduced the fluctuations in cell money rates. It has also helped in lowering reserve bank credit to central government and reserve money expansion.

5. An autonomous board for financial supervision under the umbrella of the RBI in under

consideration for revamping the bank supervision machinery.

6. A–364 treasury bill on an auction basis was introduced replacing 182-day bill in April–1992. It is not purchased or rediscounted by the RBI. It has found ready acceptance in the market and by January 1994 it had absorbed Rs. 150 billion. A 91-day auction treasury bill was introduced in January 1993.
7. The RBI has also taken a series of steps to bring about an efficient electronic clearing settlement and depository system in respect of Government securities. A system of delivery versus payment is being developed to reduce the counter party risk and risk of diversion of funds through securities transactions.
8. The funding of 364 days Treasury bills & 91 days auction Treasury Bill was effected in 1993-94 converting them into dated securities of 3 and 2 years maturity respectively.
9. Open Market Operation have been replaced by RBI with its price list using bidding patterns at its auction as a guide. Securities are purchased by RBI at competitive prices.
10. Internal Dept Management cell was created in October 1992 to carry all functions pertaining to internal debt management by RBI. It will manage market borrowings and open market operation and to promote an active and efficient Government securities market.
11. Major problem faced by the banking system was on account of constraints, mainly in terms of massive preemption of banks resources to finance Governments budgetary needs and administered interest rates. Removal of these constraints meant a planned reduction in statutory preemption and a gradual deregulation of interest rate prescriptions.

## Conclusion

To make more effective the various reforms in our financial sector the following steps should be taken immediately.

1. An auction system has been successfully implemented through the use of tenders. However, there is time gap between announcements, acceptance of bids, payment and settlement. It requires technological improvements and a lot of educational and training efforts in human resource development.
2. NRIs are permitted to invest in government securities without restriction. However, no more has been made to encourage ownership or trading of government securities by foreign investors and dealers.
3. When coupon interest payments are made to owners of securities, tax is deducted at source and a tax deduction certificate is given. Tax treatment of different institutions differs and some institutions are completely exempt from tax. This has encouraged 'voucher trading' around interest payment dates in order to develop genuine secondary market in government securities this practice should be done away with.
4. There had been a gross violations of the guidelines issued by the RBI. Financial institutions should become both autonomous and accountable. There should not be any interference in the day functioning of such institutions and more delegation of authority with accountability should be extended to this sector. The priority sector credit has increased to more than 40 per cent of the total advances with many concessions in the economy. Social responsibility should be balanced with the viability of financial institutions.

5. Scams occur in various types of financial systems. The only way to avoid such scams is really to ensure that the guilty are found out quickly and punished adequately and the system is immediately improved.

## REFERENCES

C.M. Choudhary (1996), financial sector reforms in India, sublime publications, Jaipur.

The Indian Institute of Bankers (1990), Banking Finance and Development, Quality Printers, Worli, Bombay-400018.

Debendra Kumar Das (1993), Structural Adjustment in the Indian Economy, Deep and Deep publications, New Delhi-110027.

Vasant Desai, June (1996), The Indian Financial System, Himalaya Publishing House, Bombay.

Smt. Meena Pandey (1991), Financial System of India, [volume-I banking and monetary policies-promise and performance] [volume – 2, A Profile of Sectoral Financial] Himalaya Publishing House, Bombay, Delhi.

C.M. Choudhary (1992), Dynamics of Indian Banking, Printwell, Jaipur.

Rita Swami, Shrikant Joshi, June (1992), Banking and finance, Sheth publishers, Pune.

Academic foundation (1999), Ongoing Developments in baking and financial sector, Triveni offset, Delhi.

# 18

# Changing Face of Banking Sector Real Time Gross Settlement (RTGS)

*S.K. Sharma* and Shubha Chandra***

We are passing through a phase wherein drastic changes in all spheres of life are taking place. In our normal routine life computer or information technology is increasingly used. The revolution in information technology has been so fast and so effective that it cover almost all sorts of human activities. So far, we have experienced this technology in banking through partial computerization, total branch automation (TBA), automated teller machine (ATMs) and more recently core banking solution (CBS) wherein one can have anywhere banking within CBS connected branches of same bank, no matter where account holder maintains its account.

In the banks, the current system involves settlement of payments on a "settlement day" and interest is invariably computed to accrue on a daily basis. Even in the wholesale markets for foreign exchange and money markets contracts, 'spot' transactions mean two-business days. Settlement for clearing cheque presented to the clearing houses takes place on a netting basis at a particular time either same day or on

* Reader and Head Department of Business Administration, DEI Agra.

** Research Scholar (Dayalbagh Ecucational Institute, Agra).

the next day. These conventions made sense, when book-keeping was done manually. This system gives rise to risks such as credit risk, liquidity risk, legal risk, operational risk, and systemic risk. A systemic risk is the risk that the inability of one of the participants to meet its obligations, or a disruption in the system itself, could result in the inability of other system participants or of financial institutions in other parts of the financial system to meet their obligation, as they become due. Such a failure could cause widespread liquidity or credit problems and as a result threaten the stability of the system or of financial markets.

The above apply to payment systems which would trigger or transmit systemic distruption in the financial area because of the size or nature of individual payments, which they handle because of the aggregate value of the payments processed.

Real Time Gross Settlement (RTGS) is a product of network technology being sponsored by RBI in Indian Financial Market.

RTGS is an acronym for Real Time Gross Settlement System which RBI proposes to introduce in Indian Financial Markets in the coming days.

It is a robust, secure and integrated communication network used for setting the dues on real time basis i.e. settlement takes place as and when transaction is done. This aspect one has to consider against the present settlement system. In the present system, one who is entitled to receive payment i.e. (Seller of goods/services) has to initiate action by lodging his claim by way of cheque/DD received from his customer part (buyer) to his banker. The banker collects the proceeds by sending the cheque or DD in clearing and after observing necessary period for clearance of the proceeds, the funds are made available to the customer who has lodged the instrument.

RTGS is a software package which provides online settlement of payments between financial institutions.

In this system payment instructions between banks are processed and settled individually and continuously throughout the day. This is in contrast to net settlements where payment instructions are processed throughout the day but inter-bank settlement takes place only afterwards typically at the end of the day.

Payee banks and their customers receive funds with certainty, or so-called finality, during the day, enabling them to use the funds immediately without exposing themselves to risk.

A lag between the time at which information is made available to receiving banks and the time at which settlement takes place may have important risk implications in large fund transfer systems.

To initiate a funds transfer, the sending bank dispatches a payment message which is subsequently routed to the central bank and to the receiving bank as the system process and settles the transfer. This is common in countries in the Asia-Pacific region such as Australia, Hong Kong, New Zealand, Singapore, South Korea and Taiwan.

RTGS system settles payments on a transaction-by-transaction basis as soon as they are accepted by the system.

RTGS systems do not create credit risk for the receiving participant because they settle each payment individually, as soon as it is accepted by the system for settlement.

RTGS system can require relatively large amounts of intraday liquidity because participants need sufficient liquidity to cover their outgoing payments. The cost of intraday liquidity depends on variables such as amount required, the opportunity cost of maintaining liquid balances, and the cost of intraday credit.

## Essential Components of RTGS

For using RTGS mechanism, following are the essential components:

- *Membership of Indian Financial System Network (INFINET):* For implementation of RTGS the bank should be a member of INFINET—A separate leased line network established for the exclusive use by Indian Banking & Financial System members. This network ensures that the financial messages remain secured and integrated and cannot be tampered with. The INFINET is used as a communication backbone and it is managed by Institute for Development & Research in Banking Technology (IDRBT), Hyderabad. Since general public will not have access to INFINET, it becomes a reliable communication backbone and the transactions or messages passed through this network are considered as safe and secure.
- *Establishment of Payments Gateway:* Each member bank has to open a payment gateway at their treasury so that any financial messages pertaining to the bank can be sent/received at the focal point/ centralized place for onward transmission.
- *Branch Connectivity with Payments Gateways:* The branches identified for extending RTGS remittance services will have to be connected to the payment gateway of their bank through ISDN or wide area network (WAN) or via satellite connection. The banks can use Core Banking Solution (CBS) network for messaging purpose but will have to develop an interface between their core banking systems and the RTGS application.
- *Use of Structured Financial Messaging System (SFME) as Common Message Format:* SFMS will be used as the secured messaging systems. In order to avoid ambiguity and to maintain uniformity while sending & receiving financial messages amongst the

member banks, common formats are designed under SFMS. These formats are similar to SWIFT message formats, which are used for International Fund Transfers across the world.

- *Use of Electronic Coding & Decoding Technology:* All financial messages need to be transmitted in a coded format known to and tested between the remitting and the receiving banks. For the purpose of maintaining secrecy and trustworthiness of the financial messages, Public Key Infrastructure (PKI) technology is used. This is similar to what the bankers use while coding and decoding inward/ outward Telegraphic Transfer (T/T) messages. The only difference is that the required calculations are done by the system internally and accepted only if they match with the original message sent by the remitter.
- *Unique Identification of Bank's Branch for RTGS:* Under RTGS system there is no movement of papers, however, electronic messages are exchanged between member banks. As such each participant bank branch should be recognized separately. For this purpose Indian Financial System Codes (IFSC) are sued. IFSC code is a combination of 11 digit alphanumeric characters as under:
- *First four digits denote bank name*
- *The fifth digit is a reserved digit meant for future use—presently it would be zero (0) for all the banks & branches.*
- *Last six digits provide identification for the concerned branch—it would be the six digit IBR code in vogue.*

## Procedure of RTGS

~ The bank which is a member of RTGS system has to open a separate account titled "RTGS—Settlement Account" with RBI.

~ All the remittance affected under RTGS mechanism will be settled in this account. For this purpose, the member banks will have to transfer certain amount daily in the morning from their main RBI Account and at the close of the RTGS business hours, the balance lying in this settlement account will be transferred back to the main RBI Account. Therefore, the RTGS settlement account will be an Intra-Day Account as the closing balance in this account will always be zero.

~ This arrangement will, however, create temporary mismatch as the payments and receipts of the remittances may occur randomly at any time during the business hours. To take care of such possibility and to enable members to

**Chart Depicting Movement of Message Under RTGS Scenario**

**RTGS Messages Flow**

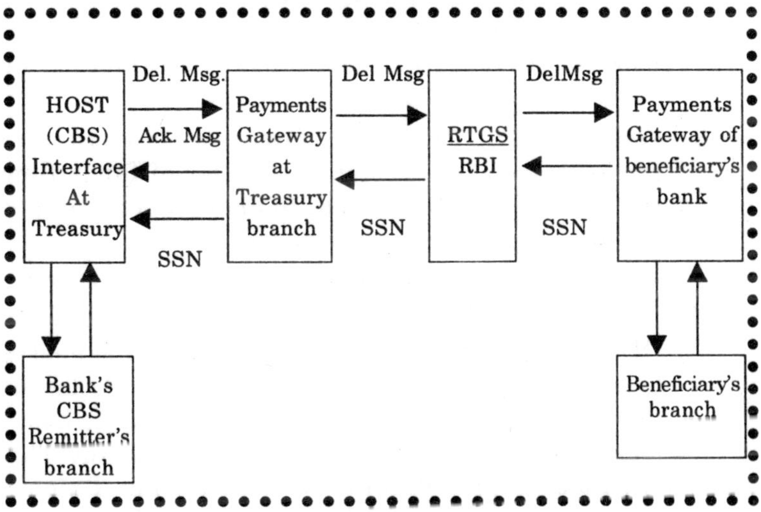


**Del. Msg**—Delivery messages from remitting branch to payments gateway & RBI through CBS.

**Ack.Msg.** —Acknowledgement Message from payments gateway outward remittance sent by branch through CBS.

**SSN**—Sender's Settlement Notification from Beneficiary's bank/branch to remitting branch through RBI.

settle their transaction on Real Time Basis, RBI will be provided them temporary funds through a facility called Intra-Day-Liquidity (IDL). This IDL facility as the name suggests, has to be adjusted by the member banks before the close of the business hours.

RTGS system would cover the payment and settlement transactions of the following types:

1. *Inter Bank Payments:* These transactions mainly arise out of treasury operations such as Money Market deals, Debt Market Operations, Foreign Exchange transactions, etc.
2. *Customer to Customer Transfer:* Customer to customer transfer transactions are the common remittance transactions happenings at branch level, which are presently done through issuance of cheque, demand draft, telegraphic transfer, etc. the RTGS mechanism is expected to take over all these tasks by settling the transactions electronically on fully being operational.
3. *Own Account Transfer :* Own account transfer transactions are relating to transfer of funds from the bank's one RBI account to another. This will be mainly handled at treasury level.
4. *Multilateral Net Settlement Batches (MNSB) :* Presently dues of the banks for collection cheque/ DDs, etc. are settle through various clearing houses by arriving at the net position (Receivable minus Payable) which is settled amongst the clearing house member banks through their RBI/SBI Account. This is called as Multilateral Net Settlement Batches (MNSB) in technological terms it is proposed under RTGS to settle the net payable or receivable on account of clearing through RTGS settlement account only at one centre. This will help the banks to manage their liquidity in a better manner as it would not require maintain RBI/SBI account at so many centres with substantial balance remaining

idle. This will be covered under RTGS in a phased manner.

It may be noted that RTGS system benefits bank and client as well. It is having such a potential that on fully being operational we can even achieve a much-dreamed scenario of paperless banking.

**Benefits to Bank**

# Optimum use of infrastructure such as CBS is already in place.

# Better management of liquidity between banks or branches and cost saving.

# Improvement in customer service.

**Benefits to Branch**

# Being front runner in RTGS implementation, more corporate clients can be brought by effective marketing strategies.

# Funds transferred through electronic message system hence lot of labor in backup like issuance of DD and its reconciliation can be avoided.

# Good source for improvement in non-interest income.

# Speedy disposal of customer's remittances gives the edge over the competitors.

**Benefits to Customers**

# Customer is the real beneficiary under RTGS as he gets the funds almost simultaneously when remitter intends to remit. Hence, both the beneficiary as well as the remitter is delighted.

In the present scenario for the banks the biggest challenge is to establish customer intimacy. Banks are looking at newer ways to make a customer's banking experience more convenient, efficient, and effective. They are using new technology tools and techniques to identify customer needs and are offering tailor—made products to match them.

At the last we can say that this network technology has enabled the banks to cross physical barrier and eventually make bank as a unit and *customer becomes a bank customer from a mere branch customer.* It will cut down on a lot of paperwork. The RTGS will give foreign investors more confidence to put money in India.

The same network technology allows bankers to enjoy the benefits of having capability to operate in a scenario where one can effect instant remittance/payments settlement even to another bank.

Trials of RTGS started in March. The system is expected to have a big impact on banks, stock markets, companies and their customers.

The first phase of the RTGS covered only four banks. But Central Bank officials say 120 institutions, including banks, primary dealers and stock exchanges, will be covered by mid-June.

## REFERENCES

Union Dhara, Vol. XXV, No. 4

www.rbi.org.in

www.sify.com/finance

www.ficci.com

www.indianbanksassociation.org

http://web1.mtnl.net.in/~pnbrscmb/whatisnew/recent1.htm

www.bankofindia.com

www.financialexpress.com

www.iba.org.in

www.statebankofindia.com

www.timesofmoney.com

# 19

# IMF and its Role in Financial Management of Developing Countries Through Capital Markets

*Kapil Sharma**

## Second Phase of Globalization – Integration of Capital Markets

The problems of financial management of the second phase of globalization, when the capital markets of the countries are being integrated, are quite different from those during the first phase. During the heyday of the Gold Standard, particularly from 1870 to 1914, when international trade and payments were conducted in currencies backed by and pegged to gold, the world witnessed high capital mobility and integration of the national economies. The system collapsed in the inter-war period and attempts to revive the gold standard failed with declines in capital mobility and disruptions in currency convertibility. When the Bretton Woods Conference re-engineered the international financial system and set up the IMF and the World Bank as the

* Faculty Finance at ICFAI Business School Indore, Jai Singh Palace, 7 Jaisingh Nagar, Rajeev Gandhi Square, Pipliapala, Indore-452017 (M.P.), India.

institutional pillars of the system, it aimed at integrating the world economy mainly through trade, but not capital movements. The IMF Articles of Agreement called for current account convertibility and full freedom of trade and payments for current transactions at fixed exchange rates. But it allowed the countries to maintain restrictions on capital flows on the assumption that complete freedom of capital movements may disrupt the orderly development of current account transactions for trade and payments. This arrangement persisted even after the fixed exchange rate system was given up in the early 1970s. But although no member of the IMF was obliged to remove their discretionary restrictions on capital account transactions, international capital movements registered a sharp increase in the 1970s and continued to increase steadily since then and many countries - especially industrial countries – relaxed restrictions on capital mobility. For those countries, the integration process went beyond the first phase through free current account transactions to the second phase of linking up through capital mobility.

For most developing countries, the integration process has not progressed much further than the first phase, as they have not completely adjusted themselves to trade liberalization and current account convertibility, although almost all of them initiated that process during the 1980s and 1990s through Fund-supported adjustment programmes. That is why most of them have not been able to take advantage of high capital mobility and the phenomenal increase in international capital flows since 1995. The bulk of such capital flows remained confined to only a few developing countries, creating problems for them in adjusting to surges in capital flows. For most other developing countries, problems remained similar to adjusting to trade and payment liberalization and currency convertibility, requiring financial support from the IMF as discussed above.

The conditions necessary for countries getting integrated through capital mobility are related to investors' confidence, with or without full convertibility of their capital accounts. Investors from abroad must believe a country's ability to sustain a process of development with stable policies and a reasonable rate of return on investment that should be transferable in foreign exchange. That is ensured when all current transactions are convertible and investment receipts are repatriable. It is not necessary that all capital inflows and outflows be allowed without any impediment. It would of course enormously help matters and contribute to investor confidence if capital accounts were fully convertible in addition to the freedom for all current transactions to be conducted in foreign exchange. But only a few countries, even in the industrial world, have such complete convertibility with all barriers on current and capital flows completely withdrawn. There would at least be some regulations imposed by supervisory agencies even in the most advanced market economies.

Most developing countries, which received large investment flows from international capital markets, had different degrees of capital accounts convertibility. Some had succeeded in adjusting their economies to the opening up of their trade accounts and to changes i the terms of trade, interest rates and exchange rates in the process of their globalization and the increasing amounts of capital flows. Even with limited capital account convertibility restricted to reparability of investment receipts and of investment incomes, they could receive large inflows of international capital and get engaged in the second phase of adjustment to globalization. The problems they faced and the financial support they required were qualitatively different from those of the first phase. For most of them the problems emerged after a reasonably long period of adjustment with growth that transformed their economies.

There were also some countries which went for capital account convertibility in order to attract increasing capital inflows from the world capital market without successfully adjusting their economies to the first phase of globalization. They soon get into problems, both of liquidity and solvency, in sustaining the process of development and servicing the investment flows. They lost credibility and the confidence of the investors, which precipitated crises of reverse capital flows that convertible capital accounts could not cope with.

Thus, measures to help developing countries face the process of opening up to the first phase of globalization adjusting to free trade and currency convertibility must be followed by policies to help them during the second phase of adjustment to high capital mobility and also capital convertibility. So long as the international capital market retains its buoyancy, investible funds, whether they are for direct investment, portfolio allocation or short-term flows, would be looking for investment outlets in developing countries where marginal productivity of capital is often very high and where the risk-weighted effective rates of return of investment could also be very high if the countries followed appropriate policies. In effect, if a country succeeds in adjusting its economy to the opening up of current accounts and is able to sustain its process of development with a stability of policies, the grounds get prepared for it to attract private capital from international markets. If there is even a marginal increase in the exposure of these countries to international capital markets, they may literally be flooded with capital flows that would quickly lead to the second phase of globalization. They will start getting integrated to the world economy not only by adjusting their productive activities to international prices of commodities and services but also by adjusting to changes in interest rates and exchange rates, to monetary and fiscal policies. As capital flows are absorbed and are deployed to earn the higher rates of return, countries move on to trajectories of higher growth of output and employment when the adjustment process is successful. Clearly such surges in capital flows can be initiated and sustained, even if capital accounts are only partially convertible, if successful adjustment of the first phase increases the productivity of investment and the confidence of investors in the sustainability of policies.

Managing the adjustment of a country to increased capital flows or the second phase of globalization would require completing the first phase of adjusting the structure of production, trade and finance to international prices, and changing interest rates and exchange rates relative to domestic and international inflation rates. All this would call for policies similar to those during the first phase of adjustment through the improvement of macro-economic stability and balance of payments viability with sustainable economic growth. This would require the kind of financial support from international organizations like the IMF as we have already discussed.

In addition to this, however, adjustment to the opening up to capital mobility may face the problem of a reversal in capital flows. The capital that came in as direct or portfolio investment or as short, medium or even long-term loans may withdraw themselves from the country, attended by capital flight or outflows of domestic savings, depending upon the degree of capital convertibility of the country. This can precipitate a major crisis in the economy. It may be very difficult to read just its production and payments system to such reversal of capital flows. An equilibrium of relationships between the growth of outputs, trade, savings and investment together with increased foreign savings, when disrupted due to the withdrawal of foreign savings and flight of domestic savings, may not just be replaced by a lower level equilibrium, but may actually be thoroughly destabilizing with sharply falling output and savings, trade and employment.

Such a disruption can take place for at least two reasons. First, policy mistakes and inability to successfully carry out the implementation of adjustment programmes may make investors lose their confidence. Secondly, either because of such loss of confidence or some exogenous developments or shocks, panic may exacerbate the loss of confidence, when investors and other economic agents compete with each other to exit with whatever funds they can secure by the sale of their assets or withdrawal of their deposits from domestic institutions.

It is important to keep the distinction between the two sources of problems in managing this second phase of globalization through capital mobility. The first is related to the problems of market development – of allowing the market forces to play their role fully in adjusting to the structure of the economy's production, trade and financial system. The second is related to the problems of market failure. If the markets fail to give the right signal to the individual agents in the economy to behave appropriately toward an equilibrium that is optimal not only for the individual but also for the whole economy, there is a problem of market failure. That cannot be solved in the same manner as solving the problems of market development through increased competition and removal of barriers on the free play of market forces. More often than not in such cases, individuals following their own 'rational' maximizing behaviour reach an outcome that is sub-optional or inefficient and unstable.

Financial markets are proverbially prone to market failure, and the most important source of that market failure is imperfect information. Joseph Stiglitz and his associates have formally modeled the effects of imperfect information on the operation of market forces to show that they are so widespread as to make market failures endemic and almost universal unless corrected by appropriate policy intervention. In the case of financial markets, the prices of financial services more often than not fail to clear the market, and prices at which markets are cleared are not always the prices at which the profits of financial service providers are maximized. Unlike commodity markets, money in the capital market is exchanged for a promise of returns in the future, which is contingent upon not only what happens in the future, but also on how the economic agent behaves. So a financial market cannot run as an auction market and lenders do not simply lend to those who offer to pay the highest interest rates. A lender has to form judgments on the basis of whatever information is available about the probability of realizing the promised return. Because the borrower's efforts affects returns on the loan and because of imperfect information, banks cannot stipulate all the actions that a borrower should undertake nor formulate the terms of the loan contract in such a manner that the borrower is induced to take the right action to make the outcomes of the loan a success. Similarly, by varying the price of loans (interest rates), banks may not be able to get the best allocation of loanable funds. Without full information about the projects, the banks cannot judge if the individuals who are willing to pay higher interest rates are not taking undue risks to undertake projects with lower probability of success but higher profits when successful.

In their classic paper of 1981, Stiglitz and Weiss showed that a loan market in a situation of imperfect information is often characterized by credit rationing, where the interest rates could be in equilibrium (in the sense that bankers would not have any incentives to change the rate once it is reached), but where there could still be an excess demand (in the sense that among loan applicants who appear to be identical, some receive a loan and other do not, and the rejected applicants would not receive a loan even if they offer to pay a higher interest rate). This is because the expected return for the bank increases less rapidly than the interest rate, and beyond a point it would actually decrease. This happens mainly because first, as interest rates increase, a higher proportion of riskier borrowers come for the loan. Second, a borrower may opt for a riskier project, because if the project succeeds he can take away the high profit but if it fails he expects to walk away with default as banks cannot fully monitor his actions. In other words, as the real interest rate increases, the probability of default on loan contracts also increases, resulting in less than proportionate increase in expected return. If the deposit rates offered by the banks are equal to their expected return, which would happen in a perfectly competitive model, the supply curve of loanable funds as a function of real interest rates would be backward bending. The real interest rates at which the demand for loans would be equal to the supply and the markets are cleared would be much higher than the rate at which the expected return would induce the maximum supply of loanable funds which would still fall short of the high demand for loans at the corresponding low real interest rates. As the market would not clear the demand and supply of loans, they would have to be naturally rationed out.

Within the framework of the Stiglitz – Weiss model, the banks that are following prudent policies would on their own put a ceiling on their interest rates without being dictated by any regulatory authority. But if there is macro-economic instability with inflationary pressures and real exchange rate uncertainty, the expected return on bank loans may fall much below the actual rate of interest. If there is no regulatory authority trying to restrain the interest rates, the banks may try to take undue risks. The incentive to make high-interest and therefore, high-risk loans can be very tempting, because a favorable outcome may lead to very high profits, while they can walk away when there are heavy losses. The default rates among the borrowers, at a time of crisis, may not be related if the banks concentrate lending to a few large borrowers. The tendency gets compounded if there is a deposit insurance cover, creating a real moral hazard. The expected profits from risky lending could be very high, because with favorable outcomes, banks would keep the extraordinary profits without paying the probability cost of incurring unusual losses, which can be passed on to insurance. The problem of moral hazard is multiplied when the banks are not privately owned, but run as public sector institutions with little risk of bankruptcy or loss of ownership claims when outcomes were unfavorable.

The problems of imperfect information, and the related adverse selection and moral hazards of a domestic financial market are many times multiplied in the international financial markets. International financial institutions could reasonably well perform the agglomeration function of pooling together the savings of individuals in different countries, and the transfer function of transferring resources from savers of one country to investors in another country. But they would find it extremely difficult to perform the selection function (finding the best user in terms of yielding the highest expected returns); and the control function, which involves the principal-agent problem of inducing prudent behaviour of those who have been provided funds. The possibility of market failures in such situations is very large, and the problems do not get solved if the flows of funds expand, or if an institution like the IMF stands ready with substantial support if market failures occur. It will be necessary to have effective regulatory authorities both in the domestic and in the international financial markets – functioning in a framework of much greater transparency and with better flows of information and more effective norms of prudential behaviour by both the lenders and borrowers across the countries.

This is easier said than done, but two issues become clear in this context that need to be highlighted. First, if the IMF is a financial player, providing funds to clients to meet their requirements, it should be as much the subject of regulation as any other international financial institution. In that case, the IMF cannot be given the regulatory function over the international capital market, as proposed by many in recent deliberations. The international regulatory authority should be independent and separate from the financing institutions, even if their ownership is inter-governmental.

Secondly, providing the IMF with more money to solve the problems of the failure of the financial markets is not going to be any help because the problems do not result from the lack of funds, but from the inability to use the funds properly. In other words, the role of the IMF in dealing with the problem of adjustment of countries to the second phase of globalization through high capital mobility and expanding international financial markets needs to be tackled differently from problems of the first phase of globalization. As seen above, the principle requirement then is increasing the IMF's financial support.

Another way of looking at the market failure problem of financial markets is to consider what Jeffrey Sachs describes as problems of multiple equilibria and problems of collective action or coordination Multiple equilibria in financial markets result from the dependence of the value of financial assets on market expectations while market expectations themselves depend upon the value of those assets. This is endemic in the nature of the assets that are traded in financial markets where current payments are made in exchange of the promises of future payments and where the value of those assets depends upon the perceived values of those promises. If the market expectations about the fulfillment of those promises change, the value of those assets will also change. Similarly, if the current value of the assets changes, market expectations about the future value of the assets also change. This circularity gives rise to the possibility of the economy landing into one or another equilibrium, in the sense that once it has landed into one, it would continue to remain in it. There is nothing in market behaviour that can move the economy from one equilibrium to another, no matter how desirable or undesirable the equilibrium position is.

The classic example of such a multiple equilibrium problem is the value of bank deposits that are supposed to be converted into cash according to their face value on demand. But since it is the job of banks to use these deposits to lend to borrowers at different maturities, these deposits can maintain their face value only if a small proportion of these deposits are demanded for encashment at any time, and if banks are not required to call back their loans to meet that demand. But if for some reasons depositors fear that banks will not be able to meet their commitments – either because they have made bad investments or because the overall conditions of the economy have deteriorated – it is quite rational for a depositor who expects the total value of the bank's assets to deteriorate to cash in his deposits before others. But if all or most depositors try to encash their deposits, the banks will have to recall their loans, lose the value of their assets and fail to meet their liabilities, leading to the depositors losing the value of their deposits. Note that even if the banks had made some bad investments, if all depositors were not rushing to withdraw their deposits, the banks should be able to meet the claims of the few depositors who might withdraw and adjust their investments to recover their position in time. The crisis is caused by the combined behavior of individual depositors expecting a fall in the value of the assets of the bank and therefore trying to be the first to redeem their deposits before others who were also expected to behave in the same way. The market expectation of a fall in the value of assets would actually lead to the fall in their value.

It may also be noted that an improvement in the banks investment policies or operational efficiency would not be able to prevent the crisis if market expectations did not change and each depositor continued to believe that other depositors expecting a fall in the market value of the banks' assets would withdraw their deposits. The only way to change the market expectation would be if the market expectations were not fulfilled – if the depositors saw that in spite of withdrawing their deposits, the value of the banks' assets did not fall, and that the banks were able to meet their commitments. This would happen if the banks had recourse to some lender of last resort – a central bank from which they could borrow to meet the demand for liquidity of the banks' depositors without recalling their own loans and impairing their values. There would then be a turn-around and the depositors would regain their confidence in the banks, expecting an improvement in the value of their assets. They would bring back their deposits, hold a larger portion of them as fixed deposits of longer maturities, facilitating the banks to lend to more long-term borrowers. All this would actually improve the value of their assets. If the bank's investment policy and efficiency improved, the turn-around would come sooner, but the basic cause of the market failure would have to be removed and the market expectations would have to be improved, in order to resolve the crisis.

Bank runs caused by panicked expectations of bank failures had been a periodic feature of the financial system of capitalist industrial countries throughout the 19th and 20th centuries. Kindleberger, who chronicled the history of such financial crisis or panics, described them as market failures caused by the irrational behaviour of market agents or manias. He also traced the evolution of central banks functioning as lenders of last resort in the industrial countries Walter Bagehot in 1873 enunciated the role that the Central Bank could play by freely lending to banks facing runs, providing them with sufficient liquidity to meet the depositors' demands. The depositors would then regain confidence that their deposits would be honoured at full value without running to the banks, which would break the expectations of panic· Accordingly, central banking institutions emerged in different countries, playing the role of lenders of last resort, helped by their roles as issuers of notes and as conductors of bank supervision. In the United Kingdom, the Bank of England was a private bank that developed into a state institution performing the functions of a Central bank. In the U.S. the Federal Reserve System was established in 1913 to play the role of a lender of last resort and of a central bank issuing notes.

Since the creation of the IMF at the Bretton Woods Conference, the international community has debated on whether the IMF would be assigned the role of a central bank of the central banks of different countries, with the power to supervise the functioning of the national central banks and their national monetary policies, as well as to issue notes as international lender of last resort. The IMF was given the power of supervising the monetary policies of the governments and the central banks that came to the Fund for financial assistance. The IMF was also allowed to issue SDRs, which are like legal tenders, but are acceptable only by central banks, and which are created not automatically by the Fund's lending but only by an accord of the member governments. The IMF was also a sort of lender of last resort to central banks or national governments in the sense that the central banks could borrow from the IMF to meet their payment needs, but there were strict limits to their total borrowing related to their quotas and subject to time-consuming negotiations and conditional ties. The IMF lending was really meant to help countries to tide over balance of payments problems that could be resolved through changes in policies. It was not meant to help countries withstand the pressures of panics or manias, which were to be resolved not so much by policy changes as by the supply of timely liquidity to resist deteriorating market expectations.

But as countries were exposed to the phenomenal growth of capital mobility in the 1990s, and more and more countries became vulnerable to panics and capital flight abroad due to a collapse of market expectations, there was an increasing clamor to give the IMF the formal role of a lender of last resort. There are several forms in which financial panics could manifest themselves in international markets, due to a collapse in market expectations. In each case, an international lender of last resort could help countries withstand the reversal of market expectations and overcome the panic and impending financial crisis.

Whether the IMF should play that role would have to be decided after carefully considering all the implications. For example, there may be a case of general creditor panic among the international banks when a sovereign government or the financial institutions of a developing country borrowed substantial funds in the short term. Under normal circumstances, with favorable market expectations and projections of growth and profitability in a stable policy framework, the short term loans would be rolled over or new loans would be made to complete the long-term investment programme. But if for some reasons the creditors lose confidence in the country's ability to pay back the loans, or to convert the domestic currency pay offs into foreign exchange or the investment programmes taken up would not be completed, they may not agree to roll over the loans, or if they do, they may insist on a sharp rise in the interest rates at which many of the investment projects already undertaken and only partially completed, may become unviable. If such investments fail, the country's ability to pay back the loans already undertaken gets impaired, and the new loans, if approved would require very high rates of return, not only to pay for themselves but also to service the past debt. If this does not appear to be feasible, it would be rational for individual creditors to withdraw before others do, and if all creditors follow their individually rational course of action the investment programmes would be disrupted, the creditors will lose their money, and the value of their assets will be grossly impaired.

There are two aspects of the problem that should be clearly distinguished. If there are policy failures leading to the impairment of investment projects already initiated or the transferability of the pay off becomes uncertain, they have to be tackled by improving policies. This would not require any lender of last resort, although international institutions like the IMF or the World Bank may have to provide financial assistance to the countries to implement the policy reform in the same manner as during the first phase of globalization. However, the problems may be caused mainly by market expectations when each creditor expects that the other creditors would withdraw because of a loss of confidence and therefore decides to withdrew himself before others do and thereby force the investment projects to be disrupted mid course. On such an occasion, a lender of last resort might be of help, allowing the investment projects to be completed and yielding enough returns to pay back both the old and the new loans. This would then break the market expectations and revive the creditors' confidence, a process that would be helped if the country also corrected the policy failures, if any during that period.

The Mexican crisis of December 1994 was an example of such creditor panic, when Mexico was unable to rollover its short-term public debts. With $29 billion in dollar-denominated debts (tesobonos) falling due in 1995, the Mexican central banks had reserves of only $6 billion and the December devaluation set off a creditor panic when each potential tesobono purchaser feared that if other creditors refused to roll over their debts, Mexico would face a default. The interest rates increased sharply to reflect the default risk, and with little roll over of the debts, Mexico was pushed into a crisis. This was met by the IMF with an unprecedented scale of support to Mexico, together with support from the United States as a loan package as if from a lender of last resort. That loan package succeeded in keeping Mexico out of default and in dissipating the creditor panic. Another possible example of the role of a lender of last resort is when there is a panic regarding the value of a country's currency. If for some reason residents lose confidence in the sustainability of the value of the domestic currency, they would reduce the holding of the currency and shift to other assets or to other currencies. If the fiscal deficit of a country is financed by seigniorage or increasing the supply of high-powered money that people are willing to hold and if there is no reduction in that fiscal deficit, it will be necessary to increase the supply of money, if the residents demand for holding money falls to finance the same deficit. As a result the value of the currency will fall further, reducing further the demand for holding that currency.

Again if the loss of confidence in the value of the currency is due to policy failures, such as uncontrolled fiscal deficits or an unviable exchange rate policy, any programme for regaining the confidence must change these policies. But if the panic leading to the flight from the currency is caused by market expectation feeding on itself – a shift from domestic currency to foreign currency in the expectation of exchange rate depreciation and fulfilling that expectation or in ensuring inflation leading to a further fall in the value of the currency and further depreciation – it could be met effectively by a lender of last resort. By increasing the supply of foreign exchange, the market expectations of exchange rate depreciation can be reversed, provided the policy failures, if any, are corrected.

Thus, if the IMF can effectively play the role of the lender of last resort, it can be very useful in solving the problems of market failure, which are caused by market exceptions and multiple equilibria. But this function of the IMF should be clearly differentiated from the IMF's role as provider of supporting finance for adjustment programmes and policy reforms of countries going through the first phase of globalization and of opening up to world trade and current payments.

There are two major requirements for the Fund to play this role effectively. First, a lender of last resort must be able to provide assistance at the first sign of crisis so that the adverse exceptions do not get a chance to be self-fulfilling. This would call for a prior clearance of the programmes or some arrangements that the countries hoping to receive such assistance would be under a policy discipline before any crisis actually hits them. In the language of the IMF, these countries should be under a shadow programme, fulfilling all the performance criteria regarding appropriate policies, but without drawing any financial support from the IMF, as capital markets would be expected to provide all the finance that is required. This would also ensure that the crisis if it hits the country would be essentially the result of market failures of adverse expectations and not very much due to policy failures or at least not due to policy mistakes that could be detected ex ante.

Secondly, the finance provided by the lender of last resort must be adequate to fight the adverse market expectations. At least the line of credit that would seem to be available to the country must be large enough to make the speculators realize that their attack on the country might be too costly for themselves. Actual drawal of the funds might turn out not to be large, if the market expectations are reversed early. But the provision of funds that could be potentially drawn upon must be sufficient to break the chain of expectations. The scale of finance necessary to effectively play such a role of lender of last resort may actually be very large. Since the countries involved would be relatively developed, receiving substantial capital inflows, a panic that reverses such flows into capital flight might need be very substantial fund to withstand the speculative pressures and revive the creditors and investors' confidence. So, if two or three countries need help at about the same time – which would often be the case because any financial crisis that hits one country has a tendency to hit several countries at a time – then most of the resources of the Fund would be exhausted, leaving very little to assist other countries facing the balance of payments problem of the first phase of globalization.

In re-engineering the international financial system, it would be necessary to address this basic question – what are the priorities in using the Fund's resources. These resources are mainly derived from the Fund's quotas, which are taxpayers' money contributed by the different governments according to some agreed criteria based on the financial strength of the different countries. Unlike the World Bank, the IMF normally does not borrow money from the capital market. The interests that have to be paid for the use of such resources are related to the average interests that treasuries of the different governments have to pay on their borrowings, plus some transaction costs, and more often than not, such interest rates are much cheaper than the market rates. Although every effort should be made to expand these resources, it would still be necessary to use these resources prudently according to priorities. It has also been seen above that the main shortcoming of the Bretton Woods system of adjustment of countries to globalization is that their programmes remain underfunded. For most developing countries the financing of these programmes on market terms may be too costly to be used effectively. Besides, most developing countries are still in their first phase of globalization, requiring substantial finance for carrying out their adjustment programmes from the IMF, supplemented by long-term development finance from the World Bank and other development agencies. The recent increases in the quotas of the Fund would still be insufficient to meet the requirements of funding such programmes. A diversion of a substantial part of these quotas to perform the task of the lender of last resort to few developing countries that have moved to the stage of adjusting to increased capital flows would leave the programmes of most of the countries under-funded, therefore under-implemented.

But if quota resources are not to be used in its functioning as a lender of last resort, how would the IMF, if it has to perform the role, secure the necessary finance that is quick disbursing and adequate? A possible answer is to replicate the existing schemes of the General Agreement to Borrow (GAB), which can be invoked to meet a "systemic" crisis. These are schemes of a prior agreement among the Central Banks and the governments, to open a line of credit when the IMF has to assist countries coming out of a systemic crisis. It is possible to have different variations of the schemes in principle, and the agreement may extend beyond the government and the central banks to major commercial banks with substantial stakes in the revival of the affected countries and resolution of their crisis. Even for normal adjustment finance of these countries, the Fund may use its limited quota resources to leverage funds from the capital market, rather than provide all the finance from its own resources. That would allow the Fund to leave most of its quotas for funding the adjustment programmes of the overwhelming bulk of the countries, which have very little access to the international capital market.

There is another form of market failure that is related to collective and coordinated action, which may require a relatively small amount of the IMF finance to catalyze other sources of funds, but needs the IMF to play a more effective role of coordinator and promoter of collective action. The classic example of such a case is the debt adjustment problem of major debtors, who for some reason or other default in their debt servicing and who would face a major crisis if creditors chose to withdraw their debts even at a loss, and were not willing to provide new loans. What would often be necessary is some debt forgiveness (when individual creditors may like to free-ride, but collectively may be willing to share in the forgiveness), some sharing of the burden by all creditors, adopting procedures of the bankruptcy courts in many countries and ascribing "seniority" to creditors providing new loans so that they can be serviced first before others, and thereby ensuring new flows of credit that are essential to revive the economy. This would require the role of a coordinator among the creditors who can bring about such collective action, which the IMF can perform effectively if authorized internationally. The IMF would not require much finance for this purpose, but would need the authority to address the problem effectively.

## Conclusion

To sum up, the IMF still has to play a major role in managing international finance in a global economy. It has to distinguish its supportive role to countries adjusting their economies and their policies to the opening up of trade and current accounts from its role of support to countries which are open to receiving substantial capital flows from international capital markets. The Fund is seriously under-funded, requiring a substantial increase in quotas. It needs to be supplemented by other development banks. But it also requires the authority to redesign adjustment programmes, taking fully into account all the failures of the market. But more importantly, the Fund can play all the roles of a market leader and coordinator, not only of policies designed carefully to meet the specific requirements of globalizing developing countries, but also of raising funds to assist their economies in adjustment.

## REFERENCES

Bagehot, Walter (1873,1962), Lambard Street: A Description of the Money Market, Richard Irvin Inc.

de Vries, Margaret (1985), The International Monetary Fund, 1972-78, IMF Washington DC.

de Vries, Margaret (1987), Balance of Payments Adjustment, 1945-1986 the IMF Experience, IMF Washington DC.

Dixit A and R. Pindyk (1994), Investment Under Uncertainty, Princeton.

Greenwald, B and J.E Stiglitz (1986), Externalities in Economics with imperfect information and incomplete markets; Quarterly Journal of Economics, May 1986. Horsefield, J. Keith(1969): The International Monetary Fund,1945-65, IMF, Washington DC.

IMF (1987), Growth Oriented Adjustment, proceedings of a Seminar,1987. James, Harold (1996): International Monetary Cooperation since Bretton Woods; IMF, Washington DC.

Kindleberger C.P. (1996), Manias, Panics and Crashes; Third Edition, John Wiley.

Robichek E.W. (1986), The IMF's Conditionality Reexamined in Adjustment Conditionality and International Finance; ed. by J. Muns) IMF, Washington DC.

Rodrik, Dani (1990), How should structural adjustment programmes be designed; World Development No. 7, 1990.

Sachs, J.(1995), Do we need an International Lender of Last Resort; F.D. Graham Lecture: Princeton.

Sachs J. and A. Warner(1995), Economic Reform and the Process of Global Integration; Brooking Papers on Economic Activity, No. 1, 1995.

Sachs J, A Tornell and A Velasco (1995), Lessons from Mexico; Memo, Harvard, MA.

Sengupta, Arjun, IMF and the LDCs; Macmillan: (forthcoming).

Sengupta, Arjun (1995), The Financial Sector and Economic Reform in India; Sir Purushottamdas Thakurdas Memorial

Lecture, 1994, Indian Institute of Bankers, reprinted in Economic and Political Weekly, Feb., 1995.

Stiglitz J.E. and A. Weiss (1981), Credit Rating in Markets with imperfect information; American Economic Review, 1981(3).

## Relevant Websites (http://www.)

worldbank.org

wto.org

imf.org

bis.org

ifc.org

# 20

# Assessment of the Impact of Financial Sector Reforms in Ghana

*J.V. Mensah* and I.K. Acheampong***

## Introduction

The economy of Ghana grew rapidly after independence on 6 March 1957. However, between the 1970s and early 1980s the economy deteriorated with the Gross Domestic Product (GDP) falling by about 13.5% percent and per capita real GDP also falling by about 22 percent. Secondly, the consumer price index rose at an average rate of 65 percent per annum (ISSER, 1991). During this period also, there was extensive government intervention in the financial sector policies and Ghana operated a repressive financial regime. As part of its repressive policies, the Bank of Ghana (BOG) imposed ceilings on interest rates, high reserve requirements, restrictions on market entry and quantity control of credit allocation in an inflationary charged economy (Aryeetey et al., 1997; Gockel et al., 1997).

The result of all these were that the real interest rate were steeply negative, thereby falling far below the

* Research Fellow Centre for Development Studies, University of Cape Coast, Ghana.

** Senior Lecturer, Department of Economics, University of Cape Coast, Ghana.

equilibrium levels. Cheap credits were given mainly to the public sector at the expense of productive investment culminating in the crowding out of the private sector. Another dimension of the crowding out effect was that government through the treasury bill mechanism also borrowed from the public thereby, having a shrinkage effect on the amount of savings available at the commercial banks for lending to the private sector. Following a considerable decline in private savings, the banking system's financial intermediation role virtually collapsed (World Bank, 2000; Leechor, 1994).

As with most developing countries that have pursued economic and structural reforms, Ghana has been undergoing a process of financial sector restructuring and transformation as an integral part of a comprehensive programme for some time. Against the background of financial shallowing and repressive measures, Ghana adopted the financial sector adjustment programme (FINSAP) in 1988 as a sequel to Structural Adjustment Programme (SAP) which was supported by the International Monetary Fund and the World Bank. Like the ERP/SAP, FINSAP was implemented in two phases. According to Gockel et al., (1997: 78), the programme of financial sector reforms (FINSAP 1) was implemented in 1988-90, *inter alia,* to:

1. restructure distressed banks to make them competitive and financially viable;
2. improve saving mobilisation and enhance efficiency in credit allocation;
3. reform banking laws;
4. restructure the regulatory framework and improve bank supervision;
5. develop money and capital/securities markets; and
6. establish a non-performing assets recovery trust.

FINSAP 2 began in 1990/91 to:

1. continue and complete any unfinished business under FINSAP 1;

2. divest state-owned banks in accordance with financial liberalisation and deregulation;
3. reform the institutional structure of Bank of Ghana (i.e. central bank); and
4. promote and strengthen the non-bank financial institutions.

In short, the financial Reform Programme was meant to bring about institutional reforms in the financial and banking sector in order to achieve improved performance or efficiency in financial intermediation. The major components of the programme included:

1. The revision of the legal and regulatory framework of the banking lending institutions;
2. Upgrading technology and introducing innovations into the whole banking process to bring about reduction in transaction cost and improve services; and
3. Introduction of measures to ensure liberalisation of exchange rate as well as interest rate deregulation.
4. Ensuring capitalisation of the banks by encouraging private sector participation, divestiture and ensuring minimum involvement of government in the sector.
5. Bringing about competition amongst the banks and improving savings or their credit formation.

Ghana government continues to observe policies adopted under FINSAP to ensure soundness and efficiency in the financial system. In addition to these policies and regulations, Bank of Ghana aims at adopting monetary and financial policies in an attempt to reduce inflation and to contain the volatility in the exchange rate of the cedi to ensure a conducive macroeconomic environment for economic activity (Republic of Ghana, 1999; Bank of Ghana, 2003a).

The objectives of the paper are to assess the effectiveness of the financial sector reforms in addressing the consequences of the pre-reform financial policies, and to examine whether the reforms have been able to foster the development of a more efficient, competitive and sound banking system. The next section looks at Ghana's Financial System. It is followed by theoretical issues on financial sector reforms and the subsequent section presents the methodology of the paper. It is then followed by an assessment of the impact of the financial sector reforms on financial development in Ghana. The last section presents the conclusions of the paper.

## Ghana's Financial System

The financial system in Ghana includes Bank of Ghana, commercial banks, insurance companies, discount houses, finance houses, leasing companies, savings and loans associations, credit unions and a stock exchange. Added to these are 115 rural banks widely dispersed throughout the country (Bank of Ghana, 2003a).

Of the seventeen banking institutions currently operating in Ghana, foreign investors hold the majority of the shares in eight commercial banks, and three banks are state-owned; there are nine purely commercial banks, five merchant banks, and three development banks (Table 1). Twelve out of the 17 banks are private.

Three commercial banks *viz.* Ghana Commercial Bank Ltd (GCB), Social Security Bank Ltd (SSB) and Barclays Bank Ltd (BB) own 57.3% share in the banking system (Table 2). While eight banks account for most financial activity, no single institution is dominant. About half of all bank branches in the interior of the country belong to a single state-owned commercial bank, the Ghana Commercial Bank (Acquah, 2003). Bank of Ghana was expected to divest all its shares in commercial banks by mid 2000 (Republic of Ghana, 1999). As at December 2003, the Non-Bank Financial Institutions (NBFIs) comprised 10 Finance Companies, 3 Discount Houses, 9 Savings and Loans Companies, 5 Leasing Companies, and 2 Venture Capital Fund Management Companies. Also, 285 Forex Bureaux were in operation (Bank of Ghana, 2003a).

**Table 1 : Structure of the Ghanaian Banking Sector as at December 2002**

| Bank | Ownership Ghanaian | Percent Foreign | Number of Branches |
|---|---|---|---|
| **Commercial Banks** | | | |
| 1. Ghana Commercial Bank Ltd | 97 | 3 | 133 |
| 2. SSB Bank Ltd. | 46 | 54 | 38 |
| 3. Barclays Bank of Ghana Ltd. | 10 | 90 | 24 |
| 4. Standard Chartered Bank | 24 | 76 | 23 |
| 5. The Trust Bank Ltd. | 39 | 61 | 6 |
| 6. Metropolitan and Allied Bank | 53 | 47 | 4 |
| 7. International Commercial Bank | 0 | 100 | 3 |
| 8. Stanbic Bank Ghana Ltd. | 9 | 91 | 1 |
| 9. Unibank | 100 | 0 | 1 |
| **Merchant Banks** | | | |
| 10. Merchant Bank Ghana Ltd. | 100 | 0 | 5 |
| 11. Ecobank Ghana Ltd. | 6 | 64 | 4 |
| 12. CAL Merchant Bank | 34 | 66 | 3 |
| 13. First Atlantic Bank | 71 | 29 | 2 |
| 14. Amalgamated Bank | 100 | 0 | 1 |
| **Development Banks** | | | |
| 15. Agricultural Development Bank | 100 | 0 | 39 |
| 16. National Investment Bank | 100 | 0 | 11 |
| 17. Prudential Bank | 100 | 0 | 5 |

*Source:* Adapted from Acquah (2003).

## Theoretical Issues on Financial Sector Reforms

This section attempts to explain the financial sector reforms from the viewpoint of theory. A major plank of the financial reforms is the financial sector liberalisation. The financial policies embodied in the standard IMF and World Bank economic reform packages are derived from most of the intellectual content of the financial repression hypothesis of McKinnon-Shaw-Fry (McKinnon, 1973; Shaw, 1973; Fry, 1988) which became the orthodoxy in the 1980s. It was viewed as conditionality under the IMF and World Bank's economic reform packages. It was argued that this strategy would deepen the financial structures and renew economic development.

**Table 2 : Assets and Liabilities of the Banking Sector in Ghana in 2002**

| *Bank* | *Total Assets = Total Liabilities (In billions of Cedis)* | *Share in banking system (Percent of total banking system)* |
|---|---|---|
| Banks 1-3 | 9763 | 57.5 |
| Banks 4-8 | 5481 | 32.3 |
| Banks 9-13 | 1474 | 8.6 |
| Others | 263 | 2.6 |
| Banking System | 16981 | 100.0 |

*Source:* Acquah (2003).

The major argument of the financial repression hypothesis is that repression is mainly attributable to government intervention particularly interest rate ceiling, and other quantity rationing devices such as the use of selective credit policies to maintain low interest rates in situation of high inflation. The McKinnon-Shaw school maintains that the adoption of low interest rate policy coupled with selective credit policy and an expansionary monetary policy are indispensable for governments seeking to control the allocation of resources to implement planning as well as to finance public sector deficits at low cost. Government deficits are invariably financed by taxing the domestic monetary system in one way or the other, a higher proportion from the financial system being transferred to the public sector than the private sector.

The McKinnon-Shaw school argues that financial liberalisation and deepening enable interest rates and exchange rates to reflect relative scarcities, stimulate savings, and discriminate more efficiently between alternative investments. This, in turn, not only induces replacement of capital intensive process and technology by labour intensive process but also provides high elasticity of substitution between labour and capital. Financial deepening will generate positive employment and distributional effects in favour of labour, thus contributing to both higher growth and more equitable distribution of income (Fry, 1988).

In their view, the most important step for success is to attain a competitive free market equilibrium level of deposit rate that will maximise growth. First, this leads to an increase in the real supply of credit and achieve a higher economic growth without raising the loan rate. Second, even if the loan rates were raised, it would mean greater efficiency per unit of investment thereby raising output sufficiently to offset the declining share of output allocated to investment (McKinnon, 1973:46).

The McKinnon-Shaw school advocates that financial liberalisation should be incorporated as part of a stabilisation package, emphasising the benign effects of interest rate policy as a stabilisation device, when the economy is repressed. They maintain that there is a double advantage in initiating financial liberalisation as part of liberalisation programmes because it avoids or at least ameliorates the contractionary effects of deflation produced solely through monetary deceleration. These policy recommendations would not only raise the rate of economic growth through an increase in credit availability but would also reduce inflationary pressures.

## Methodology

This paper utilises secondary data from official sources for analysis. The analysis of relevant issues are undertaken in a before and after scenario. It must be observed that in the context of ex-post evaluation of the impact of changes in economic policy the before situation is not equivalent to the without policy change situation since it is not satisfactory counterfactual. However, in the circumstances, the before and after approach is the simplest and most straight forward that can be used for this paper.

The results of the study are presented according to the components (see the introduction) *viz.* revision of the legal and regulatory framework; bank development and encouraging private sector participation; ensure liberalisation of exchange rate and interest rate deregulation;, divestiture and ensuring minimum involvement of government in the sector; and bringing about competition amongst the banks and improving savings mobilisation or their credit formation.

## Results - Impact of the Financial Sector Reforms

### *1. Revision of the Legal and Regulatory Framework*

As part of the financial sector reforms, the new Banking Law of 1989 (PNDCL 225) was enacted. The law provides an appropriate framework for restructuring and strengthening of banks. It defines the minimum capital requirements for various types of banks and by bank ownership. The required minimum paid-up capital for commercial banks with at least 60% Ghanaian ownership is 200 million cedis while that for foreign banks with Ghanaian ownership less than 60% is 500 million cedis. The law enjoins banks with development banking as their core business to have a minimum paid-up capital of one billion cedis. The main reason for the higher minimum capital requirement prescribed for development bank is that these banks engage in term lending, thereby exposing them to greater credit risk. The law, with reference to development banks, seems to contradict with the general provisions of banking, which include the provision of long-term loans By implications, the other banks are not qualified to grant term loans.

Secondly, the Banking Law of 1989 is explicit on capital adequacy. Although the law prescribes a minimum capital adequacy ratio of 6%, Bank of Ghana has the discretion to increase the ratio for a particular bank or the entire banking sector. Even though the Basle Accord, promulgated in July 1988 by the governors of the G-10, covered a wider spectrum of risk assets, the 1989 Banking Law recognises only two classes of risks namely assets that require no capital backing and those which must be fully backed. The riskless assets are defined as cash, Bank of Ghana and Ghana Government securities, overnight balances at discount houses, and others excluded from either side of the balance sheet. All loans and advances as well as off-balances sheet items are said to be risky and must be fully backed by the required amount of capital.

Furthermore, the 1989 Banking Law dictates explicit safeguards and penalties against excessive risk taking. These include maintenance of a reserve fund from annual profits, prohibition from excessive lending and undertaking non-bank activities, upgrading Bank of Ghana's examination and supervisory functions, and penalties in respect of non-compliance with the 1989 Banking Law.

The Bank of Ghana Law of 1992 (PNDCL 291) was promulgated to streamline structures, functions and powers of the Bank of Ghana and emphasise the Bank's role as a central force in the banking and financial system in Ghana. Later on, the Securities Industry Law of 1993 (PNDCL 333) was promulgated to regulate and maintain surveillance over the securities industry. Banks are submitting relevant financial data on a regular basis to the supervisors (Bank of Ghana) and on site inspection are being carried out.

The enactment of the Non-Bank Financial Institutions (NBFI) Law of 1993 (PNDCL 328) is another reform measure. This law covers discount houses, acceptances houses, building societies, leasing and hire-purchase companies, venture capital funding companies, mortgage financing companies, savings and loans associations, and credit unions. It also set the minimum capital requirement for the establishment of an NBFI at 100 million cedis. The minimum capital adequacy ratio is set at 10% of risk assets and the Bank of Ghana has the authority to prescribe the minimum level of liquid assets. NBFIs can accepts deposits from the public, but only for a fixed period of not less than three month unless with prior exemption from Bank of Ghana.

The enactment of the new Banking Law and NBFI Laws seemed to have streamlined the emergence of financial institutions. More private entrepreneurs have established various types of NBFIs, which emphasise private sector participation in the financial sector. The implication is that financial services are being extended beyond the range typically provided by the banks, thereby increasing competition and efficiency in financial intermediation.

2. *Bank Development and Encouraging Private Sector Participation*

Before 1998, there was an active and pervasive government involvement in monetary and credit policies motivated partly by a belief that perceived externalities and other market imperfections inherited from colonial banking arrangements worked against desirable patterns of investment and economic growth (Gockel et al., 1997). Consequently, public ownership dominated the banking system: all banks set up between the early 1950s and after independence were wholly or majority owned by the public sector, while the government also acquired 40% shares each in Standard Chartered Bank Ghana Ltd (SCBG) and Barclays Bank Ghana Ltd (BBG). Though the SCBG and BBG have majority of shares owned by overseas banks, their policies and operations were influenced by the Bank of Ghana, both banks having been incorporated in Ghana according to the Banking Act of 1970.

The period of reforms since 1990s witnessed the establishment of new banks. Before 1990, there was no licensed private bank in Ghana. Most of the staff of the new banks were experienced bank officials who had been enticed to join the new banks from the older banks. There was more private involvement in the banking industry with the divestiture of about 40% Ghana shares in Social Security Bank and Ghana Commercial Bank in the 1990s (Gockel et al, 1997). All but one of the new banks were merchants. Indeed, the new banks were of the impression that there was very little room to compete with the other banks in retail banking as this tends to be more costly. The merchant banks are typically one office-bank that specialises in export/ import business. Even though licensed as merchant banks, the new banks perform additional businesses in commercial and development banking. The introduction of sophisticated financial services and electronic purses in Ghana was due largely to the innovative and revolutionary practices of the new banks. The reforms encouraged many financial institutions to upgrade their technology, especially by computerising their operations.

The financial sector witnessed some developments in 1996. While institutional developments took place, a few new products were introduced, and infrastructural facilities were expanded and improved. Two new commercial banks were established in 1996, bringing the total number of banks operating in the country to 17. These were Prudential Bank Ltd. and International Commercial Bank Ltd. They are entirely privately owned with significant foreign participation. As at December 2003, new products and services introduced by the banks included Dial-up service, Automated Teller Machine (ATM), Phone and SMS banking, Visa Gold Card, Visa Electronic Debit Card, and Sika Text.

Developments in the non-bank financial sector in 1996 were slower than in 1995. Whereas as many as seven institutions were licensed by Bank of Ghana to commence operations in 1995, the number fell to three in 1996. This brought the total number of registered non-bank financial institutions operating in the country to 29. They were made up of 10 finance houses, 7 savings and loans companies, 4 leasing companies, 2 discount houses, 2 hire purchase companies, 2 building societies, 1 venture capital funding company and 1 mortgage finance company. Despite the growth and development of the non-bank financial institutions sector, the mismanagement of funds that Securities Discount Company Limited suffered in the course of the 1996 painted a poor picture of capacity within the financial sector, despite reforms.

The year 1997 saw relatively little activity in the financial sector, compared to the previous five years. No new banks were licensed in 1997. However, new products/services were introduced by some commercial banks. Notable among these were Barclays Bank's launching of the Barclays *Akuafo* Bond (geared toward encouraging the development of saving habits among farmers), and introduction of the Business Master, a personal computer-based system, that gives large companies access to their bank accounts by logging into the bank's computer system. Standard Chartered Bank also introduced a new service in which payment of client's utility bills could be effected through the ATM. Electronic banking was also introduced in the form of a PC-based product, VISTAPRO, which enables client's to access their account balances, and also conduct banking transactions. In the third quarter of 2003, in an attempt to reduce operational costs, the Standard Chartered Bank closed some or all of its branches in certain regional capitals such as Takoradi, Sunyani, Cape Coast and Bolgatanga.

In 1997, five new rural-community banks were licensed, bringing the total to 132. Of this number, the Bank of Ghana classified 60 as performing satisfactorily in that they were found to be complying with capital adequacy requirement, 55 as mediocre in the sense that they were capital deficient, and 17 as distressed banks. By December 2003, there were 115 rural banks, of which 99 were classified as satisfactory and 16 mediocre, based on the capital adequacy ratio of 6% (Bank of Ghana, 2003b). Six new Non-Bank Financial Institutions (NBFIs) were licensed during the 2003, bringing the total number of NBFIs to 32. Of the six, five were finance houses, and one a leasing and hire-purchase company

In line with the institutional reforms such as strengthening of internal management, operational system and control of banks, the Banking Supervision Department of the Bank of Ghana was strengthened and the National

Banking College was established in 1995 to offer training programmes with a view to enhancing the performance of middle and senior bankers in the industry (Republic of Ghana, 1999).

As a result of increasing cheque fraud in the early 1990s, the Bank of Ghana improved the quality and security of cheque paper by introducing Magnetic Ink Character Recognition (MICR) codelines on the cheques in 1997 to make them amenable to automated processing. Paralleled to the development of the MICR cheques, the Bank of Ghana completed automated interbank cheque clearing in November 1997. It also completed bureau service (or fine sorting) for commercial banks in March 1998.

3. *Ensuring Liberalisation of Exchange Rate (Exchange Rate Policy)*

Persistent exchange rate volatility resulting from internal and external forces is one of the major economic problems facing the Ghanaian economy. This phenomenon tends to impact negatively on domestic production, trade balance and employment. Until the ERP was launched in 1983, the cedi was overvalued and foreign exchange was very scarce. These were the period when Ghana maintained a highly restrictive foreign exchange rate regime, with some occasional devaluations (during 1971, 72 and 78). The ratio of the parallel to official rate rose steadily, from 1.60 in 1970 to 22.54 in 1982. In response, the real exchange rate appreciated from 27.73 to 277.62 in 1982. There was a huge depreciation of the cedi in 1983 due to an increase in demand for foreign exchange to import food items to supplement local production due to the severe drought experienced in 1983 (ISSER, various issues).

Figure 1 shows the trends in the nominal and real exchange rates from 1978 to 2000. After the introduction of the FINSAP, both nominal and real exchange rates have been increasing implying depreciation. From 1986-

1996, the growth rate of the exchange rate fluctuated around 50%. This could be attributed to the tightened financial policies and strengthened supervision of the banks and Forex Bureaux by the Bank of Ghana.

Fig. 1 : Ghana's Nominal and Real Exchange Rates: 1978-2001
*Source :* IMF (1999 - 2001) *International Financial Statistics.*

After April 1983 the government of Ghana implemented a three-stage exchange rate reform (see Table 3). The free floating policy was intended to make foreign exchange available to the private sector for the importation of inputs

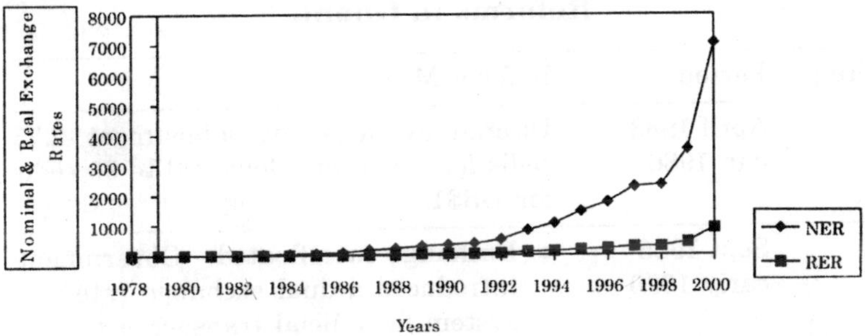


and thereby enhance private investment. The devaluation of the cedi also increased the real domestic producer price of cocoa and improved cocoa production and exports. Between 1983 and 1990, the volume of exports increased by an average of 10%, reversing the contraction in the previous two decades.

For three years in a row to 1997, the real exchange rate appreciated significantly. Very sharp depreciation in the nominal rate in the first half of the year, forced the Bank of Ghana to intervene by selling foreign currency in the markets. However, in the last quarter of 1997, its reserves ran seriously low and therefore it resorted to moral suasion and administrative management. This was responded to by collusive rate fixing by the Association of Forex Bureaux.

Both actions ignited the resurgence of the parallel market activities in foreign exchange transactions. In the first half of 1997, the nominal exchange rate depreciated by 19.4% in the interbank market and 23.4 % in the forex bureaux market. On average, the nominal exchange rate depreciated by 25.2% in the interbank market and 25.6% in the forex bureaux market in1997. These rates contrasted with much higher rates of depreciation of 36.4% and 32.1% in the interbank and forex bureaux markets respectively in 1996. In fact, the 1997 rates of nominal depreciation were the lowest since 1992.

**Table 3 : Stages in Exchange Rate Reforms in Ghana**

| Stage | Period | Reform Measure |
|---|---|---|
| 1 | April 1983 - Jan 1986 | Discrete exchange rate adjustment -2.75 cedis for US$1 was devalued to 90 cedis for US$1. |
| 2 | Sept 1986- early 1990 | • Exchange rate floated - Government introduced a dual exchange rate system for official transactions.<br>• Access to the auction was gradually broadened to include all payments and transfers for current international transactions.<br>• Parallel market for foreign exchange was absorbed - Private Forex Bureaus were in full operation and the exchange rate was free floating. |
| 3 | Early 1990 - April 1990 | • Bank of Ghana discontinued the retail auction of foreign exchange and introduced the wholesale auction.<br>• The management of exchange rates took place directly in the inter-bank markets. |

***Source :*** Bank of Ghana (various issues)

Liberalisation of the exchange rate in an inflationary environment in Ghana has led to constant depreciation of the cedi and has created a volatile foreign exchange market, which is evident by the increasing process of dollarisation in Ghana (Ziorklui, 2001). Currency substitution in Ghana has been exacerbated by the fact that most trading firms tend to quote prices of their goods in dollars (Gockel et al., 1997). Consequently, those savings which normally should have been made in cedis were made in hard currencies. Replacing the domestic currency with foreign currencies often has serious implications for the financial development of the economy. To deal with the dollarisation problem, the Bank of Ghana has included foreign currency holdings in the definition of money. Foreign demand deposits held by residents of Ghana in Ghanaian banks are referred to as foreign account, distinct from external accounts or off-shore accounts held by Ghanaians.

The instability in the exchange rates poses a problem to the businesses to plan their activities. The continuous depreciation of the cedi is the manifestation of the existence of monetary growth and inflationary growth in the economy. Three main results could be noted from Fig. 2.

Fig. 2 : Ghana's Macroeconomic Indicators: 1978-2000

- Growth in money supply (GM2S), including M1, was volatile even after the FINSAP in 1988. However, it witnessed declining trend towards 2000;

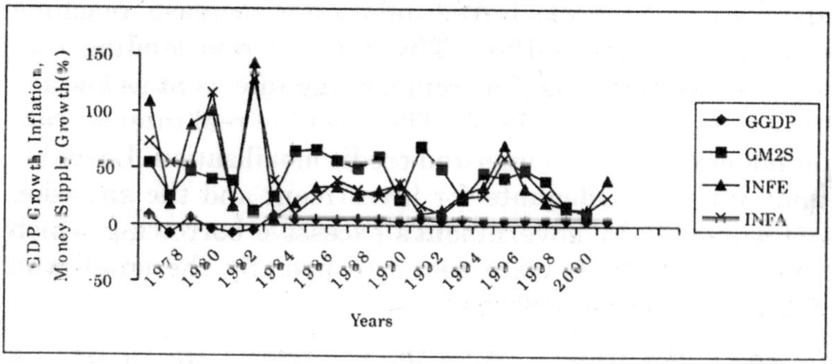


*Source :* Ghana Commercial Bank Ltd (2002).

- The growth of Gross Domestic Product (GGDP) before 1984 exhibited negative ranges but remained stagnant after 1986. Thus, the FINSAP has not been able to prepare the economy to grow at a higher rate.
- Inflation rates (INFA) were high before the FINSAP but reduced considerably even though the desired single digit rate continued to be a mirage. Inflation has been declining after late 2001 to below 25% but it is still high for effective business operation and investment as well as for mobilising savings. Ziorklui (2001) notes that the financial reform in Ghana supports the general notion that financial reforms in countries with high inflationary pressures has less chance of success than it does in those countries where macroeconomic stability prevails at the time of the reforms. The high inflationary pressures have resulted in negative real interest rates, thereby producing a disincentive for financial savings.

*4. Interest Rate Deregulation*

The pre-reform period was characterised by negative real interest rates due to excessive government borrowing and government's refusal to adjust the nominal interest rate. The lending interest rate was administratively pegged below the equilibrium level to stimulate investment. Between 1970 and 1986, the lending rate hovered around 15%. The expansionary monetary policy coupled with adverse supply shocks forced inflation to increase, reaching its peak of 123% in 1983. This left the real lending rate negative. For example, the real lending rate went as low as -108.3% in 1983 (IMF, 1990). The negative real interest rate did not encourage savings and credit mobilisation. Loanable funds were not adequate for investment and the situation was worsened by government's excessive borrowing which crowded out the private sector, especially the small and medium enterprises (SMEs).

The policy framework of the pre-reform era focused on Keynesian models that the interactive mechanism between finance and economic development proceed from low interest rates (to increase investment) to high rate of income growth, thereby increasing savings rates. The Bank of Ghana invariably used as instruments low interest rates, credit ceilings and sectoral credit controls as well as reserve requirements. Normally, the first two instruments were designed to reinforce each other to ensure that bank credit flowed to the designated priority sectors of the economy such as agriculture, manufacturing and exports.

Reforms to interest rate policy began in 1987, when limits to maximum lending rates and minimum time-deposit rates of commercial banks were abolished (ISSER, 1992; Gockel et al, 1997). The deregulation process was completed in 1988, with complete liberalisation of rates on savings deposits. Since then, commercial banks have been free to quote their own rates on deposits and loans. The Bank of Ghana has continued to set the lead rate, the Bank Rate. The bank rate is not only applied to overdrafts to banks and for the rediscounting of financial instruments but also serves as the benchmark rate for the economy-wide regime of interest rates. Changes in the bank rate are usually effected to reflect the monetary policy stance of the Bank of Ghana. The bank rate was raised steadily from 30% in 1990 to 45% by the end of 1996 as a measure to control monetary expansion.

Reserve requirements have been used to help regulate monetary expansion during the 1990-1996 period. The global reserve ratio generally remained high but the structure had been progressively changed by lowering the primary ratio and raising the secondary ratio. The purpose was to enhance banks' earnings from their reserves as an incentive for them to mobilise more financial savings (Gockel et al, 1997).

Interest rate deregulation in 1988 was based on the theoretical framework of McKinnon (1973) and Shaw (1973). The McKinnon-Shaw hypothesis shows that a low (negative) real interest rate is a disincentive to savings, thereby reducing the availability of loanable funds. The main policy prescription of the McKinnon -Shaw hypothesis is that interest rate should be determined by the interplay of demand and supply. In the financial reform process, nominal and real interest rate would increase for effective credit mobilisation.

The McKinnon-Shaw hypothesis has been challenged by Stiglitz and Weiss (1981) who are of the view that interest rates cannot function as an allocator of credit because borrowers with higher risk may be considered rather than those with potential good business with lower risks. This occurs when information asymmetry leads to market failure. According to these authors, there are two aspects of information asymmetry *viz.* adverse selection and moral hazard. Adverse selection is an *ex ante* concept which explains how lender's information on borrowers concerning the viability of an enterprise will be incomplete. The borrower with better information on his/her business concerning its high risky nature is prepared to borrow money at a high interest rate compared with the borrower whose business is less risky but not prepared to borrow money at a similar high interest rate. The lending institution will select the riskier business and this will marginalise the SMEs in the credit market and affect the lending institutions capital base. As a result, the level of investible funds will be reduced, and this will affect the performance of the entire economy.

As regards moral hazards, there is the tendency for borrowers to hide their true motives for requesting for funds. In an *ex post* sense, this means that they will misapply the loans. For example, they will put the money into speculative or consumption activities. If the investment gains are positive, the borrowers will settle their indebtedness and this reduces the lenders' risk. On the contrary, if the above does not happen, the investor will bear the full cost of the risk. There is therefore, the tendency for lending institutions to reduce the amount of loanable funds and they may even raise the interest rate to make up for losses.

Recent developments in the financial sector have shown that the Financial Sector Liberalisation has exacerbated the high interest rates and the urban bias of banks. For example, reading the 2001 Annual Budget of Ghana, the Minister of Finance and Economic Planning, remarked that the government views with concern the high cost of borrowing and lending in the banking system because the phenomenon does not augur well for private sector development. The gap between the lending and borrowing rates of 20% is a disincentive to business. The cost of credit being the high current interest rate of 47% - 57% per annum has contributed to the demise of many businesses and difficulties in recouping financial capital.

As part of efforts to minimise credit constraints, past and present governments have sponsored a lot of programmes funded through banking and non-banking institutions. Interest rates were pegged at 20% compared with an average market rate of 45% as a way of satisfying the demand of the SMEs. Although interest rates were low, loan recovery rate has not been satisfactory. Loans granted under the Poverty Alleviation Fund in 1999 has up to date not been fully paid back. Up to date, only about 40% has been paid back. This is close to moral hazard outcome of Stiglitz and Weiss (1981).

The collapse of SMEs that enhance economic development is a matter of great concern. The displacement of labour, loss of incomes and enterprise failures contribute to the weak economy and high incidence of poverty. About 40% and 32% of Ghanaians live below the upper poverty line of 900,000 cedis and the lower poverty line of 700,000 cedis respectively (Ghana Statistical Service, 2000a, 2000b).

Banking institutions have shown signs of fatigue. Indeed, some banks such as the Ghana Co-operative Bank, Bank for Housing and Construction, and several rural banks have folded up. The closure of some branches of some commercial banks in pursuit of financial rationalisation shows the de-segmentation of the activities of commercial banks albeit the creation of new commercial banks. Since 1988, nine new commercial banks have been established and these are concentrated in the capital city, Accra. This characterises the urban-bias nature of the commercial banking system and tends to crowd-out SMEs from the financial market.

5. *Improving Savings Mobilisation and Credit Formation (Financial Intermediation)*

During the ERP, the financial sector reforms intended to improve financial intermediation adopted by the Government of Ghana included the decontrol of the maximum term deposit rate in 1987; the decontrol of the maximum bank savings rate in 1988; the unification of bank cash reserve requirements on demand and time and saving deposits; the decontrol of bank charges and fees; and reduction in the required bank cash reserves in 1990; and the increase in the remuneration of the bank cash deposits with the Bank of Ghana to 5% in 1991 (ISSER, 1992).

Despite the above reforms, financial intermediation remains very low due to low level of confidence in the banking system, insufficient competition and weak financial infrastructure. The low confidence in the banking system is the result of unorthodox monetary policy measures adopted in the late 1970s and early 1980s such as currency reversion, the withdrawal of fifty-cedi notes from circulation, freezing of bank deposits in excess of 50,000 cedis pending investigation for tax liability, restricted bank loans for the financing of trade inventories, and the requirement that cheques must be used for any business transaction exceeding 1,000 cedis in 1982. Although all the restrictions imposed prior to the financial sector reforms have been gradually removed, public confidence in the banking system is still not fully restored (Gockel et al, 1997).

Stringent regulations introduced by the financial sector reforms made the banks more cautious about lending to the private sector until 1991 when credit controls were discarded (ISSER, 1992). The financial institutions have increasingly directed their funds to the acquisition of high-return earning, low-risk government papers thereby crowding out credit to the private sector. The major constraints facing the private sector in Ghana are credit availability and allocation (Popiel, 1990; Aryeetey et al., 2000). The financial sector liberalisation has led to increased allocation of credit to the private sector as shown in Table 4. Secondly, the household contributed more than 70% to the financial savings with the formal financial institutions between 1994 and 2001 as presented in Table 5.

**Table 4 : Credit Allocation to Private and Public Sectors**

| *Year* | *Central Government (¢ billion)* | *Public Enterprise (¢ billion)* | *Private Enterprise (¢ billion)* | *Total (¢ billion)* |
|---|---|---|---|---|
| 1993 | 740 (72.83) | 89 (8.76) | 187 (18.41) | 1016 (100.0) |
| 1994 | 759 (62.68) | 178 (14.70) | 274 (22.62) | 1211 (100.0) |
| 1995 | 835 (58.97) | 188 (13.28) | 393 (27.75) | 1416 (100.0) |
| 1996 | 107 (10.84) | 200 (20.26) | 680 (68.90) | 987 (100.0) |
| 1997 | 777 (39.34) | 128 (6.48) | 1070 (54.18) | 1975 (100.0) |
| 1998 | 2420 (56.90) | 194 (4.56) | 1639 (38.54) | 4253 (100.0) |
| 1999 | 3464 (54.52) | 424 (6.67) | 2466 (38.81) | 6354 (100.0) |
| 2000 | 5839 (53.68) | 1213 (11.15) | 3826 (35.17) | 10878 (100.0) |
| 2001 | 5083 (44.38) | 1775 (15.50) | 4595 (40.12) | 11453 (100.0) |

*Note* : Figures in parentheses are row percentage.
*Source:* Bank of Ghana (various issues).

**Table 5 : Household Saving Contribution**

| *Year* | *1994* | *1995* | *1996* | *1997* | *1998* | *1999* | *2000* | *2001* |
|---|---|---|---|---|---|---|---|---|
| Contribution (%) | 76.3 | 77.7 | 75.0 | 72.4 | 78.1 | 75.1 | 71.0 | 73.6 |

*Source:* Ghana Statistical Service (various issues).

However, the small scale enterprises still depend on the informal financial sector, which finance about 45% of the private sector demand for credit. Banks do not normally risk lending to new investors, large or small, who do not have a track record (Aryeetey et al., 1994). Many small enterprises do manage to finance rapid growth from their own *profits* and *supplier's credit and* from non-bank sources. Once a small enterprise was established, *advances* from customers become the most important source of finance after retained earnings (Aryeetey et al., 1994; Mensah, 2000).

The banking industry was shaken by the "A-Life Scandal" which affected three banks, namely Ghana Commercial Bank, Bank for Housing and Construction and Co-operative Bank. The scandal involving over-exposure to a single borrower to the tune of about ¢160 billion showed the weakness of the supervisory agency and the clearing system. This lending to a single borrower ensured that one company received as much as over 8% of total domestic credit.

### 6. *Monetary Policy*

During the ERP restrictive monetary policies were pursued to curb inflation. The reduction in the budget deficit coupled with the use of some indirect instruments of monetary control, such as open market operations, initially stabilised the monetary base of the economy. The government of Ghana had substantial external financial support which was used to finance public investment in 1988 and 1989. From 1989 through 1991, domestic credit policy was tightened to offset the growth in foreign assets. The fiscal surplus generated in 1989 was used to repay government's debts to the Bank of Ghana. Repayments were increased in the subsequent years and domestic credit extended by the Bank of Ghana declined. Government no longer has unrestricted access to base money. However, except in mid 1991 when Bank deposits and lending rates became positive, monetary policy in Ghana has been less successful in restoring positive real interest rates.

High monetary growth rates in Ghana have persisted for a long time (see Table 6). During 1991-96, broad money supply increased at an average rate of 40 percent per annum. The main force behind the sharp annual increases in money supply continued to be government deficit financing. The high rates of monetary growth led to a build-up of excess liquidity in the economy. This contributed to fuel inflationary pressures, with inflation averaging about 37 percent per annum during the period. Effort to control monetary expansion in order to minimise its inflationary effects had generally proved ineffective. This was due to prevailing constraints to monetary management as well as emergence of new difficulties.

**Table 6 : Key Monetary Indicators Ghana: 1961-1996**

| *Monetary Indicators* | *Period Average* | | | | | | |
|---|---|---|---|---|---|---|---|
| | *1961-66* | *1967-71* | *1972-77* | *1978-83* | *1983-86 ERP1* | *1987-91 ERP2* | *1992-96 Post ERP* |
| Private Investment/GDP | 8.4 | 8.4 | 5.5 | 2.8 | 3.8 | 7.0 | 4.3 |
| Public Investment/ GDP | 8.4 | 3.9 | 4.8 | 2.0 | 3.7 | 7.6 | 12.2 |
| Private Savings/ GDP | 7.8 | 6.3 | 13.0 | 8.5 | 5.2 | 6.7 | 7.4 |
| Public Savings/GDP | 2.4 | 1.8 | 3.9 | 2.2 | 0.5 | 5.4 | 5.7 |
| Fiscal Balance/GDP | –6.4 | –3.4 | –10.0 | –6.1 | –1.7 | 0.7 | –1.7 |
| Broad Money (M2) Growth | 41.6 | –4.1 | 36.9 | 38.9 | 55.9 | 33.9 | 42.2 |
| M2/ GDP | – | – | 24.7 | 17.6 | 12.5 | 14.5 | 17.1 |
| Growth of Private Sector Credit | 22.8 | 22.6 | 14.1 | 33.1 | 86.3 | 40.1 | 44.2 |
| Growth of Public Sector Credit | – | – | 48.3 | 54.1 | 68.9 | 49.2 | 36.4 |
| Real Lending Rate | –2.9 | 5.8 | –16.8 | –28.5 | –12.2 | –3.0 | 7.8 |
| Inflation Rate | 11.8 | 3.9 | 41.5 | 73.0 | 49.3 | 30.3 | 37.0 |

*Source:* Bank of Ghana, *Quarterly Economic Bulletin* (various issues); IMF International Financial Statistics, (various issues).

Monetary management after the introduction of the financial sector reforms covered tight monetary control, price stability, exchange rate liberalisation, interest rate liberalisation and savings mobilisation. It relied on the use of open market operations, reserve requirement and interest rates as instruments.

Open market operations (OMO) and the legal reserve requirement for the banks were used to control money supply in order to mop up excess liquidity and enhance price stability in the economy. OMO was implemented through a wholesale system where a number of instruments were sold to various financial institutions and were restrained from retailing to final buyers. The prices of various instruments were through the weekly auction of Bank of Ghana bill and other bills. Treasury bills were used to raise funds for the government and as a monetary management tool. The government indirectly influenced the prices of securities by determining the amount of securities that would be available to the participating banks.

Using the reserve requirement, the minimum cash ratio was raised from 5% to 10% in October 1996 when it was realised that inflationary pressures were mounting despite the mopping up of excess liquidity through OMO. The banks were also required to hold 37% of their deposits in secondary reserves and another 10% in temporary special reserve. Thus, banks were required to reserve a total of 57% of their deposits. However, the banks actually held 70% of their deposits in 1996. While this was good as a check on monetary expansion, it could be seen as a failure of the banks to effectively perform their financial intermediation role in the economy.

In spite of the tight monetary policies, there was an expansion in the money stock and price instability due to government deficit financing. Even though inflation has declined it has not reached the desired level for effective investment and savings mobilisation. As stated earlier, the exchange rate has been persistently depreciating due to the inability to check inflation and this poses a real challenge to the business community. Arguably, without these policy-measures, the expansion in the money stock would have been higher on account of expansionary fiscal policy.

## Conclusion

This paper has shown that Ghana has moved from an interventionist financial policy regime to a more liberalised one since 1988. The financial sector reforms have resulted in appropriate legal and regulatory framework for restructuring and strengthening the banks and Non-Bank Financial Institutions as well as strengthening the supervisory capacities of the Bank of Ghana. It has also achieved some progress in bank development and private sector participation. The public sector banks have adopted more explicitly commercial operating and credit policies with less political pressure, have strengthened credit procedures and internal controls. The two largest public sector banks (i.e. Ghana Commercial Bank and Social Security Bank) have been partially privatized with minority shares floated on the local stock market in 1995 and 1996.

Several new banks with private sector participation have been established alongside a range of NBFIs since the implementation of the reforms. This has encouraged some amount of competition in the financial sector. The new entrants have avoided retail banking outside the large cities, and the quality of service provision in retail banking still needs improvement. The financial institutions have introduced new products and services, which aim at enhancing credit allocation and savings mobilization. Some banking institutions have shown signs of fatigue as evidenced by folding up of Ghana Co-operative Bank, Bank for Housing and Construction and several rural banks. Three major commercial banks have also closed some of their branches in pursuit of financial rationalization and this may have adverse effects on financial service delivery in the affected communities.

Despite the improvements to the institutional structure of the financial system, the banking system is still shallow and perform little intermediation between savers and borrowers in the private sector. Unstable macroeconomic environment with high rates of inflation have prevented positive real interest rates to encourage financial savings. Furthermore, the liberalisation of the exchange rate in an inflationary economy has led to constant depreciation of the cedi, thereby increasing the process of dollarisation in Ghana.

## REFERENCES

Acquah, P.A. (2003), "Liberalizing Ghana's Financial Services Sector: The Role of Overseas Banks" remarks delivered at Commonwealth Business Council Banking and Financial Services Symposium, London, June 25, 2003.

Aryeetey, E., Harrigan, T. and Nissanko, M. (2000) *Economic Reforms in Ghana: The Miracle and the Mirage*, Accra: Woeli Publishing Services.

Aryeetey, E, Hettige, H., Nissanko, M. and Steel, W. F. (1997), "Financial market fragmentation and reforms in Ghana, Malawi, Nigeria and Tanzania", *The World Bank Economic Review*, Vol. 11, No. 2, pp. 195-218.

Aryeetey, E, Baah-Nuakoh, A., Duggleby, T., Hettige, H., and Steel, W. F. (1994) "Supply and Demand for Finance of Small Enterprises in Ghana", *Discussion Paper*, No. 251. Technical Department, Africa Region. Washington, D.C: World Bank.

Bank of Ghana (various issues) *Quarterly Economic Bulletin*, Accra: Bank of Ghana.

Bank of Ghana (2003a), *Annual Report 2003*, Accra: Bank of Ghana.

Bank of Ghana (2003b), *Quarterly Economic Bulletin*, Accra: Bank of Ghana.

Fry, M.J. (1988), *Money, Interest and banking in Economic Development*, Baltimore and London: The John Hopkins University Press.

Ghana Commercial Bank Ltd (2002) *Quarterly Economic Review*, Vol. 23, No. 1.

Ghana Statistical Service (various issues) *Quarterly Digest of Statistics*, Accra: Ghana Statistical Service.

Ghana Statistical Service (2000a), *Poverty Trends in Ghana in the 1990s*, Accra: Ghana Statistical Service.

Ghana Statistical Service (2000b), *Ghana Living Standard Survey Report for the Fourth Round (GLSS)*, Accra: Ghana Statistical Service.

Gockel, A.F., Kwakye, J.K. and Baffour Osei (1997), "Financial and Monetary Developments: Policies and Options", in V.K. Nyanteng (ed) *Policies and Options for Ghanaian Economic Development*, Institute of Statistical, Social and Economic Research (ISSER), Legon: University of Ghana, pp. 60-100.

International Monetary Fund (IMF) (various issues) *International Financial Statistics*, Washington D.C: IMF.

Institute of Statistical, Social and Economic Research (ISSER) (1992) *The State of Ghanaian Economy in 1991*, Legon: ISSER, University of Ghana.

Institute of Statistical, Social and Economic Research (ISSER) (1991) *The State of Ghanaian Economy in 1990*, Legon: ISSER, University of Ghana.

Leechor, C. (1994), "Ghana: Frontrunner in Adjustment", in I. Hussain and R. Faruqee (eds.) *Adjustment in Africa: Lessons from Country Case Studies*, Washington D. C: The World Bank, pp. 153-192.

McKinnon, R.I. (1973), *Monetary and Capital in Economic Development*", Washington D. C: Brookings Institution.

Mensah, J.V. (2000), *Small-Scale Industries in Ghana's Economic Development: Comparative Economic Efficiency of Rural and Urban Small-Scale Industries in the Central Region*. PhD Thesis, Bradford: University of Bradford.

Popiel, P. (1990), Developing Financial Markets in Sub-Saharan Africa", *EDI Working Paper*, Washington, D.C: EDI/World Bank.

Shaw, E.S. (1973), *Financial Deepening in Economic Development*, New York: Oxford University Press.

Stiglitz, J.E. and Weiss, A.M. (1981), "Credit rationing in markets with imperfect information", *American Economic Review*, Vol. 71, No. 3, pp. 393-410.

World Bank (2000), *Can Africa Claim The 21st Century*", Washington, D. C: The World Bank.

Ziorklui, S.Q. (2001), "The impact of financial sector reform on bank efficiency and financial deepening for savings mobilisation in Ghana", Arlington: Equity and Growth through Economic Research (EAGER).

# 21

# Micro-credit and Role of Banks Need for Initiatives and Commitment

*Amrit Patel**

In the light of implementing economic and financial sector reforms in India, need for providing micro-credit, leave alone micro-finance has gained significant importance which is reflected from the following and efforts called for to accelerate the pace of credit disbursement in the light of the year 2005 having been declared as year of micro-credit.

- The role of micro-credit in the eradication of poverty was stressed by the United Nations in agreed conclusions 1997/1 adopted by Economic and Social Council on 25th July 1997, in which the Council called for "strengthening the institutions supportive of micro-credit and recognized impor-tance of access of micro-credit of people living in poverty to enable them to undertake micro-enter-prises to generate self-employment and contribute to achieving empowerment, especially women".
- The Monterrey Consensus specifically mentions micro-finance initiatives and recognizes that micro-finance and credit for micro, small and medium-sized

* E-mail:amrit_rpatel@yahoo.com.

enterprises including in rural areas, particularly for women, as well as national savings schemes, are important for enhancing the social and economic impact of the financial sector.

- The momentum generated by the major UN conferences and summits particularly the World Summit for Social Development and the fourth World Conference on Women inspired the holding of the Micro-credit Summit in Washington in 1997 which through its Declaration and Plan of Action launched a nine-year global campaign to reach 100 million of the world's poorest families and especially the women in those families with credit for self-employment and other financial and business services by the year 2005. The latest data show that the number of poor people who benefited from micro-credit programs grew from 7.6 million in 1997 to 26.8 million by the end of 2001.
- Micro-credit and other financial services for poor people are important instruments for poverty reduction and for employing poor people, especially women.
- The provision of a range of financial services for the poor people is often referred to as micro-finance. Micro-credit or micro-finance has received increasing attention as effective anti-poverty tool and has successfully contributed to lifting people out of poverty in many developing countries.
- The concept that poor people benefit from micro-credit has evolved to the recognition that the people living in poverty deserve access to a range of financial tools that enhance their ability to increase incomes, build assets and mitigate the vulnerabi-lity in times of economic stress.

## Impact

- Sound micro-finance is having a positive impact on the lives of poor people, improving their household incomes, building assets and safeguarding them against vulnerability arising from economic and other crises, through savings, credit, insurance and other financial vehicles.
- Evidence from micro-finance programs demonstrates that access to financial services enables poor people to improve their health, nutrition, education and school enrollment of their children.
- Financial services also help to improve the stability and growth of micro-enterprises. However, poor people in most countries still do not have access to formal financial services.

## Need for

The challenge now is to expand the reach and develop more effective services for poor people on a sustainable basis.

- The observance of the year as the year of micro-credit provides a significant opportunity to raise awareness of the importance of the micro-credit and micro-finance in the eradication of poverty, share good practices and further enhance programs that support sustainable pro-poor financial sectors around the world.
- Expanding outreach can contribute to achieving the goals of major conferences and summits as well as Millennium Development Goals, particularly targets related to halving the proportion of the people living in extreme poverty by 2015, and promoting gender equality and empowerment of women.
- Establish a working group to prepare recommendations for stimulating sustainable, pro-poor financial sectors.

- To make voluntary contributions and lend other forms of support to the year, in accordance with the guidelines for international year.
- Highlight enhanced recognition to the role of micro-credit in the eradication of poverty, its contribution to social development and its positive impact on the lives of people living in poverty.
- To consider taking additional steps in the eradication of poverty including the strengthening of existing and emerging micro-credit institutions and their capacities so that credit and related services for self-employment and income-generating activities might be made available to an increasing number of people and to develop further other micro-finance institutions.
- To consider provision of unique and widely varying needs of poor people that require an extensive range of financial products and services including credit, savings, insurance and asset-building mechanisms.
- To incorporate empowerment approaches in micro-finance and building networks to advocate women's greater participation being an important priority.
- Focus is needed on promoting good practices especially building of micro-finance institutions and forging partnerships between Governments, donors, international organizations, non-govern-mental organizations, the private sectors and other stakeholders.
- Assessment and promotion of the contribution of micro-credit and micro-finance towards achieving the goals as contained in Millennium Development Goals.
- Promotion of awareness and understanding of micro-credit and micro-finance, their role in poverty eradication including achieving the MDG and how they empower people and contribute to communities.

- Identification of critical measures for Government to optimally stimulate sustainable, pro-poor financial sectors and build collective visions and strategies that position micro-credit and micro-finance as integral part of a country's financial system.
- Increase of the capacity of the micro-credit and micro-finance service providers to be more effective and efficient at addressing the needs of poor and very poor people, and strengthening the capacity of donors and Governments to support those institutions by following good practice micro-credit and micro-finance principles.
- Promotion, support and creation of innovation and strategic partnerships between and among Governments, organizations of the UN, private and public sectors, NGOs etc to build and expand the outreach and success of micro-credit and micro-finance.

**Abysmal Progress**

Despite the fact that the micro-credit program as a major policy instrument of the RBI has been under implementation for more than a decade and with a share of women being 90 per cent as well as repayment of around 98 per cent, only 71,70,00 Self-Help-Groups out of around 7 million have so far been credit-linked with formal credit agencies. Cumulative disbursements of Rs. 2,04,70 m covering 71,70,00 SHGs work out to Rs.2,85,49 per SHG

While the south continues to maintain its lead and more than half of credit-linked SHGs in the country are from the south, over 78 per cent of the total micro-credit has gone to two southern States of Andhra Pradesh and Tamil Nadu. Uttar Pradesh and Maharashtra are two other States in the country performing little better.

Not only India's performance with regard to linking SHGs with Banks has been very unsatisfactory but there has been significant disparities when the efforts of banks to link SHGs as are significantly evident in four states of Andhra Pradesh, Tamil Nadu, Uttar Pradesh and Maharashtra as against those in States of Bihar, Orissa, Rajasthan, Madhya Pradesh and North-Easter region.

**Disparities Among States in Credit-linking SHGs with Banks & Provision of Credit**

| *States* | *No. of SHGs* | *Cumulative Disbursement [Rs.in million]* |
|---|---|---|
| Andhra Pradesh | 28,10,00 [50.7] | 97,53.8 [57.2] |
| Tamil Nadu | 9,84,10 [17.8] | 42,55 [24.9] |
| Uttar Pradesh | 5,36,96 [9.7] | 8,74.6 [5.2] |
| Maharashtra | 2,80,65 [5.0] | 6,97.5 [4.2] |
| Orissa | 42272[7.7] | 510[3.0] |
| Bihar | 8161[1.6] | 120.9[0.7] |
| Rajasthan | 22742[4.1] | 462.5[2.7] |
| Madhya Pradesh | 15271[2.7] | 307.4[1.8] |
| North-Eastern Region | 4069[0.7] | 60.0[0.3] |
| Total | 553686[100] | 17041.7 [100] |

## International Year

It may be recalled that the role of micro-credit in the eradication of poverty was stressed by the United Nations in agreed conclusions 1997/1 adopted by Economic and Social Council on 25th July 1997, in which the Council called for strengthening the institutions supportive of micro-credit and recognized importance of access of micro-credit of people living in poverty to enable them to undertake micro-enterprises to generate self-employment and contribute to achieving empowerment, especially women.

The momentum generated by the major UN conferences and summits particularly the World Summit for Social Development and the fourth World Conference on Women inspired the holding of the Micro-credit Summit in Washington in 1997 which through its Declaration and Plan of Action launched a nine-year global campaign to reach 100 million of the world's poorest families and especially the women in those families with credit for self-employment and other financial and business services by the year 2005. The latest data show that the number of poor people who benefited from micro-credit programs grew from 7.6 million in 1997 to 26.8 million by the end of 2001. In this context India's performance has been the most unsatisfactory, despite India has world's large number of poor and Rural Financial Intermediaries are quite capable [and their capacity can be enhanced], if they demonstrate their willingness and commitment in this area.

United Nations has, therefore, declared the year 2005 as the international year of micro-credit focusing on following areas.

- Assessment and promotion of the contribution of micro-credit and micro-finance towards achieving the goals as contained in Millennium Development Goals [MDG], particularly targets related to halving the proportion of the people living in extreme poverty by 2015, and promoting gender equality and empowerment of women..
- Promotion of awareness and understanding of micro-credit and micro-finance, their role in poverty eradication including achieving the MDG and how they empower people and contribute to communities.
- Identification of critical measures for Government to optimally stimulate sustainable, pro-poor financial sectors and build collective visions and strategies that position micro-credit and micro-finance as integral part of a country's financial system.
- Increase of the capacity of the micro-credit and micro-finance service providers to be more effective and efficient at addressing the needs of poor and very poor people, and strengthening the capacity of donors and Governments to support those

institutions by following good practice micro-credit and micro-finance principles.

## Impact of BRI'S Approach

In this connection, our Commercial Banks and Regional Rural Banks can learn much from the experience of a committed Bank Rakyat Indonesia [BRI] which acts as a Micro-finance Institution and is now the largest financially sustainable intermediary in the developing world.

BRI's approach to micro-finance by making its services widely available and the financial intermediary profitable helped the country reduce the incidence of poverty from about 40 per cent of the population in mid 1970's to about 11 per cent in 1996. When the East Asian economic crisis began and poverty in the country started to rise in 1997, BRI concentrated on financing poor people, who had lost their jobs, for pursuing informal sector enterprises. It, also, gave secured and tailor-made deposit services to poor people in times of crisis. BRI continued its wide outreach, high repayment rate and profitability even during the 1997-99 East-Asian economic crisis as could be evident from the following

- Deposits mobilized were more than double from 7.7 trillion Ruppiah in June 1977 to 17.1 trillion Ruppiah by December 1999 with number of saving accounts having increased from 17 m to 24.2 m.
- Lending went up from 4.3 trillion Ruppiah in 2.5 m loan accounts to 6.0 trillion Ruppiah in 2.5 m accounts.
- Pre-tax profit increased from 714 billion Ruppiah to 1.2 trillion Ruppiah
- Return on assets improved from 4.9 per cent to 6.1 per cent.

World Bank says about this Bank and its operations "Program succeeded because the bank loaned at market rate, used income to finance their operations, kept operating cost low and devised appropriate savings instruments to attract depositors. Further, the vast profits of desa unit have been used to cross-subsidize bank's other divisions' wealthier clients." A survey of 1341 borrowers of this bank by an independent agency revealed that 76 per cent borrowers got loans within a week's time and only two per cent had to wait for over two weeks. About 98 per cent borrowers were satisfied with staff services and 95 per cent borrowers obtained quick guidance.

BRI adopted demand-led commercial financial system approach [in sharp contrast to supply-led system approach] for financing poor households under its micro-finance program from the year 1984 and became financially sustainable from 1986. While implementing supply-led subsidized lending approach during 1970s and early 1980s, BRI had significant loan loses and over dues. Commercial financial system approach providing both credit and savings services helped all categories of rural house-holds, more importantly low income group people, to enlarge, diversify and manage their business/enterprises, increase productivity, smoothen income flow, meet consumption needs, increase savings and provide savers with security, liquidity and returns. This system raised funds for lending from mobilizing local savings and commercial debts and covered cost of operations and acquired sustainability as well as covered large number of clients.

## Financial Restructuring

In 1970s Government invested a large share of oil wealth in agriculture for developing irrigation potential, evolving new rice technology, building infrastructure, providing education and health services in rural areas where 80 per cent population lived in mid 1970s. This investment helped agriculture and rural industries support generation of rural employment, income and growth.

Financial System in the formal sector began in 1970. In 1970s BRI opened more than 3500 village units to channel subsidized Government's credit to rice farmers under the country's rice intensification program and two other programs viz. small investment loan and small permanent working capital loan during 1970s and 1980s. However, while the rice intensification program was successful, credit components could not succeed. A large amount of subsidized loan, being at below market interest rate, was cornered by elite farmers and did not reach to poor farmers as was envisaged. Moreover, arrears and loses were high. The program was phased out in 1985.

Financial reforms were extended to rural areas and Government issued first major financial deregulation package in 1983. It abolished credit ceilings and permitted banks to set their own interest rates on loans and deposits. The Government, also, decided to convert the subsidized unit desa into a sustainable system of commercial banking at the local level to extend credit at commercial interest rate. This made possible the transformation of BRI's unit desa system from merely an channeling agent for targeted subsidized government's loans to a profitable financial intermediary providing loans and deposit services to clients in rural areas throughout the country. With the restructuring of the BRI in 1984, the unit desa [local banking system of the State owned BRI], the BRI attained nationwide coverage and financial sustainability

**BRI'S Approach**

BRI's desa unit provides credit to individuals as well as borrowers in groups, innovates new financial products suitable to borrowers and savers, adopts interest rate spreads that cover cost of lending and permit institutional profit, adopts innovative operating methods and information system. It has widely spread small outlets, specialized staff receiving need based training and incentives and finances entire loan portfolio from *locally mobilized savings*.

BRI's desa system, prior to adoption of commercial financial system approach, deliberated following issues very seriously and thoroughly.

- Would there be local demand for credit at interest rates needed for BRI to cover all its costs and earn a profit?
- Would people place their savings in BRI's village units?
- Both these issues were researched by expert teams through intensive market surveys and it was observed that there was huge demand for credit at high rate of interest. Demand for saving services was equally very high provided the deposit instruments and services were designed to meet the needs of poor.
- How long it would make the restructured commercial financial system to break even and begin to make profit?
- It achieved in less than two years as against a targeted plan of two years.

BRI's approach was entirely market based which made the system profitable since 1986 and without subsidy since 1987 and has a very high repayment rate of 98 per cent

- Unit desa offered loans up to US$ 3,400 in 1999 for any productive purpose carrying annual interest of 32 per cent, if repayment was made on time.
- Saving instruments offered a choice between different combinations of liquidity and returns. Deposits proved to be a highly stable source of funds for lending.
- Borrowers were offered considerable flexibility in respect of terms of loans to meet their credit needs. Loans were available for a variety of maturities ranging from three months to 24 months for working capital and 36 months for investment purpose. Repayment terms included monthly, seasonal and single payments to suit borrower's generation of income and capacity to repay. Investment loans with grace period of 9 months were provided. Loan packages of 36 variations indicating possible

combinations of maturities and repayments were offered to suit varying types of credit needs of borrowers. Each of these combinations was printed in the loan tables to help determine borrower's needs. This, also, made loan operations transparent, eliminated scope for corruption or favoring special customer with liberal terms.

- Loan application and appraisal procedure was very simple. Staff assisted in form filling, if required, visited customer to verify and satisfy about the credit management aspects. Large loans were granted with collaterals. No notarization and over due certificates were called for. While new borrower's loan was sanctioned within a week's time, repeat loan took two-three days and loan was disbursed immediately.
- Responsibility for loan decision was delegated to village units, whereas regional offices had to de-emphasis their control minded approach and become more oriented to development and promotion of quality of business.
- Provision of staff training helped them acquire in-depth knowledge of rural credit market and changed their behaviour and attitude towards customers; performance based cash awards and other incentives ensured high loan repayment rates. Management and organizational system aimed at capacity building to deliver financial services efficiently to low income people with wide spread outreach throughout the country. All these had impact on continuing institutional profitability without subsidy.

**Lessons to be Learnt**

From the successful operations of BRI as well as other Micro-finance Institutions our commercial/cooperatives and Regional Rural Banks may learn following lessons to create impressive impact on the rural poor households, more particularly women, through provision of micro-credit.

**Operating Procedure**

- While standardized loan program is essential, adequate flexibility in respect of loan purposes, maturities and amounts is absolutely necessary to meet borrowers' needs.
- Credit products and savings instruments need to be designed and priced in such a way that the spread/ margin ensures RFI's operational profitability.
- Credit can be provided to any credit worthy borrower for any financially viable economic activity [farm and non-farm sector] or household investment purpose. They are not limited to any sector, commodity or group a mixed package of which minimizes risk of lending.
- Credit can be extended to individuals or to self-formed small groups whose members guarantee one another's loans [not necessarily group guarantee].
- Small amount of loan is initially given to new borrowers. After establishing borrower's willing-ness and capacity to repay the credit, loans of higher amount are provided.
- A good number of borrowers are assisted for working capital with relatively small terms [typically from two months to two years] and frequent repayment of installments [weekly, biweekly or monthly], borrowers repay both principal and interest in their installments
- Credit is provided only for pursuing ongoing enterprises or borrowers experienced in specific activities reflecting a track record of good business performance.
- Borrower training, other than orientation to the loan program, is not required to receive a loan.

## Loan Approval and Disbursement

- Need based intensive training is imparted to Staff to evaluate the character of borrowers, the capacity of their enterprises to generate sufficient income to repay loans and, in case of group loans, the cohesiveness of groups and their capacity to repay.
- Loan amount is considered based on the assessment of borrower's repayment abilities from the current income flows and not necessarily from estimates of possible returns from use of the loans.
- Loan application form is simple and most of the credit decisions are made quickly at the lowest level outlets preferably within a week for new borrowers and one or two days for existing borrowers.
- Borrower transaction costs are relatively low because forms and procedures are simple, loan disbursements are timely and repeat visits to the institutions to obtain a loan are usually unnecessary.

## Loan Collection, Policies and Procedure

- RFIs should develop effective loan collection system. or should be prepared to bear the full cost of risk.
- Staff who approve and disburse loans should be responsible for recovering the loans.
- Credit officers should not monitor every borrower's business or the use of loans but concentrate on those who are in arrears. This helps each credit officer serve more clients and build up quality loan portfolio.
- Borrowers should be motivated/encouraged to maintain a god repayment record and make their enterprises credit worthy. Such borrowers can be granted another loans as well as loans of higher amount.
- As a matter of principle borrowers who do not repay on time are not sanctioned any loan. However,

there may be rare exceptions in which loans are rescheduled because of a visible catastrophic event.

- Borrowers who make timely repayment can be offered incentives [such as interest rebates]
- Borrowers who fail to repay are contacted by a staff member immediately on the next day. Borrowers in arrears are constantly followed up.
- Late repayments are recorded properly. When a loan repayment is one day late, the entire outstanding balance of the loan should be shown as delinquent. Not all sustainable institutions use this method, but they typically at least show the repayment as over due one week after its due date.

**Loan Portfolio Management**

- Loan accounting and reporting system is simple and transparent. Management information system is simple but designed to permit frequent, regular and accurate assessment of the performance of each borrower, credit officer, outlet and branch as well as of the RFIs.
- Adequate provision for loan losses is made and regularly reviewed. Bad debt is written off based on standardized aging criteria established by the RFIs, but loan collection efforts continue.
- RFIs accord highest priority for loan delinquency measurement and management and formulate policies and procedure and review them regularly. Credit officers focus on effective implementation of procedures for timely repayment of loans.
- Specialised and trained staff from controlling office visits as frequently as possible the outlets that disburse loans and carefully supervises the loan portfolio.

- Demand for loans is scientifically estimated through field surveys and supply is carefully organized to make operations cost effective.
- Asset-liability management is carried out on a frequent, regular basis and given high priority.
- Loan portfolios are diversified with regard to types of enterprises and geographical areas.

## Savings

While it is established that the poor households do save in a variety of forms and whatever small amount is possible depending upon the time, amount earned and financial exigencies, emphasis is placed on designing instruments appropriate for micro-savers and informing them about the saving instruments available and training the staff properly.

Savings are mobilized from people who live or work near the institution's outlet. This permits the institution to meet local demand for savings services. Collection of savings is not confined to poor households/micro-savers but is extended to elite community too. The bigger accounts of large savers raise the average account size, making it cost-effective for the RFIs and use savings from all sources to finance an expanding micro-loan portfolio.

Loans and savings accounts are designed , priced and managed together.

As unmet demand for saving services varies widely in different countries and regions; RFIs undertake long-range resource planning exercise based on the likelihood that at a given time number of clients demanding appropriate savings services will be more than those demanding micro-loans. Thus RFIs plan their savings and credit services in relation to the local market.

Savings from poor household borrowers is not a pre-condition for borrowing. However, poor households save and they are offered saving services for voluntary savings to suit their needs. No compulsory savings are required.

Savings instruments are available to borrowers and non-borrowers. It is not necessary to save in order to borrow.

Mobilization of voluntary public savings requires effective public supervision and regular internal supervision and audit.

RFIs consistently provide adequate security, quick and friendly service and effective cash management. Given normal expectations of withdrawals, sufficient cash is on hand during opening hours to permit services to withdraw when they come in, according to the terms of deposit instruments they hold.

Several savings and deposit instruments with different ratios of liquidity and returns are offered; opening and minimum balances are set low on savings accounts. Savers are encouraged to select an account or a combination of accounts that meets their needs.

For most small savers, security, convenience, liquidity and service are usually more important than returns.

Staff is trained to identify potential savers. They visit them, explain the available instruments and services and help them open accounts appropriate to their needs. Staff maintains ongoing relations with their clients and develop information networks through which they locate potential savers.

Locally appropriate public relation activities are emphasized. These include educating the public about the services provided and about how these can help in managing business and household activities. Promotional incentives may be offered such as lotteries in which free lottery numbers are distributed to savers according to the amount of savings they hold in the institutions.

## Conclusion

Our banks have tremendous potential and capability to provide micro-credit under the able umbrella of the National Bank for Agriculture and Rural Development and they have very well demonstrated their ability to make *Green/White/ Blue Revolution* a success. Today there is a need for initiatives and commitment from the Banks' Boards to provide directions and guidance to rural outlets in this direction.

# 22

# Financial Liberalisation and its Impact on the Determinants of Profitability of Commercial Banks in India

*V. Nagarajan Naidu* and Manju S Nair***

## Introduction

Banking sector in India had a checkered history in the process of economic development. The growth of Indian banking sector prior to nationalisation had a lackluster performance keeping in view of the socio-economic requirements of the country. After nationalisation, however, the banking sector in India has made commendable progress in extending its geographical spread and functional reach. After nationalisation, besides others, commercial banks have been entrusted with the responsibility of discharging certain social responsibilities like financing weaker sections of the society, development of the priority sectors and providing banking facilities to such areas and sectors which were hitherto neglected. In short, banks in the post-nationalisation period undertook the

* Lecturer, Department of Economics, Government College for women, Thiruvananthapuram, Kerala.

** Lecturer, Department of Economics, Christian College, Chengannur, Kerala.

responsibilities of catalysts to social change. Despite commendable progress in the post-nationalisation era, certain serious problems of the banking sector have emerged reflecting a decline in productivity and efficiency and erosion of the profitability as a consequence. The aspects of profitability, productivity and efficiency were relegated to the background in view of greater social responsibilities undertaken by the banking sector. However, banks are basically commercial organisations dealing in the public funds, which come to them solely on the basis of public confidence. Since 1991, based on the recommendations of the Narasimham Committee on Financial Services, reforms were initiated in the banking sector in India with a view to improve the operational efficiency and profitability of banks.

The policy measures initiated during the period of financial liberalisation (post 1991) was intended to offset set backs of banks during the period of financial repression period (between 1969 and 1991). The important policy measures adopted to revamp the banking sector were: The reduction of SLR and CRR, phase out the directed credit programmes and priority sector lending, increase the interest rate of government borrowing in line with market borrowing, stipulation of capital adequacy ratio linked to risk weighted assets, permission to mobilise fund from capital market, uniform accounting practices to evaluate the non-performing assets, permission to close down unviable bank branches at the discretion of commercial interest of banks and liberalised attitude toward foreign banks to open up subsidiaries. One of primary objective of initiating these policy reforms was to revamp the banking sector through increasing the profitability, productivity and efficiency. The banking sector should be prudent in its financial management and be a viable economic unit.

The present work is an attempt to evaluate the impact of these policy measures on the profitability of commercial banks. The policy impact on profitability and its determinants are assessed between pre (before 1991) and post liberalisation (after 1991) period. Since the policy impact may vary between different banks, the commercial banks were grouped into State Bank of India and Associates (SBI), Nationalised Banks (NB), and Private Banks (PB) which include both other domestic scheduled commercial banks and foreign banks.

## Determinants of Profitability of Banks

The various literature reviews on banks' profitability reveals that banks alone are not responsible for their sickness. A number of endogenous, exogenous and structural factors have affected their earnings, expenses and balance of profits. The policy variables such as changes in quantitative credit controls, credit targets, cash reserve ratio, statutory liquidity ratio, norms relating to credit to deposit ratios are the exogenous factors (Kulkarni (1979)[1], Kanthale (1984)[2], Joshi (1986)[3], Ramachandran (1992)[4]). The inefficient management of working fund, lack of administrative and operational efficiency and so on are the endogenous factors (Shah (1979)[5], Srivastava (1981)[6], Panda and Lall (1991-92)[7] Amandeep (1993)[8]). The geographical expansion, functional diffusion and changes in the pattern of deposits and credit are the structural factors (Singh (1974)[9], Goiporia (1992)[10], Dr. K. Satyanarayana (1996)[11]). The operating costs have increased on account of speedy geographical spread and shift to retail and mass banking. The unprecedented levels of over dues, bad debts and default also have adversely affected bank profitability. The financial sector reform implemented since 1991 has taken serious note on these issues and suggested drastic and far-reaching measures to improve the economic viability of banks in India.

## Trends in Profit

The profit of banks is one of the crucial indicators of their performance. The trends in profit of various groups of banks are evaluated based on operating profit. Operating profit is the difference between spread and burden of banks.

The Table 1 shows the operating profit and its index of various bank groups for the entire period between 1969 and 1999. The operating profit of banks in 1969 is much greater than the trend value for the succeeding years due to initial realignment of banks immediately after the bank nationalisation in 1969. Due to this fact, during the initial years, the index of operating profit of all banks has shown a declining trend compared to the base year 1969. For the entire period, the annual average growth rate of operating profit is maximum for OSB (59 percent) followed by SBI (55.28 percent), NB (47.11 percent) and FB (44.81 percent).

The period wise index of operating profit of various bank groups is given in the Table 1. Due to a greater operating profit of banks at the time of nationalisation in 1969, there has been a continuous decline of index of operating profit of all bank groups during the first period ie, 1969 to 1979. However, the annual average growth rate indicates the varying performance of bank groups during this period. During the first period, the FB achieved highest annual average growth rate (12.43 percent) followed by OSB (10.17 percent), NB (7.68 percent) and SBI (6.44 percent). Thus during the first period, the growth rate of operating profit of private sector banks are higher than public sector banks. During the second period of 1980 to 1991, there has been an increasing trend of operating profit of all bank groups. However, the average annual growth rate indicates that the highest progress was achieved by OSB (56.56 percent) followed by SBI (39.7 percent), FB (33.1 percent) and NB (30.64 percent). There has been a fluctuating trend of operating profit of banks particularly for SBI and NB during the third period of 1992 to 1999. During the initial periods, there was an actual decline of profit of all bank groups. However, it was overcome in the later stages. SBI has achieved the maximum annual average growth (137.76 percent) during the period of financial liberalisation followed by OSB (123.395), NB (119.03 percent) and FB (101.45). Thus compared to all other periods, the annual average growth

**Table 1: Period Wise Index of Operating Profit of Bank Groups (amount in Rs. Lakhs)**

| Year | SBI | | NB | | OSB | | FB | |
|---|---|---|---|---|---|---|---|---|
| | *Operating profit* | *Index* | *Operating profit* | *Index* | *Operating profit* | *Index* | *Operating profit* | *Index* |
| 1969 | 1224 | 100 | 2519 | 100 | 209 | 100 | 782 | 100 |
| 1970 | 323 | 26.38 | 690 | 27.39 | 240 | 114.83 | 263 | 33.63 |
| 1971 | 429 | 35.04 | 849 | 33.70 | 223 | 106.7 | 282 | 36.06 |
| 1972 | 436 | 35.62 | 755 | 29.97 | 123 | 58.85 | 390 | 49.87 |
| 1973 | 466 | 38.07 | 765 | -30.36 | 146 | 69.85 | 420 | 53.70 |
| 1974 | 523 | 42.72 | 1038 | 41.20 | 308 | 147.37 | 628 | 80.30 |
| 1975 | 682 | 55.71 | 1525 | 60.53 | 343 | 164.11 | 466 | 59.59 |
| 1976 | 879 | 71.81 | 1960 | 77.80 | 436 | 208.61 | 739 | 94.50 |
| 1977 | 886 | 72.38 | 1529 | 60.69 | 349 | 166.99 | 329 | 42.07 |
| 1978 | 968 | 79.08 | 1586 | 62.96 | 465 | 222.49 | 578 | 73.91 |
| 1979 | 1114 | 91.01 | 2272 | 90.19 | 267 | 127.75 | 780 | 99.74 |
| **Annual** average growth rate (in percent) | | **6.44** | | **7.68** | | **10.17** | | **12.43** |

*(Table Contd...)*

**Table 1 : (Contd...)**

| Year | SBI | | NB | | OSB | | FB | |
|---|---|---|---|---|---|---|---|---|
| | *Operating profit* | *Index* | *Operating profit* | *Index* | *Operating profit* | *Index* | *Operating profit* | *Index* |
| 1980 | 1316 | 100 | 2786 | 100 | 287 | 100 | 926 | 100 |
| 1981 | 1632 | 124.01 | 2954 | 106.03 | 367 | 127.87 | 1448 | 156.37 |
| 1982 | 2032 | 154.41 | 3730 | 133.88 | 413 | 143.9 | 1701 | 183.69 |
| 1983 | 2338 | 177.66 | 3827 | 137.36 | 411 | 143.21 | 1957 | 211.34 |
| 1984 | 2535 | 192.63 | 3786 | 135.89 | 952 | 331.71 | 2757 | 297.73 |
| 1985 | 3414 | 259.42 | 4589 | 164.71 | 715 | 249.13 | 3377 | 364.69 |
| 1986 | 4126 | 313.53 | 10210 | 366.47 | 984 | 342.86 | 6993 | 755.18 |
| 1987 | 4741 | 360.26 | 13531 | 485.67 | 1391 | 484.67 | 8542 | 922.46 |
| 1988-89 | 11074 | 841.49 | 25417 | 912.31 | 971 | 338.33 | 11676 | 1260.9 |
| 1989-90 | 11720 | 890.58 | 19433 | 697.52 | 5335 | 1858.9 | 15548 | 1679 |
| 1990-91 | 27739 | 2107.8 | 27221 | 977.06 | 3724 | 1297.6 | 14616 | 1578.4 |
| Annual **average growth rate (in percent)** | | 39.7 | | 30.64 | | 56.56 | | 33.1 |
| 1991-92 | 317338 | 100 | 236691 | 100 | 29408 | 100 | 110867 | 100 |
| 1992-93 | 226369 | 71.334 | 87169 | 36.83 | 24027 | 81.70 | 49847 | 44.96 |
| 1993-94 | 203200 | 64.033 | 172568 | 72.91 | 42087 | 143.11 | 126230 | 113.86 |

*(Table Contd...)*

**Table 1 : (Contd...)**

| Year | SBI | | NB | | OSB | | FB | |
|---|---|---|---|---|---|---|---|---|
| | *Operating profit* | *Index* | *Operating profit* | *Index* | *Operating profit* | *Index* | *Operating profit* | *Index* |
| 1994-95 | 258321 | 81.402 | 293735 | 124.10 | 73007 | 248.26 | 131160 | 118.3 |
| 1995-96 | 392323 | 123.63 | 364566 | 154.03 | 205626 | 699.22 | 157594 | 142.15 |
| 1996-97 | 445781 | 140.48 | 443995 | 187.58 | 127906 | 434.94 | 196915 | 177.61 |
| 1997-98 | 473234 | 149.13 | 553119 | 233.69 | 181650 | 617.69 | 254388 | 229.45 |
| 1998-99 | 464805 | 146.47 | 592945 | 250.51 | 147478 | 501.49 | 193961 | 174.95 |
| **Annual average growth rate ( in percent)** | | **137.76** | | **119.03** | | **123.39** | | **101.4** |

*Source:* Reserve Bank of India,(various years), Statistical Tables Relating to Banks in India, Bombay.

of operating profit has been highest during the period of financial liberalisation.

## Empirical Result of Determinants of Profitability

Profitability stands for profit deflated by size of the unit. In the case of banks, the size is represented by the income, deposit and assets. Hence three measures of profitability are measured: 1. profitability per unit of income 2. profitability per unit of deposit and 3. profitability per unit of total assets.

The determinants of banking sector profitability are derived by applying the tool of multiple regression. In this analysis, there are three dependent variables relating to profitability. They are

1. Profit per income
2. Profit per deposit
3. Profit per total assets

Independent variables are 1. share of credit to agriculture and small scale industry 2. investment to asset ratio 3. capital-labour ratio 4. liquid asset ratio 5. market share of total deposits 6. ratio of officers to total staff 7. ratio of rural and semi urban branches to total branches and (8) ratio of time deposit to total deposit. All these independent variables are correlated separately to each of the three dependent variables.

Data are collected for the years from 1976 to 1999 for three bank groups of State Bank of India and Associates (SBI groups), Nationalised Banks (NB), and Private Banks (PB). Both the linear and log-linear models were tried but only the log linear results are presented since they are superior. Equations are presented in Tables for all the three definitions of the dependent variables. The multiple log linear model used in the present analysis is as follows.

$$LnY = \beta_0+\beta_1 LnX_1+\beta_2 LnX_2+\beta_3 Ln\,X_3+\beta_4 Ln\,X_4+\beta_5 Ln\,X_5+\beta_6 Ln\,X_6+\beta_7 LnX_7+\beta_8 LnX_8+U_i$$

Where,

LnY = log value of dependent variable of profit per income, profit per deposit and profit per asset.

Ln $X_1$ = log value of share of credit to agriculture and small scale industry to total credit

Ln $X_2$ = log value of investment to asset ratio

Ln$X_3$ = log value of capital- labour ratio

Ln$X_4$ = log value of liquid asset ratio

Ln$X_5$ = log value of market share of total deposits

Ln$X_6$ = log value of ratio of officers to total staff

Ln$X_7$ = log value of ratio of rural and semi urban branches to total branches

Ln$X_8$ = log value of ratio of time deposit to total deposit

$\beta_1$, $\beta_2$, $\beta_3$, $\beta_4$, $\beta_5$, $\beta_6$, $\beta_7$ and $\beta_8$ are the coefficient of independent variables $\beta_0$ is the intercept and Ui is the random error term.

After performing log linear multiple regression, for the years 1979-1999, the following multiple linear regression equation is employed to examine the impact of banking reforms on selected indicators of the banking sector in India.

$$LnY = a_0 + a_1T + a_2D + U_i$$

Where,

LnY = log values of selected indicators of banking sector. These selected indicators are the independent variables considered in the first equation in the preceding regression.

T = time trend

D = dummy variables i.e., '0' for pre-liberalisation period and '1' for the post liberalisation period (1991-92 to 1998-99).

$a_0$, $a_1$ and $a_2$ are the paramotors to be estimated and

Ui = random error term.

Regression analysis is conducted separately for SBI, NB and private banks. The following section provides details of estimated results.

## Determinants of Profitability of SBI

The following Table 1 shows the values of coefficient of independent variables with respect to three dependent variables.

**Table1 : Regression Analysis of Determinants of Profitability of SBI**

| *Independent variables* | *Operational profit to income* | *Operational profit to deposits* | *Operational profit to assets* |
|---|---|---|---|
| Share of credit to agriculture and small scale industry | –0.399<br>(–0.30) | –0.0408<br>(–0.026) | –0.140<br>(–0.08) |
| Investment to asset ratio | 0.658<br>(0.771) | 0.556<br>(0.558) | 1.079<br>(1.065) |
| Capital-labour ratio | 0.964*<br>(3.132) | 1.149*<br>(3.200) | 1.102*<br>(3.017) |
| Liquid asset ratio | –2.147*<br>(–3.539) | –2.512*<br>(–3.547) | –2.363*<br>(–3.281) |
| Market share of total deposits | 6.441*<br>(1.757) | 6.482*<br>(1.575) | 6.760*<br>(1.554) |
| Ratio of officers to total staff | –0.233<br>(–0.069) | –0.0560<br>(–0.014) | –0.417<br>(–0.105) |
| Ratio rural and semi urban branches to total branches | –1.87*<br>(–2.874) | –2.09*<br>(–2.751) | –2.04*<br>(–2.641) |
| Ratio of time deposit to total deposit | 0.03017<br>(0.029) | 0.180<br>(0.147) | 0.0339<br>(0.027) |
| α | –2.967<br>(–0.418) | –4.994<br>(–0.603) | –5.013<br>(–0.596) |
| $R^2$ | 0.891 | 0.880 | 0.882 |

*Note* : Figure in the bracket shows the value of 't' statistics.
"*" shows the value of 't' statistics at 5 percent level of significance.
"**" shows the value of 't' statistics at 10 percent level of significance.

*Source* : estimated results.

Among the independent variables the share of credit to agriculture and small scale industry, liquid asset ratio, ratio of officer to total staff and ratio of rural and semi urban branches to total branches are negatively associated with the profitability indices of SBI. The variables such as investment to asset ratio, capital-labour ratio, market share of total deposits and ratio of time deposit to total deposits are positively associated. Among the negatively associated variables, the liquid asset ratio and ratio of rural and semi urban branches to total branches are significant at 5 percent level of significance. Among the positively associated variables, the capital-labour ratio and market shares of total deposits are significant at 5 percent level of significance.

The result reveals that in the case of SBI any increase in credit to agriculture and small scale industry, liquid assets, number of officers and rural and semi urban branches lead to decline in profitability. Since the credit to agriculture and small-scale industry is on a priority targeted basis at a low rate of interest, the increase in credit volume to this direction unfavourably affect the profitability performance of banks. Under the aegis of socialisation and nationalisation of commercial banks, it was the responsibility of banks to open more branches to rural and semi urban areas though they are unviable. This drive towards spatial spread of banking business on social welfare consideration might have unfavourably affected the profitability of SBI. Increasing the liquid asset reduces the fund available to deploy to more profitable long-term credit and other investment ventures by the bank. This may affect unfavourably the profitability of banks. In the case of officer employees, their growth would eat away a sizeable chunk of bank's income as establishment expenses, which will naturally erode the profitability of banks. Increasing volume of non banking activities greatly influence the profitability of banks recently. One such index is the investment ratio to total assets. Banks generally prefer to invest their funds in outside sources from which they could expect a higher return compared to interest on loans and advances. This logic explains the positive association between increase in investment and profitability of banks. Market share of total deposits is another factor, which affect the profitability. Increasing the share of mobilisation of deposit in the market involves both cost of mobilisation and yield of mobilised funds. When there is positive difference between the yield and cost of mobilisation, any increase in the market share of deposit leads of higher profit. This is particularly true in the case of SBI groups who has a large net work through out the country. Since larger the volume of time deposit to total deposit, the greater the yield of banks by advancing more funds for a longer period, any increase in time deposit will have a positive impact on profitability of banks.

Though all these independent factors show similar association with all profitability indicators, the relative influence varies. The negative impact of increasing credit to agriculture and small-scale industry is more on operational profit to income compared to operational profit to deposit and asset. In the case of liquid assets and rural and semi urban branches, both have greater negative impact on operational profit to deposit compared to other indices. The increase in the number of officers has greater negative impact on operational profit to assets compared to other indices. In the case of positive factors, the increase in investment and market share have greatly influenced operational profit to assets. The operational profit to deposit is more influenced by capital labour ratio and ratio of time deposit to total deposits.

Results of multiple regression run with time and dummy variable as independent factors and selected indicators of banking sector as dependent variable are given in the following Table 2.

**Table 2 : Regression Result of Selected Independent Variables of SBI**

| *Dependent Variables* | *Intercept* | *T* | *DumT* | $R^2$ |
|---|---|---|---|---|
| Ratio of credit to agriculture and small scale industries to total credit | -1.292<br>(-21.55)* | 0.0123<br>(1.73)* | -0.387<br>(-3.89)* | 0.524 |
| Ratio of investment to total assets | -1.509<br>(30.725)* | 0.0023<br>(0.391) | 0.280<br>(3.440)* | 0.662 |
| Capital-Labour ratio | -3.827<br>(-45.68)* | 0.132<br>(13.262)* | 0.304<br>(2.184) | 0.970 |
| Ratio of officers to total staff | -1.549<br>(-86.50)* | 0.0123<br>(5.78)* | -0.088<br>(-2.957)* | 0.656 |
| Ratio of rural and semi urban branches to total branches | -0.269<br>(33.898) | 0.010<br>(1.09) | -0.046<br>(-3.522)* | 0.734 |
| Ratio of liquid asset to total asset | -2.374*<br>(-28.034) | 0.03639*<br>(3.606) | -0.145<br>(-1.034) | 0.570 |
| Ratio of term deposit to total deposit | -0.833*<br>(-14.14) | -0.004<br>(-0.692) | 0.154<br>(1.577)* | 0.523 |

*Note* : Figure in the bracket shows the value of 't' statistics.
'*'shows the value of 't' statistics at 5 percent level of significance.
'**' shows the value of 't' statistics at 10 percent level of significance.

*Source* : estimated results.

The above Table shows that there is a positive trend with regard to credit to agriculture and small-scale industries of SBI. But a movement from the pre to the post reform period shows a decline in the share of these advances of SBI. The regression result of ratio of investment to total assets reveals a positive trend in both periods, but the coefficient of dummy variable is significant indicating that after the implementation of reforms investment has significantly increased. In the case of capital-labour ratio also, it has got increasing trend both during the pre and post reform period. There is a positive trend with regard to the ratio of officers to total staff. However, after the implementation of reforms this trend has changed as is indicated by the significant negative coefficient for the dummy. There exist a positive association between trend variable and the ratio of rural and semi urban branches to total branches of SBI. However, the influence of dummy is negative implying a change in this trend after the implementation of reforms. The liquid asset ratio has a positive trend with the trend variable and a negative association with dummy variable. The coefficient of time is significant where as the coefficient of dummy is not significant with respect to liquid asset ratio. With regard to the ratio of time deposit to total deposit the trend variable has given a negative influence. Since the implementation of banking sector reform this trend has changed and a positive significant coefficient is associated with the dummy variable. In this analysis the market share of deposit is not included since the regression result does not have a logical value with reason.

Thus the above Table indicates that all factors are moving the right direction to increase the profitability of SBI during the post reform period.

**Determinants of Profitability of NB**

The Table 3 shows the regression result of determinants of profitability of NB.

Of the eight independent variables that affect different profitability ratios of NB, credit to agriculture and small-scale industry, liquid asset ratio, market share, staff composition, branch expansion, time deposit ratio etc. negatively influence the profitability of banks. Other determinants of investment asset ratio and capital labour ratio are the only two factors, which positively contribute to profitability. Of the factors which negatively affect profitability of NB, credit to agriculture and small scale industry, liquid asset ratio, officers to total staff and rural and semi urban branches to total branches are significant. The results obtained for market share and time deposit ratio are contrary to the results obtained for SBI. For NB when the market share increases, profitability declines.

**Table 3 : Regression Analysis of Determinants of Profitability of NB**

| *Independent variables* | *Operational profit to income* | *Operational profit to deposits* | *Operational profit to assets* |
|---|---|---|---|
| Share of credit to agriculture and small scale industry | –2.037** (–1.695) | –2.585** (–1.949) | –2.596** (–1.884) |
| Investment to asset ratio | 2.162 (1.369) | 1.760 (0.966) | 2.211 (1.168) |
| Capital-labour ratio | –0.431 (–1.431) | 0.513 (1.545) | 0.504 (1.461) |
| Liquid asset ratio | –2.382** (–1.647) | –2.477** (–1.5530) | –2.459** (–1.483) |
| Market share of total deposits | –0.907 (–0.278) | –1.347 (–0.374) | –1.387 (–0.371) |
| Ratio of officers to total staff | –9.155* (–2.049) | –8.956* (–1.817) | –8.973* (–1.752) |
| Ratio rural and semi urban branches to total branches | –9.952** (–1.864) | –12.211** (–2.074) | –11.484** (–1.877) |
| Ratio of time deposit to total deposit | –0.168 (–0.132) | –0.035 (–0.025) | –0.223 (–0.153) |
| α | –9.580* (–2.681) | –12.183* (–3.091) | –11.719* (–2.862) |
| **$R^2$** | 0.924 | 0.924 | 0.922 |

*Note* : Figure in the bracket shows the value of 't' statistics.

'*'shows the value of 't' statistics at 5 percent level of significance.

'**'shows the value of 't' statistics at 10 percent level of significance.

*Source* : estimated results.

To understand the impact of banking reforms on selected indicators, mainly the independent variables in the above regression, simple regression is worked out. The results are given in the following Table 4.

**Table 4 : Regression Result of Selected Independent Variables of NB**

| *Dependent Variables* | *Intercept* | *T* | *DumT* | $R^2$ |
|---|---|---|---|---|
| Ratio of credit to agriculture and small scale industries to total credit | –1.437* (–27.13) | 0.01274* (2.025) | –0.207* (–2.361) | 0.510 |
| Ratio of investment to total assets | –1.480* (–60.620) | 0.01187* (4.082) | 0.197* (4.870) | 0.912 |
| Capital-Labour ratio | –3.419 (–31.282) | 0.119* (9.121) | 0.825* (4.547) | 0.961 |
| Ratio of liquid asset to total asset | –2.370* (–52.650) | 0.0312* (5.824) | –0.095* (–1.277) | 0.764 |
| Market share (ratio of deposit to total bank deposit) | –0.509* (–23.90) | 0.005125* (2.019) | –0.137* (–3.879) | 0.442 |
| Ratio of officers to total staff | –1.485* (–113.06) | 0.01368* (8.744) | –0.075* (–3.461) | 0.844 |
| Ratio of rural and semi urban branches to total branches | –0.417 (–37.18) | 0.00166 (1.247) | –0.074 (–3.971)* | 0.549 |
| Ratio of term deposit to total Deposit | –0.874 (–25.852) | 0.0051* (2.114) | 0.114* (2.033) | 0.683 |

*Note* : Figure in the bracket shows the value of 't' statistics.
'*'shows the value of 't' statistics at 5 percent level of significance.
'**'shows the value of 't' statistics at 10 percent level of significance.

*Source* : estimated results.

The result makes it clear that over the years credit to agriculture and small-scale industry has recorded a significant increase. However, the trend has reversed since the implementation of reforms as is indicated by the significant negative coefficient of dummy variable. The investment-asset ratio is positively associated with trend variable and the dummy and both the coefficients are significant. The capital-labour ratio has increased over the years both in the pre and post liberalisation period as is indicated by the significant positive coefficient of time and dummy. The share of liquid asset in total assets is positively associated with the trend variable for NB, however, after the implementation of banking sector reforms the situation has changed and its trend has reversed as is evident from the dummy variable. Both the coefficients are significant also. The market share of NB has increased over the years since the market share is positively correlated with the trend variable, however after the implementation of reform, the market share of NB has declined as is indicated by the negative coefficient of the dummy. Both the coefficients are significant. There exists a positive association between trend variable and ratio of officer to total staff. Rural and semi urban branches are positively associated with trend variable. But since the initiation of financial sector reforms this situation has changed. The dummy is negatively related to rural and semi urban branches and the result is significant too. The ratio of time deposit to total deposit has increased over the years. After the implementation of financial sector reforms also the same trend continues as is evident from the significant dummy variable. Thus in the case of NBs also all variables are moving in the right direction so as to improve the profitability.

## Determinants of Profitability of Private Sector Banks

Since for the initial years data regarding some variables of OSB and FB are not available separately, regression is done for these two bank groups together as regression for private banks. The Table 5 shows the regression result of determinants of profitability of private banks.

Of the factors affecting profitability of private sector banks, credit to agriculture and small-scale industry, investment to asset ratio, capital labour ratio, liquid asset ratio, and market share are positively associated. Among these, credit to agriculture and small-scale industry is the only significant variable, that too at 10 percent. The factors, which are negatively associated, are ratio of officers to total employees, number of rural and semi urban branches and ratio of time deposit to total deposit. However, these are not significant. Contrary to nationalised banks, the private sector banks could make profit out of efficient lending to agriculture and small-scale industry. Also by better management of liquid asset the private sector banks could make profit.

**Table 5 : Regression Analysis of Determinants of Profitability of Private Banks**

| *Independent variables* | *Operational profit to income* | *Operational profit to deposits* | *Operational profit to assets* |
|---|---|---|---|
| Share of credit to agriculture and small scale industry | 2.037<br>(1.695)** | 2.585<br>(1.949)** | 2.596<br>(1.884)** |
| Investment to asset ratio | 2.262<br>(1.369) | 1.760<br>(0.966) | 2.211<br>(1.168) |
| Capital-labour ratio | 0.431<br>(1.431) | 0.513<br>(1.545) | 0.504<br>(1.461) |
| Liquid asset ratio | 2.382<br>(1.647) | 2.477<br>(1.553) | 2.459<br>(1.483) |
| Market share of total deposits | 9.07<br>(0.278) | 1.347<br>(0.374) | 1.387<br>(0.371) |
| Ratio of officers to total staff | –9.155<br>(–2.047)* | –8.956<br>(–1.817)* | –8.973<br>(–1.752)* |
| Ratio rural and semi urban branches to total branches | –9.952<br>(–1.864)* | –12.211<br>(–2.074)* | –11.484<br>(–1.877)* |
| Ratio of term deposit to total deposit | –0.168<br>(–0.132) | –0.035<br>(–0.025) | –0.223<br>(–1.53) |
| $\alpha$ | –9.582<br>(–2.681)* | –12.183<br>(–3.091)* | –11.719<br>(–2.862)* |
| $R^2$ | 0.924 | 0.924 | 0.922 |

*Note* : Figure in the bracket shows the value of 't' statistics.

'*'shows the value of 't' statistics at 5 percent level of significance.

'**'shows the value of 't' statistics at 10 percent level of significance.

*Source* : estimated results.

After the analysis of the determinants of profitability of private sector banks, the impact of financial sector reforms on credit to agriculture and small-scale industry, rural and semi urban branches, investment to total assets, staff compositions, market share, liquid asset ratio of private banks is examined. The multiple regression result for the same is given in the Table 6.

**Table 6 : Regression Result of Selected Independent Variables of Private Banks**

| *Dependent Variables* | *Intercept* | *T* | *DumT* | $R^2$ |
|---|---|---|---|---|
| Ratio of credit to agriculture and small scale industries to total credit | -1.707 (-29.915)* | -0.046 (-6.80)* | 0.144 (1.518) | 0.815 |
| Ratio of investment to total assets | -1.545 (-37.460)* | 0.0015 (0.214) | 0.362 (5.297)* | 0.807 |
| Capital-Labour ratio | -3.087* (-16.011) | 0.145 (6.317)* | 1.305 (4.078)* | 0.934 |
| Ratio of liquid asset to total asset | -2.229* (-47.52) | 0.0198 (3.554)** | 0.0749 (0.963) | 0.726 |
| Market share (ratio of deposit to total bank deposit) | -2.230 (-20.741)* | -0.028 (-2.168)* | 0.775 (4.344)* | 0.513 |
| Ratio of officers to total staff | -1.539 (26.610)* | 0.0117 (1.6999)* | 0.175 (1.822)* | 0.604 |
| Ratio of rural and semi urban branches to total branches | -0.388* (-24.266) | -0.72 (-3.777)* | -0.035 (-1.316) | 0.771 |
| Ratio of term deposit to total deposit | -0.691* (7.894) | 0.00474 (0.455) | 0.174 (2.187)* | 0.411 |

*Note* : Figure in the bracket shows the value of 't' statistics.

'*'shows the value of 't' statistics at 5 percent level of significance.

'**'shows the value of 't' statistics at 10 percent level of significance.

*Source* : estimated results.

For private banks, over the years there has been a reduction in credit to agriculture and small-scale industry as is evident from the coefficient of time. However, after the implementation of reforms, credit to agriculture and small-scale industry has increased for private banks, although the result is not significant. Between the investment of private banks to total asset and the time trend, there is a positive association. But the result is not significant. However, a move from pre to post financial reform period shows that investment ratio has increased and the result is significant. Capital-labour ratio has increased over time both in the pre and post reform period. The coefficient for time and dummy are positive and significant. The liquid assets have shown an increasing trend. However since the implementation of reform this increase is not significant. The regression result reveals a negative trend with regard to market share of private banks, but a movement from the pre to post reform periods shows an increase in the market share of private banks as is indicated by the coefficient of dummy. The officer ratio has a positive trend both in the pre and post reform period. The coefficient of time and dummy are significantly positive. Between ratio of rural and semi urban branches to total branches and the time trend there exist a negative association. A movement from pre reform to post financial reform period also shows a negative influence on rural and semi urban branches of private banks. The ratio of term deposits to total deposits is positively associated with trend variable, however, this result is not significant. After the implementation of reforms this ratio has increased and the result is significant also.

## Summary Result

From this analysis of bank profitability, some interesting conclusions with far reaching policy implications can be discerned. The Table 7 summarises the nature of association of profitability with different determinants of profitability over the period 1976-1999. Social factors, which were introduced in banking such as credit to agriculture and small-scale industry, market share, staff composition and branch composition have significant impacts on profitability. Among these factors analysed, only market share is positively associated with profitability of SBI. For NB all the social factors are negatively associated with profitability. For private banks, the factors, market shares and credit to agriculture and small-scale industry are positively associated to profitability.

**Table 7 : Nature of Association of Profitability with Different Variables**

| *Variables* | *SBI* | *NB* | *Private Banks* |
|---|---|---|---|
| Ratio of credit to agriculture and small scale industry to total credit | Negative | Negative** | Positive** |
| Market share of total deposit | Positive* | Negative | Positive |
| Ratio of officers to total staff | Negative | Negative* | Negative* |
| Ratio of rural and semi urban branches to total branches | Negative* | Negative** | Negative* |
| Ratio of investment to total assets | Positive | Positive | Positive |
| Capital-labour ratio | Positive* | Positive | Positive |
| Ratio of liquid assets to total assets | Negative* | Negative** | Positive |
| Ratio of term deposit to total deposit | Positive | Negative | Negative |

*Note:* *'shows the value of 't' statistics at 5 percent level of significance.
'**'shows the value of 't' statistics at 10 percent level of significance.

Among the other factors such as capital-labour ratio, liquid asset ratio, ratio of time deposits to total deposits and investment-asset ratio, only liquid asset to total assets is negatively related to profitability of SBI. For NB only investment rate and capital-labour ratio are positively associated with profitability, that too are not significant.

Factors like liquid assets and time deposit ratio are negatively related to profitability and liquid asset is significantly related. In the case of private banks all above-mentioned factors are positively associated with profitability with the exception of time deposit ratio.

The Table 8 summarise the direction of the movement of these selected factors on account of the impact of financial sector reforms.

For SBI, the trend variable had positive influence on credit to agriculture and small-scale industries, ratio of officers to total staff, rural and semi urban branches to total branches and liquid asset ratio. However, all these variables are negatively associated with dummy variable indicating that after the implementation of reform there has been a decline in these variables. This result is very important since these are the main variables, which negatively affect the profitability of SBI. The decline of these factors would positively affect the profitability of SBI. Thus the financial sector reform enables the SBI groups to modify the rhythm of banking activities towards the direction of more profitability. For NB also the same results apply since the association of these factors with trend variables and dummy variable are same, as is the case with SBI.

For private banks the situation is different from public sector banks of SBI groups and NB. In the case of private sector banks, officer ratio, liquid asset ratio, ratio of investment to total assets, capital-labour ratio and ratio of term deposits to total deposits have increased over the years and the same trend continues even after the implementation of reform. Out of these factors except officer ratio and ratio of term deposit, all other variables has positive association with profitability. This implies that the negative impact of officer ratio and term deposit ratio could not be lessened even after liberalisation, in private sector banks. Unlike public sector banks, the credit to agriculture and small-scale industries has positive influence on profitability. But the trend indicates that overall there has

**Table 8 : Nature of Association of Profitability Determinants to Trend Variable**

| | *SBI* | | *NB* | | *Private Banks* | |
|---|---|---|---|---|---|---|
| *Dependent Variables* | *Time (T)* | *DummyT* | *Time (T)* | *DummyT* | *Time (T)* | *DummyT* |
| Ratio of credit to agriculture and small scale industries to total credit | Positive* | Negative* | Positive* | Negative* | Negative* | Positive |
| Ratio of investment to total assets | Positive | Positive* | Positive* | Positive* | Positive | Positive* |
| Capital-Labour ratio | Positive* | Positive | Positive* | Positive* | Positive* | Positive* |
| Ratio of officers to total staff | Positive* | Negative* | Positive* | Negative* | Positive* | Positive* |
| Ratio of rural and semi urban branches to total branches | Positive | Negative* | Positive | Negative* | Negative* | Negative |
| Ratio of term deposit to total deposit | Negative | Positive* | Positive* | Positive* | Positive | Positive* |
| Ratio of liquid asset to total assets | Positive* | Negative | Positive* | Negative* | Positive | Positive* |
| Market share (ratio of deposit to total bank deposit) | | | Positive* | Negative* | Negative* | Positive* |

*Note:* '*' shows the value of 't' statistics at 5 percent level of significance.
'**' shows the value of 't' statistics at 10 percent level of significance.

been a decline of credit to agriculture and small-scale industries. However, this trend has reversed after the liberalisation process. This implies that private sector banks could make profit by giving more loans to this priority sector after the reform period. The number of rural and semi urban branches is negatively associated with both trend and dummy variables. Since this factor negatively affects the profitability, the trend indicates that private banks are trying to reduce the rural and semi urban branches to increase the profitability. After reform the market share of private banks has increased and market share variable has a positive influence on profitability of private banks. Thus in the case of private sector banks except in the case of officer ratio and term deposit, for all other factors the financial sector reform could create favourable impact on profitability

Thus, from the foregoing detailed analysis on profitability and its determinants, certain useful insights are revealed. Among the determinants of profitability, the factors relating to social obligation of banking activities became a drag on profitability of public sector banks. These social objectives made them to forget about the banking objective of making more profit to become economically viable through prudential management. However, in the case of private banks, the social objectives are not a deterrent. This might be due to the non-obligatory nature of private sector banks to monetary regulation or due to the better management of resources. Though private sector banks are not lending as much percentage to priority sector and also averse to open new branches to far flung remote areas, what ever they lend to these priority sector are better managed. The restrictive regulatory framework squeezes the public sector banks of their competitive dynamism along with their counter parts. However, things are in well augur after the financial sector reforms were introduced in India. All groups of banks, both public and private sector banks are vying with each to correct their distorted behaviour since the financial sector liberalisation. This could be gleaned from the fact that those factors, which made negative impacts on the profitability of banks, have a reverse trend since the ushering of financial sector liberalisation. Thus it is amply evident that the financial sector reforms are towards the desired direction as far as profitability of banks is concerned.

## NOTES

1 Kulkarni, L.G (1979), 'Developmental Responsibility and Profitability of Banks', *Economic and Political Weekly*, Vol. 14 (34), Aug. 25, Bombay.

2 Kanthale, A.K (1984), 'The Impact of the Monetary and Credit Policies on the Working Result of Commercial Banks and Suggestions for Offsetting the Effects on their Profitability', Paper presented at Bank Economists' Meet, Hosted by Indian Bank, Madras.

3 Joshi, P.N (1986), 'Profitability and Profit Planning in Banks', *The Journal of Indian Institute of Bankers*, Vol. 57, No. 2, April-June, Indian Institute of Bankers, Bombay.

4 Ramachandran, N (1992), 'Profit Planning as a Management Tool for Profit Maximisation', *The Banker*, January, Bombay.

5 Shah, S.G.(1979), 'Bank Profitability: The Real Issues', *The Journal of the Indian Institute of Bankers*, Vol. 50, No. 3, July-Sept., Indian Institute of Bankers, Bombay.

6 Srivastava, R.B (1981), 'Profitability and Work Measurement in Banks', *Monthly Economic Review*, State Bank of India, December, Bombay, pp. 494-501.

7 Panda, J and Lall, G,S (1991), 'A Critical Appraisal on the profitability of commercial banks', *Indian Journal of Banking and Finance*, Vol. 5, Bombay.

8 Amandeep (1993), *Profits and Profitability in Commercial Banks*, Deep and Deep Publications, New Delhi.

9 Singh, P. (1974), 'Profitability of Nationalised Banks', *Economic and Political Weekly*, Vol. IX (35), August, Bombay.

10 Goiporia, M .N (1992), 'Bank Profitability-Some Issues', *Pigmy Economic Review*, Vol. 37, No. 9, April, Bombay.

11 Satyanarayana, K (1995), 'Capital Restructuring and Profitability of Banks', *Prajnan*, Vol. XXIV. No. 1, 1995-96, National Institute of Bank Management, Pune.

# 23

# Public Sector Banks in Post-Reform Period: Unfinished Agenda and the Uncertain Future

*Manoj S. Kamat* and Branda Rodrigues***

## Introduction

Public Sector Banks (PSB's) have been playing a key role in the development of the economy. In the process they have gained confidence of masses. Through branch networking and priority sector lending activities, PSB's have demonstrated their socio-economic commitment. One of the major factors, which have transformed the Indian Banking Sector, has been the launching of economic reforms. The hue and cry about redesigning the economic and financial architecture of the Indian Banking System gained momentum since the early part of 1990's. Many sectors of the economy benefited significantly from the increased integration of the sectors within the country and with the world. The traditional face of banking is also

* Lecturer in Commerce, Shree Damodar College of Commerce and Economics, Margao-Goa.

** Lecturer in Economics, Shree Damodar College of Commerce and Economics, Margao-Goa.

undergoing a change, from one of mere intermediator to one of provider of quick, efficient consumer-centric services.

The **objective** of the paper is to review the reform agenda of banking sector in India since 1991 till 2001. Secondly, the paper sets out to analyse the problems, which has threatened survival of PSBs in the post-reform period. The third part puts up an intense debate on options available to revive weak PSBs.

## Nationalisation of Banks

The concept of social control emerged after takeover of banks operating then in 1955 and 1959, in 1967 to serve better the needs of development in conformity with national priorities. The social control phase turned out to be transitory. Expectations of the government that, social control would remove objectionable banking practices of the past and would give a new sense of purpose to the banks for future were belied. The government therefore took a bold decision to bring under its direct control a substantial segment of the banking system. Twenty-eight key banks were nationalized in four stages : State Bank of India in 1955, 7 associate banks in 1959-60, 14 banks in 1969 and 6 banks in 1980. With the merger of one bank there are at present 27 banks in public sector.

With Nationalisation there has been a dramatic change in the profile of Indian Banking in terms of its length and breadth (See Table 1). A structural transformation of far reaching significance has occurred in the development of commercial bank credit. Banking has thus emerged as an effective catalytic agent of socio-economic change in the country.

## Review of Banking Sector Reforms

However by Eighties, it was clear that the operational efficiencies of PSB's was unsatisfactory. PSB's were characterized by low profitability with high & growing NPA's. There was a problem of low capital base and lack of proper disclosure system. The quality of customer services did not keep pace with increasing expectation and there was a feeling that the inefficiency of banking system was encouraging diversion of domestic financial savings away from PSB's. As the financial system of the economy underwent a complete change, NBFC's, foreign players and capital markets immerged as competitors to PSB's. As many controls weakened, selected credit flow was misused which eroded profitability, which in turn effected the deepening of financial system.

**Table 1 : Progress of Public Sector Banks**

| *Indicators* | *1964* | *1999* |
|---|---|---|
| Branches | 8262 | 66000 |
| Deposits generated (Cr.) | 4646 | 731000 |
| Loan Advanced (Cr.) | 3500 | 369000 |
| Advanced to Private Sector (Cr.) | 413 | 148000 |

*Source* : RBI Bulletins 1999.

Banking sector reforms are a means to achieve the ultimate goal of economic development and economic stability in the country. The reforms are largely intended to improve efficiency and profitability of the banks and make their financial operations more market oriented and transparent (Kaippachery, 2002). The pathetic situation of the banking sector necessitated some immediate reforms to cure all its financial ills. The banking sector reforms were implemented in two phases i.e. the first Narsimham Committee report in 1991 and second report in 1998. Added to it was the Verma Committee (Advisory Group on Banking Supervision, May, 2001). The achievements so far are substantial though a great deal remains to be done (Ahuwalia, 1999). These committees recommended various reforms to Indian Banking System. The following are the reform areas:

### *Prudential Accounting Norms*

Prudential regulation refers to the set of laws and rules designed to minimize the risks banks assume and to ensure the safety and soundness of both individual institutions and the system as a whole (D'Souza, 2000). It aims to insert best practices in the system like minimum capital adequacy guidelines, liquidity ratios, lending limits intended to improve supervision as listed by Basle Accord adopted by G-10 Industrial Countries. RBI accordingly, advised PSBs to set up Settlement Advisory Committees [SACs] for timely and speedier settlement of NPAs in small-scale sector. In 2000-01, Union Budget announced setting up of 7 more debt recovery tribunals for recovery of bad loans.

### *Capital Adequacy Ratio (CAR)*

CAR was introduced in 1992. The profitability and capital adequacy position indicated by Return on Asset [RoA] and Capital to Risk Asset Ratio [CRAR] (which is an indicator of solvency of a bank and captures prudential strengths) is indicative of the potential strength of the bank (Mathur, 2002). The CRAR was fixed at 8 %, and SLR was reduced from 15 % in 1991 to 6.5 % in October 2001.

### *Disclosure Norms*

As a move towards greater transparency, banks were directed to disclose the information regarding maturity pattern of loans and advances, investment securities, deposits and borrowings. Also, foreign currency assets and liabilities, movements in NPAs, lending to priority sector has to be disclosed in the 'notes to accounts' in the balance sheet from the accounting year end.

### *Technological Development in Banks*

Banks have entered the domain of Information Technology and computer networking. The Indian Financial Network [INFINET] is set up. It is based on satellite communication using VSAT technology and would enable faster connectivity. INFINET would severe as a backbone of Integrated Payment and Settlement System [IPSS].

*Regulatory Reform*

In order to strengthen the financial system regulation like disclosure, transparency, supervision of banking operations is been introduced. Annual Financial Inspection was introduced in 1992 as a supervisory strategy comprising on-site inspection and off-site monitoring and control systems have been instituted.

*Risk Management Guidelines*

In October 1999, RBI issued detailed guidelines for risk management systems in banks. Banks would put in place loan policies approved by their board of directors covering the methodologies for measurement, monitoring and control of credit risk. Banks were asked to form a definite time frame for moving over to Value at Risk [VaR] and duration approaches for the measurement of interest rate risks. Banks were also advised to evolve detailed policy and operative framework for operational risk management.

*Asset Liability Management System [ALMS]*

RBI came out with guidelines on ALMS in banks in 1999. These guidelines cover not only the topic of interest rate risk but also liquidity risk and a few other price risks. The objective therefore was to start with at least 60% of the assets and liabilities should be covered but 100% coverage is mandatory in due course. The three foundations of ALM were; ALM information system, ALM organization and ALM process.

*Bank Insurance*

Participation of banks in the insurance sector has taken place in India and it is now known as 'bankassurance'. It is a package of financial services which offers both the banking and insurance products under one roof.

Bankassurance is an ideal launch pad for both insurance companies and banks to increase their revenues.

*Innovative Banking*

New techniques, new methods and new schemes are being introduced in areas of deposit mobilization, bank management and deployment of credit. Merchant banking, equipment leasing, housing finance, venture capital and mutual funds are being introduced.

*Assets Securitisation Law*

Asset Securitization has been used as a risk management mechanism to mitigate the ill effects arising out of asset liability mismatching and other risks. Liabilities are of short duration while assets are created for longer duration of time. This erodes the lending institution abilities to lend further and repay. Asset securitisation involves transferring the assets from the books of lending institution to the books of Special Purpose Vehicle [SPV] for a price. Through this law the banks can recover their assets by issuing notices to defaulters and sell their loans [like shares and bonds].

## Problems of PSB's; Post-reform Period

While serving the socio-economic and development needs, some of the banks have become fundamentally weak when measured in terms of the prudential standards and financial strength. The magnitude of weakness manifested due to various reasons has threatened their survival in the post-reform period, when the accent shifted to profitability and financial strengths of the banks. Problems threatening the survival of PSB's in post-reform period are enlisted.

*Non-Performing Assets*

NPA's ceases to generate income for a bank. It refers to all those loans given by a bank where the borrower defaults or delays in repayment. The percentage of net NPA to Advances of scheduled commercial banks stood at 6.2 % on

March 31st 2001 whereas it was 5.4 % for private sector and 2.2 % for foreign banks. This high level of NPA's calls for high provisioning and thus affect profitability and operations, which makes further lending difficult. Causes for NPA's are poor recoveries, industrial recession, socio-political pressures, lack of proper follow-up, business failure, inefficient management, and banks failure to appreciate the act of good re-payer etc. The financial health of PSB's is declining because the NPA levels of PSB's are increasing. Table 2 shows the NPA's of public sector banks.

**Table 2 : NPA's of Public Sector Banks (Rs b/n)**

| **Year** | 1994 | 1995 | 1996 | 1997 | 1998 | 1999 | 2000 | 2001 |
|---|---|---|---|---|---|---|---|---|
| **NPA's** | 410.4 | 383.8 | 416.6 | 435.8 | 456.5 | 517.1 | 530.3 | 547.7 |

*Source :* RBI, Report on Trend and Progress of Banking in India 2001.

The losses that arise due to these NPAs reduce the net worth of the banks, thus making it imperative for them to raise more capital in order to comply with Capital Adequacy Ratio Norms. The resultant inadequacy of capital will restrict their activities and hence ultimately their growth. The presence of weak banks in a financial system could even lead to a systemic failure, which makes a quick turnaround of these banks inoperative.

*Interest Rate Deregulation*

In recent years most of the interest rate has being deregulated. Government securities are sold in auctions and banks are free to determine the interest rates on deposits and advances. With the changing scenario, the topic assumes a great deal of importance as market determined rates inevitably lead to volatility and hence interest rate risk. In the era of softening interest rates, borrowers were able to adjust to facilities to take advantage of lower interest rates, but the bankers have no flexibility to immediately reduce the cost of their deposits. These fluctuations in interest rate setbacks the functioning of PSB's. There is a potential for instability in the form of shifts in savings bank deposits between banks depending on the interest rates that emerge. Thus this has affected the PSBs, because of this to attract deposits they have to offer high rate of interest, which is not beneficial to PSBs.

*Burdened by Social Responsibilities*

Over the years PSBs have played an important role in industrial and agricultural development. To a large extent, the problem that the PSBs face is largely due to faithful performance of this mandate of larger social good. They have hand-held the industries and sectors that were in trouble operationally to the point that some of the problems have rubbed on to the banks. The losses that are inflicted to the PSBs are to a great extent reflective of a larger malice that afflicts the Indian industries and agriculture.

*Increase Operational Cost and Decreasing Profitability*

The cost of running the banks is going on increasing especially because of day-to-day expenses it has to incur on employees. With regard to decreasing profitability, the PSBs are running into losses due to various reasons – persistent increase in emphasis on social goals, rising industrial sickness, rapid branch expansion, unfavorable deposit mix of banks and inefficiency. Almost 2/3$^{rd}$ of the income of the bank is spent on salaries and wages. There is a problem with effective management and control especially over the branches, which are located in remote areas. This has hampered the overall efficiency of the PSBs

*Fighting the Cost of VRS*

When the nationalized banks successfully implemented an industry-wide Voluntary Retirement Scheme many problem especially regarding finances came into existence where chunk of revenues had to be used in the scheme. Secondly the efficient, experienced employees availed the facility aggravated the problem of working efficiency.

*Corporate Governance*

There is weak corporate governance practices in banks in general, and PSBs in particular. It must be appreciated that the reform process is only an enabling mechanism, leveraging it fully; is possible only if the institutional players in the system are respective to good governance. Good governance practices are a coping mechanism for an institution. Lack of such mechanism can prove to be a major source of weakness among PSBs in India (Bhide, Prasad and Ghosh, 2002].

*Competition*

In 1993, liberal licensing policy paved easy entry for foreign and private sector banks in the country. The timely entry coincided RBI granting more flexibility to the banking system wherein the regulation changed its focus from micro to macro regulation. As many as 10 private sector banks and 40 foreign banks entered the market. Emphasis of the new players was on efficiency of which modern technology was the backbone. Banks offering innovative services, flexible banking hours with pruned staffs were able to secure new generation customers and the PSB's existing 'dissatisfied' customers. As a result PSB's have faced a reduced share in assets, deposits and advances.

**Debatable Bailout Options**

Many of the weaknesses arising out of societal factors have manifested more on account of role assigned to them as PSBs; therefore it is difficult to form a single opinion on the issue relevant for the revival of weak banks. Looking to the content in which these PSBs have developed the weaknesses, we can put up an intense debate.

*Merger of Weak Banks with Strong Ones*

With a view to neutralize the loss making tendency of one bank with the profit making record of another bank a balancing act of merger can be a short-term remedy. These can bailout the weak banks. The reduction of stake by government will offer opportunities for the public sector banks to have strategic tie ups as well as strengthen the capital adequacy norms. Though the past proposed tie-up between Corporation Bank and ICICI didn't heed governments favour, attempts like Dena Bank and HDFC marriage, might trigger creation of new synergies. Merger has been found effective in allowing weak banks to continue. It is basically to protect the interest of depositors and good borrowers. Merging a weak bank with a strong bank is not a short-term solution but infact it is a long-term solution. Table 3 shows Private and Public Sector Banks merger.

**Table 3 : Public and Private Banks Involved in Mergers**

| *Public Sector Banks* | *Private Bank that were merged* |
|---|---|
| Allahabad Bank | United Industrial Bank |
| Indian Bank | Bank of Tanjavur |
| Bank of India | Paroor Central Bank |
| | Bank of Karad |
| Bank of Baroda | Barely Corporation Bank |
| | Benaras State Bank |
| Indian Overseas Bank | Bank of Tamil Nadu |
| Union Bank of India | Sikkim Bank |
| State Bank of India | Kasinath Seth Bank |
| | Bank of Cochin |
| Oriental Bank of Commerce | Punjab Co-operative Bank |

*Source* : ICFAI Press Research Centre.

The negative side of merger is that these bailout mergers may end up burdening the healthy banks affecting their future performance. Secondly, mergers may end up eroding the shareholders value of the financially sound banks. In the long run, mergers may not be a permanent solution for the sick bank; they need to make concerted efforts to enhance their productivity to sustain in future. Therefore the merging of weak banks with the strong banks will not be a tenable proposal in the long run. Moreover it may make stronger banks weaker and can eventually jeopardize the efficiency of strong banks. In the public sector the lessons from merging New Bank of India with Punjab National Bank has given sufficient inputs to RBI as also to the government in not forcing any strong bank to take over a weak bank

*Recapilalisation*

It is a fact that nationalized banks have recapitalized almost annually at least since 1984-85 till 1998-99. During this period of about a decade and a half recapitalization aggregating to Rs 20,446 crore has been provided (Mathur, *2002*). As shown in the table no 4. It is in a way the lender of the last resort position for the government. The government through special securities bonds against equity addition recapitalized the nationalized banks.

**Table 4 : Recapitalisation of Nationalised Banks**

| *Year* | *No of Banks Recapitalised* | *Amount [Rs. crore]* |
|---|---|---|
| 1985-86 | 19 | 400 |
| 1986-87 | 19 | 400 |
| 1987-88 | 18 | 200 |
| 1988-89 | 18 | 200 |
| 1989-90 | 08 | 700 |
| 1990-91 | 11 | 700 |
| 1991-92 | 15 | 700 |
| 1992-93 | 13 | 700 |
| 1993-94 | 19 | 5700 |
| 1994-95 | 13 | 5287 |
| 1995-96 | 6 | 850 |
| 1996-97 | 6 | 1509 |
| 1997-98 | 3 | 2700 |
| 1998-99 | 3 | 400 |
| 1999-00 | Nil | Nil |
| 2000-01 | Nil | Nil |
| | **Total** | **20,446** |

*Source :* RBI, Report on Trend & Progress of Banking in India 2001.

In its report on trend and progress of banking in India 2000-01 RBI has estimated that PSBs [barring the 3 weak banks] would require Rs 10,000 crore in fresh capital over the next five years. RBI had in June 2001 further recommended Rs 2,250 crore recapitilisation package for 3 weak banks of the country [Indian Bank, UCO Bank and United Bank of India].

While recapitalisation of banks is a necessary condition for dealing with weaknesses there are various disadvantages. As per RBI report, 'recapitalization of weak banks using public money is a costly and an unsustainable option. In fact it often serves to distort the incentive structure, erode discipline and reaffirm the faith of these banks in the deep pockets of the government' Recapitalization of PSBs through government budget is frequent, costly and a huge burden on the budget. The real impact on the budget falls only when interest is paid by the government to the banks on the securities held by the banks. (See table 5). Thus during the last five years [since 1996-97] interest paid by the government to the nationalized banks on special securities work out to be 7,888 crore. The government does not get any return on its investment it is rather paying for maintaining an investment. After the recapitalisation the number of banks as well as the amount paid as dividend to the government has shown a steady increase (See table 6). The dividend amount received by the government is not sufficient to compensate for the burden of interest paid to the banks.

*Narrow Banking*

The Tarapore Committee on Capital Account Convertibility (CAC) had advocated the concept of narrow banking which seeks to restrict the functioning of weak banks to making investment in government securities without lending to public. In regard to deployment of funds, the committee suggests that weak banks should not lend but restore to investment in government securities for safety of funds. This concept can be promoted to reduce intermediation costs and to avoid the incidence of NPAs.

**Table 5 : Burden of Recapitalisation on Budget**

| *Year* | *Interest paid to Banks on Recap Bonds [Rs crore]* |
|---|---|
| 1996-97 | 836 |
| 1997-98 | 1702 |
| 1998-99 | 1757 |
| 1999-00 | 1798 |
| 2000-01 | 1795 |

*Source:* RBI, Report on Trend & **Total 7888.**
Progress of Banking in India 2001.

**Table 6 : Dividends Paid by Nationalised Banks to GOI.**

| *Year* | *No of Banks out of 19* | *Amount [Rs crore]* |
|---|---|---|
| 1995-96 | 7 | 210 |
| 1996-97 | 8 | 315 |
| 1997-98 | 10 | 400 |
| 1998-99 | 14 | 399 |
| 1999-00 | 15 | 465 |
| 2000-01 | 14 | 505 |

*Source:* RBI, Report on Trend & Progress of **Total 2294.**
Banking in India 2001

The most striking limitations with this bailout proposal is that the risk free assets offer lower returns, squeezing the spread. Secondly, it will drive the employees still more unproductive as their horizons will be confined only to collection of deposits. Thirdly, the gilt securities do not enjoy the privilege of zero risk securities anymore, thus diluting the inherent rational behind the concept. Fourthly, it will be customer unfriendly. Banks known for accepting deposits and lending will find it difficult if one of its functions is stopped.

### *Closure of Weak Banks*

Banks unable to make profit from financial intermediation have no place in the commercial market. Those cannot change their style of operation to make them profitable over a fixed time frame have no option but to dissolve.

But in the case of PSBs, it is quite difficult because PSBs play a vital role in development of the economy. Secondly the closure will have bad impact on the morale of bank employees and customers. It will also lead to confidence crisis even among banks doing well.

### *Voluntary Retirement Scheme [VRS]*

The VRS is helping in reduction of the over staffed PSBs. With the announcement of Special Voluntary Retirement Scheme [SVRS], the path breaking development took place. In 2001, the 26 public sector banks together had staff strength of 8,63,214 of which 1,26,733 applied for VRS. The banks then accepted 1,61,764 application the staff strength of PSBs as on 31$^{st}$ march 2002, has dwindled to 7,46,810

The debatable issue here is whether the PSBs have really been benefited by VRS. The bank branches in rural and urban areas are faced with the challenge of coping with the same volume of business and transactions with lesser staff. With each employee having more than two to three departments to handle customer service is bound to be affected. Secondly, the VRS expenditure incurred led to increasing operating expenses. Thirdly many talented employees will leave to look for greener pastures in private banks.

### *Asset Reconstruction Commission [ARC]*

In terms of recommendation of Narsimham committee the proposal of setting up ARC by individual banks is under consideration. ARC is a possible option to shift the burden of NPAs to another organization. Formation ARCs will be able to provide relief to the banks from the follow up work and the funds locked in NPAs may be released for use at discounted rate.

But lending and recovery are an integral function of banking business. Divesting on such important function can develop a culture of disowning the responsibility of recovery of loans. The big question is who will put up the money for the ARC's? The current solution, which may see as temporary, is that the ARC will buy up assets and issue securities to the banks after ARC make the sale it will share the profits with the banks. Most observers argue that for ARC to work foreign money has to come in. Foreign funds have to be allowed to buy up bad loans restructure them and sell them at a profit.

*Privatisation*

Many studies reveal that the weak banks should be privatized and therefore management of these banks should be bailed out. The proponents of privatization of PSBs argue that privatization should take place because recapitalization through government is a burden on budget (Acharya, 2001). Secondly; state ownership of banks in India inhibits competition and consequently breeds inefficiency. Thirdly, international experience provides no evidence that state ownership lowers the probability of banking crisis and lastly, foreign banks stimulate efficiency, innovation and economic growth. Almost underway through the decade of reforms process, Joshi and Little, (1996) found that the empirical case for privatization in banking is especially strong as it is clear the public ownership has virtually paralyzed the management efficiency of banks due to political and administrative interference in the allocations of credit. It was therefore recommended that rather than go through a futile process of attempting to secure autonomy within the framework of government ownership, the government should prepare a plan to privatize several public banks.

However, privatization may not be the best option for solving the problem of weak banks for various reasons. *Firstly*, the purpose for which the banks were nationalized will be defeated once they are privatized .The motive of private banks will be profit. *Secondly*, the rural areas will be neglected. *Thirdly;* the priority sector lending will be affected because the private banks will not provide loans and advances without security therefore the result will be, financing only the big industrial concerns. Fourthly, through the public sector banks are criticized over having NPA of Rs.60,000 crore, there has not been a single government owned bank failure in our country. But in private sector there are 17 banks which has collapsed in the last 14 years (Krishnamurthy,2002). Lastly, the cost to the exchequer in terms of meeting all the liabilities before putting it at stake is doubtful.

In view of the foregoing debate on possible remedies open to the PSBs, efforts should be made to revive the banks.

## Suggestions

1. Weak banks should go for specialized banking services like housing, consumer finance, investment banking, merchant banking, credit card etc.
2. Measures should be taken by weak banks to control its expenditure by reducing its operating expenditure, which accounted for 21.3 percent to the total expenditure in year 2000.
3. Weak Banks need to be put under observation and moratorium period can be granted to revive with an action plan to be followed during the period. Verma committee's recommendation of establishing of a new monitoring and surveillance authority called Financial Restructuring Authority (FRA).
4. Weak banks should work in two shifts and follow 7 day banking to mop up remunerative business and to ensure optimum use of manpower and technology.

5. ALM needs to be further strength i.e. Bankers should adopt risk management technique this would require not only asset liability mismatch but also management of several other risks like interest rate, credit, foreign exchange and operational risk.
6. Greater transparency in banks especially with regard to provision of data on NPAs and lending. Establishing of ARC can be the first step in that direction.
7. Heavy investments should be directed towards information technology.
8. Greater emphasis should be laid on customer's satisfaction. Since customer is the kingpin utmost care should be taken with dedication, diligence and commitments.
9. The critical and immediate task before the government and RBI is to erect a credible structure of good governance. In order to provide leadership, to integrate the employees with common vision good governance is needed
10. Government should restrain itself from committing itself for free flows of recapitalization funds. Instead banks must be encouraged to explore on their own possibilities for raising funds to match the kind of business they can profitably run., which are recapitalized, should be made to adhere to stringent prudential norms and strict financial discipline.
11. PSB's be given the freedom and flexibility to choose their business and decide their priorities within the parameters of regulation laid for them. The compulsion to invest in government bonds and be allowed to choose its profitable investment portfolio.
12. PSB's should support themselves by internal fund generation or by approaching the capital market for raising capital, based on their own financials and net worth. Bailout package of the government

should be the last option for it would defeat the basic purpose of implementation of Prudential norms for Capital Adequacy.

## Conclusion

Over the years the PSB's have widened and deepened considerably. The PSB's, though not efficiently has fulfilled to some extent the objectives of providing services in rural areas which otherwise may not have been available in absence of the public sector. The reforms, proposed and implemented have marked the beginning of a new era towards financial integration of the economy with that of the worlds. These reforms desire to change the way the PSB's conduct their business. Stringent norms have forced PSB's to run on professional grounds like that of the private sector banks. The reform agenda, though unfinished, has been successful to improve the functioning and the performance in absolute terms but still a lot needs to be accomplished. Weak PSB's needed to develop better credit appraisal skills, prompt debt recovery practices and greater public accountability. The internal pressures and the external competition compel them to optimize their resources to attain technical efficiencies. Merger options and the VRS schemes may help revive weak players if the government provides reconstruction support. However the bailout packages should be short term and one time backed with long term reforms for revival of the weak players. Though new era demands that the PSB's move away from government control / ownership and closure of weak banks, its far reaching implications on the financial system as a whole should be analysed. It needs to be ensured that the reforms would not produce undesirable effects, which one generally expects under a liberated regime.

## REFERENCES


Acharya, Shankar (2001), "A Vision for Banking", the Economic Times, December 6th.

Ahuwalia, Montek (1999), India's Economic Reforms: An Appraisal, In India in The era of Economic Reforms, Scahs J., Varshney, A., & Bajpai, N. (Ed.), Oxford University Press, New Delhi.

B. Satish (2002), 'Securitisation Bill 2002', Chartered Financial Analyst, September.

Bhole, L M (1999), 'Financial Institution and Market: Structure Growth and Innovations, Tata McGraw–Hill Publishing Company Limited, New Delhi, 3rd Edn.

Bhide, M G, Prasad A, Ghosh, Saibal (2002), 'Banking Sector Reforms: A Critical Overview', EPW, Feb 2-8. Vol. 37, No 05.

Celestine, Avinash (2002), 'Making Bad Loans Good', Business World, July 15th.

Das, Abhiman (2002), 'Risk and Productivity Change of PSBs', EPW Feb 2-8, Vol. 37, No. 05.

Dessai, Vasant (2001), 'The Indian Financial System', Himalaya Publishing House, Mumbai, Fourth. Edn.

D'Souza, Errol (2000), 'Prudential Regulation in Indian Banking', EPW, Jan, Vol. 35, No. 05.

Ghosh, D N (2000), 'Weak Banks: Strategy for Self-Renewal', EPW, Jan 29, Vol. 35, No. 05.

'Is Bailout the Right Option', Chartered Financial Analyst, Jan. 2002.

Joshi, Vijay & Little, IMD (1996), 'India's Economic Reforms 1991-2001' Oxford University Press.

Jose, KG (2002), 'Non- Performing Assets Management', May, Vol. 41, No. 1.

Kaipachery, Sudhesh (2002), 'Impact of Economic Reforms on the Banking Sector', Southern Economist, July, Vol. 41, No. 5.

Krishnamurthy, S. (2002), 'De-Nationalisation of PSBs: A View', Southern Economist, May, Vol. 41, No. 1.

Mathur, K.B.L (2002), 'Public Sector Banks in Indian- should they be privatised?' EPW, June 8-14, Vol. 37, No. 23.

Majumdar, Alok (2002), 'Dealing with Surpluses', Business India, July 22- Aug. 4.

Mishra, Shashidhar (2003), 'Bank Mergers-is it the right solution', Chartered Financial Analyst, Jan.

Mohan T.T. Ram (2002), 'Deregulation and Performance of Indian PSBs' EPW, Feb 2-8, Vol. 37, No. 23.

Raghuram, G (2001), 'Narrow Banking', Chartered Financial Analyst, Feb. 1999.

Rajaram, Indira & Vasishtha, Garina (2002), 'Non–Performing Loans of PSBs', EPW Feb 2-8 ,Vol. 37, No. 05.

Rao, V.L. & Wengel, J. (2000), 'Financial and Consultancy services', Sage Publications, New Delhi.

Reddy, Y.V. (2002),'PSBs and the Governance Challenge: Indian Experience', Southern Economist, Vol. 41, No. 17.

Shekar, Chandra & Kumar, K.B.S. (2001), 'Bancassurance', Chartered Financial Analyst, Oct.

Singh, Archana Anmol (1999), 'Weak PSBs: SOS for Revival', Chartered Financial Analyst, April.

'Securitisation Act', Business World, 23rd Dec. 2002.

Shankaranarayan, (2001), 'VRS and PSBs' Southern Economist, Vol. 40, No. 12.

Shekar, K.C and Shekar, L (2000), 'Banking Theory and Practice', Vikas Publishing House, New Delhi.

Talwar S.P. (1999), 'Banking Regulation and Corporate Governance', RBI Bulletin, July, Vol. 7.

# 24
# International Financial Sector Reforms

*(Ms.) Geetanjali Sharma* and*
*(Ms.) Sandeepa Malhotra*

It is now a well recognised fact that an effective international trading and financial system has a vital role in general economic growth. In the present scenario of international economics, countries have to participate in the imports and exports of not only goods but also of services. Particularly for developing countries like India the emerging international trading system can contribute to the economic growth potential significantly. Developed countries tend to dominate with their superior technology and information systems. Developing countries have 'comparative advantage' in agricultural and primary products. By developing appropriate technology and indigenous R & D, the productivity, including quality of these products, should be increased to face the international competition and increase their market share.

Though the agreements on TRIPS, TRIMS and GATS are considered to be heavily weighted in favour of the developed countries, India can still convert these hurdles into opportunities. It will not be in the national interest to opt out of the 'rule-based' international trading system. In

* School of Studies in Economics, Jiwaji University, Gwalior.

order to increase the market share for her exports, improvement in quality of the products by intensive indigenous R & D efforts, greater productivity in the agricultural and primary goods sectors by improved technology and constant efforts towards cost control are very essential.

Development of infrastructure facilities is essential. Cumbersome procedures should be rationalised and simplified through effective administrative reforms. Besides restructuring of exporting companies the burgeoning field of modern information technology should be given special attention as information will become the crux of the emerging international trading and financial system. Needless to stress, the rates of inflation should be kept within the rates prevailing in other countries. Business ethics and ministration of corruption are also vitally necessary to ensure sustained gains of trade and economic growth.

World trade has been growing faster than world output with the result that an ever growing proportion of the world output is traded across the national borders. In the past two decades, world merchandise exports rose from 11 per cent to 18 per cent of the GDP. Trade in services has grown faster and the trend is expected to continue in future. The speed of integration, i.e., the difference between the growth rates of world output and trade, over the next decade is estimated at 207 per cent. This trend would be accelerated by the developing countries whose output and trade growth would proceed faster than that of the developed countries. The global economic integration is fostered by global sourcing and production sharing which involve many countries in the manufacturing of a product. Global sourcing is estimated to contribute nearly one-third of the world trade. Regional economic integration schemes are among the very important factors encouraging international economic integration.

The economic reforms in the developing countries have given a new dimension to the transnational financial flows.

Firms in developing countries have begun to transnationalise their financing, as is indicated by the GDR issues by Indian firms. Foreign portfolio investment in developing countries have been surging. One of the seven equity trades worldwide involves a foreigner as a counterparty. The faster rate of equity market capitalisation in developing countries encourages the portfolio investment in them. Global equity market capitalisation increased five-fold between 1984 and 1994 to $174 billion, with the share of the emerging markets rising from about 4 per cent to 10 per cent which is projected to rise above 20 per cent over the next decade. The share of developing countries in the EDI has risen from 23 per cent in mid-1980s to 40 per cent now and is projected to rise to nearly 50 per cent by 2010. The total sales of foreign affiliates may now well exceed the value of world trade and nearly one-third of the global trade is estimated to be the result of inter-company transfers. There is, thus, a growing and powerful trend towards greater global integration.

The liberalisation of international capital movements has been a widespread phenomenon in the last two decades. Liberalisation episodes have occurred a in OPCD countries and in some developing countries. Most countries continue to maintain restriction on their capital movements although they may consider liberalisation them in the near future. The most fundamental impact of a liberalisation of capital movements is the integration of the domestic financial system with international financial market. This integration will generally modify the domestic interest rate and will alter the international decision of firms and individuals and possibly public sector. In developing countries, the removal of quantitative restriction on capital flows may lead to a fundamental change in economic system. With binding quantitative capital controls, the interest rate is determined domestically and is not influenced by foreign interest rate. If a country initially faces controls on capital outflows and an interest rate lower than abroad, a removal of capital controls would lead to large net capital outlflows. In the initial situation capital outflows would occur in the opposite direction.

In recent times there has been a hightened emphasis on the part of developed countries on foreign direct investment as a source of capital flows — against the background especially of the new policy orientation of developing countries relating to liberalisation and privatisation. Foreign direct investment has many advantages particularly in the context of the globalisation of markets, rapid development in technology and export- oriented growth.

It is unlikely, however, the foreign investment will make up residual resource-gap of developing countries from inadequacy of capital flows. This would need to be a new and growth emphasis on the remaining channel for capital flows — the multilateral financial institutions, comprising the World Bank, International Monetary Fund and regional development banks. The design of the post-war monetary and financial system as reflected in the Bretton Wood institutions did not pay sufficient attention to the need of the developing countries for long term capital flows, although, the World Bank and later the regional development banks were established as source of long term capital flows. The size of the short term facilities of the International Monetary Fund, on the other hand, was established in the light of assessment of balance of payment needs.

It would be logical to rectify this shortcoming in an eventual reform or reorganisation of the international financial system. The capital needs of developing countries should not be excessively dependent on the preference, essentially political situation of donor countries or on the criteria of private foreign investors. Multilateral institution should be able to play the role of mobilising global savings surpluses and of channeling them in support of viable project and programmes in developing countries. This would require a change in present character of the existing institution where the voice of the developing countries in decision making, management and the decision of conditionality is minimal. The characteristic and scope of the international financial and monetary system of the future should indeed be the subject of study and analysis within the non-aligned movement as an important part of its economic programmes. The average assistance provided by the OECD countries has been around has been around only half of this proportion. The developing countries have consistently urged upon the fulfilment of these targets. Nevertheless, the focus of the developing countries can not be confined to ODA flows, particularly in the view of growing political constraints in major developed countries on aid budgets, the competing demand for assistance to Eastern Europe, the unbalanced distribution of ODA among developing countries.

The OPEC donor countries and OPEC institutions have contributed significantly to the financial flows among developing countries. In 2000 the total amount of development assistance provided by the Arab countries more than quadrupled as compared to 1989, reaching 6 billion dollar. Many other developing countries also provided assistance in the form of financial and technical training. China, India, Republic of Korea, Taiwan and Venezuela all extended some form of development finance. In 2000 China extended some 495 million dollar, India 180 million dollar, Republic of Korea 77 million dollar and Venezuela 41 million dollar.

Since their establishment major international development finance institutions (the World Bank and IDA and the regional development bank groups) contributed considerable financial resources to developing countries. This was particularly important in the 2000s when private lending collapsed, leading to a major outflow of financial resources from developing countries on private account. However, the net transfer (distribution on their loans to these countries less debt service-amortisation and interest) from these institutions as a group has been falling off rapidly in recent years. If the past trend continues, developing countries as a group may be facing the prospect of net financial outflows in favour of these institutions in the near future. Some countries have experienced this net outflow already.

The loan commitment of multilateral development finance agencies doubled in the last ten years from US 16.6 billion dollar in 1981 to US 33.9 billion in 2000-01. The World Bank, IDA continue to have a commanding position, although growth has been fastest in the African and Asian Development Bank groups in recent years. Disbursement i.e. the actual flow of funds have increased faster than commitment, perhaps as a result of deliberate measures to increase the share of fast-disbursing non-project loans in total lending, so as to alleviate the cash shortage in debtor countries during debt crisis. A range of realistic multi-year projections needs to be for each institution for increasing net transfers to developing countries.

Effective co-operation among developing countries is considered as indispensable and integral element of any strategy towards restructuring of the world economy. As South-South co-operation expends, the necessary leverage to emerge the North in dialogue and in actual negotiation also increases. The overview of some of the major development in economic co-operation among developing countries in the recent past suggests that progress in this regard has been substantial and a major restructuring of South-South trade is inevitable in due course of time. Besides, the positive experience of regional groupings like ASEAN and SAARC has brought about an attitudinal change in the perception of many of the developed countries. They are now keener to participate and extend due support to such co-operative efforts among developing countries provided they fulfil certain criteria which include :

(1) Formulation of outward looking market- oriented economic policies. (2) Involvement of the private business and industrial sector increasingly and substantially in the planning and implementation of regional integration/co-operation initiatives. (3) Ensuring a degree of political

stability. (4) Adoption of programmetic and realistic policies and programmes.

The financial system has undergone substantial changes in recent years. With increasing sophistication of financial needs of trade and commerce of developing countries, monetary management becomes more crucial to help control liquidity in financial system. Major international financial institutions should be more liberal to developing countries by extending facilities in supply of international liquidity in financial system and in repayment terms of developing countries' loan.

## REFERENCES

OECD, Economic Outlook, 1993, Table 31.

UNCTAD, Trade and Development p.53 Report, 1995, Table 10, p. 139.

Robert Rowthom, Capital Fomation and Unemployment, 1995, Vol. II.

World Bank, Global Economic Prospects and the Developing Countries, 1995, p. 18.

OECD, ibid., p. 122.

UNCTAD, Trade and Development Report, 2002, Table 3, p. 67.

IFC, Quarterly Review of Emerging Regional Markets, 2002, p. 13.

IFC, ibid., 2002, p. 87.